W.L. MACKENZIE KING:

A Bibliography and Research Guide

This comprehensive bibliography on William Lyon Mackenzie King, the most prominent Canadian politician in the first half of the twentieth century, will be an invaluable reference tool for researchers in archives and libraries, as well as for political scientists, historians, journalists, and book collectors.

In this volume Henderson provides comprehensive lists of books, articles, and other material written by King or about him and his era, and includes a series of appendixes relating to studies on King and miscellaneous material pertaining to his life and career. In addition, Henderson provides a list of unsigned articles by King that appeared in newspapers and periodicals, and of sound recordings and motion picture footage relating to him. Finally, he identifies all forewords and prefaces written by King, plays written about him, and books and poems dedicated to him.

GEORGE F. HENDERSON is Archivist (Public Service) at the Queen's University Archives.

W.L. MACKENZIE KING

A Bibliography and Research Guide

George F. Henderson

UNIVERSITY OF TORONTO PRESS
Toronto Buffalo London

Toronto Buffalo London

Reprinted in paperback 2014

ISBN 978-0-8020-4157-9 (cloth)
ISBN 978-1-4426-5720-5 (paper)

Printed on acid-free paper

Canadian Cataloguing in Publication Data

Henderson, George F. (George Fletcher), 1936–
W.L. Mackenzie King : a bibliography and research guide

Includes bibliographical references and index.
ISBN 978-0-8020-4157-9 (bound) ISBN 978-1-4426-5720-5 (pbk.)

1. King, William Lyon Mackenzie, 1874–1950 – Bibliography. I. Title.

FC581.K5Z9 1998 016.97106'32'092 C98-930981-9
F1033.H46 1998

This book has been published with the help of generous donations from the Davies Charitable Foundation and several departments and individuals at Queen's University.

University of Toronto Press acknowledges the financial assistance to its publishing program of the Canada Council for the Arts and the Ontario Arts Council.

TO MOTHER, with Love

Contents

Foreword

The Right Honourable John N. Turner

I am honoured to contribute a Foreword to this bibliography and research guide prepared by George Henderson, a senior archivist at Queen's University.

Mackenzie King ranks with Sir John A. Macdonald and Sir Wilfrid Laurier among Canada's three greatest prime ministers. Yet, in my judgment, almost a half century after his death, he remains perhaps our most underestimated prime minister.

For almost thirty years, from his election as leader of the Liberal Party in August 1919 until he retired as prime minister in November 1948, having served in that office for 7,829 days, longer than any other prime minister in the English-speaking world to that date, King was the towering figure of Canadian politics. He laid the foundations for Canada's social security system, played a major role in the evolution of an independent foreign policy, and maintained the unity of the country, particularly during the Conscription Crisis in the Second World War. His work with labour and industrial relations both in Canada and in the United States in association with the Rockefellers was highly regarded.

Mackenzie King was a brilliant recruiter of talent in the public service of Canada. He did this both directly, through the Liberal Party – where he recruited, for example, Louis St Laurent – and indirectly, by establishing high standards and a vibrant sense of purpose in the Canadian public service, which really had its golden age under King's aegis. Many of the giants, men like O.D. Skelton, Clifford Clark, W.A. Mackintosh, and John Deutsch, came to Ottawa from Queen's University.

King himself was a university man who had three earned degrees from the University of Toronto, attended the University of Chicago Graduate

School, and received his Doctor of Philosophy degree from Harvard. He also had a long relationship with Queen's University. In 1908 he considered the possibility of lecturing at Queen's and also holding a Kingston-area riding in the House of Commons. In 1914 he was viewed as a possible candidate for the principalship, and in 1919 he received his first honorary degree from Queen's.

My mother, the late Phyllis Gregory Ross, was part of that golden age of the Canadian public service over which King presided. She came to Ottawa in 1934 as a chief economist for the new Tariff Board and within a few years had risen to the level of deputy minister, the first female in Canada to achieve that rank. As a boy growing up in Ottawa in the 1930s and 1940s, I was privileged to meet Mr King on many occasions. I especially remember talks with him when we would meet while walking our dogs in Strathcona Park in Sandy Hill near Laurier House, his Ottawa residence.

Many years later, after I became leader of the Liberal Party in 1984, I shared another affinity with Mr King. During our careers we were the only leaders of the Liberal Party to be elected in three different provinces: King in Ontario, Saskatchewan, and Prince Edward Island and I in Quebec, Ontario, and British Columbia.

For George Henderson this bibliographical guide has been a labour of love, a project that has engaged him for almost thirty years. This is more than a bibliography. Mr Henderson has provided extensive notes on King's five books, the King diary, the official biography, and proposed books by King, as well as descriptions of the limited editions about King. In addition, this volume provides a comprehensive guide to books and articles about King as well as sound recordings, newsreel footage, and academic theses. Perhaps the most significant contribution is the identification and listing of more than three hundred unsigned articles written by King during his student days in the 1890s for the *Labour Gazette* and several Canadian newspapers. In order to locate and verify this substantial and previously unreferenced material, Mr Henderson was required to use detective skills in searching King's diary and correspondence for clues and references to these writings.

This work will be invaluable for historians, political scientists, journalists, book collectors, and researchers in all aspects of Canadian studies covering the first half of the twentieth century. Canadian history has much to teach us all. By more fully understanding the life and career of Mackenzie King and his enormous contribution to our country, Canadians will be better prepared to surmount the sometimes daunting challenges threatening our future.

Preface

Since his death in July 1950 William Lyon Mackenzie King has been the subject of a steady stream of books, articles, theses, and radio and television programs. Almost a half century after his death a great deal of interest remains in the life and times of this distinguished Canadian political figure. This continued interest can be explained by two factors. First, King dominated the political life of Canada during the first half of the twentieth century and was prime minister of this country for almost half that period. Second, Mackenzie King is a fascinating individual. Every year about 28,000 people visit Laurier House, his Ottawa home, and about 140,000 people visit his estate at Kingsmere.

The aim of this bibliography is to provide a comprehensive listing of all types of material relating to the life and work of Canada's tenth prime minister. If a book or article was published in both English and French, entries for both languages have been included. In the case of newspaper articles, several English-language papers were searched, and a number of articles from *La Presse* and *Le Devoir* have been listed as well.

The bibliography and research guide is divided into two sections. Part 1 contains a listing of books, articles, published speeches, sound recordings, and miscellaneous writings by Mackenzie King. Part 2 consists of writings and other material *about* the life and career of Mackenzie King. It includes books, articles, theses, newsreel footage, and sound recordings, as well as radio and television programs relating to King. Several appendices with additional listings and other information of potential interest to researchers have also been included.

I have attempted to produce a complete listing of the writings of Mackenzie King. In the case of his five books, full bibliographical details have been provided for each edition. A brief history of the writing of each book has also been included. Every effort has been made to list all identifiable articles written by King as well. The problem encountered in compiling this section was that most of the newspaper and early periodical articles written by King were unsigned, as were many newspaper articles at that time. On the basis of references in King's diaries and his correspondence, however, I have been able to trace 345 unsigned articles, out of a total of more than 400 of his articles in newspapers and periodicals such as *The Varsity*, *The Globe*, the *Labour Gazette*, *The Times*, and the *Mail and Empire*. The list of articles has been arranged chronologically.

In the 'Published Speeches' section, only texts of speeches published as separate items have been listed. The entries throughout this section have been arranged chronologically. The first part of the section contains references to pamphlets. The second contains a list of 'press release' copies and mimeographed copies of speeches. Texts of speeches that appeared in periodicals and newspapers or in books have not been included because most of them have been published in the *House of Commons Debates* or in compilations of King's speeches. Locations for copies of the speeches are provided.

Lists of newsreel footage relating to Mackenzie King and sound recordings of his speeches and broadcasts have been provided with dates and locations only. It has been impossible to provide details as to the actual amount of newsreel footage and the playing time of the recordings. The fact that a certain repository holds some footage or a recording of a particular event should prove adequate for anyone wishing to acquire copies of this audiovisual material for research use or for use in radio and television programs.

In the sections on books, articles, and other materials *about* Mackenzie King, items relating to his prime ministership and his political career as well as his life have been included. It was felt that the inclusion of this material would contribute to the overall value of the work. A word should also be said about the inclusion in this volume of a number of newspaper articles pertaining to King. Newspaper articles can sometimes contain significant information not to be found in books or scholarly articles. In some cases short newspaper articles summarize important aspects of King's life; in other cases, they suggest areas where more research is needed. Relatively few newspaper articles written during King's lifetime have been listed; most of the ones included here were written at the time of his death or since 1950.

Reviews of books by Mackenzie King have been included. Many significant reviews of books about King and his era have also been listed, as in many cases they are important contributions to the literature on King and on this period of Canadian history.

Messages for periodicals and commemorative issues of newspapers have not been listed. Generally speaking, this type of material would likely have been prepared by an assistant and only revised by Mr King.

A number of problems were encountered in the preparation of this work. First, despite the enormous amount of material preserved by King during his long career, he does not appear to have systematically collected his own writings. No scrapbooks of his early articles are known to exist. There are, however, several references to the preparation of scrapbooks, which may have contained copies of his early newspaper articles. For example, on September 9, 1897, he wrote in his diary: 'I pasted in clippings into my scrapbook for an hour or more.' King kept relatively few bound volumes of his speeches.

I considered preparing a list of the speeches King delivered outside the House of Commons, but decided that the finding aid for the J 5 Series of the King Papers prepared by the staff of the National Archives of Canada was adequate. While it does not contain full details of every speech, it lists most of the more important ones, and sufficient details as to dates are generally available to help locate others.

Detailed descriptions of the William Lyon Mackenzie King Papers, containing nineteen series, in the National Archives of Canada have been provided for researchers. The indexes available for each series are also briefly described.

I have added a number of appendices containing information about books that Mr King proposed to write at one time or another during his lifetime. In addition, I have provided considerable information about the official biography, which sheds light on the historiography of Mackenzie King and his era.

This bibliography and reference guide has been compiled with the hope that it will aid researchers in Canadian history, political science, economics, and journalism. The inclusion of articles from popular periodicals and newspapers as well as academic books and journals is intended to help researchers using small public libraries as well as large academic ones to locate material of interest for their work.

A detailed index containing entries for authors and the more important subjects has been included. An index of this nature is necessary to enable the researcher to make maximum use of the many sections with their various types of material.

The major source for this work was, of course, the William Lyon Mackenzie King Papers, but many large academic libraries and archival repositories were also used. A work of this kind cannot be completed without the assistance of staff members of numerous archival repositories and libraries. I wish to express my appreciation to the staff members of the Joseph R. Stauffer Library, Queen's University; the Library of Parliament; Radio Archives, Canadian Broadcasting Corporation; the National Archives of Canada; the Library of Congress; the United States National Archives; the National Sound Archive; the British Broadcasting Corporation; and the University of Toronto Archives. Special thanks go to Dr Ian McClymont and Maureen Hoogenraad of the Prime Ministers' Section of the National Archives of Canada. On numerous occasions these two individuals assisted me in countless ways, helping me find information in the Mackenzie King Papers and checking information in their indices.

Others who deserve special mention are Mike Swift, National Archives of Canada; Chris Grant, Canadian Parks Service; Mike Graham, Library of Parliament; Thomas Rosenbaum, Rockefeller Archive Center; Norma Gauld, National Library of Canada; Charlotte Stewart, McMaster University Library, William Ready Division of Archival and Research Collections; and Bob Armstrong of the Renfrew office of the National Archives of Canada. I especially wish to thank my friend Paul Rabishaw, of the latter office, who helped make it possible for me to accomplish a maximum amount of work during my research visits to Renfrew.

Professor Blair Neatby and Jacqueline Neatby helped me identify many of the memoranda prepared by several researchers for use in the official biography. I am most grateful for their assistance. I am also very grateful to Anne MacDermaid, former Queen's University Archivist, who did innumerable kind acts in helping to make funds available to me for the purchase of research collections of King Papers and related documents for the Queen's University Archives. Also on many occasions she enabled me to travel to Ottawa, often on short notice, to do research. As a friend and colleague she always encouraged me to continue my research. I wish to thank Anne's successors as well, the late Dr Shirley Spragge and Donald S. Richan, who also encouraged me in my research and were most helpful in enabling me to make trips to Ottawa when necessary.

I owe a great deal to the late Professor Frederick W. Gibson, who talked with me about the life and work of Mackenzie King on numerous occasions over a period of almost forty years. As a counsellor and friend, he always encouraged me in all aspects of my work and career. When we discussed this bibliography in the fall of 1974, Professor Gibson emphasized the need for locating King's articles in periodicals such as the *Labour Gazette.*

I am most grateful to my friend Margaret Gibson for granting me access to her husband's papers, which allowed me to include details about the memoranda prepared for the official biography. She too took a great interest in the work as it neared its final stages.

I wish to thank the staff of the Computing Centre at Queen's University for their assistance over a very long period. Special thanks go to Nicole Wakelin, who has gone far beyond the call of duty in helping me to solve countless computer problems.

To the staff of the University of Toronto Press, especially Gerald Hallowell, Emily Andrew, Robert Ferguson, Darlene Zeleney, and freelance editor Wayne Herrington, many thanks are due for their unfailing courtesy and understanding as they saw this difficult work through the Press. I am most grateful for their assistance and encouragement at all stages of the work. I owe a special debt of gratitude to Wayne Herrington, who, as copy editor, did so much to improve the overall work.

The publication of this volume was made possible by generous grants from the Davies Charitable Foundation and Queen's University. I am most grateful to these two organizations.

A very special note of appreciation goes to the Right Honourable John N. Turner, who kindly contributed the Foreword to this book.

Special thanks go to my long-time friends and colleagues, Brian Osborne, Donald Swainson, and Alan Green, who encouraged me to complete the bibliography and assisted me in many ways during the final stages of the project. In addition, I am most grateful for the encouragement and support of my friends Duncan and Nancy Edmonds. It gives me the greatest possible pleasure to record my gratitude to my friend Robert Wardhaugh, who encouraged me to complete this work. Robert's support has been most valuable and much appreciated. The pleasant memories of our many hours together and our countless conversations (which have ranged from Mackenzie King to Teemu Selanne) have helped to keep me going over the last several years. It is impossible to express in words the depth and beauty of our friendship. I am also very happy to record my warmest gratitude and appreciation to Robert's wife, Paula.

Finally, I owe an indescribable debt of gratitude to my dear mother for her support and encouragement over half a century. She helped in many ways as the work on this book progressed over the years. She was always very much aware of the work I was doing on Mackenzie King. For many years she searched through catalogues of second-hand bookdealers for new King items I might add to this work. Also she often drew my attention to articles in newspapers and periodicals about Mackenzie King. As always during our fifty-four wonderful years together she took an unusually keen interest in any research project in which I was involved. Unfortunately she did not live to see the completion of this work. This book is dedicated to her with the deepest love and appreciation for her years of hard work and concern for me.

George F. Henderson
Wilton, Ontario

Chronology of Mackenzie King's Life

1874, Dec. 17	Born at Berlin (now Kitchener), Ontario, the son of John King and Isabel Grace (Mackenzie) King
1891	Enters the University of Toronto
1893	King family moves to Toronto (147 Beverley Street)
1895	Graduates from the University of Toronto with the degree of Bachelor of Arts in political economy
1895–6	Reporter for *The Globe*
1896	Receives Bachelor of Laws degree from the University of Toronto
1896	Enters the University of Chicago Graduate School
1897	Receives Master of Arts degree from the University of Toronto
1897	Reporter for the *Daily Mail and Empire*
1897	Enters Harvard University
1898	Receives Master of Arts degree from Harvard University
1900	Appointed Deputy Minister of Labour and editor of the *Labour Gazette*
1900	Visits Kingsmere, Quebec, for the first time, with his friend Henry Albert Harper
1901	Henry Albert Harper drowns in the Ottawa River
1903	Purchases first land at Kingsmere
1904	Builds first cottage (Kingswood) at Kingsmere

1906	Publishes his first book, *The Secret of Heroism*
1908, Sept. 21	Resigns as Deputy Minister of Labour
1909	Receives Doctor of Philosophy degree from Harvard University
1909	Elected to the House of Commons in Waterloo North (Ontario)
1909, June 2	Appointed Minister of Labour
1911, Sept. 21	Defeated in Waterloo North in the general election
1914	Begins work with the Rockefeller Foundation
1915, April 4	Isabel Christina Grace King, his sister, dies
1916, Aug. 30	John King, his father, dies at Toronto
1917, Dec. 17	Defeated in the general election in North York
1917, Dec. 18	Isabel King, his mother, dies at Ottawa
1918	Publishes his second book, *Industry and Humanity*
1919, Aug. 7	Elected leader of the Liberal Party
1919, Oct. 20	Elected Member for Prince (Prince Edward Island) by acclamation
1921, Dec. 6	Elected Member for North York in general election
1921, Dec. 29	Becomes Canada's tenth prime minister and Secretary of State for External Affairs
1922, March 19	Dougall Macdougall King, his brother, dies
1923, Jan. 11	Moves into Laurier House, which was bequeathed to him by Lady Laurier
1925, Oct. 29	Defeated in North York riding in general election
1926, Feb. 15	Elected in riding of Prince Albert (Saskatchewan)
1926, Sept. 14	Elected in riding of Prince Albert in general election
1926, Sept. 25	Sworn in as prime minister
1927	Publishes *The Message of the Carillon*
1930, July 28	Liberal Party defeated in general election; King re-elected in Prince Albert
1935, Oct. 14	Liberal Party elected in general election; King re-elected in Prince Albert
1935, Oct. 23	Sworn in as prime minister

1939, Sept. 10	Canada declares war on Germany
1940, March 26	Liberal Party re-elected in general election; King re-elected in Prince Albert
1941	Publishes *Canada at Britain's Side*
1944	Publishes *Canada and the Fight for Freedom*
1945	Attends San Francisco Conference as head of Canadian delegation
1945, June 11	Liberal Party re-elected in general election; King defeated in Prince Albert
1945, Aug. 6	Re-elected to the House of Commons in a by-election in Glengarry (Ontario)
1946	Attends Paris Peace Conference as head of Canadian delegation
1948	Attends United Nations General Assembly as head of Canadian delegation
1948, April 20	Exceeds the record of Sir Robert Walpole as prime minister, becoming the longest-serving prime minister in Commonwealth history
1948, Aug. 7	Resigns as leader of the Liberal Party
1948, Nov. 15	Resigns as Prime Minister of Canada, having held office for 7,829 days, longer than any other prime minister in the English-speaking world to that date
1950, July 22	Dies at The Farm, on his estate at Kingsmere, at the age of seventy-five

Location Symbols and Abbreviations

Archives

NAC	National Archives of Canada/Archives nationales du Canada, Ottawa
QUA	Queen's University Archives, Kingston
WLMK Papers	William Lyon Mackenzie King Papers (at NAC)

Libraries

Alberta

ACU	University of Calgary
AEU	University of Alberta, Edmonton

British Columbia

BVASA	Simon Fraser University, Burnaby
BVAU	University of British Columbia, Vancouver
BVIP	British Columbia Legislative Library, Victoria
BVIV	University of Victoria

Manitoba

MBU	University of Brandon
MWU	University of Manitoba, Winnipeg
MWUC	University of Winnipeg

New Brunswick

NBFU	University of New Brunswick, Fredericton

NBSAM Mount Allison University, Sackville

Newfoundland

NFSM Memorial University of Newfoundland, St John's

Nova Scotia

NSHD Dalhousie University, Halifax
NSHP Public Archives of Nova Scotia, Halifax
NSHS Saint Mary's University, Halifax

Ontario

OGU University of Guelph
OKQ Queen's University, Kingston
OKR Royal Military College of Canada, Kingston
OLU University of Western Ontario, London
OOA National Archives of Canada/Archives nationales du Canada, Ottawa
OOC Ottawa Public Library
OOCC Carleton University, Ottawa
OOE Department of External Affairs/Ministère des affaires extérieures, Ottawa
OONDH Department of National Defence, Ottawa
OONL National Library of Canada/Bibliothèque nationale du Canada, Ottawa
OOP Library of Parliament/Bibliothèque de Parlement, Ottawa
OOU University of Ottawa
OPAL Lakehead University, Thunder Bay
OPET Trent University, Peterborough
OSTCB Brock University, St Catharines
OTAR Ontario Archives, Toronto
OTL Ontario Legislative Library, Toronto
OTMCL Metropolitan Toronto Reference Library
OTNY North York Public Library
OTU University of Toronto (Robarts Library)
OTY York University, Toronto
OWA University of Windsor
OWTL Wilfrid Laurier University, Waterloo
OWTU University of Waterloo

Quebec

QLB Bishop's University, Lennoxville

QMBM	Bibliothèque de Montréal
QMBN	Bibliothèque nationale du Québec, Montreal
QMG	Concordia University/l'Université Concordia, Montreal
QMU	Université de Montréal
QQL	Assemblée nationale du Québec, Bibliothèque, Quebec City
QQLA	Université Laval, Quebec City
QSHERU	Université de Sherbrooke

Saskatchewan

SRL	Legislative Library of Saskatchewan, Regina
SSU	University of Saskatchewan, Saskatoon

Part One

WORKS BY MACKENZIE KING

SECTION A

Books

This section contains descriptions of the five books written by Mackenzie King and published in Canada, Great Britain, the United States, and France. The books are arranged chronologically by date of publication and printings within editions.

Full bibliographic details are provided for each of the five books. In addition, a section of notes on each book outlines its publishing history, including such information as when King first conceived the idea of writing the book and other details relating to the preparation of the manuscript.

A list of reviews of King's books is provided at the end of each title.

THE SECRET OF HEROISM

First Edition:

A1 THE SECRET | OF HEROISM | A Memoir of | Henry Albert Harper | By | W. L. MACKENZIE KING | [printer's device] | New York Chicago Toronto | Fleming H. Revell Company | London and Edinburgh

161 p. 190 x 125 mm.

P. [1] blank; p. [2] inserted photograph of Henry Albert Harper facing title page; p. [3] title page as above; p. [4] Copyright, 1906, by | FLEMING H. REVELL COMPANY | [at foot] New York: 158 Fifth Avenue | Chicago: 80 Wabash Avenue | Toronto: 27 Richmond Street, W. | London: 21 Paternoster Square | Edinburgh:

100 Princes Street; p. [5] To | My Mother; p. [6] seven-line quotation from Matthew Arnold's *Rugby Chapel*; p. [7] CONTENTS; p. [8] blank; pp. 9–19 TO THE READER; inserted photograph of the Sir Galahad Monument at Ottawa facing p. 18; p. [20] blank; pp. 21–161 text.

Dark-grey cloth boards with label on spine: The | SECRET | of | HEROISM | [line] | W. L. M. KING

Published in 1906 at $1.00; number of copies unknown.

1906 (called 'Second Edition'):

A2 THE SECRET | OF HEROISM | A Memoir of | Henry Albert Harper | By | W. L. MACKENZIE KING | [printer's device] | New York Chicago Toronto | Fleming H. Revell Company | London and Edinburgh

161 p. 190 x 125 mm.

P. [1] blank; p. [2] inserted photograph of Henry Albert Harper facing title page; p. [3] title page as above; p. [4] Copyright, 1906, by | FLEMING H. REVELL COMPANY | SECOND EDITION | [at foot] New York: 158 Fifth Avenue | Chicago: 80 Wabash Avenue | Toronto: 27 Richmond Street, W. | London: 21 Paternoster Square | Edinburgh: 100 Princes Street; p. [5] To My Mother; p. [6] seven-line quotation from Matthew Arnold's *Rugby Chapel*; p. [7] CONTENTS; p. [8] blank; pp. 9–19 TO THE READER; inserted photograph of the Sir Galahad Monument facing p. 18; p. [20] blank; pp. 21–161 text.

Dark-green cloth boards stamped in gold on spine: The | SECRET | of HEROISM | [line] KING. On front cover: The SECRET of HEROISM | [line] | W. L. MACKENZIE KING

Published in 1906; price unknown; number of copies unknown.

1919 (Thomas Allen):

A3 THE SECRET | OF HEROISM | A Memoir of | Henry Albert Harper | By | W. L. MACKENZIE KING | [printer's device] | THOMAS ALLEN | TORONTO

161 p. 190 x 125 mm.

P. [1] blank; p. [2] inserted photograph of Henry Albert Harper facing title page; p. [3] title page as above; p. [4] [line]: Copyright, Canada, 1919 | by W. L. Mackenzie King [line] | [at foot] PRESS OF THE HUNTER-ROSE CO., LIMITED; p. [5] To My Mother; p. [6] seven-line quotation from Matthew Arnold's *Rugby*

Chapel; p. [7] CONTENTS; p. [8] PREFACE TO NEW EDITION; pp. 9–19 TO THE READER; p. [20] blank; pp. 21–161 text.

Dark-green cloth boards stamped in gold on spine: The | SECRET | of | HEROISM | [line] | KING | [at foot] ALLEN. On front cover: The SECRET of HEROISM | [line] | [at foot] W. L. MACKENZIE KING. Dust-jacket printed in black and white with excerpts from four reviews of previous editions of this book.

Published in 1919 at $2.50; number of copies unknown.

1919 (The Ontario Publishing Company):

A4 THE SECRET | OF HEROISM | A Memoir of | Henry Albert Harper | By | W. L. MACKENZIE KING | THE ONTARIO PUBLISHING CO., LTD. | TORONTO

161 p. 190 x 125 mm.

P. [1] blank; p. [2] blank; inserted photograph of Henry Albert Harper facing title page; p. [3] title as above; p. [4] [line] | Copyright, Canada, 1919 | by W. L. Mackenzie King | [line]; [at foot] PRINTED IN CANADA | [line] | T. H. BEST PRINTING CO., LIMITED | TORONTO, ONT.; p. [5] In Memory of | My Mother; p. [6] seven-line quotation from Matthew Arnold's *Rugby Chapel*; p. [7] CONTENTS; p. [8] blank; pp. 9–19 TO THE READER; inserted photograph of Sir Galahad Monument facing p. 18; p. [20] blank; pp. 21–161 text.

Maroon cloth board stamped in gold on spine: The | SECRET | of | HEROISM | [line] | KING | [at foot] ONTARIO PUBLISHING CO. LTD. On upper board: The SECRET of HEROISM | [at foot] W. L. MACKENZIE KING

Published in 1919; price unknown; number of copies unknown.

1938 ('Sir William Mulock Edition'):

A5 The secret of heroism: A memoir of Henry Albert Harper. Toronto: The Ontario Publishing Company, 1938. 199 p.

Published in 1938; 500 copies printed. This edition was not for sale. No copy has been located.

On December 6, 1901, Mackenzie King's closest male friend, Henry Albert Harper, drowned while attempting to rescue a young woman in the Ottawa River. King and Harper had been classmates at the University of Toronto, both graduating in 1895. In 1900 Harper became assistant editor of the

Labour Gazette. Robert MacGregor Dawson, King's official biographer, summarized the importance of Harper in King's life when he wrote: 'The place which Harper held in King's affections was never again filled.'[1]

The first mention of a book about Harper appears in King's diary on January 15, 1902, when he mentions a book of 'Bert's writings and letters.'[2] By July 1903 King had completed about two-thirds of the manuscript. At that time he told Harper's brother that he hoped to complete the book later in the year.[3]

During the summer of 1904 King was still at work on the book. As he prepared to leave Kingsmere in September he wrote: 'I would have liked especially to have completed my little memoir of Bert. This must be done before the end of another month. How well it could be done here, – alone.'[4]

By December 1905 the book had reached the proof stage. King had hoped to finish reading the proofs and to return them to the publisher by December 17, his birthday. By that date, however, he had corrected and returned only a portion of the proofs.[5]

On January 17, 1906, King received the first two copies of the book, which was entitled *The Secret of Heroism: A Memoir of Henry Albert Harper.* His diary provides this description of his feelings:

> I was very proud of the little volume which I have not cared to let out of my hands since. It is tastefully bound in grey with plain paper label on the back (This is a special edition). The bookmaking is all that can be desired, as it lies beside me I look on [it] as a first child. As I walked to the Club for lunch with it in my hand & saw the Harper monument with the sun shining on it, a wave of mingled sadness & joy each intense and inseparably blended swept over me, and I seemed to have one real word with dear old Bert. It was all intended I cannot get away from that. It was so destined, and the Will of God is evident in it all – our two lives.[6]

1 Robert MacGregor Dawson, *William Lyon Mackenzie King: A political biography, 1874–1923* (Toronto: University of Toronto Press, 1958), p. 129.

2 National Archives of Canada [hereafter listed as NAC], MG 26, J 13 Series, Diary [hereafter referred to as King Diary], January 15, 1902.

3 NAC, MG 26, J 1 Series, vol. 3, p. 2988, William Lyon Mackenzie King to Frank C. Harper, July 21, 1903.

4 King Diary, September 25, 1904.

5 King Diary, December 17, 1905.

6 King Diary, January 17, 1906.

In the autumn of 1919, shortly after he was elected leader of the Liberal Party, King contacted Thomas Allen Publishers regarding the possibility of a new edition of *The Secret of Heroism.* Writing to Thomas Allen on October 5, 1919, King noted that he had received the plates from Fleming H. Revell about two years earlier and that he was free to use them as he wished.[7]

On October 9 King and Allen had lunch together in Ottawa to discuss the new edition of the book. Allen agreed to publish the new edition. Of the effect of the book, King noted in his diary: 'I am sure the book will have a good sale at the present time. My position as Liberal Leader will cause it to attract attention & it will do good at this juncture in helping to mould the ideals of our young people. I have always felt it had a large place in Canada, if its sale could be promoted, am glad of a chance to get it out at this time.'[8] Five days later, Allen wrote to King and confirmed his company's willingness to publish the new edition. He told King that it was likely they would print about two thousand copies and bind them as they were needed.[9]

King hoped that the new edition of the book would be ready before Christmas. Although the book was on the press by November 22, delays occurred because of problems in obtaining the photographs to be used for the dust jacket. The book was published in December.

In 1938 T.H. Best Publishing Company, Limited, printed five hundred copies of *The Secret of Heroism* for Sir William Mulock, which he distributed among the schools of North York. He offered prizes of $20, $15, $10, and $5 for the best student essays on the book. Mulock gave one hundred copies to Pickering College and about forty copies to the Armitage Public School.[10]

In August 1919, a few days after his election as leader of the Liberal Party, King, in a letter to B.K. Sandwell, discussed *The Secret of Heroism*:

> As you will see in glancing over its pages, while it is ostensibly a Memoir of our friend Bert Harper, it is intended even more as a study in character likely to be of use to young men. While at the University of Toronto, I found myself

---

7 NAC, WLMK Papers, MG 26, J 1 Series, vol. 42, p. 37008, William Lyon Mackenzie King to Thomas Allen, October 5, 1919.

8 King Diary, October 9, 1919.

9 NAC, WLMK Papers, MG 26, J 1 Series, vol. 42, p. 37011, Thomas Allen to William Lyon Mackenzie King, October 14, 1919.

10 NAC, WLMK Papers, MG 26, J 8 Series, vol. 3, T. Wilbur Best to William Lyon Mackenzie King, January 26, 1938.

immensely influenced by the writings of Arnold Toynbee, and his spirit as revealed in letters and addresses collected after his death by a few friends and published in the Humboldt Library Series, along with 'The Industrial Revolution.'[11] Knowing Harper as I did, I believed that the revelation of his spirit through letters and papers in my possession might serve as a like inspiration to younger men, especially as the heroic sacrifice of self had appealed so strongly to the public imagination. This was my motive in writing the book. It is perhaps as much an expression of my own convictions on some of the fundamental things of life as it is of Harper's character and aims. What I have seen and learned in the fifteen years which have intervened since the book was written, has only helped to confirm beliefs which as a young man I cherished so strongly.[12]

Reviews of THE SECRET OF HEROISM

Canadian Churchman, August 23, 1906, p. 534; *The Globe*, April 21, 1906, Saturday Magazine Section, p. 4; *Hamilton Times*, April 30, 1906, p. 5; *Saturday Night*, March 3, 1906, p. 14; *The Spectator* [London], March 31, 1906, p. 497; *Times Literary Supplement*, March 9, 1906, p. 79; *Toronto Mail and Empire*, March 17, 1906, p. 21; *Toronto News*, March 3, 1906, p. 15; *Toronto Star*, March 3, 1906, p. 20; *The Westminister*, 8 (3), March 1906, p. 210; *The Westminster Gazette*, March 3, 1906, p. 10.

INDUSTRY AND HUMANITY

First Edition:

A6 INDUSTRY | AND HUMANITY | A STUDY | IN THE PRINCIPLES UNDERLYING | INDUSTRIAL RECONSTRUCTION | BY | HON. W. L. MACKENZIE KING, C.M.G. | M.A., LL.B. (Toronto); Ph.D. (Harvard) | FELLOW OF THE ROYAL SOCIETY OF CANADA | FORMER MINISTER OF LABOR, CANADA | AUTHOR

11 Arnold Toynbee, *Lectures on the industrial revolution of the 18th century in England* (New York: Humboldt, 1890). This 263-page book contains addresses, notes, and other fragments by Toynbee. It also contains a short memoir by B. Jowett.

12 NAC, WLMK Papers, MG 26, J 1 Series, vol. 51, pp. 43777–43778, William Lyon Mackenzie King to B.K. Sandwell, August 22, 1919.

OF "THE SECRET OF HEROISM" | [publisher's device] | TORONTO | THOMAS ALLEN | BOSTON AND NEW YORK | HOUGHTON MIFFLIN COMPANY

[xxii], [568] p. 200 x 135 mm.

P. [i] half-title; p. [ii] blank; p. [iii] title page as above; p. [iv] COPYRIGHT, 1918, BY W. L. MACKENZIE KING | ALL RIGHTS RESERVED | Published November 1918; p. [v] TO THE MEMORY | OF | MY FATHER AND MOTHER; p. [vi] blank; p. [vii] three-line quotation from Louis Pasteur; p. [viii] blank; pp. [ix–xii] PREFATORY NOTE; p. [xiii] CONTENTS; p. [xiv] blank; p. [xv–xx] INTRODUCTION; p. [xxi] half-title; p. [xxii] blank; pp. [1]-[560] text; p. [561] blank; p. [562] blank; p. [563–567] INDEX; p. [568] The Riverside Press | CAMBRIDGE. MASSACHUSETTS | U.S.A.

Dark-green boards stamped in gold on spine: INDUSTRY | AND | HUMANITY [decoration] W. L. MACKENZIE | KING [at foot] THOMAS | ALLEN [line] HOUGHTON | MIFFLIN CO. On front cover: INDUSTRY | and HUMANITY [at base] W. L. MACKENZIE KING

Published in November 1918 at $3.00; number of copies unknown.

French Edition:

A7 W.-L MACKENZIE KING | PREMIER MINISTRE DE LA CONFEDÉRATION DU CANADA | [line] | LA QUESTION SOCIALE | ET LE CANADA | [line] | INDUSTRIE ET HUMANITÉ | "La Science ... se sera efforcée, en | obéissant à cette loi d'humanité, de | reculer les frontièes de la Vie." | LOUIS PASTEUR. | Traduction de ALTIAR | [line] | Préface de Gabriel HANOTAUX | DE L'ACADEMIE FRANÇAISE | Président du Comité France-Amérique | [line] | AVEC UN PORTRAIT HORS TEXTE | PARIS | LIBRAIRIE FÉLIX ALCAN | [line] | 1925 | Tous droits de reproduction et d'adaptation réservés.

IV, [256] p. 190 x 120 mm.

[Half-title; blank page; inserted photograph of William Lyon Mackenzie King; title page as above; blank page]; pp. i–iv: PRÉFACE: pp. 1–5 INTRODUCTION; p.[6]blank; pp. 7–250 text; pp. [251]-252: TABLE DES MATIÈRES; pp. 253–256: "[LE COMITÉ] FRANCE-AMÉRIQUE."

Paperbound. On spine [line] | W.-L. MACKENZIE | KING | [line] | La Question | Sociale | et | le Canada | [line] symbol of "Librairie

Félix Alcan" | PRIX 10 francs | [line] | LIBRAIRIE | ALCAN. On cover: BIBLIOTHÈQUE FRANCE-AMÉRIQUE | [line] | W.-L MACKENZIE KING | PREMIER MINISTRE DE LA CONFÉDÉRATION DU CANADA | [line] La Question sociale | et le Canada | INDUSTRIE ET HUMANITÉ | [line] | TRADUCTION DE ALTIAR | [line] | Préface de Gabriel HANOTAUX | DE L'ACADÉMIE FRANÇAISE | Président du Comité France-Amériqe | [symbol of "Librairie Félix Alcan" | LIBRARIE FÉLIX ALCAN

Published in 1925; price unknown; number of copies unknown.

1935 (New and Shorter Edition):

A8 INDUSTRY AND | HUMANITY | A STUDY | IN THE PRINCIPLES UNDERLYING | INDUSTRIAL RECONSTRUCTION | by | THE RIGHT HONOURABLE | W. L. MACKENZIE KING, M.P., | New and Shorter Edition | [publisher's device] | TORONTO: THE MACMILLAN COMPANY | OF | CANADA LIMITED, AT ST. MARTIN'S HOUSE | 1935

xxii, 269 p. 220 x 145 mm.

P. [i] half-title; p. [ii] blank; inserted photograph of William Lyon Mackenzie King facing title page; p. [iii] title page as above; p. [iv] [at about mid-page] Copyright, Canada, 1918 and 1935 | by | W. L. Mackenzie King | All rights reserved | [at foot] Printed in Canada; p. [v] TO THE MEMORY | OF | MY FATHER AND MY MOTHER; p. [vi] blank; p. [vii] three-line quotation from Louis Pasteur; p. [viii] blank; p. ix PUBLISHER'S NOTE; p. [x] blank; pp. xi–xiii PREFACE TO NEW AND ABRIDGED EDITION; p. [xiv] blank; p. [xv] CONTENTS; p. [xvi] blank; pp. xvii–xx INTRODUCTION TO FIRST EDITION; p. [xxi] half-title; p. [xxii] blank; pp. 1–265 text; p. [266] blank; pp. 267–269 INDEX.

Dark-red cloth boards stamped in gold on spine: INDUSTRY | AND | HUMANITY | [line] | MACKENZIE | KING | A study in | the Principles | Underlying | Industrial | Reconstruction | [at foot] MACMILLAN. Upper board also stamped: INDUSTRY AND HUMANITY | A Study in the Principles | Underlying Industrial Reconstruction | THE RIGHT HONOURABLE | W. L. MACKENZIE KING, M.P.

Publisher's note: 'The present book is an abridgement of the original. It is not, however, in any sense a revision.' [p. ix].

In the Preface, King writes: 'I have thought it advisable not to alter anything in the nature of a revision, beyond abridgment of the text as originally published' [p. xi]. He added: 'The present volume is about half the size of the original' [p. xi].

Published in 1935 at $2.50; number of copies unknown.

1947 (Macmillan):

A9 INDUSTRY AND | HUMANITY | A study in the principles underlying | Industrial Reconstruction | by | THE RIGHT HONOURABLE | W. L. MACKENZIE KING, M.P. | TORONTO | THE MACMILLAN COMPANY | OF CANADA LIMITED | 1947

xxix, 270 p. 225 x 145 mm.

P. [i] half-title; p. [ii] By the same Author | THE SECRET OF HEROISM | THE MESSAGE OF THE CARILLON | CANADA AT BRITAIN's SIDE | CANADA AND THE FIGHT FOR FREEDOM | ETC.; inserted photograph of William Lyon Mackenzie King facing title page; p. [iii] title page as above; p. [iv] Copyright, Canada | by | W. L. Mackenzie King | Original Edition, 1918 | Abridged Edition, 1935 | Re-issue, with new material, 1947 | All rights reserved | [at foot]: PRINTED AND BOUND IN CANADA | T. H. Best Co., Limited, Toronto; p. [v] TO THE MEMORY | OF | MY FATHER AND MY MOTHER; p. [vi] blank; p. [vii] three-line quotation from Louis Pasteur; p. [viii] blank; pp. ix–x PUBLISHER'S NOTE; p. xi CONTENTS; p. [xii] blank; pp. xiii–xxix; Introduction; p. [xxx] blank; pp. 1–265 text; p. [266] blank; pp. 267–270 INDEX.

Light-blue cloth boards stamped in gold on spine: INDUSTRY | AND | HUMANITY | KING | [at foot] MACMILLAN. On front cover: INDUSTRY | AND | HUMANITY/ W. L. MACKENZIE KING. Blue, black, and white dust jacket, picturing line of workers meeting employers.

Publisher's note: 'This present book, which is an abridgement of the original, is furnished with a new introduction by the author. This Introduction alone, which sums up what still remains of the problems he first stated in 1918, would seem to justify this re-issue were one not otherwise convinced of its desirability.' [p. x].

Published in October 1947 at $4.00; number of copies unknown.

1973 Edition:

A10 Industry and humanity | A STUDY IN THE PRINCIPLES | UNDERLYING INDUSTRIAL RECONSTRUCTION | WILLIAM LYON

MACKENZIE KING | WITH AN INTRODUCTION BY DAVID JAY BERCUSON | UNIVERSITY OF TORONTO PRESS

xxiv, [357] p. 210 x 135 mm.

P. [i] The social history of Canada | MICHAEL BLISS, EDITOR; pp. [ii–iii] title page as above; p. [iv] © University of Toronto Press 1973 | Toronto and Buffalo | Printed in Canada | ISBN (clothbound) 0-8020-1947-1 | ISBN (paperbound) 0-8020-6174-5 | LC 72-95460; [at foot] The original edition of this work appeared in 1918; p. [v] An introduction | BY DAVID JAY BERCUSON; pp. vi–xxiv Introduction; p. [1] Industry and Humanity | WILLIAM LYON MACKENZIE KING | p. [2] To the memory of my father and my mother; p. [3] Contents; p. [4] two-line quotation from Louis Pasteur; p. [5]–8 Prefatory note; pp. 9–12 Introduction; pp. [13]–[357] text.

Black cloth boards lettered in white. Down spine: Industry and humanity | King | Toronto. White dust jacket with red, blue, and black lettering.

Published in 1973 at $15.00; number of copies unknown. Also published in a paperback edition.

In the Preface to *Industry and Humanity*, King describes the purpose of his book:[13]

> Hopeful of being constructively helpful ... I decided to make a personal investigation into the root causes of some of the existing industrial controversies in America, and to contribute, by suggestion or otherwise, as opportunity offered, to working out improvements between Capital and Labor. I also decided to prepare, on the basis of my own experience and the literature available, a statement of underlying principles which are finding expression in the organization of industrial society, and which should obtain in all efforts at reconstruction. This volume marks the completion of that endeavour.

King began work with the Rockefeller Foundation as Director of Industrial Relations in October 1914. Of his work with the Foundation, J.W. Pickersgill has written: 'The original purpose of Mackenzie King's associa-

13 *Industry and humanity: A study in the principles underlying industrial reconstruction* (Toronto: Thomas Allen; and Boston and New York: Houghton Mifflin Company, 1918), pp. ix–x.

tion with the Rockefeller Foundation was the preparation of a book on industrial relations.'[14] It is impossible to determine precisely when King first decided to write *Industry and Humanity*. In August 1918 he wrote that it had involved 'about three years, pretty constant research and writing.'[15] This would place the date sometime during 1915. As the diary is somewhat sketchy for this period, it is impossible to be more precise as to the beginning of the work.

By the summer of 1916 King, who was spending several weeks at Kingsmere, was hard at work on the book.[16] The time spent on the writing was, however, reduced by several events during the summer of 1916, notably a trip to New York City for business with the Rockefeller Foundation and the death of his father on August 30. While he devoted considerable time to the book during the summer of 1917, several factors diverted his attention. His mother was seriously ill, and he spent as much time as possible with her at his cottage at Kingsmere. By the late fall he was campaigning for the December 17 federal election. His mother died on December 18 at Ottawa.

In February 1918 King was still looking for a publisher for the book. On February 23 he met with a representative of Macmillan in New York. King noted in his diary that Mr Brett 'seemed on the whole to think well of the outline I gave him, though he was careful to reserve judgement till seeing the mss. which he suggested my sending him at any time.'[17]

King was still hard at work on the book in June 1918. On June 28 he wrote: 'I have got up near to the end now, I see the stretch that leads to the finish.'[18] By July Houghton Mifflin had accepted the book, and word had been received from the publishing company that they were ready for the manuscript.[19]

King had high hopes for the book. The idea occurred to him that it might open the way to his obtaining a seat in the British Parliament. 'I believe my book,' he wrote, 'is going to be of real service and to be appreciated. It is a great thing to be at liberty, to write without restraint and yet

14 John Whitney Pickersgill, 'Mackenzie King spurned Rockefeller for an unknown career in politics,' *The Globe and Mail*, December 15, 1962, p. 22.

15 NAC, WLMK Papers, MG 26, J 1 Series, vol. 38, p. 33551, William Lyon Mackenzie King to Thomas Allen, August 5, 1918.

16 King Diary, June 22, 1916.

17 King Diary, February 23, 1918.

18 King Diary, June 28, 1918.

19 King Diary, July 12, 1918.

with the prestige which association of one kind or another & opportunity have brought.'[20] A few days later he wrote: 'I believe the book will have a wide circulation & will be of real service at this juncture in the world's affairs.'[21]

He was pleased to learn in August that Thomas Allen, a Toronto publisher, had arranged to take the book from Houghton Mifflin for publication in Canada. King continued to write and revise many hours every day during the summer and early fall of 1918. He had hoped to have the book completed by September 15, the anniversary of his father's birth, so that the Preface could be dated that day. However, he was unable to meet this deadline.

At one stage of the work King considered having a preliminary edition published for private distribution. This edition would have enabled him to circulate it among a few friends in order to obtain their comments.[22] While he ultimately abandoned this idea he did send drafts of several chapters to John D. Rockefeller and to his brother, Dr Dougall Macdougall King.[23]

In the period from September to November drafts, galley proofs, and page proofs continued to go back and forth between Ottawa and Houghton Mifflin in Boston. The Preface is dated October 3. As late as November 4 index proofs and charts were being relayed between the author and the publisher. Several delays occurred. In addition to King's finding it necessary to make several trips to Boston and Washington in connection with his work for the Rockefeller Foundation, the influenza epidemic of that year hit the employees of the publishing company.

Fred McGregor, who had been King's secretary since 1914, helped King a great deal with the writing and revising of his work,[24] typing and retyping the numerous drafts. By December 4 advance copies of *Industry and Humanity* had been sent to the author from Boston. King was in possession of what was to be his best-known book.

King summarized the thesis of the book in these words:

---

20 King Diary, July 18, 1918.

21 King Diary, August 22, 1918.

22 Frederick Alexander McGregor, *The fall and rise of Mackenzie King, 1911–1919* (Toronto: Macmillan of Canada, 1962), p. 224.

23 Ibid., pp. 224–225.

24 For a description of the writing of *Industry and Humanity*, see Frederick Alexander McGregor, *The fall and rise of Mackenzie King, 1911–1919* (Toronto: Macmillan of Canada, 1962), pp. 215–229.

> The main thesis of the book is that in *Reason* not in *Force* must be found the method of preventing and settling industrial disputes, and that any of the partners to industry: Labour, Capital, Management, and the Community, the interests of *the Community* must at all times be regarded as the over-riding interest since all other parties to industry owed to the community such rights and opportunities as are theirs. [King's emphasis][25]

A French edition of *Industry and Humanity* was published in Paris in 1925.

In 1935, as the general election appeared on the horizon, King began to think of a new edition of *Industry and Humanity*. Early in January he began to reread the book. 'The time has come I believe,' he wrote, 'to turn it to full as well as good account in Parliament & on the platform if need be.'[26] He decided that he should prepare an edition of excerpts from the book.[27] A few weeks later he received a letter from Houghton Mifflin informing him that the plates of the original edition had been melted down three years earlier. On receiving this news he wrote: 'I should have bought them then – & would have had it not been for weight & storage.' He added: 'I believe I shall yet get it reprinted at least in part.'[28]

In January 1935 King contacted Thomas Allen, the publisher of the Canadian edition, about the possibility of a new edition. 'It now looks,' he wrote, 'as if that book were at last coming into its own, and I imagine will be much discussed and widely read in the course of the next few months, as the book itself will become a main subject of discussion in the forthcoming general elections.' King believed that a new edition of *Industry and Humanity* 'would be a most profitable venture for any publishing house.'[29]

Thomas Allen was unable to undertake a new edition because of the cost of setting up and printing a book of that length; he had learned that Houghton Mifflin had destroyed the plates. His company was agreeable, however, to allow another publisher to publish a new edition of the work.[30]

Early in March the Macmillan Company decided that it would publish

25 NAC, MG 26, J 1 Series, vol. 424, p. 385129, William Lyon Mackenzie King to John Gray, March 8, 1947.
26 King Diary, January 7, 1935.
27 King Diary, January 7, 1935.
28 King Diary, February 3, 1935.
29 NAC, WLMK Papers, MG 26, J 3 Series, vol. 2, William Lyon Mackenzie King to Thomas Allen, January 26, 1935.
30 Ibid., Thomas Allen to William Lyon Mackenzie King, February 22, 1935.

an abridged edition of the book. King was amused that Macmillan now ageed to publish a new edition: 'What is more remarkable – this firm (the McMillan's [*sic*] in New York) rejected the MSS before it was accepted by Houghton Mifflin. Now it accepts an abridged edition after several of the other the original have been published by their competitors and the book is no longer in print.'[31]

In April Macmillan decided to proceed with the publication of the new edition without the guaranteed sale of one thousand copies. The company agreed to a three-hundred-page volume. In a meeting with Hugh S. Eayrs of Macmillan, King selected the type and paper. At the same time King and Eayrs agreed on 'a warm red almost a maroon for the colour of the cover, a sort of fine ribbed effect, gold lettering on front & back ...'[32]

King agreed to write a new Foreword, do the abridging, and look over the page proofs. With the new agreement with Macmillan, he recorded his feelings in his diary: 'This should be & doubtless is one of the great days of my life – a new edition of *Industry and Humanity*. I shall be able to put into a foreword what will give it point in these times & for a general election – but most of all – its page will help to fulfil the purpose for which they were written.'[33]

By early May King was at work on the revision of the book. On May 8 he wrote: 'It is a great relief to my mind to get this far under way – or rather, too, at last, have begun in earnest of [on] this task which is an important and exacting one.'[34] As he proceeded with the abridgment, he wrote: 'I confess I wish I had had the time to rewrite it as much of it read at this time is not equal to the present day need. Still enough remains to make it a worth while contribution to present day problems.' Of the work and its likely reception by the public, he wrote: 'It was a difficult and painful process, amputating chapter after chapter, and cutting out some of the material that involved most in the way of research. Still I think what remains makes a better volume, more compact and readable and saleable. I shall be surprised if at this date the book sells, & a full edition gets across. However, it may.'[35]

By May 15 the work on the book was almost completed. It was, he wrote,

31 King Diary, March 6, 1935.
32 King Diary, April 15, 1935.
33 King Diary, April 15, 1935.
34 King Diary, May 8, 1935.
35 King Diary, May 11, 1935.

'another memorable day.' He added: 'That work will soon be complete – the 15th edition.'[36] King gave his sister this description of the new edition of the book:

> It has gone through fifteen editions in all, and this is the sixteenth. It took up practically a solid week to make the revision necessary to cut the original book in half. I feel, however, immensely pleased that this firm is re-publishing a book which was published by the Houghton Mifflin Company in the first instance, and am delighted that they are doing so wholly on their own, and even allowing me a royalty of ten per cent.[37]

A few days later, as the first section of his ruins was being constructed on his estate at Kingsmere, the proof for the dust jacket of the book arrived. King was very pleased with it. Of the title, he wrote: 'The title will hold its own. There is something about it in keeping with the view from the hill.'[38]

King received the first copies of the new edition on July 25. After looking at the book before photographs of his mother and Woodside, he wrote: 'I prayed very earnestly for God's guidance & help, and offered the book as on an altar to His service.'[39]

Late in January 1947 King learned that the Macmillan Company of Canada was interested in publishing a revised edition of *Industry and Humanity*, with a new Introduction of about fifteen pages. The publishing company hoped to release the new edition in the autumn of 1947. Ill health prevented King from beginning work on the Introduction immediately. As late as April 12 he was still having difficulty getting the work under way.[40] In addition to a bout of influenza, the heavy parliamentary session and a four-week vacation in the United States delayed work on the writing.

By May 23 the Introduction was complete. The prime minister was pleased to see that it ran to exactly seventeen pages. He gave it the date of June 10, 1947 – the day on which he completed twenty years in office as

---

36 King Diary, May 15, 1935. King should have written that the new edition would be the sixteenth, since it was first published in 1918. The Preface states that it was the sixteenth edition.

37 NAC, WLMK Papers, MG 26, J 7 Series, vol. 13, p. 599, William Lyon Mackenzie King to Jennie, May 17, 1935.

38 King Diary, May 17, 1935.

39 King Diary, July 25, 1935.

40 King Diary, April 12, 1947.

prime minister. Of this date he wrote: 'I trust [it] may help to add significance to its words.'[41] He mailed the Introduction to Gray on May 24.[42]

The newly designed jacket for the book was ready in September. On September 21 King described his feelings about the jacket: 'I am immensely pleased with the jacket design for *Industry and Humanity*. Nothing could be better.'[43]

On October 30, just as he was leaving for a European visit that included the wedding of Princess Elizabeth and Prince Philip, King received the first copy of the new edition. 'It has been a great pleasure,' he wrote, having the new edition of my Industry and Humanity in its final form, coming out at this time.' He added: 'That will be a real help.'[44]

Reviews of INDUSTRY AND HUMANITY

1918 Edition:

American Economic Review, 9 (3), September 1919, p. 582; *Catholic World*, March 1919, p. 819; *The Globe*, December 24, 1918, p. 6; *The Nation*, 109, August 16, 1919, p. 229; *New Republic*, 19, July 2, 1919, p. 293; *New York Times*, November 16, 1919, p. 661; *North American Review*, 209, March 1919, p. 423; *Outlook*, 122, June 25, 1919, p. 340; *Times Literary Supplement*, April 24, 1919, p. 227; *Times Literary Supplement*, June 26, 1919, p. 343.

1935 Edition:

American Journal of Sociology, 42 (1), July 1936, p. 145; *Financial Post*, October 26, 1935, p. 24; *Manchester Guardian*, December 9, 1935, p. 5; *Montreal Gazette*, August 3, 1935, p. 3; *Vancouver Sun*, August 16, 1935, p. 6.

1947 Edition:

Halifax Chronicle, December 13, 1947, p. 4; *Ottawa Morning Journal*, November 18, 1947, p. 4; *The Times* [London], November 15, 1947, p. 3; *Vancouver Daily Province*, Saturday Magazine, January 10, 1948, p. 4.

41 King Diary, May 23, 1947.

42 NAC, WLMK Papers, MG 26, J 1 Series, vol. 424, pp. 385138–385139, William Lyon Mackenzie King to John Gray, May 24, 1947.

43 Ibid., vol. 424, p. 385153, William Lyon Mackenzie King to John Gray, September 21, 1947.

44 King Diary, November 17, 1947.

THE MESSAGE OF THE CARILLON

First Canadian Edition:

A11 The MESSAGE | of the CARILLON | And Other Addresses | BY | THE RIGHT HONOURABLE | W. L. MACKENZIE KING, | C.M.G., LL.D., D.C.L., M.P. | PRIME MINISTER OF CANADA | AUTHOR OF | "INDUSTRY AND HUMANITY," "THE SECRET OF HEROISM," ETC. | [publisher's device] | TORONTO: THE MACMILLAN COMPANY OF | CANADA LIMITED, AT ST. MARTIN'S HOUSE | 1927

x, 274 p. 220 x 145 mm.

P. [i] half-title; p. [ii] blank; inserted photograph of William Lyon Mackenzie King facing title page; p. [iii] title page as above; p. [iv] Copyright, Canada, 1927, by | THE MACMILLAN COMPANY OF CANADA LIMITED | [at foot] PRINTED IN CANADA | T. H. BEST PRINTING CO. LIMITED, TORONTO; p. [v] four-line quotation from Shakespeare's *King Henry VIII*; p. [vi] blank; pp. vii–viii PREFACE; pp. ix–x CONTENTS; pp. 1–274 text.

Maroon cloth boards; stamped in gold on spine: The | MESSAGE | of the | CARILLON | [line] | MACKENZIE | KING | [at foot] MACMILLAN

Published on December 1, 1927; price unknown; 2,000 copies printed.

Contents: p. 1: [half-title] I Confederation Addresses – p. [2] blank – pp. 3–13: The Message of the Carillion – pp. 14–29: Canada – pp. 30–37: H.R.H. The Prince of Wales – pp. 38–45: The Prime Minister of Great Britain – pp. 46–60: Laurier – pp. 61–71: Growth and Expansion – pp. 72–89: The Diamond Jubilee of Confederation – pp. 90–93: Progress – p. [94] blank; p. 95: [half-title] II Canada and the Empire – p. [96] blank: pp. 97–99: Symbols of Sovereignty – pp. 100–104: Canadian Unity – pp. 105–111: The Freedom of London – pp. 112–116: The British Commonwealth of Nations – pp. 117–129: Historical Records and Personalities – pp. 130–150: Citizenship – pp. 151–153: The British Commonwealth – pp. 154–160: Imperial Unity – p. 161 [half-title] III International and Industrial Peace – p. [162] blank – pp. 163–168: One Hundred Years of Peace I – pp. 169–173: One Hundred Years of Peace II – pp. 174–178: One Hundred Years of Peace III – pp. 179–190: Canada and the United States – pp. 191–221:

Industrial Peace – p. [222] blank – p. 223: [half-title] Appreciations – p. [224] blank – pp. 225–232: The University and Public Life – pp. 233–239: Canada and France – pp. 240–242: Marshal Foch – pp. 243–248: Recognition – pp. 249–257: The University and Service – pp. 258–269: Thomas D'Arcy McGee – pp. 270–274: The Supremacy of Ideals.

First British Edition:

A12 The MESSAGE | OF THE CARILLON | And Other Addresses | BY | THE RIGHT HONOURABLE | W. L. MACKENZIE KING, | C.M.G., LL.D., D.C.L., M.P. | PRIME MINISTER OF CANADA | AUTHOR OF | "INDUSTRY AND HUMANITY," "THE SECRET OF HEROISM," ETC. | [publisher's device] | MACMILLAN AND CO., LIMITED | ST. MARTIN'S HOUSE, LONDON | 1927

x, 274 p. 220 x 145 mm.

Maroon cloth boards stamped in gold on spine: The | MESSAGE | of the | CARILLON | [line] MACKENZIE | KING | [at foot] MACMILLAN

Identical text except for title page.

1928 Reprint:

A13 The MESSAGE | of the CARILLON | And Other Addresses | BY | THE RIGHT HONOURABLE | W. L. MACKENZIE KING | C.M.G., LLD., D.C.L., M.P. | PRIME MINISTER OF CANADA | AUTHOR OF | "INDUSTRY AND HUMANITY," "THE SECRET OF HEROISM," ETC. | [publisher's device] | TORONTO: THE MACMILLAN COMPANY OF | CANADA LIMITED, AT ST. MARTIN'S HOUSE | 1928

x, 274 p. 220 x 145 mm.

Maroon cloth boards stamped in gold on spine: The | MESSAGE of the | CARILLON | [line] MACKENZIE | KING | at foot] MACMILLAN

Indentical text except for title page.

1928 (Carillon Book Club):

A14 The MESSAGE | of the CARILLON | And Other Addresses | BY | THE RIGHT HONOURABLE | W. L. MACKENZIE KING | C.M.G., LL.D., D.C.L., M.P. | PRIME MINISTER OF CANADA | AUTHOR OF | "INDUSTRY AND HUMANITY," "THE SECRET

OF HEROISM," ETC. | [publisher's device] | TORONTO: THE MACMILLAN COMPANY OF | CANADA LIMITED, AT ST. MARTIN'S HOUSE | 1928

x, 274 p. 220 x 145 mm.

Identical text except for title page.

Dark-blue cloth boards stamped in gold on spine: The | MESSAGE | of the | CARILLON | [line] | MACKENZIE KING | [at foot] [double line] CARILLON with sketch of Peace Tower blocked in darker blue on cover. Patterned endpapers.

'This book has been chosen as the second to be distributed to the Booklovers of the Carillon Book Club Canada.'

On July 1, 1927, Mackenzie King presided at ceremonies on Parliament Hill in Ottawa at which the carillon in the Peace Tower was dedicated. On that occasion King made a major address, which he entitled 'The Message of the Carillon.' He issued the address in pamphlet form.[45]

On October 6 King, who was in Toronto to deliver an address at the University of Toronto on the occasion of its centenary, visited the Macmillan Company to discuss the possibility of a 250-page book of speeches. King suggested two titles: 'Confederation and other addresses' or 'The message of the carillon and other addresses.' However, he confided to his diary that he had had the latter title in mind from the beginning.[46]

Three days later the prime minister was at work on preparing an outline for the book.[47] Within a few days he was sorting speeches, making a provisional table of contents, and beginning to edit and revise the Confederation speeches. 'I find Baldwin's "On England"[48] a good guide,' he wrote; 'it gives me a feeling of justification in what I am attempting.'[49]

As he reread the speeches, he became dissatisfied. 'Indeed I am in some doubt about the publication at all of the speeches,' he wrote on October 17, 'save that they help in a way to bring up to date & preserve in permanent form literary efforts up to 1897 [1927] inclusive, & are a sort of souvenir of Confederation Year.'[50] King continued, however, to revise the speeches.

45 See item F36.

46 King Diary, October 6, 1927.

47 King Diary, October 9, 1927.

48 Stanley Baldwin, *On England, and other addresses* (London: P. Allen and Co. Ltd., 1926).

49 King Diary, October 10, 1927.

50 King Diary, October 17, 1927.

By the third week of October, the first proofs had arrived. King's diary contains this reaction to their arrival: 'It is a quite thrilling experience to see another book thus quickly underway.'[51] King was pressed to complete his work on the book before the opening of the Dominion–Provincial Conference on November 3. As he continued on with the Preface, title page, and table of contents he told his diary: 'There is great joy in seeing a book gradually taking shape.' The Preface was dated November 11, 1927.[52]

While the final work of proofreading was interrupted by the conference, he was able to write on November 12: 'It is just 5 weeks since the contract was concluded & a volume of 275 pages or thereabouts has been prepared. I am greatly pleased, tho' tired after the work. On the whole it has been pleasant & very publishable.'[53]

When Mackenzie King returned to Ottawa from talks in Washington on November 27, 1927, he received the first copies of *The Messsage of the Carillon.* His diary describes his reaction:

> To my delight Measures[54] was at the train with copies of his book under his arm. These I opened at Laurier House. I was prouder than I can say of the appearance of the book. Read through several chapters and was more than pleased at the way they appeared in print. I believe that the book will do myself & the party great good. I gave the first copy to Joan [Patteson] whose birthday is today and who the suggestion for the text on the big bell, which has led to the title of the book, its first address etc. etc. I shall always believe this book was inspired, that it was dear Mother who brought it and many features of the July 1 celebrations into being.[55]

On November 29 he wrote: 'More copies of my book received today. I am delighted with it.' He sent out over four hundred copies as Christmas gifts in 1927.

At year's end King's diary contains these comments about the book: 'I shall ever believe the *Message of the Carillon* was a direct inspiration from dear Mother, that her spirit was in all that therein is found expressed.'[56] As he summarized the year on New Year's Eve, King wrote that the book was 'a

---

51 King Diary, October 22, 1927.
52 King Diary, October 29, 1927.
53 King Diary, November 12, 1927.
54 King's secretary.
55 King Diary, November 27, 1927.
56 King Diary, December 16, 1927.

real gift to the Nation and will prove of incalculable value to myself, in my political life.'[57]

The book contains twenty-eight addresses delivered in the period from June 30, 1909 (at commencement ceremonies at Harvard University) to October 6, 1927 (at centenary ceremonies at the University of Toronto).

Reviews of THE MESSAGE OF THE CARILLON

Canadian Historical Review, 9 (2), June 1928, pp. 181–182; *Charlottetown Patriot*, January 7, 1928, p. 4; *London Advertiser*, December 21, 1927, p. 6; *Mail and Empire*, December 24, 1927, p. 18; *Manitoba Free Press*, January 24, 1928, p. 11; *Ottawa Citizen*, December 17, 1927, p. 35; *Ottawa Citizen*, January 13, 1928, p. 27; *Ottawa Journal*, January 9, 1928, p. 6; *Renfrew Mercury*, March 1, 1928, p. 6; *Saskatoon Daily Star*, December 7, 1927, p. 4; *Vancouver Sun*, January 7, 1928, p. 6; *Vancouver Sunday Province*, December 18, 1927, p. 4; *Willison's Monthly*, 3 (8), January 1928, p. 282.

CANADA AT BRITAIN'S SIDE

First Edition:

A15 CANADA | AT BRITAIN'S SIDE | BY | THE RIGHT HONOURABLE | W. L. MACKENZIE KING, M.P. | TORONTO | THE MACMILLAN COMPANY | OF CANADA LIMITED | 1941

xii, 332 p. 218 x 139 mm.

P. [i] half-title; p. [ii] blank; inserted photograph of William Lyon Mackenzie King facing title page; p. [iii] title page as above; p. [iv] [at about mid-page] COPYRIGHT, CANADA, 1941 | By | THE MACMILLAN COMPANY OF CANADA LIMITED | [at foot] PRINTED IN CANADA | T. H. BEST PRINTING CO., LIMITED | TORONTO, ONT.; p. [v] fourteen-line quotation from speech by William Lyon Mackenzie King; p. [vi] blank; p. [vii] prefatory statement by the publishers; p. [viii] blank; pp. ix–x CONTENTS; p. [xi] half-title; pp. [xii]–332 text.

57 King Diary, December 31, 1927.

Red cloth boards; stamped in gold on spine: CANADA | at | BRITAIN'S | SIDE | W. L. | MACKENZIE | KING | [at foot] | MACMILLAN. Red dust jacket with blue and white lettering.

Published on September 17, 1941, at $2.50; 1,500 copies printed.

Contents: pp. [ix–xi], 1–4: At Britain's Side – pp. 5–24: Canada Enters the War – pp. 25–40: The Issue – pp. 41–56: The Organization of Canada's War Effort – pp. 57–70: The British Commonwealth Air Training Plan – pp. 71–82: National Unity and the Defence of Freedom – pp. 83–88: The Late Lord Tweedsmuir – pp. 89–102: The Spring of 1940 – Canada's War Effort – pp. 103–118: New Situations and Responsibilities – pp. 119–126: Italy Enters the War – pp. 127–136: Midsummer 1940 – Canada's War Effort in Review – pp. 143–152: Labour and the War – pp. 153–158: Japan and the New Order – pp. 159–178: Canada–United States Joint Defence – The Ogdensburg Agreement – pp. 179–192: Lights and Shadows – The War in Perspective – pp. 193–200: The Old Year and the New – pp. 201–222: Brighter Skies and Gathering Storms – The War in Review – pp. 223–228: A Milestone of Freedom – The Lend–Lease Act – pp. 228–234: A New World Order – pp. 235–242: Canada's Contribution to Freedom – pp. 243–250: The Invasion of Yugoslavia and Greece – pp. 251–258: The Conflict in the Middle East – pp. 259–270: Co-operation in Economic Defence – The Hyde Park Declaration – pp. 271–278 – Changing Phases of World-Wide War – pp. 287–294: The Universities – The Trustees of Liberty – pp. 295–308: Canada's War Effort Outlined in the United States – pp. 309–314: Germany Attacks Russia – pp. 315–332: The World-Encircling Danger.

British Edition:

A16 CANADA | AT BRITAIN'S SIDE | BY | THE RIGHT HONOURABLE | W. L. MACKENZIE KING, M.P. | LONDON | MACMILLAN AND CO., LTD | 1941

P. [i] half-title; p. [ii] blank; inserted photograph of William Lyon Mackenzie King facing title page; p. [iii] title page as above; p. [iv] [about mid-page] COPYRIGHT, CANADA, 1941 | By | THE MACMILLAN COMPANY OF CANADA LIMITED | [at foot] PRINTED IN CANADA | T. H. BEST PRINTING CO., LIMITED | TORONTO, ONT.; p. [v] fourteen-line quotation from speech by William Lyon Mackenzie King;

p. [vi] blank; p. [vii] prefatory statement by the publishers; p. [viii] blank; pp. ix–x CONTENTS; p. [xi] half-title; pp. [xii]–332 text.

Indentical text to First Edition.

Red cloth boards; stamped in gold on spine: CANADA | at | BRITAIN'S | SIDE | W. L. | MACKENZIE | KING | [at foot] MACMILLAN

Published in 1941; price unknown; 250 copies contained the London imprint.

French Edition:

A17 W.-L MACKENZIE KING, MP. | PREMIER MINISTRE DU CANADA | Le | Canada | et la | guerre | ÉDITIONS BERNARD VALIQUETTE | MONTRÉAL

[343] p. 190 x 125 mm.

P. [1] blank; p. [2] blank; p. [3] half-title; p. [4] blank; p. [5] title as above; p. [6] blank; p. [7] twelve-line quotation from a Mackenzie King speech; p. [8] blank; p. [9] note from 'Les éditeurs.'; p. [10] blank; pp. [11] [half-title]; pp. 12–341 text; p. [342] blank; p. [343] TABLES DES MATIÈRES.

Published in 1941; price unknown; 2,000 copies printed.

Contents: pp. [11]–16: Le Canada allié de la Grande Bretagne; pp. [17]–36: L'entrée en guerre du Canada; pp. [37]–53: La question en jeu; p. [54] blank; pp. [55]–72: L'organisation de l'effort de guerre du Canada; pp. [73]–87: Plan d'entraînement des aviateurs du Commonwealth britannique; p. [88] blank; pp. [89]–101: Unité nationale et défense de la liberteé; p. [102] blank; pp. [103]–108: Feu Lord Tweedsmuir; pp. [109]–123: Printemps 1940: L'effort de guerre du Canada; p. [124] blank; pp. [125]–141: Nouvelles situations et nouvelles responsabilités; p. [142] blank; pp. [143]–150: L'entrée de l'Italie dans la guerre; pp. [151]–160: Administration de guerre; pp. [161]–166: Eté 1940: L'effort de guerre du Canada; pp. [167]–177: Le travail et la guerre; p. [178] blank; pp. [179]–184: Le Japon et l'ordre nouveau; pp. [185]–203: Défense conjointe du Canada et des États-Unis: Accord d'Ogdensbourg; p. [204] blank; pp. [205]–220: Ombres et lumières: La guerre qui nous attend; pp. [221]–228: L'année qui fait; L'année qui arrive; pp. [229]–238: Effort total contre guerre totale; pp. [239]–251: Rayons et ombres: Revue de la guerre; p. [251] blank; pp. [252]–258: Le bill de prêt-location.

Tourant de la liberté; pp. [259]–264: Un nouvel ordre dans le monde; pp. [262]–273: L'apport du Canada à la liberté; p. [274] blank; pp. [275]–282: L'invasion de la Yougoslavie et de la Grèce; pp. [283]–290: Le conflit dans le Moyen-Orient; pp. [291]–301: La déclaration de Hyde-Park; Coopération de défense économique; p. [302] blank; pp. [303]–311: Vers la victoire; p. [312] blank; pp. [313]–320: Aspects multiple de la guerre mondiale; pp. [321]–325: L'Allemagne attaque la Russie: p. [326] blank; p. [326] blank; pp. [327]–341: Le danger d'encerclement mondiale.

Paperbound; white cover with red and black lettering; on spine: W.-L | MACKENZIE | KING, M.P. | [line] | Le | Canada | et la guerre | [line] | EDITIONS | BERNARD | VALIQUETTE

1943 (United States Office of War Information Edition):

A18 Le Canada et la guerre. New York: Les Éditions de la Maison Française, 1943.

Published in 1943; 2,750 copies printed.

No copy has been located.

King may have conceived the idea of this collection of wartime addresses when he saw Winston Churchill's first book of wartime speeches.[58] A few days after the publication of *Canada at Britain's Side*, King wrote to Churchill: 'I cannot claim that the accompanying volume is worthy of a place on your shelves near "Into Battle," or its American alternate, "Blood, Sweat and Tears." It does, however, belong to the same family, and I am not at all sure that, feeble as it may be in comparison, the contents do not owe their publication in book-form to the example set by yourself or rather by Randolph in his publication of your exceptional speeches and addresses.'[59] Earlier in the year, on June 13, King received two publications with chap-

58 The English edition was entitled *Into Battle* and was published by Cassell and Company Limited on April 14, 1941. The American edition, *Blood, Sweat, and Tears*, was published by G.P. Putnam's Sons in February 1941. William Ready Division of Archives and Research Collections, McMaster University Library, Hamilton, Canada, Macmillan Company of Canada Archives [hereafter Macmillan Company of Canada Archives], William Lyon Mackenzie King to Robert Huckvale, June 25, 1941.

59 NAC, WLMK Papers, MG 26, J 1 Series, vol. 302, p. 255594, William Lyon Mackenzie King to Winston Churchill, September 30, 1941.

ters contributed by him. They were *Let's Face the Facts*[60] and *Canada Fights: An American Democracy at Work.*[61]

The first mention of a book occurs in his diary on June 21, 1941. On that date the prime minister telephoned Mr Robert Huckvale, vice-president of the Macmillan Company of Canada in Toronto. King told Huckvale that he believed several of the addresses he had delivered since the beginning of the war would make 'a readable volume.' He suggested the title 'Canada and the War.' Huckvale told King that the company would be pleased to accept it for publication and that it could be out by September. 'I am delighted,' King wrote, 'for I am sure the volume will disclose a fine record and a war effort that is indeed worthy of our country.'[62]

On June 24 King left for a nineteen-day tour of western Canada. He wrote to Huckvale on June 25 from the train en route to the West. He told Huckvale that a ring binder containing the speeches and broadcasts that he thought might make up the published volume had been prepared. He believed that there should be 'a brief statement of about half a page which would serve to link up one address with the other, each address constituting as it were a separate chapter.' He had asked Leonard Brockington, his assistant, to prepare something in the way of these introductory sections.[63]

King believed that the book would 'prove to be a helpful contribution to our war effort.' It would explain, he wrote, 'principles underlying the conflict, the progress of the war, and Canada's contribution thereto.'[64]

The original material submitted to the publisher amounted to about 164,000 words. The publisher suggested that it would be necessary to reduce the length to about 86,000 words in order to keep the price down to a level where substantial sales could be expected.[65] When King returned

---

60 *Let's face the facts: Four addresses from a series of radio broadcasts by internationally promiment men and women, delivered over the national network of the Canadian Broadcasting Corporation.* Ottawa: Director of Public Information, 1940. 46 p.

61 John Wesley Dafoe, *Canada fights: An American democracy at work* (New York and Toronto: Farrar & Rinehart, Inc., 1941), vi, 280 p.

62 King Diary, June 21, 1941.

63 Macmillan Company of Canada Archives, William Lyon Mackenzie King to Robert Huckvale, June 25, 1941.

64 Ibid.

65 NAC, MG 26, J 1 Series, vol. 304, pp. 257186–257187, Ellen Elliott to William Lyon Mackenzie King, July 9, 1941.

to Ottawa from his trip to western Canada he 'was greatly pleased to see that it is going to be accepted, and that suggested abbreviations accorded with my own ideas.'[66]

During the final illness of his Irish terrier, Pat, King attempted to work on the manuscript. He devoted a good deal of time to working at the collection of speeches. By July 14, only a day before Pat died, King had a talk with J.W. Pickersgill regarding the book. By this time he mentioned the title 'At Britain's Side.'

A few days after Pat's death, King was able to return to his work on the book, including the reading of page proofs. He was concerned about the size of the type. On July 28 he received the promise of a larger type from the publisher.[67] On August 2 he mentions for the first time the final title – 'Canada at Britain's Side.'[68]

Work progressed on the book during the first week of August. The writing of the prefatory notes for each chapter took a great deal of time. On August 8 the contract for the book was signed.[69] In the days following the signing of the contract, King continued to work on the table of contents and frontispiece and the final reading of proofs. On August 13, just as he was planning for a flight to Britain, the prime minister was informed that sixty pages still had to be cut from the manuscript.[70] The last proofs were mailed to Macmillan on August 17. He summarized his feelings when he described the final stage: 'This was an immense relief.'[71] The prime minister had daily talks by telephone with the publisher. On the following day, amid delays in the delivery of proofs to Macmillan, King learned that reductions had to be made to some sections, and additions to others. 'I found this very exacting and trying, having to follow galley proofs while conversing over the telephone ...'[72] Finally, on August 19, he left by air for Britain on his first transatlantic flight.

King received the first copies of the book on September 9, 1941. His feelings about it are recorded in his diary: 'The great event of the day – and as I record it the two hands of the clock are together, near twenty to

66 King Diary, July 12, 1941.
67 King Diary, July 28, 1941.
68 King Diary, August 2, 1941.
69 King Diary, August 8, 1941.
70 King Diary, August 13, 1941.
71 King Diary, August 17, 1941.
72 King Diary, August 18, 1941.

eight[73] – was the arrival exactly at six, at the Farm, of the first copies of my book "Canada at Britain's Side." I am greatly pleased with the appearance and make-up of the volume which is quite a substantial one. It is coming out at exactly the right moment. For this, too, I am most grateful to God.'[74]

On September 25 he inscribed the first copies of the book, which had just arrived with the dust jacket. The first he inscribed to himself, the second to Joan Patteson, and the third to Lord Athlone, the governor general.[75]

King described the book in this way: 'It is really a compilation of speeches and addresses delivered since the beginning of the war.'[76] In writing to King George VI's private secretary, King described the value of the book: 'I do not claim any special merit for the book other than that I think it may serve to answer those critics who claim that Canada has not, from the beginning, appreciated the significance and magnitude of the present world conflict, or that her effort in the war has been all that, in the circumstances, it might have been expected to be.'[77]

---

73 For a considerable portion of his life, Mackenzie King paid attention to the position of the hands of the clock when important events occurred. His diary contains hundreds of references to this phenomenon. The positions were when the hands were together, at right angles, or in a straight line. The first reference in the diary to the hands of the clock occurred on September 16, 1918, the day he completed the writing of *Industry and Humanity*.

Several of King's biographers, including Dawson, Neatby, and Stacey, have discussed King's interest in the position of the hands of the clock. Dawson suggests that the frequency of references to the phenomenon became 'something in the nature of a fixed obsession' with King. For Dawson's analysis of this subject, see his *William Lyon Mackenzie King: A political biography, 1874–1923* (Toronto: University of Toronto Press, 1958), pp. 252–253. For Neatby's discussion, see his *William Lyon Mackenzie King: The lonely heights, 1924–1932* (Toronto: University of Toronto Press, 1963), pp. 201–202. Stacey believes that King gave something of a key to an explanation of this interest when he describes a conversation he had with Violet Markham in 1944: 'As I ... went to take the watch out of my pocket, to show her how the face had been broken, I looked at it and the two hands were exactly at 10 to 10. I mentioned it to her as an illustration of my belief that some presence was making itself known to me. That I was on the right line, and that the thought was a true one which I was expressing.' Charles Perry Stacey, *A very double life: The private world of Mackenzie King* (Toronto: Macmillan of Canada, 1976), p. 161.

74 King Diary, September 9, 1941.

75 King Diary, September 25, 1941.

76 NAC, WLMK Papers, MG 26, J 1 Series, vol. 305, p. 257762, William Lyon Mackenzie King to Sir Eric Mielville, September 30, 1941.

77 Ibid.

The book consisted of fourteen addresses delivered by King from September 3, 1939, to June 22, 1941. All of the speeches were published as pamphlets. Several of them in appeared in the 'Canada and the War' series.[78]

Macmillan Company considered the publication of a paper-bound edition of the book. Discussion with booksellers, however, showed that there was little enthusiasm for a reprint edition.[79]

A French edition was published early in 1942 by Éditions Bernard Valiquette of Montreal.

In 1943, 2,750 copies of *Le Canada et la guerre* were distributed around the world under the auspices of the United States Office of War Information. The edition was printed by Éditions de la Maison Française of New York City.[80]

Reviews of CANADA AT BRITAIN'S SIDE

Brandon Daily Sun, September 30, 1941, p. 4; *Financial Post*, October 11, 1941, p. 5; *The Globe and Mail*, September 20, 1941, p. 6; *Labour World*, January 24, 1942, p. 6; *Le Droit*, January 22, 1942, p. 3; *Montreal Gazette*, October 9, 1941, p. 8; *Ottawa Citizen*, September 27, 1941, p. 19; *Ottawa Evening Journal*, September 27, 1941, p. 21; *Toronto Star*, September 20, 1941, p. 6; *Vancouver Sun*, October 11, 1941, Magazine Section, p. 4.

CANADA AND THE FIGHT FOR FREEDOM

First Edition:

A19 CANADA | AND THE | FIGHT FOR FREEDOM | By | THE RIGHT HONOURABLE | W. L. MACKENZIE KING, M.P. | TORONTO | THE MACMILLAN COMPANY | OF CANADA LIMITED | 1944

78 About thirty-seven of King's wartime speeches were issued by the King's Printer in the 'Canada and the War' and 'Le Canada et la guerre' series between 1940 and 1945. They are listed in the 'Published Speeches' section of this bibliography.

79 NAC, WLMK Papers, MG 26, J 1 Series, vol. 323, p. 275418, Ellen Elliott, Macmillan Company of Canada Limited, to William Lyon Mackenzie King, April 22, 1942.

80 Ibid., vol. 353, p. 306524, Bernard Valiquette to William Lyon Mackenzie King, August 6, 1943.

[xxvi], 326 p. 215 x 140 mm.

P. [i] half-title; p. [ii] blank; inserted photograph of William Lyon Mackenzie King facing title page; p. [iii] title page as above; p. [iv] COPYRIGHT, CANADA, 1944 | BY | THE MACMILLAN COMPANY OF CANADA LIMITED | [at foot] PRINTED IN CANADA | T. H. BEST CO., LIMITED, TORONTO; pp. v–xv INTRODUCTION [by Eric Estorick]; pp. xvi–xxiv INTRODUCTION [by B. K. Sandwell]; p. [xxv] CONTENTS; p. [xxvi] blank; pp. 1–326 text.

Contents: pp. 1–12: Canada and the Fight for Freedom – pp. 13–29: Servitude or Freedom – pp. 30–41: Controlling the Cost of Living – pp. 42–90: The Real Meaning of a Total War Effort – pp. 91–101: Keeping Faith With the People – pp. 102–121: National Selective Service – pp. 122–129: The Defence of Canada – pp. 130–141: National Security in Time of War – pp. 142–152: National Unity and National Survival – pp. 153–182: I. Overseas Service – Historical Considerations – pp. 183–197: II. Overseas Service in Relation to a Total War Effort – pp. 198–220: Nothing Matters Now but Victory – pp. 221–232: The Defence of Common Liberties – pp. 233–244: Temperance and a Total War Effort – pp. 245–258: Canada's Fighting Men – pp. 259–265: Canadian Forces in Alaska and the Aleutians – pp. 266–274: Four Years of War 1939–1943 – pp. 275–298: Politics and the War – pp. 299–309: The Battle Against Inflation – pp. 310–326: "The Glory and the Dream."

Published in 1944 at $3.50; number of copies unknown.

Red cloth boards; stamped in gold on the spine: CANADA | AND THE | FIGHT | FOR | FREEDOM | [line] | KING | MACMILLAN

Dust jacket: Red, white, and blue with black. Front: with white lettering on blue background: CANADA | AND THE | FIGHT | FOR | FREEDOM | [black lettering on red background]: THE RIGHT HONOURABLE | W. L. MACKENZIE KING | M.P. | On spine: [white lettering on red background]: CANADA | AND THE | FIGHT | FOR FREEDOM | [black letters]: W. L. | MACKENZIE | KING | M.P. | [white lettering on red background]: MACMILLAN

Back cover contains an excerpt from Winston Churchill's introduction of Mackenzie King on the occasion of King's address to both Houses of the British Parliament, London, May 11, 1944. Front flap contains a quotation from the writings of Emil Ludwig on King's political career and comments from the London *Times* and the *New*

York Times on King's 1944 address to the British Parliament. The back flap contains a biographical sketch of Mackenzie King.

American Edition:

A20 CANADA | AND THE | FIGHT FOR FREEDOM | By | THE RIGHT HONOURABLE | W. L. MACKENZIE KING, M.P., | NEW YORK | DUELL, SLOAN AND PEARCE | 1944

[xxvi], 326 p. 215 x 140 mm.

P. [i] half-title; p. [ii] blank; inserted photograph of William Lyon Mackenzie King facing title page; p. [iii] title page as above; p. [iv] COPYRIGHT, CANADA, 1944 | BY | THE MACMILLAN COMPANY OF CANADA LIMITED | [at foot] PRINTED IN CANADA | T. H. BEST PRINTING CO., LIMITED, TORONTO; pp. v–xv INTRODUCTION [by Eric Estorick]; pp. xvi–xxiv INTRODUCTION [by B.K. Sandwell]; p. [xxv] CONTENTS; p. [xxvi] blank; pp. 1–326 text.

Dark-blue cloth boards; stamped in gold on the spine: CANADA | AND THE | FIGHT | FOR | FREEDOM | W. L. | MACKENZIE | KING | M.P. [at foot] | DUELL, SLOAN | AND PEARCE

Published in 1944; $3.50; number of copies unknown.

1972 (Essay Index Reprint Series):

A21 CANADA | AND THE | FIGHT FOR FREEDOM | THE RIGHT HONOURABLE | WILLIAM L. MACKENZIE KING | Essay Index Reprint Series | Originally Published by | DUELL, SLOAN AND PEARCE | NEW YORK | [printer's device] | BOOKS FOR LIBRARIES PRESS | FREEPORT, NEW YORK

[xvi], 326 p. 215 x 140 mm.

P. [i] half-title; p. [ii] portrait of William Lyon Mackenzie King; p. [iii] title page as above; p. [iv] Copyright, Canada, 1944 by | The Macmillan Company of Canada Limited | Reprinted 1972 by arrangement with | Hawthorn Books, Inc. | [at centre] [eight lines of Library of Congress Cataloguing in Publication data] | [at foot] PRINTED IN THE UNITED STATES OF AMERICA | pp. v–xv INTRODUCTION [by Eric Estorick]; pp. xvi–xxiv INTRODUCTION [by B.K. Sandwell]; p. [xxv] CONTENTS; p. [xxvi] blank; pp. 1–326 text.

Dark-blue cloth boards; stamped in silver on a dark-red panel on spine reading down: CANADA AND THE | FIGHT FOR FREEDOM | [dot] KING | [Symbol of Books for Libraries]

Published in 1972; price unknown; number of copies unknown.

Early in 1944 Eric Estorick, an American writer, proposed that a second collection of Mackenzie King's wartime speeches should be published by Duell, Sloan and Pearce of New York City. Estorick was prepared to write the Introduction and to undertake the necessary editorial work. Early in January King signed a contract for the book with Duell, Sloan and Pearce, Incorporated.[81]

The Macmillan Company of Canada, publishers of *Canada at Britain's Side*, learned of the proposal. Macmillan pointed out that the contract for the publication of *Canada at Britain's Side* contained a clause giving that company the option of King's next book.[82] On February 12, 1944, King wrote to Macmillan and agreed that they could print and publish the book. Macmillan would supply Duell, Sloan and Pearce either with sheet or bound stock. The prime minister made it clear that the proposal to publish a second volume of speeches had come from Estorick and that he personally had not taken any initiative in the matter.[83]

King found it 'very gratifying' to have a second book of his wartime speeches published.[84] He considered it as a companion volume to *Canada at Britain's Side.*[85]

King signed the contract for the book on March 14, 1944. By this time B.K. Sandwell, the well-known Canadian journalist and writer, had also agreed to write an introduction to the book.[86]

King originally suggested the title 'Canada's Fight for Freedom.'[87] By

81 NAC, WLMK Papers, MG 26, J 1 Series, vol. 359, pp. 311573–311576, 'Agreement between Right Honourable William Lyon Mackenzie King and Duell, Sloan & Pearce, Inc. for the publication of Book on Canada, dated January 4, 1943 [*sic*].'

82 Ibid., J 1 Series, vol. 359, p. 311516, Eileen Elliott to William Lyon Mackenzie King, January 28, 1944.

83 NAC, WLMK Papers, MG 26, J 1 Series, vol. 359, pp. 311520–311521, William Lyon Mackenzie King to Eileen Elliott, February 12, 1944.

84 King Diary, February 12, 1944.

85 Queen's University Archives [hereafter listed as QUA], Bernard Keeble Sandwell Papers, vol. 1, William Lyon Mackenzie King to Bernard Keeble Sandwell, March 4, 1944.

86 NAC, WLMK Papers, J 1 Series, vol. 359, p. 311522, Eileen Elliott to William Lyon Mackenzie King, February 17, 1944; and p. 311523, H.R.L. Henry [Private Secretary to Mr King], February 19, 1944.

87 Ibid., vol. 359, p. 311521, William Lyon Mackenzie King to Eileen Elliott, February 12, 1944.

late June the title had been changed to 'Canada and the Fight for Freedom.'[88]

This book consists of twenty-one addresses delivered by Mackenzie King from September 4, 1941, to May 11, 1944. It includes radio broadcasts, speeches in the House of Commons, and formal addresses such as one delivered to the British Parliament. Most of these addresses were issued as pamphlets in the 'Canada and the War' and 'Le Canada et la guerre' series. The book contains introductions by Eric Estorick and B.K. Sandwell.

Reviews of CANADA AND THE FIGHT FOR FREEDOM

Catholic World, July 1945, pp. 358–359; *Churchman*, June 15, 1945, pp. 18, 20; *Financial Post*, April 21, 1945, p. 20; *Montreal Gazette*, April 28, 1945, p. 7; *The Narrator*, May 1945, p. 9; *New York Times*, April 22, 1945, Book Review Section, p. 20; *Ottawa Evening Citizen*, April 21, 1945, p. 13; *Ottawa Morning Journal*, April 14, 1945, p. 8; *Saturday Night*, 60 (13), April 21, 1945, p. 30; *Toronto Daily Star*, April 14, 1945, p. 20; *Winnipeg Free Press*, May 5, 1945, p. 10.

88 NAC, WLMK Papers, MG 26, J 4 Series, vol. 287, p. 198090, 'Memorandum on "Canada and the Fight for Freedom."'

SECTION B

Articles

This section contains a chronological listing of the newspaper and periodical articles written by Mackenzie King from his days as a university student until shortly before his death.

Most of the newspaper and journal articles written by Mackenzie King were unsigned. They have been identified by comparing references in the diary and correspondence with the appropriate newspaper or journal for the days following their mention in either of the above sources.

An asterisk before an article indicates that it was unsigned.

B1 *'Football. Varsity's second defeats Upper Canada College by 29 to 2.' *The Toronto Mail,* October 5, 1893, p. 2.
Reference: King Diary, October 4, 1893.

B2 *'Midst the Mortar Boards.' *The Varsity,* 13 (2), October 18, 1893, p. 8.
Reference: King Diary, October 14, 1893.

B3 *'Y.M.C.A.' *The Varsity,* 13 (3), October 25, 1893, p. 8.
Reference: King Diary, October 17, 1893.

B4 *'Hallowe'en: A farce in five acts.' *The Varsity,* 13 (5), November 8, 1893, p. 8. Signed 'ONE WHO IS REAPING ITS BENEFIT.'
Reference: King Diary, November 4, 1893.

B5 *'Midst the Mortar Boards.' *The Varsity,* 13 (6), November 15, 1893, p. 8.
Reference: King Diary, November 4, 1893.

B6 *'Midst the Mortar Boards.' *The Varsity*, 13 (7), November 22, 1893, p. 8.
Reference: King Diary, November 18, 1893.

B7 *'Midst the Mortar Boards.' *The Varsity*, 13 (9), December 6, 1893, p. 8.
Reference: King Diary, December 1 and 2, 1893.

B8 *'The Varsity and the students.' [Letter to the Editor]. *The Varsity*, 13 (9), December 6, 1893, p. 5. Letter signed 'Justice.'
Reference: King Diary, December 2, 1893.

B9 *'University Glee Club.' [Description of visit to Lindsay]. In 'Music and the Drama' column, *The Globe*, December 19, 1893, p. 8.
Reference: King Diary, December 18, 1893.

B10 *'University Glee Club.' [Description of visit to Peterborough]. In 'Music and the Drama' column, *The Globe*, December 20, 1893, p. 6.
Reference: King Diary, December 19, 1893.

B11 *'The Club in Ottawa.' *The Globe*, December 22, 1893, p. 8.
Reference: King Diary, December 21, 1893.

B12 *[Article on the annual tour of the University of Toronto Glee Club, Banjo and Guitar Club and Mandolin Quartette through eastern Ontario]. In 'Social and Personal' column, *Saturday Night*, 7 (7), January 6, 1894, p. 3.
Reference: King Diary, December 30, 1893.

B13 *'Varsity sports.' *The Varsity*, 14 (1), October 11, 1894, pp. 5–6.
Reference: King Diary, October 4, 1894.

B14 *'Varsity sports.' *The Varsity*, 14 (3), October 24, 1894, pp. 20–21.
Reference: King Diary, October 22, 1894.

B15 'Greek letter societies.' *The Varsity*, 14 (2), October 17, 1894, pp. 9–10.
Reference: King Diary, October 13, 15, and 17, 1894.

B16 'Hallowe'en.' *The Varsity*, 14 (5), November 7, 1894, pp. 33–35.
Article signed 'Rex.'
Reference: King Diary, November 3 and 5, 1894.

B17 *'Varsity Glee Club.' *The Globe*, December 19, 1894, p. 3.
Reference: King Diary, December 18, 1894.

B18 *'Varsity Glee Club at St Mary's.' [In 'Music and the Drama' column]. *The Globe,* December 21, 1894, p. 6.
Reference: King Diary, December 20, 1894.

B19 *'The Varsity Glee Club winds up at Stratford.' [In 'Music and the Drama' column]. *The Globe,* December 22, 1894, p. 17.
Reference: King Diary, December 21, 1894.

B20 'The Varsity trouble – A correction.' [Letter to the editor regarding strike meeting]. *The Toronto World,* January 25, 1895, p. 2.
Reference: King Diary, January 24, 1895

B21 'A little thought, a little word.' [Eight-line untitled poem]. *The Varsity,* February 1, 1895, p. 124.
Reprinted: Robert MacGregor Dawson, *William Lyon Mackenzie King: A political biography, 1874–1923,* p. 32.
Reference: King Diary, February 1, 1895.

B22 *'Abolish the reformatory. The Prisoners' Aid Association have no use for the institution.' *Evening News,* October 28, 1895, p. 3.
Reference: King Diary, October 27, 1895.

B23 *[Inquest relating to smothering of five-month-old child in Toronto]. [In 'Latest local briefs']. *Evening News,* October 29, 1895, p. 3.
Reference: King Diary, October 28, 1895.

B24 *'A new departure. Mail and Empire to be sold for a cent. No alteration in size.' *Evening News,* October 31, 1895, p. 3.
Reference: King Diary, October 30, 1895.

B25 *'The Princess Theatre. How it is run and why the attendance is meagre.' *Evening News,* November 1, 1895, p. 3.
Reference: King Diary, October 30, 1895.

B26 *'Pedlars in police court.' *The Globe,* November 6, 1895, p. 10.
Reference: King Diary, November 5, 1895.

B27 *'Shorthand lecture.' *The Globe,* November 8, 1895, p. 8.
Reference: King Diary, November 7, 1895.

B28 *'Mr Mulock re-elected.' *The Globe,* November 9, 1895, p. 20.
Reference: King Diary, November 8, 1895.

B29 *'St Joseph's High School. Annual distribution of prizes and certificates. Archbishop Walsh on Roman Catholic Schools.' *The Globe,* November 9, 1895, p. 7.
Reference: King Diary, November 8, 1895.

B30 *'University Notes. Meeting of Literary and Scientific Society. Arrangements for the Winter. Victoria Conversat.' *The Globe,* November 9, 1895, p. 8.
Reference: King Diary, November 8, 1895.

B31 *'Manslaughter. Mrs Mercier Beer committed for trial. The death of Percy Beck. Christian Science treatment discussed. The boy's father and mother testify. What the post-mortem examination showed. Magistrate Denison's remarks. The prisoner bailed.' *The Globe,* November 13, 1895, p. 1.
Reference: King Diary, November 12, 1895.

B32 *'Trinity College. Proceedings of the Annual Convocation. A brilliant gathering at the banquet. Speeches by the new Provost. Hon. G.W. Ross, Principal Parkin, the Chancellor, and others.' *The Globe,* November 13, 1895, p. 2.
Reference: King Diary, November 12, 1895.

B33 *'At the police court.' *The Globe,* November 14, 1895, p. 2.
Reference: King Diary, November 12, 1895.

B34 *'Mr R.S. White in Toronto. The ex-Member for Cardwell discusses the impending bye-elections and the political situation.' *The Globe,* November 15, 1895, p. 2.
Reference: King Diary, November 14, 1895.

B35 *'Mr Armstrong's funeral.' *The Globe,* November 15, 1895, p. 8.
Reference: King Diary, November 14, 1895.

B36 * [Review of 'A Midsummer Night's Dream.'] [In 'Music and the Drama' column]. *The Globe,* November 15, 1895, p. 9.
Reference: King Diary, November 14, 1895.

B37 *'Political Science Club.' *The Globe,* November 15, 1895, p. 8.
Reference: King Diary, November 14, 1895.

B38 *'University of Toronto. Formal opening of Biological Museum. Addresses by Vice-Chancellor Mulock and Hon. George W. Ross.' *The Globe,* November 16, 1895, p. 18.
Reference: King Diary, November 15, 1895.

B39 * 'Police Court.' *The Globe*, November 18, 1895, p. 10.
Reference: King Diary, November 16, 1895.

B40 * 'Police Court.' *The Globe*, November 19, 1895, p. 10.
Reference: King Diary, November 18, 1895.

B41 * [Review of Miss Nellie Ganthony's Concert at Massey Hall]. [In 'Music and the Drama' column], *The Globe*, November 19, 1895, p. 2.
Reference: King Diary, November 18, 1895.

B42 * 'Dental College dinner. The annual banquet held last night at the Rossin House – Speeches by Hon. George W. Ross and Wm. Mulock, M.P.' *The Globe*, November 20, 1895, p. 8.
Reference: King Diary, November 19, 1895.

B43 * 'Police Notes.' *The Globe*, November 20, 1895, p. 10.
Reference: King Diary, November 19, 1895.

B44 'To heal the sick: The new addition to St Michael's Hospital.' *The Globe*, November 21, 1895, p. 7.
Reference: King Diary, November 20, 1895.

B45 * 'United Harvest Service [at St James Cathedral]. *The Globe*, November 22, 1895, p. 8.
Reference: King Diary, November 21, 1895.

B46 * 'Canadians in danger. Congregation missionaries being protected by a United States cruiser – Names of those concerned.' *The Globe*, November 22, 1895, p. 8.
Reference: King Diary, November 21, 1895.

B47 * 'Theological Conference. Important gathering at Victoria University. Papers by distinguished theologians – Economic questions.' *The Globe*, November 26, 1895, p. 7.
Reference: King Diary, November 25, 1895.

B48 * 'Theological Conference. Important gathering of Methodists at Victoria.' *The Globe*, November 27, 1895, p. 10.
Reference: King Diary, November 26, 1895.

B49 * 'Vaughan Township fire.' *The Globe*, November 28, 1895, p. 10.
Reference: King Diary, November 27, 1895.

B50 * 'University Notes.' *The Globe*, November 27, 1895, p. 7.
Reference: King Diary, November 26, 1895.

B51 *'Found drowned.' *The Globe,* November 28, 1895, p. 10.
Reference: King Diary, November 26, 1895.

B52 *'Prison Gate Mission.' *The Globe,* November 29, 1895, p. 8.
Reference: King Diary, November 28, 1895.

B53 *'Theological Conference.' *The Globe,* November 29, 1895, p. 8.
Reference: King Diary, November 26, 1895.

B54 *'Their labours ended.' [Theological Conference]. *The Globe,* November 30, 1895, p. 20.
Reference: King Diary, November 29, 1895.

B55 *'Caught in the act.' *The Globe,* December 2, 1895, p. 8.
Reference: King Diary, November 30, 1895.

B56 *'A Trinity of doctrine. Rev. W.W. Weeks' first sermon in Walmer Road Baptist Church an able effort.' *The Globe,* December 2, 1895, p. 2.
Reference: King Diary, December 1, 1895.

B57 *'The Hyams conspiracy trial.' *The Globe,* December 3, 1895, p. 10.
Reference: King Diary, December 2, 1895.

B58 *[Review of the Third Annual Concert under the auspices of Toronto Legions at Massey Hall]. [In 'Music and the Drama' column]. *The Globe,* December 4, 1895, p. 10.
Reference: King Diary, December 3, 1895.

B59 *[Review of Violin and Song Recital by Mr and Mrs H. Klingerfeld at St George's Hall.] [In 'Music and the Drama' column]. *The Globe,* December 4, 1895, p. 10.
Reference: King Diary, December 3, 1895.

B60 *'Athenian statesmen. Able lecture by Prof. Maurice Hutton – Political phases of ancient and modern times compared.' *The Globe,* December 5, 1895, p. 8.
Reference: King Diary, November 29, 1895.

B61 *'Varsity's teams. The Athletic Club honours the champions. An enjoyable reception.' *The Globe,* December 5, 1895, p. 4.
Reference: King Diary, December 4, 1895.

B62 *'Rescue Home for Girls.' [Special meeting of the Woman's Christian Temperance Union]. *The Globe,* December 5, 1895, p. 12.
Reference: King Diary, December 4, 1895.

B63 *'Two fires yesterday.' *The Globe,* December 7, 1895, p. 24.
Reference: King Diary, December 6, 1895.

B64 *'Was a police spy. William McCarthy placed in a police cell to listen to conversation between prisoners. The McMillan arson case.' *The Globe,* December 7, 1895, p. 17.
Reference: King Diary, December 5, 1895.

B65 *'George Eliot. A brilliant lecture by Provost Welch of Trinity. The last of the series of St Hilda's lectures.' *The Globe,* December 7, 1895, p. 21.
Reference: King Diary, December 6, 1895.

B66 *'Life at Oxford. Dr Parkin of Upper Canada College gives his impressions of the great English university.' *The Globe,* December 9, 1895, p. 5.
Reference: King Diary, December 7, 1895.

B67 *'The body identified.' *The Globe,* December 7, 1895, p. 24.
Reference: King Diary, December 6, 1895.

B68 * [Brief note regarding inquest on body of Henry Parkinson]. *The Globe,* December 7, 1895, p. 12.
Reference: King Diary, December 6, 1895.

B69 *'Police court doings.' *The Globe,* December 9, 1895, p. 10.
Reference: King Diary, December 7, 1895.

B70 *'A merry evening. The smoker in honor of Varsity Rugby team. It proves a great success. Silver souvenirs presented by Mr Mulock. A capital programme presented and executed. Some notes on the entertainment provided for the evening.' *The Globe,* December 11, 1895, p. 8.
Reference: King Diary, December 10, 1895.

B71 * [Review of a promenade and musical under the auspices of the John Eaton Company in aid of the poor of the city of Toronto]. *The Globe,* December 13, 1895, p. 7.
Reference: King Diary, December 12, 1895.

B72 *'Sackville Street School.' *The Globe,* December 14, 1895, p. 24.
Reference: King Diary, December 13, 1895.

B73 * [Review of annual concert of the University Glee Club at Massey Hall]. *The Globe,* December 14, 1895, p. 11. [In the 'Music and the Drama' column].
Reference: King Diary, December 13, 1895.

B74 *'Mary Aitkin's death. Frank Smith and William Broom held responsible. Will be sentenced today.' *The Globe,* December 14, 1895, p. 5.
Reference: King Diary, December 14, 1895.

B75 *'Industrial Room Society.' *The Globe,* December 21, 1895, p. 24.
Reference: King Diary, December 18, 1895.

B76 *'Trinity Convocation. Bishop Rowe of Alaska invested with an honorary degree by Trinity University, his Alma Mater.' *The Globe,* December 21, 1895.
Reference: King Diary, December 20, 1895, p. 34.

B77 *'Newfoundland affairs. An interesting interview with a prominent Presbyterian pastor from the ancient colony.' *The Globe,* December 25, 1895, p. 8.
Reference: King Diary, December 24, 1895.

B78 * [Review of recital at the eleventh annual convention of the Canadian Society of Musicians]. *The Globe,* December 27, 1895, p. 8.
Reference: King Diary, December 26, 1895.

B79 *'The Hyams twins. Conspiracy to murder and forgery charged. Evidence for Crown began. Another remand for a week.' *The Globe,* December 31, 1895, p. 5.
Reference: King Diary, December 30, 1895.

B80 *'Licence Commissioners.' *The Globe,* December 31, 1895, p. 1.
Reference: King Diary, December 30, 1895.

B81 *'The Orphan's Home. A most enjoyable entertainment given the children yesterday. Many visitors present. Santa Claus delights everyone.' *The Globe,* January 1, 1896, p. 6.
Reference: King Diary, December 31, 1895.

B82 *'Government House. Over five hundred visitors at the New Year's

reception – Some of those present.' *The Globe*, January 2, 1896, p. 7.
Reference: King Diary, January 1, 1896.

B83 *'The McCall Auxiliary.' *The Globe*, January 3, 1896, p. 8.
Reference: King Diary, January 2, 1896.

B84 *'Two for Fleming. Excellent meetings in Daws' and Dingman's Halls. A comparison of records. Mr Fleming's definite stand on the gas question.' *The Globe*, January 3, 1896, p. 3.
Reference: King Diary, January 2, 1896.

B85 *'Hyams case again. Conspiracy charges now under investigation. The preliminary inquiry. Placing the insurance on Mrs Hyams' life. Agent O'Leger's suspicions. Dr Field in the witness box. The case again remanded.' *The Globe*, January 7, 1896, p. 3.
Reference: King Diary, January 6, 1896.

B86 *'The Hyams Brothers. Evidence of Mrs Harry Hyams to be heard this morning. A note regarding Dr Fel's evidence.' *The Globe*, January 8, 1896, p. 3.
Reference: King Diary, January 7, 1896.

B87 *'Yacht Club Ball. Brilliant society function at the Pavilion. Magnificent decorations. Over five hundred invited guests participate. The old Pavilion presents a carnival appearance. A list of those [present].' *The Globe*, January 11, 1896, p. 17.
Reference: King Diary, January 10, 1896.

B88 *'Overdose of morphine.' *The Globe*, January 15, 1896, p. 10.
Reference: King Diary, January 14, 1896.

B89 *'City Hall figures. The losses and vital statistics for 1895. Not so many marriages. Final meeting of Council this afternoon. The chairmanship slate is rapidly filling up. The mayor will not likely be present.' *The Globe*, January 16, 1896, p. 7.
Reference: King Diary, January 15, 1896.

B90 * [Account of Presbyterian Church meetings]. 'Church meetings. Progress of Presbyterians in Toronto. The record for the year. Satisfactory conditions of most congregations.' *The Globe*, January 16, 1896, p. 9.
Reference: King Diary, January 15, 1896.

B91 * [Review of Jennie O'Neill Potter's monologues at the Princess Theatre]. *The Globe,* January 16, 1896, p. 12.
Reference: King Diary, January 15, 1896.

B92 * 'Queen Street Methodists. Rev. A.B. Simpson of the International Missionary Alliance preaches the annual foreign mission sermon.' *The Globe,* January 20, 1896, p. 2.
Reference: King Diary, January 19, 1896.

B93 * 'The Hyams case. Harry Hyams discharged and called as a witness against his brother. Ste Marie refuses to come.' *The Globe,* January 21, 1896, p. 5.
Reference: King Diary, January 20, 1896.

B94 * 'To foreign lands! Ordination of two young missionaries. For China and Thibet [*sic*]. Impressive and earnest services held. Speeches by the two volunteers for the foreign field. Afternoon and evening sessions.' *The Globe,* January 21, 1896, p. 7.
Reference: King Diary, January 20, 1896.

B95 * 'Licence Commissioners.' *The Globe,* January 22, 1896, p. 10.
Reference: King Diary, January 21, 1896.

B96 * 'House of Industry. Monthly meeting of the Board – A large number of families relieved. The different reports.' *The Globe,* January 22, 1896, p. 6.
Reference: King Diary, January 21, 1896.

B97 * 'Death from exposure.' *The Globe,* January 23, 1896, p. 10.
Reference: King Diary, January 22, 1896.

B98 * 'University claims. An influential deputation waits on the Ontario Government. Impact at claims presented.' *The Globe,* January 24, 1896, p. 2.
Reference: King Diary, January 23, 1896.

B99 * 'Burns Birthday. Prof. Clark on the famous Scottish poet. A lecture at Trinity. Interesting phases of the poet's life. The beauty of his poems. Patriotism and love their characteristics.' *The Globe,* January 25, 1896, p. 5.
Reference: King Diary, January 24, 1896.

B100 * 'Nerve cells.' *The Globe,* January 27, 1896, p. 8.
Reference: King Diary, January 26, 1896.

B101 *'Mrs Hyams' evidence. The police magistrate holds court in Mr E.W. Aylesworth's house. No important testimony elicited.' *The Globe,* January 29, 1896, p. 9.
Reference: King Diary, January 28, 1896.

B102 *'George Eliot. A brilliant lecture by Provost Welch. The novelist's character. Ennobling influence of her famous books. Students' hall crowded with a delightful audience. Some character representations.' *The Globe,* February 3, 1896, p. 8.
Reference: King Diary, February 2, 1896.

B103 *'Hyamses' bailed. A special train takes them out of the country. They may never return. Bail granted by Mr Hugh Miller. Case to be called today. Remand to be asked until Thursday. Bonds of 1,150 put up. Brief outline of the famous criminal trial.' *The Globe,* February 3, 1896, p. 3.
Reference: King Diary, February 2, 1896.

B104 *'The Globe's new home. A year after the fire. Back in its accustomed location. A model newspaper office with every appropriate convenience and comfort. ' *The Evening Telegram,* February 11, 1896, p. 3.
Reference: King Diary, February 4 and 5, 1896.

B105 *'Pressmen gather. Meeting of the Canadian Press Association. Newspapers and mails. Discussions of interest to the craft. The questions of the cable service. Nominations and elections. A number of excellent papers read.' *The Globe,* February 7, 1896, p. 7.
Reference: King Diary, February 6, 1896.

B106 *'Tried in Toronto. Marvellous feats of the new photography. Excellent experiments. Pictures of objects taken through opaque bodies. Toronto University professors make use of the Cathode light. Possibilities of the discovery.' *The Globe,* February 10, 1896, p. 9.
Reference: King Diary, February 9, 1896.

B107 *'Focusing the ray. Splendid result of experiments at the University. Reflection obtained. Instantaneous photographs of invisible objects. A decided advance for which Toronto University deserves credit. Interesting experiments by Dr Ellis.' *The Globe,* February 12, 1896, p. 6.
Reference: King Diary, February 11, 1896.

B108 * 'The farm pupil problem.' *The Globe,* February 13, 1896, p. 8.
Reference: King Diary, February 12, 1896.

B109 * 'The new photography.' *The Globe,* February 13, 1896, p. 10.
Reference: King Diary, February 13, 1896.

B110 * 'University Conversazione.' *The Globe,* February 14, 1896, p. 10.
Reference: King Diary, February 14, 1896.

B111 * 'Suggestions for art study.' *The Globe,* February 20, 1896, p. 10.
Reference: King Diary, February 20, 1896.

B112 * 'Mr Macdonnell's burial.' *The Globe,* February 21, 1896, p. 10.
Reference: King Diary, February 20, 1896.

B113 * 'The Rontgen Rays.' *The Saturday Globe,* February 22, 1896, pp. 1–2.
Reference: King Diary, February 15, 1896.

B114 * [Review of plays at Grand Opera House]. *The Globe,* February 22, 1896, p. 7.
Reference: King Diary, February 21, 1896.

B115 * 'Shakespeare's Imogen first of a series of lectures on Shakespeare's heroines by Canon Sutherland at Trinity University.' *The Globe,* February 24, 1896, p. 10.
Reference: King Diary, February 22, 1896.

B116 * [Rev. Albert Gilray's sermon on the death of Rev. D.J. Macdonnell], in a series of summaries of several sermons. 'A beloved pastor. Honor done to Rev. D.J. Macdonnell's memory.' *The Globe,* February 24, 1896, p. 10.
Reference: King Diary, February 23, 1896.

B117 * 'Classical Association. An open meeting held yesterday. Dr Park in the chair and Prof. Cody the lecturer of the day.' *The Globe,* February 26, 1896, p. 5.
Reference: King Diary, February 25, 1896.

B118 * 'Armenian atrocities. A native of Armenia appeals to Canadians on behalf of his suffering countrymen. Immediate relief imperative.' *The Globe,* February 26, 1896, p. 10.
Reference: King Diary, February 25, 1896.

B119 * 'Leaped to his death. Another fatality at the Glen Road Bridge.

Arthur Long the victim. Leaves a letter telling of his intention. Deceased was a waiter at the Albany Club. He had nearly $500 in the bank. Despondency caused the deed.' *The Globe*, February 27, 1896, p. 10.
Reference: King Diary, February 26, 1896.

B120 *'Ontario Land Surveyors.' *The Globe*, February 28, 1896, p. 8.
Reference: King Diary, February 27, 1896.

B121 *'At Massey Hall.' [Sermon by Rev. G.C. Grubb]. *The Globe*, February 28, 1896, p. 8.
Reference: King Diary, February 27, 1896.

B122 *'Epworth League. The annual convention closed. Officers elected at the afternoon session. A successful closing meeting.' *The Globe*, February 28, 1896.
Reference: King Diary, February 28, 1896.

B123 *'Shakespearean lectures.' *The Globe*, March 2, 1896, p. 10.
Reference: King Diary, February 29, 1896, and March 1, 1896.

B124 *'The late Mr Macdonnell. Touching reference to the deceased pastor by Rev. D.R. Drummond. His life and inspiration.' *The Globe*, March 2, 1896, p. 8.
Reference: King Diary, March 1, 1896.

B125 *'The late Lady Smith. The funeral attended by many prominent citizens. The Premier and several Cabinet Ministers present.' *The Globe*, March 5, 1896, p. 8.
Reference: King Diary, March 4, 1896.

B126 *'The non-day discourse. Canon Du Moulin contrasts practical unbelief with practical Christianity. A word to Sunday bicylists.' *The Globe*, March 6, 1896, p. 5.
Reference: King Diary, March 5, 1896.

B127 *'Q.O.R. The Sergeants Mess celebrates their 13th annual dinner. A jolly time spent by those present.' *The Globe*, March 7, 1896, p. 11.
Reference: King Diary, March 6, 1896.

B128 *'Firemen injured.' *The Globe*, March 9, 1896, p. 10.
Reference: King Diary, March 7, 1896.

B129 *'Macbeth. Rev. Canon Sutherland lectures on Shakespeare's

greatest tragedy. He compares it to the story of Eden.' *The Globe*, March 9, 1896, p. 5.
Reference: King Diary, March 8, 1896.

B130 * 'God and man. The relationship of the Creator to the creature – Rev. Canon Du Moulin's mid-day discourse.' *The Globe*, March 10, 1896, p. 6.
Reference: King Diary, March 9, 1896.

B131 * 'The local courts. Yesterday's proceedings at the Civil Assizes, Court of General Sessions and County Court – Some important cases.' *The Globe*, March 10, 1896, p. 5.
Reference: King Diary, March 9, 1896.

B132 * 'The Monday service. Rev. Du Moulin continues his discourse on God and man. – The destroyer of happiness.' *The Globe*, March 11, 1896, p. 3.
Reference: King Diary, March 10, 1896.

B133 * 'The noonday service. Rev. Canon Du Moulin continues his discourses on God and man. The destroyer of happiness.' *The Globe*, March 11, 1896, p. 3.
Reference: King Diary, March 10, 1896.

B134 * 'The local courts. Yesterday's proceedings at the Civil Assizes, Court of General Sessions and County Court. Today's lists.' *The Globe*, March 11, 1896, p. 6.
Reference: King Diary, March 10, 1896.

B135 * 'Death of John J. Vickers. The well-known founder of Vickers Express Company passes away. One of Toronto's pioneers.' *The Globe*, March 12, 1896, p. 7.
Reference: King Diary, March 11, 1896.

B136 * 'The local courts. James McKearnd sentenced to be lashed. Miss Cline's action against the city dismissed. Noverre claims $3,000 damages.' *The Globe*, March 12, 1896, p. 5.
Reference: King Diary, March 11, 1896.

B137 * 'The prodigal's sin. When lovely woman brings disaster and misery. Canon Du Moulin's noon discourse.' *The Globe*, March 13, 1896, p. 5.
Reference: King Diary, March 12, 1896.

B138 * 'Canada's resources. An intersting lecture by Mr C.C. James. The chief features and natural products of the country ably detailed.' *The Globe*, March 13, 1896, p. 5.
Reference: King Diary, March 12, 1896.

B139 * 'Laid to rest. The funeral of the late J.J. Vickers largely attended. A long and useful career brought to a close.' *The Globe*, March 14, 1896, p. 15.
Reference: King Diary, March 13, 1896.

B140 * 'Rosalind. Canon Sutherland's lecture on the heroine of "As You Like It" in the Trinity Lecture series.' *The Globe*, March 16, 1896, p. 6.
Reference: King Diary, March 15, 1896.

B141 * 'Canon Du Moulin. His noon discourse at St James. The Christian home built on the Master's plan.' *The Globe*, March 17, 1896, p. 3.
Reference: King Diary, March 16, 1896.

B142 * 'Mr John Bailie's funeral. It is largely attended by citizens and members of the I.P.B.S. A letter from Goldwin Smith.' *The Globe*, March 17, 1896, p. 7.
Reference: King Diary, March 16, 1896.

B143 * 'Jesus in social life. Where're He walked He left only good behind. Canon Du Moulin's noonday discourse.' *The Globe*, March 18, 1896, p. 5.
Reference: King Diary, March 17, 1896.

B144 * 'Massey's Magazine. The issue for March contains a number of interesting articles. Many illustrations and poems.' *The Globe*, March 18, 1896, p. 8.
Reference: King Diary, March 17, 1896.

B145 * 'The model for all. Jesus was a teacher, physician and a workingman. Canon Du Moulin's noonday discourse.' *The Globe*, March 19, 1896, p. 5.
Reference: King Diary, March 18, 1896.

B146 * 'George Frederick Watts. A brilliant lecture on the life and works of the great portrait painter. The characteristics of his art described.' *The Globe*, March 19, 1896, p. 5.
Reference: King Diary, March 18, 1896.

B147 *'Literary Society elections.' *The Globe*, March 21, 1896, p. 20.
Reference: King Diary, March 20, 1896.

B148 *'Missionary conference.' *The Globe*, March 24, 1896, p. 10.
Reference: King Diary, March 23, 1896.

B149 *'Awarded a scholarship. Mr A.M. Scott's valuable contributions to science. A student of exceptional ability and promise.' *The Globe*, March 24, 1896, p. 5.
Reference: King Diary, March 23, 1896.

B150 *'Military Law.' [Lecture by Judge Davidson at the Military Institute]. *The Globe*, March 24, 1896, p. 5.
Reference: King Diary, March 23, 1896.

B151 *'Missionary convention.' *The Globe*, March 25, 1896, p. 10.
Reference: King Diary, March 24, 1896.

B152 *'An awful mockery. The six court trials our Saviour suffered where perjury and subordination prevailed.' *The Globe*, March 26, 1896, p. 5.
Reference: King Diary, March 25, 1896.

B153 *'Decorative art. An able lecture delivered by Professor Huntingford before the Woman's Art Association.' *The Globe*, March 26, 1896, p. 5.
Reference: King Diary, March 25, 1896.

B154 * [Review of Miss A. Ramsay's costume recital at St George's Hall]. *The Globe*, March 27, 1896, p. 10.
Reference: King Diary, March 27, 1896, p. 10.

B155 *'The Canadian Institute. Prof. Wrong speaks of the discovery of America by John Cabot. An interesting paper by Mr F.F. Payne on the seasons in Hudson's Straits.' *The Globe*, March 30, 1896, p. 7.
Reference: King Diary, March 28 and 29, 1896.

B156 *'The City Council. A session from three till half past nine. The aqueduct agreement. Important changes made in the committee. Discussions on Mr Hardy's bill regarding Council and Board of Manufactures Committee.' *The Globe*, March 31, 1896, p. 6.
Reference: King Diary, March 30, 1896.

B157 *'Burglars sentenced.' *The Globe*, April 2, 1896, p. 12.
Reference: King Diary, April 1, 1896.

B158 *'The problem of beauty. A lecture by Professor Mavor on the art of seeing and the seeing of art.' *The Globe*, April 2, 1896, p. 8.
Reference: King Diary, April 1, 1896.

B159 *'Knox College. Annual closing exercises of the institution. Addresses by Rev. Dr Caven. Graduates who have secured diplomas. List of scholarship winners. Special degrees conferred. Remarks by Dr Robertson.' *The Globe*, April 3, 1896, p. 5.
Reference: King Diary, April 2, 1896.

B160 *'Music at Easter.' [Mackenzie King wrote the sections on music in the Roman Catholic churches for Easter Sunday]. *The Globe*, April 4, 1896, p. 18.
Reference: King Diary, April 3, 1896.

B161 *'Vestry meetings.' [Mackenzie King wrote the sections on St George's and the Church of the Ascension]. *The Globe*, April 7, 1896, p. 9.
Reference: King Diary, April 6, 1896.

B162 * [Review of play, 'The Waifs of New York,' at the Toronto Opera House]. [In 'Music and the Drama' column]. *The Globe*, April 28, 1896, p. 2.
Reference: King Diary, April 27, 1896.

B163 *'Police court notes.' *The Globe*, April 30, 1896, p. 12.
Reference: King Diary, April 30, 1896, p. 12.

B164 *'Criminal assizes.' *The Globe*, April 30, 1896, p. 12.
Reference: King Diary, April 29, 1896.

B165 *'Non-jury sittings.' *The Globe*, April 30, 1896, p. 12.
Reference: King Diary, April 30, 1896.

B166 *'House of Industry. The annual meeting held yesterday afternoon. Very satisfactory reports by the various committees.' *The Globe*, April 30, 1896, p. 7.
Reference: King Diary, April 29, 1896.

B167 *'On trial for murder. James Healy faces a jury charged with killing Thomas Corrigan last February. Evidence taken.' *The Globe*, May 1, 1896, p. 8.
Reference: King Diary, May 1, 1896.

B168 *'Religious instruction.' *The Globe*, May 4, 1896, p. 10.
Reference: King Diary, May 3, 1896.

B169 *[Review of play, 'Fatherland,' at Toronto Opera House]. *The Globe*, May 5, 1896, p. 12.
Reference: King Diary, May 4, 1896.

B170 *'A young man's tragic end.' *The Globe*, May 6, 1896, p. 12.
Reference: King Diary, May 5, 1896.

B171 *'Exhibition of pictures' [at St George's Hall]. *The Globe*, May 7, 1896, p. 12.
Reference: King Diary, May 6, 1896.

B172 *'Police court notes.' *The Globe*, May 8, 1896, p. 10.
Reference: King Diary, May 7, 1896.

B173 *'Varsity notes. How the faculty will put in summer. The medical and law examinations.' *The Globe*, May 8, 1896, p. 10.
Reference: King Diary, May 7, 1896.

B174 'St Michael's Cathedral. Rev. Father Ryan pays a graceful tribute to the late Hon. T.W. Anglin.' *The Globe*, May 11, 1896, p. 11.
Reference: King Diary, May 10, 1896.

B175 *'Police court notes.' *The Globe*, May 12, 1896, p. 12.
Reference: King Diary, May 11, 1896.

B176 *'U. E. Loyalists.' *The Globe*, May 12, 1896, p. 12.
Reference: King Diary, May 11, 1896.

B177 *'Baccalaureate. Rev. Dr Lorimer in Walmer Road Church. Annual McMaster sermon. An eloquent and inspiring discourse. The distinguished Boston divine preaches on the darkness of light. Annual commencement exercises.' *The Globe*, May 13, 1896, p. 4.
Reference: King Diary, May 12, 1896.

B178 *'Honors awarded. Degrees and diplomas bestowed by McMaster University. Commencement exercises. Addresses by eminent divines and teachers. Miss Dryden's achievement. A numerous company entertained at a collation. Toasts and college songs.' *The Globe*, May 14, 1896, p. 4.
Reference: King Diary, May 13, 1896.

B179 *'"The French Revolution." A brilliant lecture by Dr Geo. C. Lorimer

of Boston at Massey Hall last night. The subject treated in a novel and interesting manner.' *The Globe*, May 15, 1896, p. 7.
Reference: King Diary, May 14, 1896.

B180 *'Upper Canada College. Annual games held yesterday afternoon. Distribution of prizes. Lists of events and winners.' *The Globe*, May 16, 1896, p. 12.
Reference: King Diary, May 18, 1896, p. 2.

B181 *'Pharmacy examinations. The list of those who have passed and taken honors. Nearly 100 graduates will obtain diplomas.' *The Globe*, May 18, 1896, p. 2.
Reference: King Diary, May 16, 1896.

B182 *'Influence of ideals. An interesting lecture by Rev. Dr Lloyd of New York in the Elm Street Methodist Church.' *The Globe*, May 19, 1896, p. 4.
Reference: King Diary, May 18, 1896.

B183 *'Model School games. Annual sports held yesterday afternoon. List of prize-winners. Other races to come.' *The Globe*, May 23, 1897, p. 19.
Reference: King Diary, May 22, 1896.

B184 * [Review of musical recital at St George's Hall]. *The Globe*, May 28, 1896, p. 12.
Reference: King Diary, May 27, 1896.

B185 *'Found dead in bed. A young medical student who used morphine. An overdose of the drug proved fatal.' *The Globe*, May 30, 1896, p. 17.
Reference: King Diary, May 29, 1896.

B186 *'Protestant Orphans' Home. The forty-fifth annual meeting held yesterday. Presentation of addresses to Miss Wheelwright.' *The Globe*, June 3, 1896, p. 12.
Reference: King Diary, June 2, 1896.

B187 *'The fallen raised. Social work of the Salvation Army. The institutions visited. Commandant Booth makes a farewell inspection. Many prominent citizens given an insight into the practical work. How the under strata are being helped.' *The Globe*, June 5, 1896, p. 4.
Reference: King Diary, June 4, 1896.

B188 *'Police court notes.' *The Globe,* June 6, 1896, p. 26.
Reference: King Diary, June 5, 1896.

B189 *'City Hall notes.' *The Globe,* June 10, 1896, p. 12.
Reference: King Diary, June 9, 1896.

B190 *'Board of Health. Special meeting of the Provincial Branch held yesterday. Important matters dealt with. Resolution of condolence.' *The Globe,* June 10, 1896, p. 3.
Reference: King Diary, June 9, 1896.

B191 *'Women's Auxiliary.' *The Globe,* June 11, 1896, p. 12.
Reference: King Diary, June 10, 1896.

B192 *'Farewell and welcome.' *The Globe,* June 12, 1896, p. 12.
Reference: King Diary, June 11, 1896.

B193 *'Class of 1896.' *The Globe,* June 15, 1896, p. 12.
Reference: King Diary, June 12, 1896.

B194 *'In the East End. Big Robertson meeting at the Pavilion. A voice from Winnipeg. The Tupper candidates across the Don. Mr Coatsworth speaks in Dingman's Hall. The electors of East Toronto listen to rival nominees.' *The Globe,* June 17, 1896, p. 12.
Reference: King Diary, June 13, 1896.

B195 *'Y.W.C.G. Summerholn.' *The Globe,* June 15, 1896, p. 12.
Reference: King Diary, June 13, 1896.

B196 *'Robertson mass meeting.' *The Globe,* June 16, 1896, p. 12.
Reference: King Diary, June 15, 1896.

B197 *'Women's Council.' *The Globe,* June 17, 1896, p. 12.
Reference: King Diary, June 16, 1896.

B198 *'Lively at Clarke's meeting. West Toronto Conservatives threaten interrupters with police interference. Few new points raised.' *The Globe,* June 18, 1896, p. 8.
Reference: King Diary, June 17, 1896.

B199 *'Electrical association. The annual convention still in progress. The banquet held at Lorne Park. Work of the day.' *The Globe,* June 19, 1896, p. 9.
Reference: King Diary, June 17, 1896.

B200 * 'Sons of Ireland.' *The Globe,* June 19, 1896, p. 12.
Reference: King Diary, June 18, 1896.

B201 * 'Kearney guilty. Sentenced to be hanged on the first of October. The Agnew murder trial. Moral irresponsibility the defence's plea. The case against Patrick Kearney results in acquittal. Able defence to the jury.' *The Globe,* June 22, 1896, p. 3.
Reference: King Diary, June 20, 1896.

B202 * 'Nearly drowned' [Account of two near drownings]. *The Globe,* June 23, 1896, p. 10.
Reference: King Diary, June 22, 1896.

B203 * 'University notes. Alexander Mackenzie Fellows in Political Science appointed. The subjects of various competitions announced.' *The Globe,* June 27, 1896, p. 21.
Reference: King Diary, June 26, 1896.

B204 * [Description of the Ontario Parliament Buildings] in 'Parliament Buildings of Canada.' *The Globe,* June 27, 1896, p. 4.
Reference: King Diary, June 16, 1896.

B205 * 'De La Salle Institute. The annual commencement excercises held yesterday. The programme an interesting and varied one.' *The Globe,* June 30, 1896, p. 5.
Reference: King Diary, June 29, 1896.

B206 * 'Public Library Board.' *The Globe,* July 10, 1896, p. 20.
Reference: King Diary, July 10, 1896.

B207 * [Account of the sermon of Rev. Dixon] in 'Orange lilies. Anniversary of the Boyne celebration on Saturday.' *The Globe,* July 13, 1896, p. 7.
Reference: King Diary, July 12, 1896.

B208 * 'Rev. Alexander Brown. An eminent Glasgow divine preaches at St James' Square Church. Brilliant discourses given at both services.' *The Globe,* July 20, 1896, p. 10.
Reference: King Diary, July 19, 1896.

B209 * 'Drowned in the Don.' *The Globe,* June 20, 1896, p. 10.
Reference: King Diary, July 19, 1896.

B210 * 'Mrs Finucane's death.' *The Globe,* July 21, 1896, p. 10.
Reference: King Diary, July 21, 1896.

B211 * 'The Boy's Brigade. Pellatt Cup presented by the Lieutenant-Governor. St Joseph's Company wins this year.' *The Globe*, July 23, 1896, p. 10.
Reference: King Diary, July 21, 1896.

B212 * 'A terrible death. Cut to pieces beneath the wheels of a trolley. A woman the victim. The motorman's account of the fatality. An inquest conducted on Saturday night. The husband hears the news while at the hospital.' *The Globe*, July 27, 1896, p. 6.
Reference: King Diary, July 25, 1896.

B213 * 'Narrow escape from death.' *The Globe*, July 27, 1896, p. 10.
Reference: King Diary, July 25, 1896.

B214 'Husband and wife. Mrs Rowatt says her husband deliberately shot her. Evidence taken at the General Hospital.' *The Globe*, July 27, 1896, p. 5.
Reference: King Diary, July 25, 1896.

B215 * 'Weary of living. A young man comes home from a picnic and puts an end to his life. He was ill and in poverty.' *The Globe*, July 27, 1896, p. 10.
Reference: King Diary, July 25 and 26, 1896.

B216 * 'Police court notes.' *The Globe*, July 29, 1896, p. 10.
Reference: King Diary, July 28, 1896.

B217 * 'Sons of York. Enthusiastic reception to its representatives. Reception to Mr Mulock. He is returned again by acclamation. Hon. E.J. David welcomed. Address by prominent Liberals on live issues. "An honest government," the burden of the speeches. The Postmaster-General speaks of cold storage.' *The Globe*, July 31, 1896, p. 5.
Reference: King Diary, July 30, 1896.

B218 * 'Police court notes.' *The Globe*, August 8, 1896, p. 24.
Reference: King Diary, August 7, 1896.

B219 * 'A mad bull at large. Tosses little girl on University Ave. and breaks her collar-bone. A bicycle smashed to bits.' *The Globe*, August 8, 1896, p. 17.
Reference: King Diary, August 7, 1896.

B220 * 'Scotland's sons. The annual celebration and games at Brantford.

Many camps represented. The visitors given a royal reception. Large gatherings witness the day's proceedings. The events equal to any of previous years.' *The Globe*, August 11, 1896, p. 2.
Reference: King Diary, August 10, 1896.

B221 * 'Dogs and ponies.' *The Globe*, August 13, 1896, p. 12.
Reference: King Diary, August 12, 1896.

B222 * 'Bicycle tourney. A brillant spectacle at Niagara-on-the-Lake. The parade of the wheels. Prizes for the most handsomely decorated. A brave turnout of holiday makers. A cotillion to wind up the first day.' *The Globe*, August 15, 1896, p. 20.
Reference: King Diary, August 13, 1896.

B223 * 'A gruesome discovery. The bodies of two infants found. One at Hanlon's Point and one in the Bay.' *The Globe*, August 26, 1896, p. 8.
Reference: King Diary, August 25, 1896.

B224 * 'Student volunteers.' *The Globe*, August 31, 1896, p. 12.
Reference: King Diary, August 31, 1896.

B225 * [Opening of Robinson's Musee under new management] and [Review of 'A Happy Little Home' at the Toronto Opera House] in 'Theatre opened. The season inaugurated most successfully. A laughing audience at the Toronto. A most auspicious opening of the Musee. The Princess will unlock its doors with "superbs."' *The Globe*, September 1, 1896, p. 3.
Reference: King Diary, August 31, 1896.

B226 * 'Very sudden death. Mr George L. Guilbert lies down in his store and dies before medical aid can reach him.' *The Globe*, September 4, 1896, p. 4.
Reference: King Diary, September 3, 1896.

B227 * 'Mr Donald's death. Sudden demise of the well-known King Street merchant. A useful and honourable career.' *The Globe*, September 5, 1896, p. 24.
Reference: King Diary, September 4, 1896.

B228 * [Review of 'An American Beauty,' a new comic opera]. *The Globe*, September 22, 1896, p. 10.
Reference: King Diary, September 21, 1896.

B229 [Review of] *Province of Quebec and the early American Revolution: A study in English-American colonial history.* By Victor Coffin. Madison: University of Wisconsin, 1896. xvii, 287 p. *Journal of Political Economy*, 5, December 1896, pp. 105–109.

B230 * 'In Chicago slums. The work of Hull House among the poor. A mixed settlement. Evils of sweating system and overcrowding. Cleaning up the 14th Ward. Much educational work being done. Art exhibitions and musical entertainments. Many social clubs. Review of the House's work.' *The Globe*, January 16, 1897, p. 9.
Reference: King Diary, January 18, 1897.

B231 'Trade-union organization in the United States.' *Journal of Political Economy*, 5, March 1897, pp. 201–215.

B232 * 'Charities and correction. The General Secretary of the National Conference speaks at Jarvis Street Church. The call for organization.' *The Globe*, July 5, 1897, p. 6.
Reference: King Diary, July 5, 1897.

B233 * 'The British Association.' *The Times*, August 24, 1897, p. 7.
Reference: King Diary, August 23, 1897.

B234 * 'The British Association.' *The Times*, August 25, 1897, p. 4.
Reference: King Diary, August 24, 1897.

B235 * 'The British Association.' *The Times*, August 26, 1897, p. 4.
Reference: King Diary, August 25, 1897.

B236 * 'Advances made in higher education. A PhD course established at the university. Law curriculum changed. Christmas examinations at Osgoode Hall. What the Principal has to say. Important additions made to the courses at Varsity and Trinity. The standard in some instances materially raised.' *Daily Mail and Empire*, September 9, 1897, p. 6.
Reference: King Diary, September 8, 1897.

B237 * 'Eaton liquidator not yet appointed. Claims of Mr Clarkson and Mr Campbell reviewed. The Master-in-Ordinary kept busy all day yesterday and will sit again to-day. Mr Clarkson to be called.' *Daily Mail and Empire*, September 9, 1897, p. 8.
Reference: King Diary, September 8, 1897.

B238 * 'Creameries Association.' *Daily Mail and Empire*, September 9, 1897, p. 6.
Reference: King Diary, September 8, 1897.

B239 * 'Big assignments made yesterday. American operators suspend their business. J.B. Willard & Company, of New York, have heavy liabilities. The International Commission Company also suspended.' *Daily Mail and Empire*, September 10, 1897, p. 5.
Reference: King Diary, September 9, 1897.

B240 * 'Red River Expedition. The Association holds a pleasant reunion at Webb's. Interesting reminiscences related.' *Daily Mail and Empire*, September 10, 1897, p. 7.
Reference: King Diary, September 9, 1897, p. 6.

B241 * 'Poultry Breeders confer.' *Daily Mail and Empire*, September 10, 1897, p. 7.
Reference: King Diary, September 9, 1897.

B242 * 'Accidental death. Jury's verdict in children's drowning case. Nearly three hours taken to arrive at a decision. Important recommendations made.' *Daily Mail and Empire*, September 11, 1897, p. 6.
Reference: King Diary, September 10, 1897.

B243 * 'A new Baptist church opened. The dedication service was held yesterday. Erected in memory of a devoted Christain worker and presented to the congregation. The generous gift of a well-known citizen.' *Daily Mail and Empire*, September 13, 1897, p. 5.
Reference: King Diary, September 12, 1897.

B244 * 'The crowd leaving town.' *Daily Mail and Empire*, September 13, 1897, p. 6.
Reference: King Diary, September 11, 1897.

B245 * 'Annual meeting of the Central W.C.T.U. A review of the work of the year. Election of officers.' *Daily Mail and Empire*, September 14, 1897, p. 2.
Reference: King Diary, September 13, 1897.

B246 * 'Memorial Church opening ceremonies. Many visitors present. Mr Wm. Davies spoke.' *Daily Mail and Empire*, September 14, 1897, p. 8.
Reference: King Diary, September 12, 1897.

B247 'The International Typographical Union.' *Journal of Political Economy*, 5, September 1897, pp. 458–484.

B248 'Crowded housing, its evil effects. The conditions in Toronto a menace to the public and a grave source of danger. The problems of great cities here in embryo. What has been done to meet the evils which are becoming greater. Remedies which are available to the city and its inhabitants.' *Daily Mail and Empire*, September 18, 1897, p. 7.

B249 * 'Cowan-Downie. A very pretty wedding held at Trinity Church, Watford. The contracting parties well known.' *Daily Mail and Empire*, September 23, 1897, p. 5.
Reference: King Diary, September 22, 1897.

B250 * 'Foreigners who live in Toronto. Another phase of the great city problems which deserves careful attention. The people who make up the city's population. An historical sketch of the nationalities represented and a summary of their social, economic and political condition.' *Daily Mail and Empire*, September 25, 1897, p. 7.
Reference: King Diary, September 20–September 24, 1897.

B251 * 'Foreigners who live in Toronto. A further account of residents who have come here from other countries. Cosmopolitan elements in the city population. Social and economic conditions of foreign residents. A worthy class, by whose presence Toronto, if wisely guided, may prosper.' *Daily Mail and Empire*, October 2, 1897, Part 2, p. 10.
Reference: King Diary, October 6, 1897.

B252 * 'Toronto and the sweating system. An investigation of the matter by a representative of the Mail and Empire. Statements by the contractors and workers. Dangers which may arise and evils which already exist clearly described. The warnings of other cities.' *Daily Mail and Empire*, October 9, 1897, Part 2, p. 10.
Reference: King Diary, October 11, 1897.

B253 'The story of Hull House.' *Westminster* [Toronto], November 6, 1897, pp. 356–359.

B254 'Sweating system in Montreal. Nearly all the ready-made clothing that is worn is sweater-made. Starvation prices paid. Two classes of sub-contracting – small shops and home workers. Much work is done in villages.' *The Herald* [Montreal], April 16, 1898, p. 9.

B255 'Sweating system in Montreal city. Practically no factory inspector reaches the sweat shops, although an effort is being made. System spreads diseases. Measures taken everywhere to curtail the evils, but the remedy is in the hands of the purchaser. "White Lists" of N.Y. League.' *The Herald* [Montreal], April 23, 1898, p. 2.

B256 'The sweating system in Canada. Conditions which obtain in the manufacture of ready-made clothing. Effects of competition under some features of the industrial system. An investigation into the various processes by which ready-made clothing is obtained by the contractor. The economics of present conditions. Revelations with regard to the employment of women and children. Prices paid for the work done,' *The Globe*, November 19, 1898, p. 5.

B257 * 'Anti-sweating regulations in government contracts.' *Labour Gazette*, 1 (1), September 1900, pp. 5–13.

B258 * 'Règlements pour supprimer le système de "sweating" dans les contrats du gouvernement.' *La Gazette du travail*, 1 (1), septembre 1900, pp. 5–14.
Reference: King Diary, August 22 and 28, 1900.

B259 * 'Conciliation et arbitrage volontaires.' *La Gazette du travail*, 1 (1), septembre 1900, pp. 29–35.

B260 * 'Voluntary conciliation and arbitration.' *Labour Gazette*, 1 (1), September 1900, pp. 28–34.
Reference: King Diary, July 26, 30, and 31, 1900.

B261 * 'Bureau du Travail dans Ontario.' *La Gazette du travail*, 1 (1), septembre 1900, p. 35.

B262 * 'Bureau of Labour in Ontario.' *Labour Gazette*, 1 (1), September 1900, p. 34.
Reference: King Diary, August 29 and 30, 1900.

B263 * 'Application de la loi relative au travail des étrangers.' *La Gazette du travail*, 1 (1), septembre 1900, pp. 27–28.

B264 * 'Enforcement of the Alien Labour Act.' *Labour Gazette*, 1 (1), September 1900, pp. 26–27.
Reference: King Diary, August 30, 1900.

B265 * 'Fair wages in public contract work.' *Labour Gazette*, September 1900, pp. 15–26.

B266 * 'Gages raisonnables pour les travaux publics par contrat.' *La Gazette du travail*, 1 (1), septembre 1900, pp. 16–27.
Reference: King Diary, August 20, 21, and 29, 1900.

B267 * 'Rapports de Départements et de Bureaux.' *La Gazette du travail*, 1 (1), septembre 1900, p. 36.

B268 * 'Reports of Departments and Bureaus.' *Labour Gazette*, 1 (1), September 1900, p. 35.
Reference: King Diary, September 4, 1900.

B269 * 'La Gazette du travail.' *La Gazette du travail*, 1 (1), septembre 1900, pp. 1–2.

B270 * 'The Labour Gazette.' *Labour Gazette*, 1 (1), September 1900, pp. 1–2.
Reference: King Diary, August 1, 1900.

B271 * 'Difficultés ouvrières durant le mois d'octobre.' *La Gazette du travail*, 1 (3), novembre 1900, pp. 120–122.

B272 * 'Trade disputes of the month of October.' *Labour Gazette*, 1 (3), November 1900, pp. 117–118.
Reference: King Diary, November 9, 1900.

B273 * 'Difficultés ouvrières à Valleyfield, Qué.' *La Gazette du travail*, 1 (3), novembre 1900, pp. 100–103.

B274 * 'The labour difficulties at Valleyfield, Que.,' *Labour Gazette*, 1 (3), November 1900, pp. 101–103.
Reference: King Diary, November 9, 1900.

B275 * [Editorial on the features of the *Labour Gazette*]. *Labour Gazette*, 1 (3), November 1900, p. 85.

B276 * [Editorial sur la nature de *La Gazette du travail*]. *La Gazette du travail*, 1 (3), novembre 1900, p. 87.
Reference: King Diary, November 9, 1900.

B277 * 'Unions formed during October, 1900.' *Labour Gazette*, 1 (3), November 1900, pp. 103–104.

B278 * 'Unions formées durant le mois d'octobre 1900.' *La Gazette du travail,* 1 (3), novembre 1900, pp. 139–140.
Reference: King Diary, November 10, 1900.

B279 * 'Règlement de la grève des faiseurs de noyaux d'après l'acte de conciliation canadien.' *La Gazette du Travail,* 1 (5), janvier 1901, pp. 237–239.

B280 * 'Settlement of coremakers' strike under Canadian Conciliation Act.' *Labour Gazette,* 1 (5), January 1901, pp. 230–232.
Reference: King Diary, December 17 and 18, 1900.

B281 * 'Difficultés ouvrières durant le mois de décembre.' *La Gazette du travail,* 1 (5), janvier 1901, pp. 260–262.

B282 * 'Trade disputes of the month of December.' *Labour Gazette,* 1 (5), January 1901, pp. 248–250.
Reference: King Diary, December 18, 1900.

B283 'Life, labor, and love' in 'The significance to Canadians of the last Christmas day of the century.' *Toronto Daily Star,* December 22, 1900, p. 9.

The newspaper had sent requests to a number of leading men in all the various fields of intellectual and commercial activity in Canada for comments on 'what the last Christmas day of the nineteenth century should signify to mankind and to Canadians.'

B284 * [Editorial reviewing main features of the January issue of the *Labour Gazette*]. *Labour Gazette,* 1 (5), January 1901, pp. 199–200.

B285 * [Editorial à propos des articles du numéro de janvier de *La Gazette du travail*]. *La Gazette du travail,* 1 (5), janvier 1901, pp. 209–210.
Reference: King Diary, January 8, 1901.

B286 * [Introduction to] 'Legislation for the protection of employees in shops and stores.' *Labour Gazette,* 1 (5), January 1901, pp. 248–249.

B287 * [Introduction à] 'Législation pour la protection des employés dans les boutiques et dans les magasins.' *La Gazette du travail,* 1 (5), janvier 1901, pp. 253–254.
Reference: King Diary, January 4, 1901.

B288 * 'Tarif de gages et heures de travail dans les métiers et l'imprimerie au Canada.' *La Gazette du travail*, 1 (5), janvier 1901, pp. 244–250.

B289 * 'Wages and hours in the printing trades, Canada.' *Labour Gazette*, 1 (5), January 1901, pp. 233–239.
Reference: King Diary, January 9 and 10, 1901.

B290 * 'Unions formed during December, 1900.' *Labour Gazette*, 1 (5), January 1901, pp. 238–240.

B291 * 'Unions formées durant le mois de décembre 1900.' *La Gazette du travail*, 1 (5), janvier 1901, pp. 250–251.
Reference: King Diary, January 10, 1901.

B292 * 'Gages et heures dans les manufactures de cigares au Canada.' *La Gazette du travail*, 1 (6), février 1901, pp. 325–329.

B293 * 'Wages and hours in the cigarmaking trade.' *Labour Gazette*, 1 (6), February 1901, pp. 310–313.
Reference: King Diary, January 16, February 6, 7, and 11, 1901.

B294 * [Editorial on the extent to which arbitration and conciliation are being put forward in the settlement of disputes]. *Labour Gazette*, 1 (6), February 1901, pp. 259–260.

B295 * [Editorial sur le degré auquel l'arbitration et la conciliation sont proposées dans la résolution des disputes]. *La Gazette du travail*, 1 (6), février 1901, pp. 273–274.
Reference: King Diary, January 31 and February 1, 1901.

B296 * [Introduction to] 'Reports from local correspondents.' *Labour Gazette*, 1 (6), February 1901, p. 261.

B297 * [Introducton aux] 'Rapports de correspondants locaux.' *La Gazette du travail*, 1 (6), février 1901, p. 275.
Reference: King Diary, February 1, 1901.

B298 * 'The arbitration award concerning the boot and shoe industry, Quebec, Que.' *Labour Gazette*, 1 (6), February 1901, pp. 294–297.

B299 * 'Sentence arbitrale concernant l'industrie des chausseurs à Québec.' *La Gazette du travail*, 1 (6), février 1901, pp. 309–312.
Reference: King Diary, February 1, 1901.

B300 * 'Difficultés ouvrières durant le mois de janvier.' *La Gazette du travail*, 1 (6), février 1901, pp. 321–323.

B301 * 'Trade disputes of the month of January.' *Labour Gazette*, 1 (6), February 1901, pp. 306–308.
Reference: King Diary, February 4, 1901.

B302 * 'Unions formed during month of January.' *Labour Gazette*, 1 (6), February 1901, pp. 305–306.

B303 * 'Unions formées durant le mois de janvier.' *La Gazette du travail*, 1 (6), février 1901, pp. 320–321.
Reference: King Diary, February 4, 1901.

B304 * 'Gages et heures de travail dans les métiers des métaux en Canada.' *La Gazette du travail*, 1 (6), fevrier 1901, pp. 371–378.

B305 * 'Wages and hours in the metal industry, Canada.' *Labour Gazette*, 1 (7), March 1901, pp. 355–362.
Reference: King Diary, February 26, 27, and April 2, 1901.

B306 * [Editorial relating to articles in the *Labour Gazette*]. *Labour Gazette*, 1 (8), April 1901, pp. 287–388.

B307 * [Editorial à propos des articles du numéro d'avril de *La Gazette du travail*]. *La Gazette du travail*, 1 (8), avril 1901, pp. 409–410.
Reference: King Diary, April 2, 1901.

B308 * [Introduction to] 'Reports from local correspondents.' *Labour Gazette*, 1 (8), April 1901, pp. 388–389.

B309 * [Introduction aux] 'Rapports de correspondants locaux.' *La Gazette du travail*, 1 (8), avril 1901, pp. 410–411.
Reference: King Diary, April 3, 1901.

B310 * 'Directory of labour organizations in Canada.' *Labour Gazette*, 2 (3), September 1901, pp. 181–189.

B311 * 'Indicateur des organisations ouvrières en Canada.' *La Gazette du travail*, 2 (3), septembre 1901, pp. 187–195.
Reference: King Diary, August 21, 22, and 23, 1901.

B312 * [Editorial on features of the September issue of the *Labour Gazette*]. *Labour Gazette*, 2 (3), September 1901, pp. 131–132.

B313 [Editorial sur les articles du numéro de septembre de *La Gazette du travail*]. *La Gazette du travail*, 2 (3), septembre 1901, pp. 131–132.
Reference: King Diary, September 5, 1901.

B314 * [Introduction] to 'Reports from local correspondents.' *Labour Gazette*, 2 (3), September 1901, p. 132.

B315 * [Introduction aux] 'Rapports de correspondants locaux.' *La Gazette du travail*, 2 (3), septembre 1901, p. 136.
Reference: King Diary, September 5, 1901.

B316 * 'La grève des hommes d'équipe du Chemin de fer du Pacifique canadien.' *La Gazette du travail*, 2 (3), septembre 1901, pp. 178–184.

B317 * 'The strike of the trackmen on the C.P.R.' *Labour Gazette*, 2 (3), September 1901, pp. 172–178.
Reference: King Diary, September 6, 1901.

B318 * 'Directory of labour organizations in Canada (continued).' *Labour Gazette*, 2 (4), October 1901, pp. 243–255.

B319 * 'Indicateur des organisations ouvrières au Canada' [suite]. *La Gazette du travail*, 2 (4), octobre 1901, pp. 251–263.
Reference: King Diary, October 4, 1901.

B320 * 'Difficultés ouvrières du mois de septembre.' *La Gazette du travail*, 2 (4), octobre 1901, pp. 246–247.

B321 * 'Trade disputes during September.' *Labour Gazette*, 2 (4), October 1901, pp. 210–211.
Reference: King Diary, October 4, 1901.

B322 * 'Décisions judiciaires récentes affectant le travail.' *La Gazette du travail*, 2 (4), octobre 1901, pp. 248–251.

B323 * 'Recent legal decisions affecting labour.' *Labour Gazette*, 2 (4), October 1901, pp. 239–243.
Reference: October 4, 1901.

B324 * 'Association internationale pour la législation ouvrière.' *La Gazette du travail*, 2 (4), octobre 1901, pp. 216–217.

B325 * 'International Association for Labour Legislation.' *Labour Gazette*, 2 (4), October 1901, pp. 226, 227.
Reference: King Diary, October 4, 1901.

B326 * 'British Columbia cases. Convictions under Alien Labour Act.' *Labour Gazette*, 2 (4), October 1901, pp. 242–243.

B327 * 'Cas de la Colombie anglaise [*sic* for britannique]. Condamnation en vertu de la loi sur le travail des étrangers.' *La Gazette du travail,* 2 (4), octobre 1901, pp. 250–252.
Reference: King Diary, October 8, 1901.

B328 * [Editorial relating to the articles in the *Labour Gazette*]. *Labour Gazette,* 2 (4), October 1901, pp. 191–192.

B329 * [Editorial sur les articles de *La Gazette du travail*]. *La Gazette du travail,* 2 (4), octobre 1901, pp. 197–198.
Reference: King Diary, October 4, 1901.

B330 * 'Le Congrès des métiers et du travail du Canada.' *La Gazette du travail,* 2 (4), octobre 1901, pp. 222–233.

B331 * 'The Trades and Labour Congress of Canada.' *Labour Gazette,* 2 (4), October 1901, pp. 212–222.
Reference: King Diary, September 26 and October 1, 1901.

B332 * 'Application de la résolution relative aux gages raisonnables par le Ministère des Postes.' *La Gazette du travail,* 2 (5), novembre 1901, pp. 292–294.

B333 * 'Enforcement of Fair Wages resolution by Post Office Department.' *Labour Gazette,* 2 (5), November 1901, pp. 282–285.
Reference: King Diary, October 11, 1901.

B334 * 'Règlement par conciliation de la grève des fileurs de coton à Valleyfield, Qué. *La Gazette du travail,* 2 (5), novembre 1901, pp. 285–286.

B335 * 'Settlement by conciliation of Valleyfield Spinners' strike.' *Labour Gazette,* 2 (5), November 1901, pp. 285–286.
Reference: King Diary, October 16, 1901.

B336 * 'Feu Henry A. Harper.' *La Gazette du travail,* 2 (6), décembre 1901, p. 336.

B337 * 'The late Henry A. Harper.' *Labour Gazette,* 2 (6), December 1901, p. 325.
Reference: The King Diary does not contain any reference to this article. There is, however, a corrected draft of the article in the King Papers, J 7 Series, Box 3, pp. 1571A–1573A.

B338 * 'La situation à Rossland.' *La Gazette du travail*, 2 (6), décembre 1901, pp. 373–376.

B339 * 'The Rossland situation.' *Labour Gazette*, 2 (6), December 1901, pp. 362–365.
Reference: The King Diary does not contain any reference to this article, but the published article contains Mackenzie King's report, as Deputy Minister of Labour, relating to the Rossland Miners' Union at Rossland, B.C.

B340 * [Introduction to] 'Legislation in Canada for the protection of employees on ships.' *Labour Gazette*, 2 (5), November 1901, pp. 286–287, 2 (6), December 1901, p. 350, 2 (7), January 1902, p. 408.

B341 * [Introduction à] 'Législation pour la protection de personnes employées sur les navires.' *La Gazette du travail*, 2 (5), novembre 1901, pp. 295–296, 2 (6), décembre 1901, p. 360, 2 (7), janvier 1902, p. 413.
Reference: King Diary, January 4, 1902.

B342 * 'Gages et heures de travail dans les métiers du bois au Canada.' *La Gazette du travail*, 2 (5), novembre 1901, pp. 309–319, 2 (6), décembre 1901, pp. 355–361, 2 (7), janvier 1902, pp. 417–424.

B343 * 'Wages and hours in the woodworking trades, Canada.' *Labour Gazette*, 2 (5), November 1901, pp. 299–309, 2 (6), December 1901, pp. 345–351, 2 (7), January 1902, pp. 399–408.
Reference: King Diary, January 4, 1902.

B344 * 'Règlement de la grève des facteurs de pianos à Toronto, d'après l'acte de Conciliation.' *La Gazette du travail*, 2 (7), janvier 1902, pp. 412–413.

B345 * 'Settlement of piano-makers' strike, Toronto, under Conciliation Act, 1900.' *Labour Gazette*, 2 (7), January 1902, pp. 407–408.
Reference: King Diary, January 4, 1902.

B346 * 'Difficultés ouvrières du mois de décembre.' *La Gazette du travail*, 2 (7), janvier 1902, pp. 425–426.

B347 * 'Trade disputes during the month of December.' *Labour Gazette*, 2 (7), January 1902, pp. 412–413.
Reference: King Diary, January 4, 1902.

B348 * [Introduction to] 'Reports from local correspondents.' *Labour Gazette*, 2 (7), January 1902, p. 380.

B349 * [Introduction aux] 'Rapports des correspondants locaux.' *La Gazette du travail*, 2 (7), janvier 1902, p. 392.
Reference: King Diary, January 7, 1902.

B350 * [Editorial relating to the features of the January issue of the *Labour Gazette*]. *Labour Gazette*, 2 (7), January 1902, p. 379.

B351 * [Editorial sur les articles du numéro de janvier de *La Gazette du travail*]. *La Gazette du travail*, 2 (7), janvier 1902, p. 391.
Reference: King Diary, January 7, 1902.

B352 * 'Législation au Canada relative aux apprentis.' *La Gazette du travail*, 2 (9), mars 1902, pp. 492–496.

B353 * 'Legislation in Canada in regard to apprentices.' *Labour Gazette*, 2 (8), February 1902, pp. 470–475, 2 (9), March 1902, pp. 526–530.
Reference: King Diary, January 16 and 21, 1902.

B354 * 'Fair wages on public contract work – Canada.' *Labour Gazette*, 2 (8), February 1902, pp. 475–481.

B355 * 'Gages raisonnables dans les travaux publics à l'entreprise, Canada.' *La Gazette du travail*, 2 (8), fevrier 1902, pp. 467–472.
Reference: King Diary, January 27 and 28, 1902.

B356 * 'Conciliation au Canada, d'après la loi de 1900.' *La Gazette du travail*, 2 (8), février 1902, pp. 487–492.

B357 * 'Conciliation in Canada – Experience under Act, 1900.' *Labour Gazette*, 2 (8), February 1902, pp. 466–470.
Reference: King Diary, January 27 and 28, 1902.

B358 * 'La besogne du Département du Travail.' *La Gazette du travail*, 2 (8), février 1902, pp. 473–480.

B359 * 'The work of the Department of Labour.' *Labour Gazette*, 2 (8), February 1902, pp. 459–465.
Reference: King Diary, January 27 and 28, 1902.

B360 * [Introduction to] 'Wages and hours in the carriage and wagon-making trades – Canada.' *Labour Gazette*, 2 (8), February 1902, p. 452.

B361 * [Introduction à] 'Gages et heures de travail dans les métiers se rapportant à la fabrication des voitures.' *La Gazette du travail*, 2 (8), février 1902, p. 480.
Reference: King Diary, February 1, 1902.

B362 * 'Directory of labour organizations in Canada.' *Labour Gazette*, 2 (8), February 1902, p. 487.

B363 * 'Indicateur des organisations ouvrières au Canada.' *La Gazette du travail*, 2 (8), février 1902, p. 503.
Reference: King Diary, February 1, 1902.

B364 * [Introduction to] 'Reports from local correspondents.' *Labour Gazette*, 2 (8), February 1902, p. 434.

B365 * [Introduction aux] 'Rapports des correspondants locaux.' *La Gazette du travail*, 2 (8), février 1902, p. 448.
Reference: King Diary, February 1, 1902.

B366 * [Editorial relating to the appointment of Robert Hamilton Coats as assistant editor of the *Labour Gazette* and a summary of articles in the current issue]. *Labour Gazette*, 2 (8), February 1902, p. 433.

B367 * [Editorial sur le nomination de M. Robert Hamilton Coats comme rédacteur-adjoint de *La Gazette du travail* et un résumé des articles du numéro de février]. *La Gazette du travail*, 2 (8), février 1902, p. 447.
Reference: King Diary, February 1, 1902.

B368 * 'Difficultés ouvrières du mois de janvier.' *La Gazette du travail*, 2 (8), février 1902, pp. 497–499.

B369 * 'Trade disputes during month of January.' *Labour Gazette*, 2 (8), February 1902, pp. 481–483.
Reference: King Diary, February 1, 1902.

B370 * 'Gages et heures de travail des employés du chemin de fer au Canada.' *La Gazette du travail*, 3 (3), septembre 1902, pp. 178–183.

B371 * 'Wages and hours of railway employees, Canada.' *Labour Gazette*, 3 (3), September 1902, pp. 165–170.
Reference: King Diary, September 30, 1902.

B372 * 'Labour organization in Canada – Its growth and present position – II. The Province of Quebec.' *Labour Gazette*, 3 (4), October 1902, pp. 238–246.

B373 * 'L'organisation ouvrière au Canada – Sa croissance et sa position actuelle. II – La Province du Québec.' *La Gazette du travail*, 3 (4), octobre 1902, pp. 274–282.
Reference: King Diary, September 30, 1902.

B374 * [Editorial relating to articles in the October issue of the *Labour Gazette*]. *Labour Gazette*, 3 (4), October 1902, pp. 189–190.

B375 * [Editorial sur les articles du numéro d'octobre de *La Gazette du travail*]. *La Gazette du travail*, 3 (4), octobre 1902, pp. 197–198.
Reference: King Diary, September 30, 1902.

B376 * 'Canadian Conference of Charities and Corrections.' *Labour Gazette*, 3 (4), October 1902, pp. 259–260.

B377 * 'Conférence canadienne pour la charité et la correction.' *La Gazette du travail*, 3 (4), octobre 1902, p. 254.
Reference: King Diary, September 30, 1902.

B378 * 'Difficultés ouvrières du mois de septembre.' *La Gazette du travail*, 3 (4), octobre 1902, pp. 255–258.

B379 * 'Trade disputes during the month of September.' *Labour Gazette*, 3 (4), October 1902, pp. 268–272.
Reference: King Diary, October 1, 1902.

B380 * 'The organizer gives evidence. James Baker before the Commissioners. President of Ladysmith Union also on stand. Many witnesses to be examined.' *Victoria Daily Times*, May 7, 1903, p. 1.
Reference: King Diary, May 6, 1903.

B381 'Interview with the Union officials. Commissioners met executive committee. James Baker on strike and arbitration. Two miners give evidence. Sit here Monday.' *Victoria Daily Times*, May 8, 1903, p. 1.
Reference: King Diary, May 7, 1903.

B382 * 'Were compelled to live at Ladysmith. More miners before Royal Commission. Company's counsel says he will show why men were required to live there.' *Victoria Daily Times*, May 9, 1903, p. 1.
Reference: King Diary, May 9, 1903.

B383 * 'Mr Dunsmuir and his employees. Will lay proposals before the miners. Meeting of committee representing the men and President of coal company.' *Victoria Daily Times,* May 19, 1903, p. 1.
Reference: King Diary, May 18, 1903.

B384 * 'The labor commission. Member of the Ladysmith miners' executive examined. A warning.' *Victoria Daily Times,* May 23, 1903.
Reference: King Diary, May 21, 1903.

B385 * 'Labour unions and British industry.' *Labour Gazette,* 4 (8), February 1904, pp. 796–797.

B386 * 'Unions ouvrières et l'industrie anglaise.' *La Gazette du travail,* 4 (8), février 1904, pp. 823–824.
Reference: King Diary, January 12 and 13, 1904.

B387 * 'Apprenticeship articles of Employers' Association of Toronto.' *Labour Gazette,* 4 (9), March 1904, pp. 899–901.

B388 * 'Contrat d'apprentissages de l'Association des Patrons de Toronto.' *La Gazette du travail,* 4 (9), mars 1904, pp. 930–933.
Reference: King Diary, February 19, 1904.

B389 'The National Transcontinental Railway of Canada.' *Quarterly Journal of Economics,* 19, November 1904, pp. 136–148.

B390 * 'Grève des machinistes de la Compagnie de chemin de fer du Grand Tronc.' *La Gazette du travail,* 6 (5), novembre 1905, p. 607.

B391 * 'Strike of machinists on Grand Trunk Railway.' *Labour Gazette,* 6 (5), November 1905, pp. 580–581.
Reference: King Diary, November 4 and 6, 1905.

B392 * 'Investigation au sujet des prétendues menées frauduleuses, en Angleterre, afin d'induire des imprimeurs à venir au Canada.' *La Gazette du Travail,* 6 (10), avril 1906, pp. 1134–1142.

B393 * 'Investigation of alleged fraudulent practices in England to induce printers to come to Canada.' *Labour Gazette,* 6 (10), April 1906, pp. 1122–1130. [With the exception of three introductory paragraphs the article contains the text of Mackenzie King's report to the Minister of Labour.]

B394 'Rapport du Sous-Ministre du travail sur les causes de l'affluence des Italiens à Montréal en 1904.' *La Gazette du travail*, 6 (12), juin 1906, pp. 1371–1375.

B395 * 'Report of the Deputy Minister of Labour on causes of influx of Italians to Montreal during 1904.' *Labour Gazette*, 6 (12), June 1906, pp. 1347–1351.

B396 * 'False representations to induce or deter immigrants.' *Labour Gazette*, 7 (3), September 1906, pp. 290–291.

B397 * 'Fausses représentations pour promouvoir ou détourner l'immigration.' *La Gazette du travail*, 7 (3), septembre 1906, pp. 290–291.
Reference: King Diary, September 10, 1906.

B398 'Règlement de la grève des houilleurs, à Lethbridge, Alberta, sous l'Acte de Médiation.' *La Gazette du travail*, 7 (6), décembre 1906, pp. 708–724.

B399 'Settlement of the coal miners strike at Lethbridge, Alberta, under Conciliation Act.' *Labour Gazette*, 7 (6), December 1906, pp. 647–662.
Reference: King Diary, December 8 and 9, 1906.

B400 [Letter to the editor relating to the correspondence between D. Hibner and Mackenzie King]. *Berlin Telegraph*, August 26, 1911.

B401 'The Canadian Combines Investigation Act.' *Annals of the American Academy of Political and Social Science*, 42, July 1912, pp. 149–155.

B402 * 'How Canada prevents strikes.' *World's Work*, 26, August 1913, pp. 438–444.

B403 * 'The European War.' *Canadian Liberal Monthly*, 1 (12), August 1914, pp. 134–152.

B404 * 'La guerre européenne.' *Le mois Libéral canadien*, 1 (12), août 1914, pp. 134–148.
Reference: King Diary, August 11, 13, 14, 15, 16, and 17, 1914.

B405 * 'L'attitude des Libéraux [à la guerre européenne].' *Le mois Libéral canadien*, 1 (12), août 1914, p. 134.

B406 * 'The Liberal attitude [to the European War].' *Canadian Liberal Monthly*, 1 (12), August 1914, p. 134.
Reference: King Diary, August 16, 1914.

B407 'The aim of the Liberal Party in Canada to-day.' *Maclean's Magazine*, 34 (2), January 15, 1921, pp. 20–21, 37.

B408 'If I am re-elected?' *Maclean's Magazine*, 38 (19), October 1, 1925, pp. 28, 44.

B409 'The issues as I see them.' *Maclean's Magazine*, 39 (17), September 1, 1926, pp. 7, 32, 36.

B410 'The election issues as I see them.' *Maclean's Magazine*, 43 (14), July 15, 1930, pp. 9, 37–39, 41.

B411 'Liberalism in Canada.' *Jewish Daily Eagle*, July 8, 1932, pp. 25–26. [In the Centennial Jubilee Edition commemorating the centenary of Jewish emancipation in Canada and the twenty-fifth anniversary of the *Jewish Daily Eagle*].

B412 'King met Laurier as Globe scribe in 1896 election. Memorable night at Sir William Mulock's home recalled by Liberal leader. King's varied work while on staff of Globe.' *The Globe*, March 28, 1934, p. 15.

In this article King describes his work as a reporter for *The Globe* from 1894 to 1896.[89]

B413 'The issues in this election.' *Monetary Times*, 104 (10), March 9, 1940, pp. 302, 304.

The article also contains sections by W.D. Herridge, J.S. Woodsworth, and R.J. Manion.

B414 'The issue as I see it.' *Maclean's Magazine*, 53 (6), March 15, 1940, pp. 12, 53.

B415 'What is the election issue?' *Liberty*, March 23, 1940, pp. 4, 6.

B416 'What do the Liberals stand for?' *Maclean's Magazine*, 58 (3), February 1, 1945, pp. 10–11, 38–40. [Interview with Blair Fraser].

B417 'Canadian citizenship and the larger world.' *International Journal*, 2, Spring 1947, p. 95.

B418 [Draft of an article on the early history of the *Labour Gazette* and the

89 See Appendix 1 for the text of this article.

Department of Labour]. *Labour Gazette,* 50 (9), September 1950, pp. 1312–1313.

B419 [Brouillon d'un article sur les débuts de *La Gazette du travail* et du Ministère du travail]. *La Gazette du travail,* 50 (9), septembre 1950, pp. 1311–1313.

The Editor noted that this was 'the first draft of a message which might have appeared in this issue under the signature of the Rt. Hon. William Lyon Mackenzie King.' He added that King was deeply interested in the plans for the celebration of the fiftieth anniversary of the *Labour Gazette.* He continued: 'The draft was prepared, a few weeks before his death, along lines which he himself indicated. It received his general approval, subject to the kind of revision to which he subjected every statement that might be ascribed to him. Unfortunately, in the week of his last illness it was beyond his strength to attempt even such a revision and the message was left, in its present form, unfinished.'

References to the following articles have been located in the King Papers, but the actual texts of them have not been found:

B420 [Report on the election in the riding of Jacques-Cartier, Quebec, for the Associated Press], December 30, 1895. [Text not located].

Reference: WLMK Papers, J 1 Series, vol. 1, William Lyon Mackenzie King to Henry Albert Harper, December 1, 1895.

B421 [Report on the fight between 'Tommy' Dixon and Frank Zimpfer at the Princess Theatre, Toronto, for the Associated Press], May 23, 1896. [Text not located].

Reference: King Diary, May 23, 1896.

B422 [Report on the races at Woodbine Track, Toronto, for the Associated Press], May 25, 1896. [Text not located].

Reference: King Diary, May 25, 1896.

B423 [Report on the races at Woodbine Track, Toronto, for the Associated Press], May 26, 1896. [Text not located].

Reference: King Diary, May 26, 1896.

B424 [Report on the races at Woodbine Track, Toronto, for the Associated Press], May 28, 1896. [Text not located].

Reference: King Diary, May 28, 1896.

B425 [Report on the races at Woodbine Track, Toronto, for the Associated Press], May 29, 1896. [Text not located].
Reference: King Diary, May 29, 1896.

B426 [Report on the races at Woodbine Track, Toronto, for the Associated Press], May 30, 1896. [Text not located].
Reference: King Diary, May 30, 1896.

B427 'Canada's position as a manufacturing country.' *Encyclopedia Americana,* 1904.
Reference: King Papers, J 4 Series, vol. 21, pp. 14127–14139.

SECTION C

Government Reports

While still a student at Harvard University, Mackenzie King was asked by Sir William Mulock, the federal postmaster general, to prepare a report on Canadian government clothing contracts. Later King was the sole commissioner of six royal commissions appointed to investigate subjects ranging from the hours of employment at Bell Telephone Company of Canada to industrial disputes in the province of Quebec. In addition, King wrote reports on several other special subjects for the federal government.

The reports in this section are arranged chronologically.

Separate Reports

C1 Report to the Honourable the Postmaster General of the methods adopted in Canada in the carrying out of the government clothing contracts. Ottawa: Government Printing Bureau, 1898. 31 p.

C2 Report of the Royal Commission on a dispute respecting hours of employment between the Bell Telephone Company of Canada, Ltd., and operators at Toronto, Ontario. Ottawa: Government Printing Bureau, 1907. x, 102 p.

C3 Rapport par W.L. Mackenzie King, C.M.G., sous-ministre du travail, relatif à sa mission en Angleterre pour conférer avec les autorités britanniques sur l'immigration de l'Orient au Canada, et plus particulièrement sur l'immigration de l'Inde. Ottawa: Imprimeur du Roi, 1909. 10 p.

C4 Report by W.L. Mackenzie King, C.M.G., Deputy Minister of Labour, on mission to England to confer with the British authorities on the subject of immigration to Canada from the Orient and immigration from India in particular. Ottawa: King's Printer, 1908. 10 p.

The British Government also issued this report as a Command Paper.

C5 Report of Mr W.L. Mackenzie King on his mission to England in connection with the immigration of Asiatics into Canada. London: His Majesty's Stationery Office, 1908. 7 p. [Command Paper 4118].

C6 Memorandum accompanying report of W.L. Mackenzie King, C.M.G., Deputy Minister of Labour, on his mission to England to confer with the British authorities on the subject of immigration to Canada from the Orient, and immigration from India in particular. Ottawa: King's Printer, 1908. 15 p.

C7 Rapport par W.L. Mackenzie King, C.M.G., sous-ministre du travail, sur la nécessité de supprimer le commerce de l'opium au Canada. Ottawa: Imprimeur du Roi, 1908. 13 p.

C8 Report by W.L. Mackenzie King, C.M.G., Deputy Minister of Labour, on the need for the suppression of the opium traffic in Canada. Ottawa: King's Printer, 1908. 13 p.

C9 Rapport de W.L. Mackenzie King, C.M.G., sous-ministre du Travail, commissaire, nommé pour s'enquérir des pertes subies par la population japonaise de Vancouver, C.-B., lors des émeutes qui ont en lieu dans cette ville au mois de septembre. Ottawa: Imprimeur du Roi, 1908. 21 p.

C10 Report by W.L. Mackenzie King, C.M.G., Deputy Minister of Labour, Commissioner, appointed to investigate into the losses sustained by the Japanese population of Vancouver, B.C., on the occasion of the riots in that city in September, 1907. Ottawa: King's Printer, 1908. 22 p.

C11 Report of the Royal Commission appointed to inquire into the methods by which Oriental labourers have been induced to come to Canada. W.L. Mackenzie King, C.M.G., Commissioner. Ottawa: Government Printing Bureau, 1908. 81 p.

C12 Rapport de W.L. Mackenzie King, C.M.G., sous-ministre du Travail, commissaire, nommé pour s'enquérir des pertes subies par la population chinoise de Vancouver, C.-B., lors des émeutes qui ont en lieu dans cette ville au mois de septembre 1907. Ottawa: Imprimeur du Roi, 1908. 18 p.

C13 Report of W.L. Mackenzie King, C.M.G., Deputy Minister of Labour, Commissioner, appointed to investigate into the losses sustained by the Chinese population of Vancouver, B.C., on the occasion of the riots in that city in September, 1907. Ottawa: King's Printer, 1908. 18 p.

C14 Rapport de la commission royale chargée de s'enquérir des diffeérends industriels survenus dans les industries textiles de coton de la Province du Québec. Commissaire: W.L. Mackenzie King, C.M.G., sous-ministre du Travail. Ottawa: Imprimeur du Roi, 1909. xi, 36 p.

C15 Report of Royal Commission to inquire into industrial disputes in the cotton factories of the Province of Quebec. Commissioner: W.L. Mackenzie King, C.M.G., Deputy Minister of Labour. Ottawa: King's Printer, 1909. x, 32 p.

Annual Report of the Department of Labour

From September 18, 1900, to September 21, 1908, King was not only editor of the *Labour Gazette*, but also Deputy Minister of Labour. His work in the latter position included drafting and virtual writing the annual report of the department. The following reports are signed 'W.L. Mackenzie King, Deputy Minister of Labour.'

C16 *Rapport du Département du travail pour l'exercice clos le 30 juin 1901.* Ottawa: Imprimeur du Roi, 1902. 67 p.

C17 *Report of the Department of Labour for the fiscal year ended June 30, 1901.* Ottawa: King's Printer, 1902. 67 p.

C18 *Rapport du Ministère du travail pour l'exercice clos le 30 juin 1902.* Ottawa: Imprimeur du Roi, 1903. 94 p.

C19 *Report of the Department of Labour for the fiscal year ended June 30, 1902.* Ottawa: King's Printer, 1903. 96 p.

C20 *Rapport du Ministère du travail pour l'exercice clos le 30 juin 1903.* Ottawa: Imprimeur du Roi, 1904. 95 p.

C21 *Report of the Department of Labour for the fiscal year ended June 30, 1903.* Ottawa: King's Printer, 1904. 99 p.

C22 *Rapport du Ministère du travail pour l'exercice clos le 30 juin 1904.* Ottawa: Imprimeur du Roi, 1905. 107 p.

C23 *Report of the Department of Labour for the fiscal year ended June 30, 1904.* Ottawa: King's Printer, 1905. 107 p.

C24 *Rapport du Département du travail pour l'exercice clos le 30 juin 1905.* Ottawa: Imprimeur du Roi, 1906. 130 p.

C25 *Report of the Department of Labour for the fiscal year ended June 30, 1905.* Ottawa: King's Printer, 1905. 136 p.

C26 *Rapport du Ministère du travail pour l'exercice clos le 30 juin 1906.* Ottawa: Imprimeur du Roi, 1906. 127 p.

C27 *Report of the Department of Labour for the fiscal year ended June 30, 1906.* Ottawa: King's Printer, 1906. 136 p.

C28 *Rapport du Ministère du travail pour les neuf mois compris entre le 1 janvier 1906 et le 31 mars 1907.* Exercice de 1906–07. Ottawa: Imprimeur du Roi, 1907. 168 p.

C29 *Report of the Department of Labour for the fiscal year 1906–07.* Ottawa: King's Printer, 1907. 170 p.

C30 *Rapport du Ministère du travail pour l'exercice 1907–1908.* Ottawa: Imprimeur du Roi, 1909. 423 p.

C31 *Report of the Department of Labour for the fiscal year 1907–1908.* Ottawa: King's Printer, 1908. 408 p.

SECTION D

The Mackenzie King Diaries

On September 6, 1893, Mackenzie King, who was just beginning his third year at the University of Toronto, purchased a diary. Later that same day he made the first entry in it: 'After having been told by many that I could never keep a diary, I decided to make, at least, an attempt.'[90]

On page 1 he wrote:

> This diary is to contain *a very brief sketch* of the events, actions, feelings and thoughts of my daily life. It must above all be *a true and faithful account.* The chief object of my keeping this diary is that I may be ashamed to let even one day have nothing worthy of its showing, and it is hoped that through its pages the reader may be able to trace how the author has sought to *improve his time.* Another object must here be mentioned and is this, the writer hopes that in future days – be they far or near – he may find great pleasure both for himself and friends in *the remembrance of events recorded,* surrounded, as they must be, by many an unwritten association. If either aim is reached this present diary will not have been in vain.
>
> W.L. Mackenzie King [emphasis in original][91]

Almost fifty-seven years later, on July 19, 1950, three days before his death and on the day he became unconscious, King wrote the last entry in his diaries. After a page-long description of the day's events, the last paragraph is: 'When it came to getting up for dinner, found myself alone to

90 King Diary, September 6, 1893.
91 Ibid.

give me clothing, part of which had been taken away. Lafleur [Rolland O. Lafleur, assistant secretary] came to the rescue. I got what was needed and later signed letters. Then, went downstairs for dinner, at quarter to eight, dictating diary to date. Very very sorry to have kept Lafleur all that time.'[92]

For the most part the King diaries are arranged chronologically each year. There are a few exceptions. There are separate volumes dealing with his work relating to Japanese claims after the Vancouver riots in 1908, the work with the Rockefeller Foundation in 1913 to 1914, his international relations including a mission to Great Britain, the United States, and Japan in 1908, a visit to Europe in 1919, and a mission to the Orient in 1908 and 1909. For the first half of 1934 he kept two diaries.

Until 1938 King wrote most of the diaries by hand. However, during that year he began dictating the diaries to a secretary, who then produced a typewritten copy. From time to time, especially in later years, King placed copies of correspondence, memoranda, and clippings in his diaries.

J.W. Pickersgill has described the King diary this way:

> Because he was unmarried and without close family ties, Mackenzie King confided the day-to-day impressions and secrets that other men would have given to their wives or intimate friends to what must surely be the most remarkable diary ever kept by a Canadian. This diary is an amazing combination of intimate personal details with the most careful and painstakingly accurate reporting of the events in which he had a part. On the personal side, the diary undoubtedly served the need that most human beings have for sharing their experiences with others; on the public side, it was deliberately designed to provide a faithful record of Mackenzie King's part in public affairs of which he had hoped, one day, to write his own account. Though in his public utterances he tried always to maintain a nineteenth-century decorum, he could and often did express his views, in private conversation and in his diary, without moderation and even with vehemence, and no one had a more acute consciousness of the frailties of others, or a greater readiness in private to point them out.[93]

The diaries contain several references to King's reasons for keeping this record. In 1901, shortly after the death of his friend Henry Albert Harper, he wrote that the diary was 'a means of keeping [me] true to my purpose ...

92 King Diary, July 19, 1950.
93 J.W. Pickersgill, ed., *The Mackenzie King record*, vol. 1, p. 3.

it has helped to clear me in my thoughts and convictions, and it has been a real companion and friend.'[94] In 1941 he wrote: 'Like my friend Bert Harper before me I have sought to keep a record of thought, beliefs and actions which might serve later to myself, if the chance should come to go through the papers, something of the influences which shape human lives and have influenced my own for better or worse.'[95]

Mackenzie King's will contained the following clause: 'I direct my Literary Executors to destroy all my diaries except those parts which I have indicated are and shall be available for publication or use.'[96] The literary executors, however, decided not to destroy the diaries.[97] Several reasons account for the decision to make the diaries available for research. First, after it was decided to use the diaries in the official biography, it was felt that they should be made available to other biographers. Second, the Department of Justice handed down a decision stating that the estate was not required to destroy the diaries. Third, a member of the Public Archives staff microfilmed the diaries and made a copy (or copies) available outside of the institution. Finally, the diaries constitute one of the most important historical documents for Canadian history in the first half of the twentieth century.

There are indications that King really did not intend to have the diaries destroyed. He believed that the diaries would be a substitute for his memoirs if the latter were not completed. He is quoted as telling Fred McGregor: 'Why worry about it, McGregor, the book is practically written.'[98] '"Why, the whole story of my life," he said, "is in the diaries, fifty-eight years of them."'[99]

One volume of the diary covering the period from November 10 to

94 King Diary, January 1, 1902.

95 Public Archives of Canada. Manuscript Division. Prime Ministers Section. Archives publiques du Canada. Division des manuscrits. Section des Archives des premiers ministres. King, William Lyon Mackenzie. MG 26, J 13 Series. Diaries. Finding aid no. 502/Instrument de recherche no. 502. Ottawa: Public Archives of Canada/Archives publiques du Canada, 1981, p. 4.

96 NAC, WLMK Papers, MG 26, J 17 Series, vol. 1, Folder 1, Copy of the Last Will and Testament of the Rt. Hon. W.L. Mackenzie King, Clause 10.

97 For a detailed analysis of the reasons for deciding to preserve the original diary, see Jean Dryden, 'The Mackenzie King Papers: An archival odyssey.' *Archivaria*, 6, Summer 1978, pp. 52–57.

98 McGregor, *The fall and rise of Mackenzie King: 1911–1919*, p. 15.

99 Ibid.

December 31, 1945, is missing. It is the only volume in the entire period 1893 to 1950 that has not been accounted for in the King Papers.

The official biography of Mackenzie King covers the years 1874 to 1939. It was decided that it would not extend beyond the beginning of the Second World War. To cover the remaining years of Mackenzie King's life, an edited edition of the diary was issued. Edited by J.W. Pickersgill and Donald F. Forster, four volumes were published by the University of Toronto Press from 1960 to 1970.

An edited version of the diaries for the period 1939 to 1948 was published in hardcopy by the University of Toronto Press:

D1 Pickersgill, John Whitney, ed. *The Mackenzie King Record. Volume l: 1939–1944.* Toronto: University of Toronto Press, 1960. xiv, 723 p.

D2 – and Donald Frederick Forster, ed. *The Mackenzie King Record. Volume 2: 1944–1945.* Toronto: University of Toronto Press, 1968. xi, 495 p.

D3 – *The Mackenzie King Record. Volume 3: 1945–1946.* Toronto: University of Toronto Press, 1970. viii, 424 p.

D4 – *The Mackenzie King Record. Volume 4: 1947–1948.* Toronto: University of Toronto Press, 1970. v, 472 p.

The Mackenzie King Record (Volume 1) was serialized in *Weekend Magazine*:

D5 [Part 1] 'Mackenzie King and World War II: His bitter feeling about political enemies.' *Weekend Magazine,* 10 (41), October 8, 1960, pp. 14–15, 55–56.

D6 [Part 2] 'Mackenzie King and World War II: Boos from the troops.' *Weekend Magazine,* 10 (42), October 15, 1960, pp. 26–27, 29–31, and 54.

The University of Toronto Press has published a microfiche edition of the King diaries. The collection, which was published between 1973 and 1980, consists of 492 microfiches. It contains the complete manuscript entries and the typewritten transcripts, the original typewritten diaries, and other original typewritten journals.

The set consists of two series: the transcript series (275 microfiches) and the manuscript series (217 microfiches). As the transcript series, which was prepared for the use of the official biographer, does not contain the complete text of the handwritten diaries, it is possible to go to the manuscript series to read the omitted sections, which are indicated by '(...)' in the transcripts.

Two brief guides to the diary were also published by the University of Toronto Press:

D7 *The Mackenzie King diaries, 1893–1931: Introduction and index.* Toronto and Buffalo: University of Toronto Press, 1973. 8 p.

D8 *The Mackenzie King diaries, 1932–1949: Introduction and index.* Toronto, Buffalo, and London: University of Toronto Press, 1980. 8 p.

It is impossible to exaggerate the importance of the Mackenzie King diaries for scholars in twentieth-century Canadian political, social, and economic history. C.P. Stacey has called the diaries 'the most important Canadian political document of the twentieth century.'[100] Robert Fulford, the well-known Canadian journalist, has written that the diaries 'might turn out to be the only Canadian work of our century that someone will look at in 500 years ... The material is terrific, the cast of characters magnificent.'[101]

There is no doubt that the diaries are one of the most fascinating documents ever produced by a human being. The 64,000 pages provide the biographer with an unparalleled biographical source. At the same time, historians, political scientists, economists, and other researchers have invaluable material to use from this document.

---

100 C.P. Stacey, [Review of *The Mackenzie King record*, Volume 1], *Canadian Historical Review*, 50 (3), September 1969, p. 309.

101 Robert Fulford, 'Mackenzie King left literary monument,' *Toronto Daily Star*, August 30, 1980, p. H5.

SECTION E

Editorial Work

During his lifetime Mackenzie King was editor of three periodicals. The entries for the three periodicals are arranged chronologically.

The Labour Gazette

E1 *The Labour Gazette: The journal of the Department of Labour.* Volumes 1–8, 1900/1901–1907/1908. Ottawa: King's Printer, 1900–1908. 8 v.

E2 *La Gazette du travail: Le Journal du Département du travail.* Volumes 1–8, 1900/1901–1907/1908. Ottawa: Imprimeur du Roi, 1900–1908. 8 v.

King was editor of the *Labour Gazette* from September 1900 to September 1908.

Canadian Liberal Monthly

E3 *The Canadian Liberal Monthly.* Volume 1: September 1913–August 1914. Published by the Central Information Office of the Canadian Liberal Party. Ottawa, 1913–1914.

E4 *Le mois Libéral canadien.* Volume 1: septembre 1913–août 1914. Publié par Le Bureau central d'information du parti Libéral canadian. Ottawa, 1913–1914.

Of his work with the *Canadian Liberal Monthly* King once wrote: 'The Liberal Monthly, I have edited & written most of.'[102]

The Message

E5 *The Message.* Published by the Men's Association of St Andrew's Church, Ottawa. Volume 1, no. 1–Volume 1, no. 5, January 1904–May 1904.

King was listed as chairman of the Board of Management.

This publication, which was the official journal of the Men's Association, was founded on October 12, 1903. It contained a sermon by the pastor, a record of work of the several societies and organizations of the church, and events and happenings of interest to members and adherents of the congregation.

2 King Diary, October 4, 1914.

SECTION F

Published Speeches

This section contains a chronological list of the speeches of Mackenzie King that were published separately, as pamphlets. It does not include texts of speeches or excerpts of speeches contained in periodicals or other publications.

Locations of copies of the speeches in Canadian libraries have been provided. If no copy has been located in a Canadian library, the location in the King Papers has been indicated.

F1 House of Commons Debates. Second Session – Eleventh Parliament. Speech of Hon. W.L. Mackenzie King, M.P., (Minister of Labour) on technical education, Ottawa, Monday, December 6, 1909. [Ottawa, 1909]. 9 p.
Location: WLMK Papers, J 5 Series, vol. 1, Folder 1, Item 1.

F2 House of Commons Debates. Second Session – Eleventh Parliament. Speech of Hon. W.L. Mackenzie King, Minister of Labour, on Combines Investigation Act, Ottawa, Tuesday, April 12, 1910. [Ottawa, 1910]. 31 p.
Location: No library copy located.

F3 The Combines Investigation Act. Abstract of speech by the Honourable the Minister of Labour in the House of Commons on the Second Reading of the Bill, April 12, 1910. [N.p., n.d.] 7 p.
Location: WLMK Papers, J 5 Series, vol. 1, Folder 1, Item 2.

F4 House of Commons Debates. Third Session – Eleventh Parliament.

Speech of Hon. W.L. Mackenzie King on the manufacture of white phosphorus matches, Ottawa, Thursday, January 19, 1911. [Ottawa, 1911]. 12 p.
Location: WLMK Papers, J 5 Series, vol. 1, Folder 1, Item 3.

F5 House of Commons Debates. Third Session – Eleventh Parliament. Speech of Hon. W.L. Mackenzie King on prohibition of opium and other drugs, Ottawa, January 26, 1911. [Ottawa, 1911]. 7 p.
Location: WLMK Papers, J 5 Series, vol. 1, Folder 1, Item 4.

F6 The Grand Trunk Strike. The position of the government with reference to the big industrial dispute. Speech delivered in the House of Commons by Hon. W.L. Mackenzie King, March 21, 1911. [Ottawa, 1911]. 23 p.
Location: OONL, OWTU.

F7 Eight hour day. Speech by Hon. W.L. Mackenzie King. [Address at the Auditorium, Berlin, September 2, 1911]. [N.p., n.d.] 4 p.
Location: WLMK Papers, J 5 Series, vol. 6, pp. 3344–3347.

F8 Achtstunden tag. Rede des Achtb. W.L. Mackenzie King. [Wahrend einer am 2 Sept. 1911 in Berlin gehaltenen rede.] [Berlin 1911]. 4 p.
Location: WLMK Papers, J 5 Series, vol. 6, pp. 3348–3351.

F9 Address of the President, Hon. W.L. Mackenzie King, at the Eighth Annual Meeting of the General Reform Association for Ontario on October 8, 1912. [N.p., n.d.] 8 p.
Location: WLMK Papers, J 5 Series, vol. 1, Folder 1, Item 6.

F10 The Canadian method of preventing strikes and lockouts. Address by Hon. W.L. Mackenzie King, former Canadian Minister of Labour, delivered at the Annual Meeting of the Railway Business Association, together with an abstract of the Canadian Industrial Disputes Act, December 19, 1912. [New York: Railway Business Association, 1912]. 20 p.
Location: OOA, OTMCL, OWTU.

F11 Industrial Peace. Address delivered by Hon. William Lyon Mackenzie King, former Minister of Labor for the Dominion of Canada and author of the Industrial Disputes Investigation Act of the Dominion. Banquet given in his honor by representative business and labor men of Cincinnati, at Sintin Hotel, Thursday Evening,

September 18, 1913. Address of Judge James B. Swing, Toastmaster of the occasion, introducing Mr King. Together with some appropritate notes regarding the reception tendered the distinguished visitor. Published by the Publicity Bureau of the 'No Strike' or Industrial Peace Ass'n., October, 1913. Editors, Matt Glaser and Frank E. Tunison, Managers, Publicity Bureau. [Cincinnati, 1913]. 20 p.
Location: OONL.

F12 Address of the President of the General Reform Association for Ontario, delivered at the Ninth Annual Meeting held on Toronto on November 28th, 1913. [N.p., n.d.] 11 p.
Location: OONL.

F13 President's address delivered at the Tenth Annual Meeting of the General Reform Association for Ontario, held at Toronto, November 27, 1914. [N.p., n.d.] 11 p.
Location: OONL.

F14 The four parties to industry. Address before the Empire Club of Canada at the King Edward Hotel, Toronto, March 13, 1919. [N.p., n.d.] 32 p.
Location: AEU, OKQ, OOC, OONL, OOU, OPAL, OPET, OSTCB, OTAR, OTU, OTY, OWTL, OWTU, SRL, SSU.

F15 Canada. House of Commons Debates. Official Report. Speech of Hon. W.L. Mackenzie King, Esq., Member for Prince, P.E.I., on the Address in Reply to Governor General's Speech, in the House of Commons, on Monday, March 1, 1920. [Ottawa: King's Printer, 1920]. 14 p.
Location: WLMK Papers, J 5 Series, vol. 26, pp. 4224–4237.

F16 Canada. House of Commons Debates. Official Report. Speech of Hon. W.L. Mackenzie King, Esq., Member for Prince, P.E.I., on status of Canada as a nation (Bulgarian Treaty) in the House of Commons, Ottawa, on Tuesday, March 16, 1920. [Ottawa, 1920]. 11 p.
Location: WLMK Papers, J 5 Series, vol. 1, Folder 1, Item 13.

F17 Canada. House of Commons Debates. Official Report. Speech of Hon. W.L. Mackenzie King, M.P., Leader of the Opposition, in reply to misrepresentations concerning his services in the adjustment of relations between workers and employers in war

industries during the period of the war, House of Commons, Ottawa, Tuesday, April 20, 1920. [Ottawa: King's Printer, 1920]. 12 p.
Location: OOU.

F18 Canada. Débats des Communes. Compte rendu officiel. Discours de l'honorable W.L. Mackenzie King, Député, leader de l'opposition, en réponse aux fausses répresentations faites à l'égard de l'établissement de meilleurs rapports entre travailleurs et employeurs dans les industries de guerre durant la guerre, Chambre des communes, Ottawa, 20 avril 1920. [Ottawa: Imprimeur du Roi, 1920]. 12 p.
Location: OKQ, QMBN.

F19 Canada. Débats. Communes. Compte rendu officiel. Discours de l'hon. W.L. Mackenzie King, M.P., Leader de l'Opposition, sur le rétablissement des pensions naguère constituées en faveur des employés du Chemin de fer du Grand-Tronc, Chambre des Communes, Ottawa, les vendredi 16 avril et jeudi 22 avril 1920. [Ottawa: Imprimeur du Roi, 1920]. 32 p.
Location: QMBN.

F20 Canada. House of Commons Debates. Official Report. Speeches of Hon. W.L. Mackenzie King, M.P., Leader of the Opposition, on the restoration of pensions to Grand Trunk Railway employees, House of Commons, Ottawa, Friday, April 16 and Thursday, April 22, 1920. [Ottawa, 1920]. 32 p.
Location: OONL.

F21 Canada. House of Commons Debates. Official Report. Speech of Hon. W.L. Mackenzie King, Member for Prince, P.E.I., on address in reply to Govenor General's speech, in the House of Commons, Ottawa, on Tuesday, February 15, 1921. [Ottawa, 1921]. 19 p.
Location: WLMK Papers, J 5 Series, vol. 1, Folder 1, Item 16.

F22 Speech of Hon. W.L. Mackenzie King on tariff revision and taxation. Budget debate, House of Commons, Ottawa, Thursday, May 19, 1921. [Ottawa, 1921]. 24 p.
Location: OTAR.

F23 Canada. House of Commons Debates. Official Report. Speech of Hon. W.L. Mackenzie King, Prime Minister, on the Address, in

the House of Commons, Ottawa, on Monday, March 13, 1922. [Ottawa: King's Printer, 1922]. 12 p.
Location: WLMK Papers, J 6 Series, vol. 205.

F24 The Liberal Party and the tariff: A review of Liberal policy and achievement outlined in a concluding speech on the budget debate, by Rt. Hon. W.L. Mackenzie King, Prime Minister, in the House of Commons, Ottawa, on Wednesday, May 23, 1923. 'What we have done in this budget is to carry out the spirit of the platform as laid down in 1919, in the light of conditions as we see them at the present time.' [Ottawa, 1923]. 11 p.
Location: WLMK Papers, J 6 Series, vol. 205.

F25 Progress and achievement. A review of two years of steady improvements in national finances and national development under Liberal Administration, by Right Hon. W.L. Mackenzie King, Prime Minister, in reply to the Conservative leader in the House of Commons debate on the Address in Reply to the Speech from the Throne, March 3, 1924. [Ottawa: King's Printer, 1924]. 18 p.
Location: OKQ.

F26 Le parti libéral et le tarif. Une revue des propositions budgétaires de 1924 et des principes fondamentaux de la politique libérale, par le très hon. W.L. Mackenzie King, premier ministre du Canada. Après deux années de gouvernement libéral par l'honorable Ernest Lapointe, Ministre de la Justice. Discours prononcé pendant le débat sur le budget, à la Chambre des communes, le 15 mai 1924. [Ottawa, 1924]. 94 p.
Location: AEU, OONL, OOU, QMU.

F27 The Liberal Party and the tariff: A review of the 1924 budget proposals and principles underlying Liberal policy, by the Rt. Hon. W.L. Mackenzie King, M.P., Prime Minister of Canada. A speech delivered in reply to the Leader of the Opposition in the debate on the budget, House of Commons, May 15th, 1924. [Ottawa, 1924]. 71 p.
Location: BVAU, BVIP, OKQ, OOC, OOCC, OOP, OOU, OPET, OSTCB, OTU, OTY.

F28 Church union in Canada. Remarks by Rt. Hon. W.L. Mackenzie King, M.P., in the House of Commons, June 26, 1924, upon con-

sideration in Committee of the whole of the bill to incorporate the United Church of Canada. [Ottawa, 1924]. 6 p.
Location: OKQ, OONL.

F29 Liberal government: A review of the record and policies of the administration since 1922: A contrast with the preceding Conservative regime, by the Rt. Hon. W.L. Mackenzie King, Prime Minister. Reduced expenditures, lessened taxation, lowered cost of living, steady improvement in immigration, industrial and trade expansion, a more economic and equitable tariff. Replies of the Prime Minister to the Leader of the Opposition in the debate on the address in reply to the speech from the throne and in the budget debate during the session of Parliament, 1925. [Ottawa, 1925]. 78 p.
Location: AEU, OKQ, OOE, OONL, OOP, OTAR, OTU, OTY, QMU, SSU.

F30 Citizenship: An address delivered on August 4th 1925, by the Right Honourable W.L. Mackenzie King, Prime Minister of Canada, at the complimentary luncheon in his honour on the occasion of the Old Boys' Reunion, Kitchener, Ontario, 1925. Under the auspices of the Canadian, Rotary and Kiwanis Clubs. Printed for distribution among members. [Kitchener, 1925]. 15 p.
Location: OKQ, OONL, OOP, OTMCL.

F31 Pillars of world peace: Mackenzie King, Prime Minister of Canada, discusses the problem of the Pacific and gives a formula for interracial good relations. By Edward Price Bell. Chicago: Chicago Daily News Company, 1925. 12 p. (The Chicago Daily News Reprints, No. 20).
Location: AEU, NBSAM, NSHD, OOA, OOU, OONL, OSTCB, OTAR, SSU.

F32 Speech on the budget, by Rt. Hon. W.L. Mackenzie King, P.C., C.M.G., LL.D., Leader of the Liberal Party of Canada, delivered in the House of Commons, May 18, 1926. 'What is unquestionably a more popular budget than any that has ever been submitted to Parliament – a budget that means more in the way of reduction in taxation than any other which it has been the good fortune of this country to receive.' Ottawa: National Liberal Committee, 1926. 31 p.
Location: OONL, OOP, OTY.

F33 The Parliament of 1926 and the constitutional issue. Speech by the Rt. Hon. W.L. Mackenzie King, P.C., C.M.G., LL.D., Leader of the Liberal Party of Canada, at the Auditorium, Ottawa, Ontario, July 23rd, 1926. [Ottawa: Dominion Loose Leaf Company, 1926]. 47 p.
Location: AEU, OONL, OSTCB, OWTU, SSU.

F34 Discours prononcé à Ottawa le vendredi 24 juillet 1926. [Montréal: Imprimerie populaire, 1926]. 63 p.
Location: OKQ, OONL, OTU, OWTL, SSU.

F35 Confederation. Address by Right Honourable W.L. Mackenzie King, P.C., C.M.G., LL.D., Prime Minister of Canada, Parliament Hill, July 1, 1927. Diamond Jubilee of Confederation. [Ottawa, 1927]. 8 p.
Location: AEU, OKQ, OONL, OTAR, OWTU.

F36 The message of the carillon. Address by Right Honourable W.L. Mackenzie King, Parliament Hill, P.C., C.M.G., LL.D., Prime Minister of Canada, July 1, 1927. Diamond Jubilee of Confederation. [Ottawa, 1927]. 6 p.
Location: OONL, OSTCB, OTAR, OWA, QSHERU.

F37 An address of welcome to the Right Honourable Stanley Baldwin, P.C., M.P., LL.D., Prime Minister of Great Britain. [August 2, 1927]. Diamond Jubilee of Confederation. [Ottawa, 1927]. 3 p.
Location: WLMK Papers, J 5 Series, vol. 25, pp. 13874–13876.

F38 Address of welcome on behalf of the government of Canada to His Royal Highness the Prince of Wales. Diamond Jubilee of Confederation. [August 2, 1927]. [Ottawa, 1927]. 2 p.
Location: OKQ, OPAL, OWA, OWTU, QSHERU.

F39 1841. Laurier. 1941. Address by Right Honourable W.L. Mackenzie King, P.C., C.M.G., LL.D., Prime Minister of Canada, on the occasion of the Unveiling of the statue of Sir Wilfrid Laurier by His Royal Highness the Prince of Wales, Parliament Hill, August 3, 1927. Diamond Jubilee of Confederation. [Ottawa, 1927]. 7 p.
Location: OKQ, OONL, OSTCB, OWA.

F40 Liberalism: The principle of the future. An address by the Right Honourable W.L. Mackenzie King, Prime Minister of Canada,

delivered on April 18th, 1928, to the National Federation of Liberal Women in assembly at Ottawa. [Ottawa, 1928]. 10 p.
Location: AEU, OONL.

F41 Address delivered by the Right Hon. W.L. Mackenzie King, C.M.G., M.A., LL.B., LL.D., on November 9th, 1928, at a banquet of the League of Nations Society in Canada at the Chateau Laurier, Ottawa, League of Nations Society in Canada. [Ottawa: League of Nations Society in Canada, 1928]. 23 p.
Location: OONL.

F42 Some recent developments in Canada's external relations. Address by Rt. Honourable W.L. Mackenzie King, Prime Minister of Canada, before Toronto Board of Trade, Hart House, Toronto, November 22, 1928. [Richmond Hill, Ontario: Liberal Printing Company, 1928]. 29 p.
Location: OONL, OSTCB, OTU.

F43 Canada's progress under Liberal administration, 1921–1929, from gloom to unparalleled prosperity. Conservative fallacies and misrepresentations exposed; the tariff situation explained. Reeducation in debt and in taxation – Organization and improved condition of Canadian National Railways – Expansion in industry and trade. Speech by the Prime Minister in the House of Commons, April 9, 1929, in reply to the Acting Leader and Financial Critic of the Opposition; together with an appendix showing reductions in the rates of customs duties under the Liberal Administration. [Ottawa: National Liberal Organization, 1929]. 78 p.
Location: AEU, OONL, OOP, OSTCB, SSU.

F44 The university and leadership, by the Right Honourable W.L. Mackenzie King. A speech delivered at the McGill convocation, May 29th, 1929. [Montreal, 1929]. 8 p.
Supplement to the *McGill News*, September 1929.
Location: WLMK Papers, J 5 Series, vol. 27, pp. 15564–15571.

F45 Canada. House of Commons Debates. Official Report. Speech of Right Hon. W.L. Mackenzie King, Prime Minister, on export of liquor. Refusal of releases and clearances to countries where importation forbidden. Delivered in the House of Commons, on Friday, March 14, 1930. [Ottawa: King's Printer, 1930]. 20 p.
Location: WLMK Papers, J 6 Series, vol. 205.

F46 Press summary of Mr King's opening speech at Brantford, Ont., June 16th, 1930. [Ottawa: The Liberal-Conservative Party]. 6 p.
Location: OOA.

F47 William Lyon Mackenzie King, Chef du Parti Libéral. Discours prononcé à Brantford, le lundi 16 juin 1930. [Montréal, 1930]. (Traduction intégrale). 72 p.
Location: OOA, OONL, OOP, OTY.

F48 The Speech from the Throne, 1931 and the Imperial Economic Conference, 1930: A contrast in Liberal and Conservative methods and policies, by the Rt. Hon. W.L. Mackenzie King, Leader of the Opposition. Reprinted from the Official Record, House of Commons Debates, Ottawa, March 16, 1931. Ottawa: King's Printer, 1931. 45 p.
Location: WLMK Papers, J 5 Series, vol. 31, pp. 18010–18054.

F49 The budget of 1931: finances, tariff, trade, unemployment: a contrast in Liberal and Conservative methods, policies and mentality; outstanding features and tendencies, by the Right Hon. W.L. Mackenzie King, Leader of the Opposition. [Ottawa: King's Printer, 1931]. 45 p.
Location: WLMK Papers, J 5 Series, vol. 31, pp. 18010–18054.

F50 Unemployment in Canada: A contrast in Liberal and Conservative methods and policies. Complete failure of Bennett government to redeem pledges made at general elections, 1930. Speech by the Right Hon. W.L. Mackenzie King, Leader of the Opposition. Reprinted from Official Report, House of Commons Debates, Ottawa, March 1, 1932. Ottawa: King's Printer, 1932. 17 p.
Location: WLMK Papers, J 6 Series, vol. 205.

F51 The Liberal Party's position on some immediate problems. Ottawa: National Liberal Federation of Canada, 1933. 5 p.
'Extracted from the official report of Mr Mackenzie King's speech in the House of Commons on February 27, 1933.'
Location: WLMK Papers, J 5 Series, vol. 84, p. 53792.

F52 Canada. Débats de la Chambre des communes. Compte rendu officiel. Discours par le très honorable W.L. Mackenzie King, Leader de l'Opposition sur les solutions proposées par les partis politiques du Canada aux problèmes qui se posent à l'heure actuelle; les visées et les propositions de la Fédération du Commonwealth

coopératif et celles du parti conservateur en comparison de celles du parti libérale prononcé le 27 février 1933. (Traduction). Ottawa: Imprimeur du Roi, 1933. 23 p.
Location: QQL.

F53 Canada. House of Commons Debates. Official Report. Speech by Right Hon. W.L. Mackenzie King, Leader of the Opposition, on policies of political parties in Canada in relation to present-day needs. The aims and proposals of the Co-operative Commonwealth Federation compared with those of the Liberal Party. Delivered in the House of Commons on Monday, February 27, 1933. [Ottawa: King's Printer, 1933]. 24 p.
Location: OOA.

F54 Canada. House of Commons Debates. Official Report. Speech by Right Hon. W.L. Mackenzie King, Leader of the Opposition, upon loss of confidence by country in Bennett administration. Failure of government's policies with respect to unemployment, trade and agriculture – Contrast afforded by Liberal Recovery Plan, also banking and monetary policies – Restoration of titles in defiance of the House of Commons – Prime Minister's campaign of misrepresentation – Challenge to government's right to continue longer in office. Delivered in the House of Commons on Monday, January 29, 1934. Ottawa: King's Printer, 1934. 46 p.
Location: OOA.

F55 Canada. House of Commons Debates. Official Report. Speech by Right Hon. W.L. Mackenzie King, Leader of the Liberal Party, on social and industrial reform and the position of the Conservative and Liberal Parties with respect thereto. Loss of confidence in Bennett Government – The changing social order – Electorate deprived of its right to a general election – The meaning of laissez-faire and state intervention – Liberal labour legislation – Liberal Party's policies – Co-operation by Liberals on reform measures – Methods of expediting reform. Delivered in the House of Commons on Monday, January 21, 1935. Ottawa: King's Printer, 1935. 36 p.
Location: WLMK Papers, J 6 Series, vol. 206, File 1.

F56 Mr King replies to Mr Bennett, September 17th, 1935. Ottawa: National Liberal Federation, 1935. 19 p.
Location: OONL, OTU.

F57 La voix du peuple. Texte de la déclaration faite aux journaux par le très honorable Mackenzie King, le soir des élections générales, le 14 octobre 1935. Ottawa: Fédération libérale nationale du Canada, 1935. 6 p.
Location: OONL.

F58 The voice of the people. A reprint of statement to the press, issued by the Rt. Hon. Mackenzie King on the night of the general elections, October 14th, 1935. Ottawa: National Liberal Federation, 1935. 8 p.
Location: BVIP, OKQ, OONL, OSTCB, OTY, OWA, OWTU, SSU.

F59 Mackenzie King to the Canadian people, 1935. A reprint of the series of radio broadcasts delivered by the Rt. Hon. Mackenzie King, leader of the Liberal Party of Canada, to the people of Canada. Toronto: National Liberal Publicity Committee, 1935. 56 p.
Contents: Political parties and tendencies: Democracy versus dictatorship [First radio broadcast from Ottawa on July 31, 1935]; Principles and policies versus platforms and promises: The Liberal Party's position on present day problems [Second radio address from Ottawa on August 2, 1935]; Unemployment – Canada's most urgent national problem: A statement of Liberal policy [Third radio address from Ottawa on August 5, 1935].
Location: BVAU, OONL, OPAL, OPET, OSTCB, OTAR, OTY, OWTL, OWTU, QMU, QQLA, SSU.

F60 The Italo-Ethiopian conflict and the League of Nations. Statement of Canada's position by the Right Hon. W.L. Mackenzie King, Prime Minister and Secretary of State for External Affairs, House of Commons, Ottawa, June 18, 1936. Ottawa: King's Printer, 1936. 27 p.
Location: BVIP, OKQ, OONL, OOP.

F61 Message from the Prime Minister of Canada on the occasion of the unveiling of the memorial at Vimy, July 26, 1936. Address of welcome by the Prime Minister of Canada on the occasion of the visit of President Roosevelt to Quebec, July 31, 1936. [Ottawa, 1936]. 6 p.
Location: BVIP, OOP.

F62 Attitudes de la Société des Nations. Discours du très hon. W.L. Mackenzie King, M.P., Premier ministre du Canada, à la dix-septième séance de l'Assemblée de la Société des Nations, Genève, le 29 septembre 1936. Ottawa: Imprimeur du Roi, 1936. 12 p.
Location: OOP.

F63 League of Nations policies. Address by the Right Hon. W.L. Mackenzie King, M.P., Prime Minister of Canada, at the Seventeenth Session of the Assembly of the League of Nations, Geneva, Sept. 29, 1936. Ottawa: King's Printer, 1936. 10 p.
Location: OKQ, OONL, OOP.

F64 Address by the Rt. Hon. W.L. Mackenzie King, M.P., Prime Minister of Canada, on the occasion of the Canadian Legion Remembrance Day broadcast, November 11, 1936. [Ottawa, 1936]. 3 p.
Location: OKQ, OOP.

F65 Canada. House of Commons Debates. Official Report. Speech by Right Hon. W.L. Mackenzie King, Prime Minister of Canada, on the defence of Canada. Proposals of the government examined in the light of the world situation. Delivered in the House of Commons on Friday, February 19, 1937. Ottawa: King's Printer, 1937. 21 p.
Location: OKQ, OOP.

F66 Crown and Commonwealth. An address on the Coronation, the Imperial Conference, and visit to the Continent of Europe, by the Right Hon. W.L. Mackenzie King, M.P., Prime Minister of Canada, delivered over the National Network of the Canadian Broadcasting Corporation, Ottawa, July 19, 1937. Ottawa: King's Printer, 1937. 16 p.
Location: NBFU, NBSAM, OKQ, OOP, OOU, OTL, OTU, SRL.

F67 La Couronne et le Commonwealth. Discours sur le Couronnement, la Conférence imperiale et le voyage en Europe continentale, par le très hon. W.L. Mackenzie King, M.P., Premier ministre du Canada, prononcé sur le Réseau national de la Société Radio Canada, à Ottawa, le 19 juillet 1937. Ottawa: Imprimeur du Roi, 1937. 16 p.
Location: OONL, OOP.

F68 Principles underlying peace. Address by the Right Hon. W.L. Mackenzie King, M.P., Prime Minister of Canada, at the luncheon given by the University of Toronto at the York Club, Toronto, in honour of the Honourable Cordell Hull, Secretary of State of the United States, October 22, 1937. [Ottawa: King's Printer, 1937]. 7 p.
Location: BVIP, BVIV, OKQ, OONL, OOP, OTL, OTU, OWTU.

F69 Principes directeurs de la paix. Discours du très honorable W.L. Mackenzie King, M.P., Premier ministre du Canada, au déjeuner offert par l'Université de Toronto, au Club York, Toronto, en l'honneur de l'honorable Cordell Hull, Secrétaire d'État des États-Unis, le 22 octobre 1937. [Ottawa: Imprimeur du Roi, 1937]. 7 p.
Location: OONL, QQLA.

F70 Canadian foreign policy. Statement of Canada's position with respect to external affairs, by the Rt. Hon. W.L. Mackenzie King, Prime Minister and Secretary of State for External Affairs, House of Commons, Ottawa, May 24, 1938. Ottawa: King's Printer, 1938. 36 p.
Location: OKQ, OOP.

F71 Politique étrangère du Canada. Déclaration sur l'attitude du Canada relative aux affaires extérieures par le très honorable W.L. Mackenzie King, Premier ministre et Sécretaire d'État aux Affaires extérieures, Chambre des communes, Ottawa, 24 mai 1938. Ottawa: Imprimeur du Roi, 1938. 40 p.
Location: OOP.

F72 The struggle for enduring peace. Address by the Right Hon. W.L. Mackenzie King, M.P., Prime Minister of Canada, at the Canadian Corps Reunion, Toronto, July 30th, 1938. Ottawa: King's Printer, 1938. 5 p.
Location: OKQ, OONL, OOP, OTL, OTU.

F73 The bridge-builders. Address by Rt. Hon. W.L. Mackenzie King, M.P., Prime Minister of Canada, at the dedication of the Thousand Islands International Bridge at Ivy Lea, Ontario, and Collin's Landing, New York, August 18th, 1938. Ottawa: King's Printer, 1938. 9 p.
Location: OKQ, OONL, OOP, OOU, OTL, OTU, SRL.

F74 Les constructeurs de ponts. Discours prononcé par le très honorable W.L. Mackenzie King, M.P., Premier ministre du Canada lors de l'inauguration du pont international des Mille-Iles, à Ivy-Lea (Ontario) et Collins Landing (New-York), le 18 août 1938. Ottawa: Imprimeur du Roi, 1938. 9 p.
Location: OONL, OOP.

F75 Les États-Unis et le Canada. Réciprocité dans la défense. Déclaration par le Président des États-Unis, à l'Université Queen's, Kingston, Ontario, le 18 août 1938, et réponse par le premier ministre

du Canada, dans un discours à Woodbridge, Ontario, le 20 août 1938. Ottawa: Imprimeur du Roi, 1939. 9 p.
Location: OKQ, OOP.

F76 The United States and Canada. Reciprocity in defence. Declaration by the President of the United States at Queen's University, Kingston, Ontario, August 18, 1938 and acknowledgment and reply by the Prime Minister of Canada, in a speech at Woodbridge, Ontario, August 20, 1938. Ottawa: King's Printer, 1938. 8 p.
Location: BVIV, OKQ.

F77 'The voices of silence.' Address by the Rt. Hon. W.L. Mackenzie King, M.P., Prime Minister of Canada, on the occasion of the Canadian Legion Remembrance Day broadcast, November 11, 1938. [Ottawa, 1938]. 3 p.
Location: OKQ.

F78 Canada. House of Commons Debates. Official Report. Speech by Right Hon. W.L. Mackenzie King, Prime Minister of Canada, on the Canada–United States trade agreement. Its far-reaching advantages and its international significance, delivered in the House of Commons, February 14, 1939. [Ottawa: King's Printer, 1939]. 18 p.
Location: WLMK Papers, J 5 Series, vol. 59, pp. 35782–35799.

F79 The international situation. Canada's attitude towards present day world problems. Statements by the Right Hon. W.L. Mackenzie King, Prime Minister and Secretary of State for External Affairs. I. House of Commons, Ottawa, March 20th, 1939. II. House of Commons, Ottawa, March 30, 1939. Ottawa: King's Printer, 1939. 53 p.
Location: AEU, OKQ, OONL, OOP, OTL, SSU.

F80 La situation internationale. L'attitude du Canada devant les problèmes actuels du monde. Déclaration du très honorable W.L. Mackenzie King. Premier ministre et Secrétaire d'État aux Affaires Extérieures. I. Chambre des communes, Ottawa, le 20 mars 1939. II. Chambre des communes, Ottawa, le 30 mars 1939. Ottawa: Imprimeur du Roi, 1939. 59 p.
Location: OOP.

F81 Discours du premier ministre du Canada au déjeuner offert par le gouvernement de Sa Majesté au Canada, au Château Frontenac de Québec, le lundi 15 mai 1939, pour souhaiter la bienvenue au

Roi George VI et à la Reine Elizabeth à l'occasion de l'arrivée de leurs Majestés au Canada. [N.p., n.d.] 4 p.
Location: WLMK Papers, J 5 Series, vol. 60, pp. 37276–37279.

F82 The speech of the Prime Minister of Canada at the luncheon given by His Majesty's Government in Canada, at the Chateau Frontenac, Quebec, Wednesday May 17, 1939[103] to welcome King George VI and Queen Elizabeth, on the occasion of Their Majesties' arrival in Canada. [N.p., n.d.] 4 p.
Location: WLMK Papers, J 5 Series, vol. 39, pp. 22253–22256.

F83 Twenty years of Liberal leadership. Speech by the Right Honourable W.L. Mackenzie King, Leader of the Liberal Party of Canada, delivered at the Royal York Hotel, Toronto, August 8, 1939, in response to the toast proposed by the Honourable Ernest Lapointe on the occasion of the complimentary banquet tendered Mr King on completion of his 20 years of leadership of the party. [N.p., 1939]. 16 p.
Location: BVAU, BVIP, OONL, OOP, OTY.

F84 Canada at the side of Britain. Broadcast by Right Hon. W.L. Mackenzie King, M.P., Prime Minister of Canada, Sunday, September 3, 1939 (the day upon which H.M. The King proclaimed a state of war between the United Kingdom and Germany). Ottawa: King's Printer, 1939. 5 p.
Location: OOE, OOP, OOU.

F85 Le Canada aux côtes de la Grande-Bretagne. Discours à la radio par le très honorable W.L. Mackenzie King, M.P., Premier ministre du Canada, dimanche 3 septembre 1939 (le jour ou S.M. le Roi a proclamé l'existence d'un état de guerre entre le Royaume-Uni et l'Allemagne). Ottawa: Imprimeur du Roi, 1939. 5 p.
Location: OOA, OOP.

F86 Canada. House of Commons Debates. Official Report. Speech by Right Hon. W.L. Mackenzie King, Prime Minister of Canada, on

103 The date printed in the text of the documents is 'Monday May 15.' A typewritten change to 'Wednesday May 17' was made on the copy in the King Papers. The ship carrying King George and Queen Elizabeth was delayed by bad weather in the North Atlantic and Their Majesties arrived in Canada two days late.

Canada and the war, delivered in the House of Commons, September 8, 1939. [Ottawa: King's Printer, 1939]. 25 p.
Location: OOE.

F87 Canada. Débats de la Chambre des communes. Discours par le très honorable W.L. Mackenzie King, Premier ministre du Canada, sur le Canada et la guerre, prononcé à Chambre des communes, le 8 septembre 1939. [Traduit de l'anglais]. Ottawa: [Imprimeur du Roi, 1939]. 26 p.
Location: OOP.

F88 La question en jeu dans la guerre actuelle. Discours à la radio par le très honorable W.L. Mackenzie King, M.P., Premier ministre du Canada, vendredi, 27 octobre 1939. [Ottawa: Imprimeur du Roi, 1939]. 15 p.
Location: OKQ, OOE, OONDH, OONL, OOP, OOU, OSTCB, SRL, SSU.

F89 The issue in the present war. Broadcast by Right Hon. W.L. Mackenzie King, M.P., Prime Minister of Canada, Friday, October 27, 1939. Ottawa: King's Printer, 1939. 14 p.
Location: OKQ, OKR, OOE, OONDH, OONL, OOP, OOU, OSTCB, OTAR, OTMCL, SRL, SSU.

F90 The organization of Canada's war effort. Parliament and the government. Broadcast by Right Hon. W.L. Mackenzie King, M.P., Prime Minister of Canada, Tuesday, October 31, 1939. Ottawa: King's Printer, 1939. 16 p.
Location: OKQ, OOE, OONL, OOP, OOU, OSTCB, OTMCL, SSU.

F91 L'organisation de l'effort de guerre du Canada. Le Parlement et le gouvernement. Discours à la radio, par le très honorable W.L. Mackenzie King, M.P., Premier ministre du Canada, mardi, le 31 octobre 1939. [Ottawa: Imprimeur du Roi, 1939]. 16 p.
Location: OOA, OONL, OOP.

F92 The British Commonwealth Air Training Plan. Broadcast by Right Hon. W.L. Mackenzie King, M.P., Prime Minister of Canada, Sunday, December 17, 1939. Ottawa: King's Printer, 1939. 17 p.
Location: OKQ, OKR, OOE, OOP, OOU, OTMCL.

F93 Plan d'entraînement des aviateurs du Commonwealth Britannique. Discours à la radio par le très honorable W.L. Mackenzie King,

M.P., Premier ministre du Canada, le dimanche 17 decembre 1939. Ottawa: Imprimeur du Roi, 1939. 15 p.
Location: OOA, OOP.

F94 Canada. House of Commons Debates. Official Report. Dissolution of Parliament. Speech from the Throne and speech by the Right Hon. W.L. Mackenzie King, Prime Minister of Canada, delivered in House of Commons, January 25, 1940. [Ottawa: King's Printer, 1940]. 8 p.
Location: OKQ.

F95 Canada and the war. Parliament and the people: Unity and freedom. A radio address by Right Hon. W.L. Mackenzie King, Ottawa, 7th February, 1940. [Ottawa: National Liberal Federation, 1940]. 18 p.
Location: OONL, OTNY, OWA.

F96 Tributes to the late Lord Tweedsmuir, Governor General of Canada, by Right Hon. W.L. Mackenzie King, Prime Minister of Canada. I. Broadcast over the National Network of the Canadian Broadcasting Corporation, Sunday, February 11, 1940. II. To the press of Canada, Monday, February 12, 1940. Ottawa: King's Printer, 1940. 6 p.
Location: OKQ, OOC, OONL, OOP, OTL, SRL.

F97 Canada and the war. War record of the Mackenzie King administration. A radio address by Right Honourable W.L. Mackenzie King, Ottawa, 21st February, 1940. [Ottawa: National Liberal Federation, 1940]. 20 p.
Location: OONL, OTNY.

F98 Canada and the war. Canada's war effort – how best promoted. 'National' versus 'Union' government. A radio address by Right Honourable W.L. Mackenzie King, Ottawa, 23rd February, 1940. [Ottawa: National Liberal Federation, 1940]. 20 p.
Location: AEU, OONL, OTNY, OOU.

F99 Un gouvernement national: ce qu'il doit être, ce qu'il ne saurait être. Discours prononcé à la radio le vendredi 23 février 1940 par le très hon. W.L. Mackenzie King. Ottawa: Fédération libérale nationale, 1940. 15 p.
Location: OONL.

F100 Canada and the war. The training of British pilots and the joint air training plan. Mackenzie King replies to Dr Manion. A radio address by Right Honourable W.L. Mackenzie King, 8th March, 1940. [Ottawa: National Liberal Federation, 1940]. 14 p.
Location: OONL, OTNY.

F101 Canada and the war. The choice that lies before the electors; a final word to the Canadian people. A radio address by Right Honourable W.L. Mackenzie King, Ottawa, 21st March, 1940. [Ottawa: National Liberal Federation, 1940]. 19 p.
Location: OONL, OTNY.

F102 Canada and the war. The defence of freedom at home and abroad: Significance of the 1940 campaign, a radio address by Right Honourable W.L. Mackenzie King, Ottawa, 23rd March, 1940. [Ottawa: National Liberal Federation, 1940]. 18 p.
Location: OONL.

F103 Canada and the war. Mackenzie King to the people of Canada, 1940. A series of radio broadcasts by Prime Minister Mackenzie King from Ottawa, February–March, 1940. [Ottawa: National Liberal Federation of Canada, 1940]. 104 p.
Contents: Parliament and the people: Unity and freedom [First of a series of radio broadcasts from Ottawa, February 7, 1940]; War record of the Mackenzie King Administration: National defence and international co-operation [Second of a series of radio broadcasts from Ottawa, February 21, 1940]; Canada's war effort – how best promoted. 'National' versus 'Union' Government [Third of a series of radio broadcasts from Ottawa, February 23, 1940]; The training of British pilots and the Joint Air Training Plan: Mackenzie King replies to Dr Manion [Fourth of a series of radio broadcasts from Ottawa, March 8, 1940]; The choice that lies before the electors: A final word to the Canadian people [Fifth of a series of radio broadcasts from Ottawa, March 21, 1940]; The defence of freedom at home and abroad: Significance of the 1940 campaign [Sixth of a series of radio broadcasts from Ottawa, March 23, 1940]; A word of thanks to the people of Canada [Radio broadcast from Ottawa, March 26, 1940, following the return of the government to office in the general election of that day].
Location: BVIP, NBFU, OKQ, OONL, OOU, OSTCB, OTNY, OWTL, OWTU, QMG, QQLA, SSU.

F104 Canada. House of Commons Debates. Official Report. Speech of

Right Hon. W.L. Mackenzie King, Prime Minister of Canada. War effort. Delivered in the House of Commons, Monday, May 20, 1940. [Ottawa: King's Printer, 1940]. 10 p.
Location: OOE.

F105 Facts about Canada's war effort. Extracts from an address by the Prime Minister, Rt. Hon. W.L. Mackenzie King, House of Commons, 20th May, 1940. [Ottawa: King's Printer, 1940]. 8 p.
Location: OKQ.

F106 L'effort de guerre du Canada. Extraits d'un discours prononcé à la Chambre des communes à Ottawa, le 20 mai 1940, par le très Hon. W.L. Mackenzie King, Premier ministre. [Ottawa: Imprimeur du Roi, 1940]. 8 p.
Location: No library copy located.

F107 Canada and the war. New situations and responsibilities. I. Canada's war effort viewed in relation to the war effort of the Allied Powers. II. Italy's entry into the war. Broadcasts by Right Hon. W.L. Mackenzie King, M.P., Prime Minister of Canada, Friday, June 7, and Monday, June 10, 1940. Ottawa: King's Printer, 1940. 18 p.
Location: OONL, OOP, OTU.

F108 Le Canada et la guerre. Nouvelles situations et nouvelles responsabilités. I. L'effort de guerre du Canada en regard de l'effort de guerre des puissances alliées. II. L'entre de l'Italie dans la guerre. Discours à la radio du très hon. W.L. Mackenzie King, M.P., Premier ministre du Canada, le vendredi 7 juin et le lundi 10 juin 1940. Ottawa: Imprimeur du Roi, 1940. 20 p.
Location: OOP.

F109 Canada and the war. An outline of the organization of the war administration. Reconstruction of the Cabinet. Statement by Right Hon. W.L. Mackenzie King, M.P., Prime Minister of Canada, House of Commons, Monday, July 8, 1940. Ottawa: King's Printer, 1940. 33 p.
Location: OKQ, OOE, OOP.

F110 Canada and the war. Labour and the war: Two significant anniversaries. Broadcast by Right Hon. W.L. Mackenzie King, M.P., Prime Minister of Canada, Sunday, September 1, 1940. Ottawa: King's Printer, 1940. 10 p.
Location: OOP.

F111 Let's face the facts, No. 7. Address to the men and women of Canada, by the Rt. Hon. W.L. Mackenzie King, Prime Minister of Canada, over a national network of the Canadian Broadcasting Corporation, Sunday night, Sept. 1, 1940, at the invitation of the Director of Public Information for Canada. [Ottawa, 1940]. 4 p.
Location: OONL, OOU.

F112 Canada and the war. The voices of mercy: An appeal for the Canadian Red Cross. Broadcast by Right Hon. W.L. Mackenzie King, M.P., Prime Minister of Canada, Sunday, September 29, 1940. Ottawa: King's Printer, 1940. 4 p.
Location: OOP.

F113 Canada. House of Commons Debates. Official Report. The Ogdensburg agreement: Reprint from speech by Right Hon. W.L. Mackenzie King, Prime Minister, delivered in the House of Commons, November 12, 1940. [Ottawa: King's Printer, 1940]. 8 p.
Location: OOE, OONL, OOP, OTAR, SRL.

F114 Canada. Débats de la Chambre des communes. Compte rendu officiel. L'entente d'Ogdensburg. Réimpression d'un discours prononcé par le très honorable W.-L. Mackenzie King, Premier ministre, à la Chambre des communes, le 12 novembre 1940. [Ottawa: Imprimeur du Roi, 1940]. 8 p.
Location: WLMK Papers, J 5 Series, vol. 92, pp. 58579–58586.

F115 Canada and the war. The old year and the new. 1. Christmas greetings to Canada's Armed Forces. 2. A new year message to the Canadian people. Broadcasts by Right Hon. W.L. Mackenzie King, M.P., Prime Minister of Canada, Wednesday, December 25, and Tuesday, December 31, 1940. Ottawa: King's Printer, 1941. 12 p.
Location: AEU, OOE.

F116 Le Canada et la guerre. L'année qui fuit; l'année qui arrive. 1. Voeux de Noël aux forces armées du Canada. 2. Message de nouvelle année à la population du Canada. Discours prononcés à la radio par le très honorable W.L. Mackenzie King, M.P., Premier ministre du Canada, mercredi, le 25 décembre et mardi, le 31 décembre 1940. Ottawa: Imprimeur du Roi, 1941. 12 p.
Location: OOP.

F117 Canada and the war. Total war and total effort. An appeal for war savings. Broadcast by Right Hon. W.L. Mackenzie King, M.P., Prime Minister of Canada, Sunday, February 2, 1941. Ottawa: King's Printer, 1941. 12 p.
Location: AEU, BVAU, OKQ, OOE, OONDH, OONL, OOP, OOU, OSTCB, OTAR, OWTU, SRL, SSU.

F118 Le Canada et la guerre. Effort total contre guerre totale. Un appel en faveur de l'épargne de guerre. Radiodiffusion par le très hon. Mackenzie King, M.P., Premier ministre du Canada le dimanche 2 février 1941. Ottawa: Imprimeur du Roi, 1941. 12 p.
Location: OOA, OOP, OOU.

F119 Canada and the war. A new world order. Welcome to Mr Wendell Willkie. Speech by Right Hon. W.L. Mackenzie King, M.P., Prime Minister of Canada, at the opening of the Canadian War Services Fund Campaign, Toronto, March 24, 1941. Ottawa: King's Printer, 1941. 10 p.
Location: BVIV, OKQ, OOE, OONL, OOP, OTAR, SSU.

F120 Le Canada et la guerre. Un nouvel ordre dans le monde. Bienvenue à M Wendell Willkie. Discours prononcé par le très honorable W.L. Mackenzie King, M.P., Premier ministre du Canada, à l'ouverture de la Campaign de la Caisse des Services de guerre canadiens, Toronto, le 24 mars 1941. Ottawa: Imprimeur du Roi, 1941. 10 p.
Location: OOP.

F121 Canada and the war. What Canada is doing. A tribute to the Canadian people. Statement by Right Hon. W.L. Mackenzie King, M.P., Prime Minister of Canada, House of Commons, March 25, 1941. Ottawa: King's Printer, 1941. 12 p.
Location: NBFU, OKQ, OKR, OONL, OOP, OOU, OSTCB, OTAR, SSU.

F122 Le Canada et la guerre. Le Canada à l'oeuvre: Hommage au peuple du Canada. Déclaration faite par le très honorable W.L. Mackenzie King, M.P., Premier ministre du Canada, Chambre des communes, 25 mars 1941. Ottawa: Imprimeur du Roi, 1941. 12 p.
Location: OOP.

F123 Canada and the war. The Hyde Park Declaration. Cooperation in economic defence. Statement by Right Hon. W.L. Mackenzie

King, M.P., Prime Minister of Canada, House of Commons, April 28, 1941. Ottawa: King's Printer, 1941. 15 p.
Location: BVASA, BVIV, OKQ, OKR, OLU, OOE, OONL, OOP, OOU, OSTCB, OTAR, OWA, OWTU, SRL, SSU.

F124 Le Canada et la guerre. Déclaration de Hyde Park. Plan commun de défense économique. Déclaration faite par le très honorable W.L. Mackenzie King, M.P., Premier ministre du Canada, à la Chambre des communes, le 28 avril 1941. Ottawa: Imprimeur du Roi, 1941. 15 p.
Location: OKQ, OOP, OOU.

F125 'Till the hour of victory.' Addresses by Right Honourable W.L. Mackenzie King, Prime Minister of Canada, Right Honourable Winston Churchill, Prime Minister of Great Britain, the Honourable Ernest Lapointe, Minister of Justice. Delivered over the national network of the Canadian Broadcasting Corporation, 1st June, 1941. Ottawa: King's Printer, 1941. 11 p.
Location: BVIV, OOE, OONL, OOP.

F126 Vers la victoire. Discours des très honorable W.L. Mackenzie King, Premier ministre du Canada, très honorable Winston Churchill, Premier ministre de la Grande-Bretagne, très honorable Ernest Lapointe, Ministre de la Justice, Discours prononcé à la radio, 1er juin 1941. Ottawa: Imprimeur du Roi, 1941. 12 p.
Location: OOP.

F127 Canada and the war. To-day's situation and Canada's contribution; sunlight and shadows. Statement by Right Hon. W.L. Mackenzie King, M.P., Prime Minister of Canada, House of Commons, June 13, 1941. [Ottawa: King's Printer, 1941]. 10 p.
Location: BVIV, OOE, OOP.

F128 Le Canada et la guerre. La situation actuelle et l'effort canadien: ombres et lumières. Déclaration du très honorable W.L. Mackenzie King, Premier ministre du Canada, Chambre des communes, le 13 juin 1941. Ottawa: Imprimeur du Roi, 1941. 11 p.
Location: OOP.

F129 Canada and the war. Canada's contribution to freedom. Speech by Rt. Hon. W.L. Mackenzie King, M.P., Prime Minister of Canada, at a dinner tendered in his honour by the Associated Canadian Organizations of New York City, New York, June 17, 1941. Ottawa: King's Printer, 1941. 18 p.

Location: BVIV, OOE, OONL, OOP.

F130 Aggression in Hitler's mind has no limits, by Rt. Hon. Mackenzie King, P.C., M.P., Prime Minister of Canada. My duty, as I see it, is to seek above all else to preserve national unity. Speech delivered before the Winnipeg Board of Trade and the Canadian Club, at the Royal Alexandra Hotel, Winnipeg, Canada, Thursday noon, July 10, 1941, and broadcast over the CBC [Winnipeg: The Universal Life Assurance and Annuity Company, 1941]. 23 p.
Location: BVIV, OOE, OONL, OSTCB, OWA, OWTU.

F131 Canada and the war. The Lord Mayor's luncheon in honour of the Prime Minister of Canada. Addresses by Right Hon. Sir George Henry Wilkinson, Lord Mayor of London, Right Hon. W.L. Mackenzie King, M.P., Prime Minister of Canada and Right Hon. Winston S. Churchill, C.H., M.P., Prime Minister of Great Britain, The Mansion House, London, England, September 4, 1941. Ottawa: King's Printer, 1941. 16 p.
Location: BVIV, NBFU, OKQ, OKR, OONL, OOP, OOU, OSTCB, OTAR.

F132 Le Canada et la guerre. Dîner offert par le Lord-maire en l'honneur du premier ministre du Canada. Discours des très honorable Sir George-Henry Wilkinson, Lord-maire de Londres, très honorable W.-L. Mackenzie King, M.P., Premier ministre du Canada, et du très honorable Winston Churchill, C.H., M.P., Premier ministre de la Grande-Bretagne, à Mansion House, Londres, Angleterre, le 4 septembre 1941. Ottawa: Imprimeur du Roi, 1941. 16 p.
Location: OONDH, OOP.

F133 Canada and the war. Servitude or freedom. The present position of the war. Speech by Right Hon. W.L. Mackenzie King, M.P., Prime Minister of Canada, at a dinner tendered in his honour by the Canadian Clubs of Ottawa, The Chateau Laurier, Ottawa, September 17, 1941. Ottawa: King's Printer, 1941. 14 p.
Location: BVIV, MWU, NBFU, OKQ, OKR, OONL, OOP, OOU, OSTCB, OTAR, OWTU, SRL, SSU.

F134 Le Canada et la guerre. Servitude ou liberté. Situation actuelle de la guerre. Discours prononcé par le très honorable W.L. Mackenzie King, M.P., Premier ministre du Canada, à un dîner offert en son honneur par les 'Canadian Clubs' d'Ottawa, au Château Laurier,

Ottawa, le 17 septembre, 1941. Ottawa: Imprimeur du Roi, 1941. 14 p.
Location: OKQ, OOP.

F135 Let free men face reality! by the Right Honourable W.L. Mackenzie King. An address delivered before the Canadian Club of Ottawa, September 17th, 1941. [Ottawa, 1941]. 30 p.
Location: BVIV, OONL, OTU.

F136 Norman McLeod Rogers. Address delivered by Rt. Hon. W.L. Mackenzie King, Prime Minister of Canada, on the occasion of the presentation to the city of Kingston of a portrait of the late Honourable Norman McLeod Rogers, Kingston, Ont., October 17, 1941. [Kingston, 1941]. 10 p.
Location: OKQ.

F137 Canada and the war. Controlling the cost of living. The stabilization of prices and wages. Broadcast by Right Hon. W.L. Mackenzie King, M.P., Prime Minister of Canada, October 18, 1941. Ottawa: King's Printer, 1941. 12 p.
Location: BVAU, BVIP, OKQ, OONL, OOP, OOU, OSTCB, OTAR, OTU, OTY.

F138 Le Canada et la guerre. Réglementation du coût de la vie. La stabilisation des prix et des salaires. Discours prononcé à la radio par le très hon. Mackenzie King, M.P., Premier ministre du Canada, samedi, le 18 octobre 1941. Ottawa: Imprimeur du Roi, 1941. 13 p.
Location: OONL, OOP.

F139 Canada and the war. War on all continents. 1. Declaration of existence of state of war between Canada and Hungary, Roumania and Finland. 2. Declaration of the existence of a state of war between Canada and Japan. 3. Declaration of the existence of a state of war between the United States and Japan, Germany and Italy. Statements by Right Hon. W.L. Mackenzie King, M.P., Prime Minister of Canada, December 6, 8, and 11, 1941. Ottawa: King's Printer, 1941. 14 p.
Location: OKQ, OONL, OOP.

F140 Le Canada et la guerre. Guerre des continents. 1. Déclaration de l'existence d'un état de guerre entre le Canada et la Hongrie, la Roumanie et la Finlande. 2. Déclaration de l'existence d'un

état de guerre entre le Canada et le Japon. 3. Déclaration de l'existence d'un état de guerre entre les États-Unis et le Japon, l'Allemagne et l'Italie. Déclarations faites par le très hon. W.L. Mackenzie King, M.P., Premier ministre du Canada, 6, 8, et 11 décembre 1941. Ottawa: Imprimeur du Roi, 1941. 14 p.
Location: OOP.

F141 Canada. House of Commons Debates. Official Report. Speech of Right Hon. W.L. Mackenzie King, Prime Minister of Canada, on the real meaning of a total war effort, delivered in the House of Commons on Monday, January 26, 1942. [Ottawa: King's Printer, 1942]. 20 p.
Location: OKQ.

F142 Canada and the war. The inauguration of the Second Victory Loan. Addresses broadcast by Right Hon. W.L. Mackenzie King, M.P., Prime Minister of Canada, and Franklin D. Roosevelt, President of the United States, February 15, 1942. Ottawa: King's Printer, 1942. 8 p.
Location: OKQ, OKR, OOE, OONL, OOP, SSU.

F143 Le Canada et la guerre. Inauguration du deuxième emprunt de la victoire. Discours prononcés à la radio par le très hon. W.L. Mackenzie King, Premier ministre du Canada, et Franklin-D. Roosevelt, Président des États-Unis, le 15 février 1942. Ottawa: Imprimeur du Roi, 1942. 8 p.
Location: OOP.

F144 Keeping faith with the people. A speech by Rt. Hon. W.L. Mackenzie King, M.P., Prime Minister of Canada, in the House of Commons, February 25, 1942. Ottawa: King's Printer, 1942. 15 p.
Location: OOE, OOP, OOU, OTMCL, SSU.

F145 Canada. House of Commons Debates. Official Report. Speech of Rt. Hon. W.L. Mackenzie King, M.P., Prime Minister of Canada, on National Selective Service, delivered in the House of Commons on Tuesday, March 24, 1942. [Ottawa: King's Printer, 1942]. 8 p.
Location: OOE, OONDH, OOP.

F146 Canada. Débats de la Chambre des communes. Compte rendu officiel. Discours du très hon. Mackenzie King, M.P., Premier ministre du Canada, sur le Service Sélectif National, déclaration faite à la Chambre des communes, le 24 mars 1942. Ottawa: Imprimeur du Roi, 1942. 8 p.

Location: No library copy located.

F147 Canada. House of Commons Debates. Official Report. Speech of Rt. Hon. W.L. Mackenzie King, M.P., Prime Minister of Canada, on the defence of Canada, delivered in the House of Commons on Wednesday, March 25, 1942. [Ottawa: King's Printer, 1942]. 4 p.
Location: BVAU, OKQ, OOE, OOP, OTAR.

F148 Canada. Débats de la Chambre des communes. Compte rendu officiel. La défense du Canada. Discours du très hon. W.L. Mackenzie King, M.P., Premier ministre du Canada, sur la défense du Canada, prononcé à la Chambre des communes, le mercredi 25 mars 1942. [Ottawa: Imprimeur du Roi, 1942]. 4 p.
Location: No library copy located.

F149 National security – the issue in the plebiscite. An appeal to the Canadian electorate for an affirmative vote on April 27th. An address broadcast by the Right Honourable W.L. Mackenzie King, M.P., Prime Minister of Canada, over the Canadian Broadcasting Corporation Network, April 7th, 1942. Ottawa: King's Printer, 1942. 12 p.
Location: AEU, BVAU, OKQ, OKR, OOE, OONDH, OONL, OOP, OSTCB, OTAR, SRL, SSU.

F150 Une mesure de sécurité nationale. La question du plébiscite. Les chefs disent pourquoi et comment voter. Discours prononcés par le très Honorable W.L. Mackenzie King, Premier minsistre du Canada et l'honorable P.J.A. Cardin, Ministre des Transports. Irradies par le Réseau français de Radio-Canada, les 7 et 9 avril 1942. Ottawa: Imprimeur du Roi, 1942. 16 p.
Location: OKQ, SSU.

F151 National unity and national survival: Responsibilities to our own and future generations. A second appeal to the Canadian electorate for an affirmative vote on April 27th. An address broadcast by the Right Honourable W.L. Mackenzie King, M.P., Prime Minister of Canada, over the Canadian Broadcasting Corporation network, April 24th, 1942. Ottawa: King's Printer, 1942. 11 p.
Location: OOE, OOP.

F152 Canada. House of Commons Debates. Official Report. Speech by Rt. Hon. W.L. Mackenzie King, M.P., Prime Minister of Canada, on overseas service in the Canadian Army. Amendment of the

National Resources Mobilization Act. Delivered in the House of Commons on Wednesday, June 10, 1942. [Ottawa: King's Printer, 1942]. 20 p.
Location: OOE, OOP, OTAR.

F153 Discours prononcé par le très Hon. W.L. Mackenzie King, M.P., Premier ministre du Canada, à la Chambre des communes, le mercredi 10 juin 1942, sur le sens de l'amendment au sujet du service militaire outre-mer. [Ottawa: Imprimeur du Roi, 1942]. 20 p.
Location: QMU, QQL.

F154 Canada and the war. Manpower and a total war effort. National Selective Service. Broadcast by Right Hon. W.L. Mackenzie King, M.P., Prime Minister of Canada, August 19, 1942. Ottawa: King's Printer, 1942. 12 p.
Location: AEU, BVAU, OKQ, OOE, OONL, OOP, OSTCB, OTAR, SRL, SSU.

F155 Le Canada et la guerre. Ressources humaines et effort de guerre total: Service Sélectif National. Discours prononcé à la T.S.F. par le très honorable W.L. Mackenzie King, M.P., Premier ministre du Canada, le 19 août 1942. Ottawa: Imprimeur du Roi, 1942. 13 p.
Location: OOP.

F156 Canada and the war. Three years of war. The real issue in the struggle. Broadcast by Right Hon. W.L. Mackenzie King, M.P., Prime Minister of Canada, September 10, 1942. Ottawa: King's Printer, 1942. 12 p.
Location: BVIV, OKQ, OKR, OOE, OONL, OOP, OSTCB, OTAR, OTL, OTU, SRL, SSU.

F157 Le Canada et la guerre. Trois ans de guerre. Le véritable enjeu de cette lutte. Discours prononcé à la T.S.F. par le très honorable W.-L. Mackenzie King, M.P., Premier ministre du Canada, le 10 septembre 1942. Ottawa: Imprimeur du Roi, 1942. 12 p.
Location: BVAU, BVIV, OKQ, OOE, OONL, OSTCB, OTU, SRL, SSU.

F158 Canada and the war. Labour and the war. An address to the American Federation of Labour 1942 Convention, by Right Hon. W.L. Mackenzie King, M.P., Prime Minister of Canada, Toronto, October 9, 1942. Ottawa: King's Printer, 1942. 11 p.
Location: OOP, OTAR.

F159 Le Canada et la guerre. Le travail et la guerre. Discours prononcé à la convention de 1942 de la Fédération américaine du travail, par le très hon. W.L. Mackenzie King, M.P., Premier ministre du Canada, Toronto, le 9 octobre 1942. Ottawa: Imprimeur du Roi, 1942. 12 p.
Location: OOP, QMBM, QQL.

F160 Canada and the war. Nothing matters now but victory. An address on the opening of the 1942 Victory Loan Campaign, by Right Hon. W.L. Mackenzie King, M.P., Prime Minister of Canada, Montreal, October 16, 1942. Ottawa: King's Printer, 1942. 11 p.
Location: BVAU, BVIV, OKQ, OOE, OONL, OOP, OSTCB, OTY, SRL, SSU.

F161 Le Canada et la guerre. Plus rien n'importe, sauf la victoire. Discours inaugurant la campagne de 1942 pour l'emprunt de la victoire, par le très hon. W.L. Mackenzie King, Montreal, le 16 octobre 1942. Ottawa: Imprimeur du Roi, 1942. 11 p.
Location: No library copy located.

F162 Canada and the war. The military occupation of French North Africa and the withdrawal of recognition of the Government at Vichy. Statements by Right Hon. W.L. Mackenzie King, M.P., Prime Minister of Canada, Ottawa, November 8 and 9, 1942. [Ottawa: King's Printer, 1942]. 4 p.
Location: AEU, BVAU, BVIP, OKQ, OONDH, OONL, OOP, OTAR, SSU.

F163 Le Canada et la guerre. L'occupation militaire de l'Afrique du Nord française et la cessation de la reconnaissance du gouvernement de Vichy. Déclaration faite par le très hon. W.L. Mackenzie King, M.P., Premier ministre du Canada, Ottawa, les 8 et 9 novembre 1942. Ottawa: Imprimeur du Roi, 1942. 3 p.
Location: OOP, QMBM.

F164 Canada and the war. The defence of common liberties. An address to the Pilgrims of the United States, by Right Hon. W.L. Mackenzie King, M.P., Prime Minister of Canada, New York, December 2, 1942. Ottawa: King's Printer, 1942. 11 p.
Location: AEU, BVAU, BVIV, OKQ, OKR, OOE, OONL, OOP, OOU, OSTCB, OTAR, SSU.

F165 Le Canada et la guerre. La défense de nos communes libertés. Dis-

cours prononcé lors du dîner des 'Pilgrims of the United States' par le très hon. W.L. Mackenzie King, M.P., Premier ministre du Canada, New York, le 2 décembre 1942. Ottawa: Imprimeur du Roi, 1942. 12 p.
Location: OONL, OOP, QMBM, QQL.

F166 Canada and the war. Temperance and a total war effort. Broadcast by Right Hon. W.L. Mackenzie King, M.P., Prime Minister of Canada, Ottawa, December 16, 1942. Ottawa: King's Printer, 1942. 11 p.
Location: NBFU, OKQ, OKR, OOE, OONDH, OONL, OOP, OTAR, OTU, OTY, SSU.

F167 Le Canada et la guerre. Temperance et effort de guerre total. Discours prononcé à la radio, par le très honorable W.L. Mackenzie King, M.P., Premier ministre du Canada, Ottawa, le 16 décembre 1942. Ottawa: Imprimeur du Roi, 1942. 12 p.
Location: OOP, QQL.

F168 Canada. House of Commons Debates. Official Report. Speech of Rt. Hon. W.L. Mackenzie King, M.P., Prime Minister of Canada, on proposal to withhold calling up of men under the National Resources Mobilization Act, delivered in the House of Commons on Friday, February 19, 1943. [Ottawa: King's Printer, 1943]. 7 p.
Location: OOE.

F169 Canada and the war. Canada's fighting men. An address on the opening of the Fourth Victory Loan Campaign, by Right Hon. W.L. Mackenzie King, M.P., Prime Minister of Canada, Toronto, April 19, 1943. Ottawa: King's Printer, 1943. 15 p.
Location: OKQ, OKR, OOE, OONL, OOP, SSU.

F170 Le Canada et la guerre. Les forces combattantes du Canada. Discours prononcé à la ouverture de la campagne du quatrième emprunt de la victoire, Toronto, par le très honorable W.-L. Mackenzie King, Premier ministre du Canada, Toronto, le 19 avril 1943. [Ottawa: Imprimeur du Roi, 1943]. 15 p.
Location: OOP.

F171 Canada and the war. Canadian forces in the North Pacific, Alaska and the Aleutians. Broadcast by Right Hon. W.L. Mackenzie King, M.P., Prime Minister of Canada, Quebec, August 21, 1943. Ottawa: King's Printer, 1943. 7 p.
Location: OOE, OOP.

F172 Canada and the war. Visit of the President of the United States to the capital of Canada. Addresses by the Right Honourable W.L. Mackenzie King, M.P., Prime Minister of Canada, Franklin D. Roosevelt, President of the United States, the Honourable Thomas Vien, K.C., Speaker of the Senate, The Honourable James Allison Glen, K.C., M.P., Speaker of the House of Commons, Parliament Hill, August 25, 1943. Ottawa: King's Printer, 1943. 14 p.
Location: OKQ, OOE, OOP.

F173 Canada and the war. The unconditional surrender of Italy (September 3, 1943). Four years of war, 1939–1943. Broadcasts by Right Honourable W.L. Mackenzie King, M.P., Prime Minister of Canada, from Ottawa, September 8 and 10, 1943. Ottawa: King's Printer, 1943. 10 p.
Location: OOE, OOP.

F174 Discours du très honorable W.L. Mackenzie King, Premier ministre du Canada, devant la Fédération libérale nationale au Château Laurier, Ottawa, le 27 septembre 1943. [Ottawa: La Fédération libérale nationale, 1943]. 22 p.
Location: QUA, Charles Gavan Power Papers, vol. 99.

F175 Politics and the war. Address by the Rt. Honourable W.L. Mackenzie King, Prime Minister of Canada, to the National Liberal Federation, Chateau Laurier, Ottawa, September 27, 1943. [Ottawa: National Liberal Federation, 1943]. 29 p.
Location: BVIP, OOP.

F176 Le Canada et la guerre. La lutte contre l'inflation. Discours du très honorable W.L. Mackenzie King, M.P., Premier ministre du Canada, radiodiffusé d'Ottawa, le 4 décembre 1943. [Ottawa: Imprimeur du Roi, 1943]. 11 p.
Location: WLMK Papers, J 5 Series, vol. 96, pp. 61290–61299.

F177 Canada and the war. The battle against inflation. Broadcast by Right Hon. W.L. Mackenzie King, M.P., Prime Minister of Canada, Ottawa, December 4, 1943. Ottawa: King's Printer, 1943. 11 p.
Location: OOE, OONL, SSU.

F178 A better future for mankind. An address by Right Hon. W.L. Mackenzie King, M.P., Prime Minister of Canada, before both Houses of Parliament of the United Kingdom, London, May 11, 1944. [Ottawa: National Liberal Federation of Canada, 1944]. 12 p.
Location: BVAU, BVIP, OOA.

F179 Canada and the war. Proceedings on the occasion of an address by Rt. Hon. W.L. Mackenzie King, M.P., Prime Minister of Canada, to the Members of both Houses of the Parliament of the United Kingdom. Addresses by the Right Honourable Winston Churchill, C.H., M.P., Prime Minister of the United Kingdom, the Right Honourable W.L. Mackenzie King, M.P., Prime Minister of Canada, the Right Honourable Viscount Simon, G.C.S.I., G.C.V.O., Lord Chancellor of the United Kingdom, the Right Honourable Clifton Brown, M.P., Speaker of the House of Commons of the United Kingdom, Westminster, London, England, May 11, 1944. Ottawa: King's Printer, 1944. 22 p.
Location: BVIP, BVIV, OKQ, OOE, OONDH, OONL, OSTCB, OTL, OWTU, SSU.

F180 Le Canada et la guerre. Cérémonie tenue à l'occasion d'un discours prononcé par le très honorable W.L. Mackenzie King, M.P., Premier ministre du Canada, devant les deux chambres du parlement de Westminster. Discours prononcés par le très honorable Winston Churchill, C.H., M.P., Premier ministre du Royaume-Uni, le très honorable W.L. Mackenzie King, M.P., Premier ministre du Canada, le très honorable Vicomte Simon, G.C.S.I., G.C.V.O., Lord Chancellor, le très honorable Clifton Brown, M.P., Président de la Chambre des communes du Royaume-Uni, Westminster, Londres, Angleterre, le 11 mai 1944. Ottawa: Imprimeur du Roi, 1944. 23 p.
Location: OOP.

F181 Canada. House of Commons Debates. Official Report. Speech of Rt. Hon. W.L. Mackenzie King, M.P., Prime Minister of Canada, on the Address in Reply to the Speech from the Throne – Regarding position of Leader of the Opposition – Elections in wartime – Commonwealth relations. Delivered in the House of Commons on Monday, January 31, 1944. [Ottawa: King's Printer, 1944]. 13 p.
Location: OONL.

F182 Pour le bonheur de l'humanité. Discours prononcé par le très hon. W.L. Mackenzie King, Premier Ministre du Canada, devant les deux chambres du Parlement de Westminster, le 11 mai 1944. Ottawa: La Fédération Libérale Nationale du Canada, 1944. 15 p.
Location: No library copy located.

F183 Canada's provision for her fighting forces. Broadcast by Rt. Hon. W.L. Mackenzie King, M.P., Prime Minister of Canada, from Ottawa on the CBC Network, August 16, 1944. [Ottawa: National Liberal Federation of Canada, 1944]. 12 p.
Location: OOE.

F184 Le Canada et l'avenir de ses forces combattantes. Discours prononcé à la radio par le très hon. W.L. Mackenzie King, à Ottawa, sur le réseau de Radio-Canada, le 16 août 1944. [Hull: Cauvin, 1944]. 14 p.
Location: QMBN.

F185 Canada and the war. Canada's support of the Army overseas. Broadcast by Right Hon. W.L. Mackenzie King, M.P., Prime Minister of Canada, Ottawa, November 8, 1944. Ottawa: King's Printer, 1944. 11 p.
Location: AEU, BVAU, NBFU, OKQ, OONL, OOP, OSTCB, OTAR, OTU, SSU.

F186 Le Canada et la guerre. Appui du Canada à son armée d'outre-mer. Causerie radiophonique du très honorable W.L. Mackenzie King, M.P., Premier ministre du Canada, Ottawa, 8 novembre 1944. Ottawa: Imprimeur du Roi, 1944. 12 p.
Location: OOP.

F187 Canada and the war. General elections and the war: The government's plans for the coming months. Broadcast by Right Hon. W.L. Mackenzie King, M.P., Prime Minister of Canada, Ottawa, Friday, March 2, 1945. Ottawa: King's Printer, 1945. 11 p.
Location: OOE.

F188 Proposals for the establishment of a general international organization for the maintenance of international peace and security. Statement in the House of Commons, Ottawa, by the Right Honourable William Lyon Mackenzie King, M.P., Prime Minister of Canada, March 20, 1945. Ottawa: King's Printer, 1945. 24 p.
Location: BVASA, OOE.

F189 Propositions en vue de l'établissement d'une organisation internationale générale pour le maintien de la paix et de la sécurité internationales. Déclaration à la Chambre des communes, Ottawa, du très honorable W.L. Mackenzie King, M.P., premier

ministre du Canada, 20 mars 1945. Ottawa: Imprimeur du Roi, 1945. 24 p.
Location: No library copy located.

F190 Canada and the war. Victory, reconstruction and peace. Mackenzie King to the people of Canada, 1945. A series of addresses by Rt. Hon. W.L. Mackenzie King, Prime Minister of Canada, May–June 1945. [Ottawa: National Liberal Federation of Canada, 1945]. 142 p.
Contents: An appeal for a renewed expression of national confidence [Nationwide broadcast, from Vancouver, May 16, 1945]; International co-operation essential to peace, security and prosperity [Address at Edmonton, May 18, 1945]; Election issues and social legislation [Address at Prince Albert, May 19, 1945]; Employment, prosperity and national unity [Address at Winnipeg, May 24, 1945]; Government planning for war and peace [Nationwide broadcast from London, Ontario, May 30, 1945]; The Liberal Party and Quebec [Address at Montreal, June 2, 1945]; Significant factors in the election campaign [Nationwide broadcast from Ottawa, June 8, 1945]; The verdict of the people [Nationwide broadcast from Ottawa, June 11, 1945]; The end of the war against Nazi Germany [Broadcast from San Francisco, May 8, 1945]; The end of the war against militarist Japan [Statement issued in Ottawa, August 14, 1945].
Location: BVASA, BVAU, BVIV, NSHD, NSHS, OGU, OKQ, OKR, OOA, OOC, OOE, OONDH, OONL, OOP, OOU, OPAL, OSTCB, OTNY, OTU, OTY, OWTU, QLB, SRL, SSU.

F191 Canada. Débats de la Chambre des communes. Compte rendu officiel. Discours du très honorable W.L. Mackenzie King, Premier Ministre du Canada, sur la Déclaration de Washington concernant l'énergie atomique, prononcé à la Chambre des Communes, le lundi 17 décembre 1945. [Ottawa: Imprimeur du Roi, 1945]. 8 p.
Location: WLMK Papers, J 5 Series, vol. 78, pp. 49560–49567.

F192 Canada. House of Commons Debates. Official Report. Speech of Rt. Hon. W.L. Mackenzie King, M.P., Prime Minister of Canada, on the Washington declaration on atomic energy, delivered in the House of Commons, Monday, December 17, 1945. [Ottawa: King's Printer, 1945]. 8 p.
Location: WLMK Papers, J 5 Series, vol. 101, pp. 64647–64653.

F193 Government policy on price and wage control in the transition period. Statement by Right Hon. W.L. Mackenzie King, Prime Minister of Canada, together with a statement by Hon. Humphrey Mitchell, Minister of Labour, on changes in wage control, Ottawa, January 31, 1946. Ottawa: King's Printer, 1946. 14 p.
Location: OKQ.

F194 Address of welcome by the Prime Minister of Canada (The Rt. Hon. W.L. Mackenzie King) to His Excellency Field Marshal the Rt. Hon. Viscount Alexander of Tunis, G.C.B., G.C.M.G., C.S.I., D.S.O., M.C., LL.D., A.D.C., Governor-General of Canada. [Ottawa, 1946]. 4 p.
Location: WLMK Papers, J 5 Series, vol. 87, pp. 56163–56166.

F195 Le parti libérale: Personnalités et principes. Discours du très honorable W.L. Mackenzie King, Premier ministre du Canada et chef du parti libérale du Canada et du très honorable Louis-S. Saint-Laurent, Ministre de la Justice et Secrétaire d'État aux Affaires extérieures, prononcé au Château Frontenac, Québec, le 29 novembre 1946 à l'occasion du banquet offert en l'honneur de M. Saint-Laurent. [Ottawa: La Fédération libérale nationale, 1946]. 29 p.
Location: OOP.

F196 The Liberal Party: Personalities and policies. Speeches by the Right Honourable W.L. Mackenzie King, Prime Minister and Leader of the Liberal Party of Canada, and the Honourable Louis S. St Laurent, Minister of Justice and Secretary of State for External Affairs, delivered at the Chateau Frontenac, Quebec, November 29, 1946, on the occasion of the complimentary banquet in honour of Mr St Laurent. [Ottawa: National Liberal Federation, 1946]. 26 p.
Location: OONL.

F197 Unity, security, freedom. Fundamental principles of Liberalism, by Right Honourable W.L. Mackenzie King, M.P., Prime Minister and Leader of the Liberal Party. [National broadcast, Ottawa, December 1, 1946]. [Ottawa: National Liberal Federation of Canada, 1946]. 7 p.
Location: WLMK Papers, J 5 Series, vol. 82, pp. 52810–52814.

F198 Canada. House of Commons Debates. Official Report. Speech of Right Hon. W.L. Mackenzie King, Prime Minister, on the Address in Reply to the Speech from the Throne, delivered in the House of Commons, on Monday, February 3, 1947. [Ottawa: King's Printer, 1947]. 15 p.
Location: WLMK Papers, J 5 Series, vol. 102, p. 65553.

F199 The Geneva trade agreements: An address by Right Hon. W.L. Mackenzie King, Prime Minister of Canada, over the CBC Network, November 17, 1947. 3 p. (Canada. Department of External Affairs, Statements and Speeches series 47/50).
Location: OKQ, OOE.

F200 Text of an address made by the Right Honourable W.L. Mackenzie King, Prime Minister of Canada, over the CBC Network at 10.15 p.m. E.S.T., on November 17, 1947. 4 p. (Canada. Department of External Affairs, Official Statements and Speeches, no. 9).
Location: OOE.

F201 Texte du discours qu'a prononcé le très honorable W.L. Mackenzie King, premier ministre du Canada, sur le réseau de Radio-Canada, le 17 novembre 1947, à 10h. 15 de l'apres midi, h.n.e. 4 p. (Ministre des affaires extérieures. Déclarations et discours officiels, no. 9).
Location: OOE.

F202 Call for a national Liberal convention; the international situation, the problem of prices. Address by the Right Honourable W.L. Mackenzie King, Prime Minister and Leader of the Liberal Party of Canada, on the occasion of the meeting of the Advisory Council of the National Liberal Federation of Canada, the Chateau Laurier, Ottawa, January 20, 1948. [Ottawa: National Liberal Federation of Canada, 1948]. 22 p.
Location: AEU, OONL, OPAL, OSTCB, SSU.

F203 Convocation d'un congrès libérale nationale. 'La situation internationale.' 'Le probleme de l'augmentation des prix.' Discours du très honorable W.L. Mackenzie King, Premier ministre et chef du parti libérale canadien, à l'occasion de la réunion du Conseil consultatif de la Fédération libérale nationale du Canada. Prononcé au Château Laurier, à Ottawa, le 20 janvier 1948. [Ottawa: La Fédération libérale nationale du Canada, 1948]. 24 p.
Location: OONL, OOP.

F204 Statement by the Prime Minister on health services and health insurance, House of Commons, May 14, 1948. [N.p., n.d.] 16 p.
Location: BVIP.

F205 A message from our leader, 1919–1948. Rt. Hon. W.L. Mackenzie King: Unity – security – freedom. [Ottawa, 1948]. 7 p.
Location: OONL, OPAL, OTY, OWTU, SSU.

F206 Un message de notre chef (1919–1948). Le très honorable W.L. Mackenzie King, P.C., O.M., M. P. Unité – sécurité – liberté. [Ottawa, 1948]. 7 p.
Distributed with a recording to the delegates to the National Liberal Convention, August 1948.
Location: OWA.

F207 Unité, sécurité, liberté. Principes fondamentaux du libéralisme. Ottawa: Fédération libérale nationale du Canada, 1948. 8 p.
Location: No library copy located.

F208 Congrès libéral national, 1948. Discours du très honorable W.L. Mackenzie King, premier ministre et chef du parti libérale du Canada, sur ses années à la direction et les raisons de sa retraité comme chef du parti, le Colisée, Ottawa, 6 août 1948. [Ottawa, 1948]. 16 p.
Location: OONL, QSHERU.

F209 National Liberal Convention, 1948. Address by the Right Honourable W.L. Mackenzie King, Prime Minister of Canada and Leader of the Liberal Party of Canada, on his years of leadership – and reasons for retirement as leader of the Party, The Coliseum, Ottawa, August 6, 1948. [Ottawa, 1948]. 16 p.
Location: OOA, OONL, OWA, QSHERU.

F210 A statement by the Right Hon. W.L. Mackenzie King, Prime Minister of Canada, at the United Nations General Assembly in Paris, on September 28, 1948. 6 p. (Canada. Department of External Affairs, Statements and Speeches series 48/50).
Location: OKQ, OOE.

Press Release Copies of Speeches

During Mackenzie King's tenure as prime minister his office issued relatively few mimeographed speeches in the sense of today's 'press releases.' Two reasons can be suggested for this. First, the organized public-relations aspect of today's leader's office was virtually non-existent in the days of Mackenzie King. Second, King's method of preparing speeches, a substantial portion of which he did himself, made it impossible to have a text ready for release to the press prior to its delivery by King. While the staff assembled material for speeches and did a considerable amount of drafting, King continued to revise his speeches until the time came to speak.

With the exception of items F354 to F360, the following speeches were issued in mimeographed form by the Prime Minister's Office. They were not, however, printed and issued as pamphlets. Copies are located in the King Papers, J 5 Series.

F211 [Speech delivered at the League of Nations, Geneva, September 29, 1936]. 14 p.
Location: OKQ.

F212 Radio address re the Abdication of King Edward VIII, December 10, 1936. 7 p.
Location: WLMK Papers, J 5 Series, vol. 44, pp. 26021–26027.

F213 Address by the Right Honourable W.L. Mackenzie King, M.P., Prime Minister of Canada, on the occasion of the inauguration of the World Economic Co-operation Campaign sponsored by the National Peace Conference of the United States and the League of Nations Society in Canada. Delivered over the networks of the Canadian Broadcasting Corporation and the Columbia Broadcasting System, Ottawa, September 19, 1937. 4 p.
Location: WLMK Papers, J 5 Series, vol. 45, pp. 26648–26652.

F214 Red Cross broadcast by the Prime Minister, November 12, 1939. 3 p.
Location: WLMK Papers, J 5 Series, vol. 39, pp. 22334–22336.

F215 Outline of speech by Mackenzie King, Montreal, March 12, 1940. 8 p.
Location: WLMK Papers, J 5 Series, vol. 83, pp. 53563–53570.

F216 Statement by Prime Minister, House of Commons, December 2, 1940. The present situation. 17 p.
Location: No library copy located.

F217 Address by the Prime Minister. Opening of the Dominion–Provincial Conference, January 14, 1941. 21 p.
Location: WLMK Papers, J 5 Series, vol. 92, pp. 58842–55862.

F218 Address by Right Honourable W.L. Mackenzie King, Prime Minister of Canada, Victory Loan Broadcast, Wednesday, June 24 [1941], 10 p.m. EDST, National Network. 2 p.
Location: OOE.

F219 Allocution prononcée par le très honorable W.L. Mackenzie King, premier ministre du Canada, le 25 juin 1941, a 10 hr. du soir, heure d'été, sur le reseau nationale de Radio Canada. 2 p.
Location: OOE.

F220 Canada's war effort. Speech by the Prime Minister in the Debate on the Address, House of Commons, January 26, 1942. 70 p.
Location: OOE.

F221 L'effort de guerre canadien. Discours prononcé par le premier ministre, au cours du débat sur l'Adresse, à la Chambre des communes, le 26 janvier 1942. 30 p.
Location: No library copy located.

F222 Speech by the Prime Minister, closing the Debate on the Second Reading of the Bill to amend the National Resources Mobilization Act, July 7, 1942. 36 p.
Location: OOE.

F223 Aid to Russia campaign. Montreal, January 19, 1943. Remarks by the Prime Minister of Canada, Rt. Hon. W.L. Mackenzie King, in introducing Mrs Franklin D. Roosevelt. 8 p.
Location: WLMK Papers, J 5 Series, vol. 95, pp. 60431–60438.

F224 Statement of the policy of the Canadian Government on civil air transport made in the House of Commons on April 2, 1943, by the Prime Minister, the Right Honourable W.L. Mackenzie King. 4 p.
Location: WLMK Papers, J 5 Series, vol. 95, pp. 60948–60951.

F225 Statement by the Prime Minister, Rt. Hon. W.L. Mackenzie King, on the fourth Victory Loan [May 17, 1943]. 3 p.
Location: WLMK Papers, J 5 Series, vol. 95, pp. 60502–60504.

F226 Remarks by Prime Minister in connection with Victory Loan Broadcast, Sunday, 7:30 p.m., May 23, 1943. 2 p.
Location: OOE.

F227 Déclaration du Premier ministre concernant la défense de la région du Bas Saint-Laurent [le 8 juin 1943]. 4 p.
Location: WLMK Papers, J 5 Series, vol. 95, pp. 60975–60981.

F228 [Statement by the Prime Minister on the defences of the Lower St Lawrence Region, House of Commons, June 8, 1943]. 3 p.
Location: WLMK Papers, J 5 Series, vol. 95, pp. 60962–60965.

F229 United Nations Food Conference. [Statement in the House of Commons, June 14, 1943]. 8 p.
Location: WLMK Papers, J 5 Series, vol. 96, pp. 61026–61033.

F230 Introduction of Mme Chiang Kai-Shek, to the Houses of Parliament, Ottawa, June 16, 1943, by the Prime Minister, Right Honourable W.L. Mackenzie King. 3 p.
Location: WLMK Papers, J 5 Series, vol. 95, pp. 60928–60931.

F231 Statement by the Prime Minister on international relief, Ottawa, June 18th, 1943. 3 p.
Location: WLMK Papers, J 5 Series, vol. 96, pp. 61139–61141.

F232 Canadian–Soviet Friendship Rally, Toronto, June 22, 1943. Introduction of Honourable Joseph E. Davies, by Right Hon. W.L. Mackenzie King, Prime Minister of Canada. 12 p.
Location: WLMK Papers, J 5 Series, vol. 76, pp. 47633–47644.

F233 Dominion Day [Address in the House of Commons, July 1, 1943]. 7 p.
Location: OOE.

F234 Statement by the Prime Minister on The Wartime Information Board [House of Commons, July 13, 1943]. 19 p.
Location: OOE.

F235 Déclaration du premier ministre sur la participation de l'Armée Canadienne à la campagne de Sicile. [17 juillet 1943]. 5 p.
Location: WLMK Papers, J 5 Series, vol. 96, pp. 61118–61122.

F236 The War and Italy. Broadcast by the Prime Minister, Rt. Hon. W.L. Mackenzie King, M.P., 8.30 p.m., August 2, 1943. 11 p.
Location: WLMK Papers, J 5 Series, vol. 86, pp. 55315–55324.

F237 Discours radiodiffusé par le premier ministre, le très hon. W.L. Mackenzie King, sur le rôle joué par les troupes canadiennes en Alaska et dans les Aleoutes, 21 août 1943. 3 p.
Location: WLMK Papers, J 5 Series, vol. 95, pp. 60635–60637.

F238 Adresse de bienvenue au président des États-Unis par le premier

ministre du Canada, Colline du parlementaire, Ottawa, 25 août 1943. 5 p.
Location: WLMK Papers, J 5 Series, vol. 95, pp. 60630–60634.

F239 Address by the Rt. Honourable W.L. Mackenzie King, Prime Minister of Canada, to the National Liberal Federation, Chateau Laurier, Ottawa, September 27, 1943. 36 p.
Location: OOE.

F240 Thirtieth National Foreign Trade Convention. Message of the Right Honourable W.L. Mackenzie King, Prime Minister of Canada, to the World Trade Dinner at Hotel Pennsylvania on October 26, 1943, delivered through Brooke Claxton, M.P. 4 p.
Location: WLMK Papers, J 5 Series, vol. 96, pp. 61212–61215.

F241 Trentième convention nationale du commerce éxterieur. Message du très honorable W.L. Mackenzie King, premier ministre du Canada, prononcé au banquet du commerce mondial, à l'hôtel Pennsylvania, le 26 octobre 1943, par M. Brooke Claxton, député. 4 p.
Location: WLMK Papers, J 5 Series, vol. 96, pp. 61232–61235.

F242 Discours de remerciements du premier ministre pour l'accueil fait au cinquième emprunt de la Victoire, radiodiffusé le 14 novembre 1943. 3 p.
Location: WLMK Papers, J 5 Series, vol. 96, pp. 61236–61237.

F243 Expression of thanks by the Prime Minister for the response to Fifth Victory Loan, broadcast on November 14, 1943. 13 p.
Location: WLMK Papers, J 5 Series, vol. 96, pp. 61238–61240.

F244 Statement by the Prime Minister in regard to amendments to Wartime Wages Order (P.C. 9384 of December 9, 1943). 4 p.
Location: WLMK Papers, J 5 Series, vol. 98, pp. 62256–62259.

F245 Christmas message from Prime Minister Mackenzie King broadcast to Canada's armed forces in the Mediterranean area, December 25, 1943. 2 p.
Location: WLMK Papers, J 5 Series, vol. 96, pp. 61546–61547.

F246 Canada's New Year message, by Prime Minister Mackenzie King, December 31, 1943. 2 p.
Location: WLMK Papers, J 5 Series, vol. 96, pp. 61550–61551.

F247 Address by the Prime Minister. Opening of the Dominion–Provincial Conference, January 14, 1941. 21 p.
Location: WLMK Papers, J 5 Series, vol. 92, pp. 58842–58862.

F248 Address by Rt. Hon. William Lyon Mackenzie King, Prime Minister of Canada, at the presentation of a tree to Rt. Hon. Sir William Mulock, on his one hundredth birthday anniversary, by the Men of the Trees, Toronto, January 19, 1944. 3 p.
Location: WLMK Papers, J 5 Series, vol. 76, pp. 47179–47181.

F249 Statement by the Prime Minister made in the House of Commons, Friday, January 28, 1944. [Re treatment of Japanese prisoners of war]. 5 p.
Location: OOE.

F250 Foreign policy. Statement made in the House of Commons on January 31, 1944 by the Prime Minister of Canada. 4 p.
Location: WLMK Papers, J 5 Series, vol. 97, pp. 62040–62043.

F251 Expulsion of German and Japanese diplomatic agents from Ireland. [March 13, 1944]. [Statement in the House of Commons]. 3 p.
Location: WLMK Papers, J 5 Series, vol. 98, pp. 62120–62122.

F252 Speech by Prime Minister Mackenzie King, [House of Commons], 13th March, 1944 [on Wartime Alcoholic Beverages Order]. 9 p.
Location: WLMK Papers, J 5 Series, vol. 97, pp. 61960–61968.

F253 Prime Minister Curtin's visit. Address of welcome by Right Hon. W.L. Mackenzie King, Prime Minister of Canada. Ottawa, June 1, 1944. 4 p.
Location: WLMK Papers, J 5 Series, vol. 97, pp. 62019–62022.

F254 Statement by Prime Minister W.L. Mackenzie King, June 6, 1944. 1 p. [Broadcast on Allied landing in Europe].
Location: WLMK Papers, J 5 Series, vol. 97, p. 61733.

F255 Introduction by Prime Minister Mackenzie King of Prime Minister Peter Fraser of New Zealand, House of Parliament, June 30, 1944. 4 p.
Location: WLMK Papers, J 5 Series, vol. 97, pp. 62085–62088.

F256 Présentation de M Peter Fraser, premier ministre de la Nouvelle-Zélande par le premier ministre du Canada, M Mackenzie King, Parlement du Canada, 30 juin 1944. 2 p.
Location: WLMK Papers, J 5 Series, vol. 97, pp. 62089–62090.

F257 Allocution à publier une fois prononcé, Colline du parlementaire, Ottawa, 11 juillet 1944. Présentation du général de Gaulle, par le premier ministre M Mackenzie King. 2 p.
Location: WLMK Papers, J 5 Series, vol. 97, pp. 61738–61739.

F258 Introduction by Prime Minister Mackenzie King of General de Gaulle, Parliament Hill, July 11, 1944. 4 p.
Location: WLMK Papers, J 5 Series, vol. 97, pp. 61756–61759.

F259 Expression of thanks by the Prime Minister for the response of the Seventh Victory Loan, Broadcast on November 19, 1944. 2 p.
Location: WLMK Papers, J 5 Series, vol. 97, pp. 61950–61951.

F260 Remerciements du Prime Ministre pour la réponse à la campagne de souscription en faveur du Septième Emprunt de la Victoire. Radio-émission du 19 novembre [1944]. 1 p.
Location: WLMK Papers, J 5 Series, vol. 97, p. 61954.

F261 Statement re war policy. [April 4, 1945]. 9 p.
Location: WLMK Papers, J 5 Series, vol. 98, pp. 62472–62481.

F262 Statement by the Prime Minister, Mr Mackenzie King, in the House of Commons, Ottawa, [on the death of President Franklin D. Roosevelt], April 12, 1945. 2 p.
Location: WLMK Papers, J 5 Series, vol. 77, pp. 48577–48578.

F263 Statement by Prime Minister Mackenzie King, in House of Commons, Ottawa, April 13, 1945. [Re business of the House of Commons]. 3 p.
Location: WLMK Papers, J 5 Series, vol. 98, pp. 62282–62284.

F264 Discours prononcé par le premier ministre du Canada, le très honorable William Lyon Mackenzie King, à la deuxième séance plénière de la Conférence de San-Francisco, le 27 avril 1945. 4 p.
Location: WLMK Papers, J 5 Series, vol. 98, pp. 62683–62686.

F265 Broadcast from San Francisco by Right Hon. W.L. Mackenzie King, Prime Minister of Canada, 8th May, 1945. 7 p.
Location: WLMK Papers, J 5 Series, vol. 87, pp. 55934–55940.

F266 Radio-diffusion prononcée de San-Francisco, par le très honorable W.L. Mackenzie King, premier ministre du Canada. 7 p. [May 8, 1945].
Location: WLMK Papers, J 5 Series, vol. 98, pp. 62714–62720.

F267 Nationwide broadcast by the Rt. Hon. W.L. Mackenzie King, Prime Minister of Canada, Vancouver, May 16, 1945. 16 p.
Location: WLMK Papers, J 5 Series, vol. 99, pp. 63193–63208.

F268 Address by the Rt. Hon. W.L. Mackenzie King, Prime Minister of Canada. Edmonton, May 18, 1945. 15 p.
Location: WLMK Papers, J 5 Series, vol. 99, pp. 63242–63256.

F269 Nationwide broadcast by the Rt. Hon. W.L. Mackenzie King, London, May 30, 1945. 15 p.
Location: WLMK Papers, J 5 Series, vol. 99, pp. 63326–63340.

F270 Broadcast by the Rt. Hon. W.L. Mackenzie King, Prime Minister of Canada, Montreal, June 6, 1945. 20 p.
Location: WLMK Papers, J 5 Series, vol. 99, pp. 63417–63436.

F271 Address by the Rt. Hon. W.L. Mackenzie King, M.P. (Election campaign speech – Saint John, N.B.), June 6, 1945. 13 p.
Location: WLMK Papers, J 5 Series, vol. 99, pp. 63492–63505.

F272 Nationwide address by the Rt. Hon. W.L. Mackenzie King, Prime Minister of Canada, Ottawa, June 8, 1945. 16 p.
Location: WLMK Papers, J 5 Series, vol. 99, pp. 63112–63126.

F273 Déclaration du premier ministre, M Mackenzie King, Ottawa, le 11 juin 1945 [à propos des résultats des élections générales]. 6 p.
Location: WLMK Papers, J 5 Series, vol. 99, pp. 63583–63588.

F274 Statement by the Prime Minister, Mr Mackenzie King, June 11, 1945. [Re the results of the general election]. 5 p.
Location: WLMK Papers, J 5 Series, vol. 99, pp. 63563–63567.

F275 Bienvenue au major-general Hoffmeister. Radio-allocution du premier ministre, M Mackenzie King, Ottawa, le 14 juin 1945. 6 p.
Location: WLMK Papers, J 5 Series, vol. 98, pp. 62726–62731.

F276 Welcome to Major General Hoffmeister. Ottawa, June 14, 1945. 5 p.
Location: WLMK Papers, J 5 Series, vol. 98, pp. 62721–62725.

F277 Statement by Rt. Hon. W.L. Mackenzie King, Prime Minister of Canada, San Francisco, Cal., June 26, 1945. [On signing the United Nations Charter]. 1 p.
Location: WLMK Papers, J 4 Series, vol. 340, p. 235335.

F278 Speech by Right Hon. W.L. Mackenzie King at Alexandria, Ontario, July 17, 1945. 35 p.
Location: WLMK Papers, J 5 Series, vol. 99, pp. 63590–63624.

F279 Conférence fédérale–provinciale sur la reconstruction. Discourse d'ouverture du premier ministre du Canada, le très honorable W.L. Mackenzie King, Ottawa le 6 août 1945. 7 p.
Location: WLMK Papers, J 5 Series, vol. 98, pp. 62798–62804.

F280 Dominion–Provincial Conference on Reconstruction. Opening remarks by the Prime Minister of Canada, Right Honourable W.L. Mackenzie King, Ottawa, August 6, 1945. 16 p.
Location: WLMK Papers, J 5 Series, vol. 98, pp. 62741–62756.

F281 Welcome to General Crerar. Remarks by the Prime Minister in presenting Address of Welcome, Parliament Hill, August 7, 1945. 7 p.
Location: WLMK Papers, J 5 Series, vol. 99, pp. 62808–62814.

F282 Bienvenue au Général Crerar. Remarques du premier ministere en guise de présentation d'une adresse de bienvenue au général Crerar, sur la Colline parlementaire, le 7 août 1945. 6 p.
Location: WLMK Papers, J 5 Series, vol. 99, pp. 62829–62835.

F283 Statement by Prime Minister Mackenzie King on the occasion of his visit to Europe, House of Commons, September 27, 1945. 3 p.
Location: WLMK Papers, J 5 Series, vol. 78, pp. 49490–49492.

F284 Introduction of the Prime Minister of the United Kingdom by the Prime Minister, Right Hon. W.L. Mackenzie King, Ottawa, Nov. 19, 1945. 4 p.
Location: WLMK Papers, J 5 Series, vol. 98, pp. 62563–62566.

F285 Statement by the Prime Minister, House of Commons, 23rd November, 1945. [Regarding the rationing of meat, fats, and oils]. 4 p.
Location: WLMK Papers, J 5 Series, vol. 100, pp. 63762–63765.

F286 Dominion–Provincial Conference on Reconstruction. Co-ordinating Committee. Opening statement by the Prime Minister of Canada, November 26, 1945. 5 p.
Location: WLMK Papers, J 5 Series, vol. 99, pp. 63016–63020.

F287 Statement regarding persons of Japanese origin in Canada by the Prime Minister, Rt. Hon. W.L. Mackenzie King, House of Com-

mons, December 17, 1945. 5 p. [Three orders-in-council were attached to the prime minister's mimeographed text].
Location: WLMK Papers, J 5 Series, vol. 100, pp. 63726–63737.

F288 Vote of thanks to General Eisenhower, Canadian Club, Ottawa, by Right Honourable W.L. Mackenzie King, Prime Minister of Canada. [January 10, 1946]. 5 p.
Location: WLMK Papers, J 5 Series, vol. 100, pp. 63867–63871.

F289 Dominion–Provincial Conference. Co-ordinating Committee. Statement by the Prime Minister of Canada (Rt. Hon. W.L. Mackenzie King), at the opening session, January 28, 1946. 7 p.
Location: WLMK Papers, J 5 Series, vol. 79, pp. 49904–49910.

F290 Conférence Fédérale–Provinciale. (Séance pléniere). Déclaration du premier ministre du Canada, le très honorable W.L. Mackenzie King, M.P., le 29 avril 1946. 15 p.
Location: WLMK Papers, J 5 Series, vol. 100, pp. 63943–63957.

F291 Dominion–Provincial Conference (Plenary Session). Statement by the Prime Minister of Canada, Rt. Hon. W.L. Mackenzie King, M.P., April 29, 1946. 14 p.
Location: WLMK Papers, J 5 Series, vol. 100, pp. 63973–63986.

F292 Address of welcome to Hon. Herbert Hoover, by Rt. Hon. W.L. Mackenzie King, Prime Minister of Canada, Chateau Laurier, Ottawa, June 28, 1946. 3 p.
Location: WLMK Papers, J 5 Series, vol. 100, pp. 64002–64004.

F293 The first year of peace. Broadcast by Rt. Hon. W.L. Mackenzie King, M.P., Leader of the Liberal Party, CBC National Network, Ottawa, July 3, 1946. 9 p.
Location: WLMK Papers, J 5 Series, vol. 100, pp. 64005–64013.

F294 'La première année de paix.' Discours prononcé à la radio, par le très honorable W.L. Mackenzie King, M.P., Chef du parti Libéral, Ottawa, le 3 juillet 1946. 6 p.
Location: WLMK Papers, J 5 Series, vol. 100, pp. 64034–64039.

F295 Address by Rt. Hon. W.L. Mackenzie King, Prime Minister of Canada, before the plenary session of the Peace Conference, Paris, August 2, 1946. 6 p.
Location: WLMK Papers, J 5 Series, vol. 82, pp. 52874–52880.

F296 Discours prononcé par M W.L. Mackenzie King, premier ministre du Canada, à la séance plénière de la Conférence de Paris, le 2 août 1946. 7 p.
Location: WLMK Papers, J 5 Series, vol. 82, pp. 64083–64089.

F297 Cérémonie nationale de citoyenneté, Edifice de la Cour Suprême, Ottawa, le 3 janvier 1947. Discours du très honorable W.L. Mackenzie King, M.P., premier ministre du Canada. Bienvenue aux nouveaux citoyens. 10 p.
Location: WLMK Papers, J 5 Series, vol. 101, pp. 64810–64820.

F298 National Citizenship Ceremony, Supreme Court Building, January 3, 1947. Address by Right Honourable W.L. Mackenzie King, M.P., Prime Minister of Canada. Welcome to new citizens. 8 p.
Location: WLMK Papers, J 5 Series, vol. 101, pp. 64802–64809.

F299 Statement made in the House of Commons on defence cooperation with the United States. [February 12, 1947]. 2 p.
Location: WLMK Papers, J 5 Series, vol. 102, pp. 65613–65614.

F300 Comments made in the House of Commons following the agreed statement on defence, February 12, 1947. 3 p.
Location: WLMK Papers, J 5 Series, vol. 102, pp. 65615–65616.

F301 Statement by the Prime Minister of Canada, the Rt. Hon. W.L. Mackenzie King, on the second anniversary of the establishment of the International Service of the CBC [February 25, 1947]. 2 p.
Location: WLMK Papers, J 5 Series, vol. 88, pp. 56285–85286.

F302 Bell Centennial, Brantford, March 3, 1947. Greetings broadcast from Ottawa, by Rt. Hon. W.L. Mackenzie King, M.P., Prime Minister of Canada. 2 p.
Location: WLMK Papers, J 5 Series, vol. 101, pp. 64881–64882.

F303 Centenaire de Bell, Brantford, le 3 mars 1947. Émission radiophonique de salutations d'Ottawa, par le très honorable W.L. Mackenzie King, M.P., premier ministre du Canada. 2 p.
Location: WLMK Papers, J 5 Series, vol. 101, pp. 64887–64888.

F304 Statement by the Prime Minister, Rt. Hon. W.L. Mackenzie King. Re: Withdrawl of occupational forces from Germany [March 10, 1947]. 13 p.
Location: WLMK Papers, J 5 Series, vol. 80, pp. 50879–50889.

F305 Statement by Prime Minister. Re resignation of Mr Donald Gordon as Chairman of Wartime Prices and Trade Board, House of Commons, March 19, 1947. 2 p.
Location: WLMK Papers, J 5 Series, vol. 103, pp. 65917–65918.

F306 Déclaration du premier ministre. Au sujet de la résignation de M Donald Gordon comme président de la Commission des prix et du commerce en temps de guerre, Chambre des communes, le 19 mars 1947. 3 p.
Location: WLMK Papers, J 5 Series, vol. 103, pp. 65917–65919.

F307 Canada's immigration policy. Statement by the Prime Minister, House of Commons, May 1st, 1947. 12 p.
Location: WLMK Papers, J 5 Series, vol. 102, pp. 65724–65735.

F308 Statement by the Prime Minister, visit of President Truman [June 2, 1947]. 3 p.
Location: WLMK Papers, J 5 Series, vol. 103, pp. 65870–65873.

F309 Cérémonie du dévoilement, le 10 juin 1947. Remarques du premier ministre, le très honorable W.L. Mackenzie King. 5 p.
Location: WLMK Papers, J 5 Series, vol. 103, pp. 65911–65915.

F310 Unveiling ceremony, June 10, 1947. Remarks by the Prime Minister, Rt. Hon. W.L. Mackenzie King. 4 p. [Unveiling of portraits of Sir Robert L. Borden and the Right Honourable William Lyon Mackenzie King].
Location: WLMK Papers, J 5 Series, vol. 103, pp. 65839–65842.

F311 President Truman's visit. Address of welcome by Rt. Hon. W.L. Mackenzie King, Prime Minister of Canada, House of Commons Chamber, Ottawa, June 11, 1947. 6 p.
Location: WLMK Papers, J 5 Series, vol. 103, pp. 65843–65848.

F312 Visite du president Truman. Discours de bienvenure du tres hon. W.L. Mackenzie King, premier ministre du Canada, Chambre des communes, Ottawa, le 11 juin 1947. 6 p.
Location: WLMK Papers, J 5 Series, vol. 103, pp. 65861–65866.

F313 Reception – Chateau Laurier – June 18th, 1947. Remarks by the Rt. Honourable W.L. Mackenzie King. 6 p. [Civil reception for the Marian Congress].
Location: WLMK Papers, J 5 Series, vol. 101, pp. 64897–64902.

F314 Réception au Château Laurier, le 18 juin 1947. Allocution du très honorable W.L. Mackenzie King. 7 p. [Réception au Congrès marial].
Location: WLMK Papers, J 5 Series, vol. 101, pp. 64903–64909.

F315 Statement by the Prime Minister regarding the Newfoundland delegation, House of Commons, June 23, 1947. 7 p.
Location: WLMK Papers, J 5 Series, vol. 102, pp. 65698–65704.

F316 Statement by the Prime Minister, House of Commons, Tues. June 24th [1947] Statement on Post-UNRRA relief. 3 p.
Location: WLMK Papers, J 5 Series, vol. 103, pp. 65874–65876.

F317 Meeting between delegates from the National Convention of Newfoundland and representatives of the Government of Canada. Opening statement by Rt. Hon. W.L. Mackenzie King, Prime Minister of Canada, Parliament Buildings, Ottawa, June 25, 1947. 7 p.
Location: WLMK Papers, J 5 Series, vol. 102, pp. 65677–65683.

F318 Réunion des délegués de la Convention nationale de Terre-Neuve et des représentations du gouvernement du Canada. Discours d'ouverture par le très honorable W.L. Mackenzie King, premier ministre du Canada, Édifices du Parlement, Ottawa, le 25 juin 1947. 6 p.
Location: WLMK Papers, J 5 Series, vol. 102, pp. 65705–65710.

F319 Statement by the Prime Minister, House of Commons, June 27, 1947 [on the death of R.B. Bennett]. 8 p.
Location: WLMK Papers, J 5 Series, vol. 103, pp. 65736–65743.

F320 Statement by the Prime Minister of Canada regarding approval of treaties of peace with Italy, Roumania, Hungary and Finland, House of Commons, June 30, 1947. 7 p.
Location: WLMK Papers, J 5 Series, vol. 103, pp. 65791–65797.

F321 Déclaration du premier ministre du Canada aux sujet de la ratification des traités de paix conclus avec l'Italie, la Roumania, la Hongrie et la Finlande, Chambre des communes, le 30 juin 1947. 3 p.
Location: WLMK Papers, J 5 Series, vol. 103, pp. 65812–65814.

F322 Statement by the Prime Minister, House of Commons, July 9, 1947 [Regarding engagement of Princess Elizabeth and Lieutenant Philip Mountbatten]. 1 p.
Location: WLMK Papers, J 5 Series, vol. 103, p. 65816.

F323 Radio address by the Prime Minister on the second anniversary of the surrender of Japan, August 14, 1947. 2 p.
Location: WLMK Papers, J 5 Series, vol. 88, pp. 56302–56303.

F324 Address by the Right Honourable W.L. Mackenzie King, Prime Minister, at the official opening of the Canadian National Exhibition, Toronto, August 22, 1947. 12 p.
Location: WLMK Papers, J 5 Series, vol. 102, pp. 64954–64965.

F325 Allocution prononcée par le très honorable W.L. Mackenzie King, premier ministre, à l'ouverture officielle de l'exposition nationale du Canada, Toronto, le 22 août 1947. 12 p.
Location: WLMK Papers, J 5 Series, vol. 102, pp. 64966–64977.

F326 Remarks by the Rt. Hon. W.L. Mackenzie King, Prime Minister, at official ceremony opening the British Section of the Canadian National Exhibition under the auspices of the British Empire Overseas Branch of the Toronto Board of Trade, Toronto, August 22, 1947. 3 p.
Location: WLMK Papers, J 5 Series, vol. 80, pp. 51241–51243.

F327 Quelques pensées sur le Canada et le monde d'aujourd' hui. Discours du très honorable W.L. Mackenzie King, premier ministre, à la fete champêtre annuelle de la Fédération agricole du comte de Waterloo, Waterloo Park, Waterloo, Ontario, le 8 septembre 1947. 20 p.
Location: WLMK Papers, J 5 Series, vol. 102, pp. 65158–65177.

F328 Some thoughts on Canada and the world of today. Speech by the Rt. Hon. W.L. Mackenzie King, Prime Minister, at the annual field day of the Waterloo County Federation of Agriculture, Waterloo Park, Waterloo, Ontario, September 8, 1947. 18 p.
Location: WLMK Papers, J 5 Series, vol. 81, pp. 51271–51288.

F329 Address by the Rt. Hon. W.L. Mackenzie King, Prime Minister, to the newly admitted Barristers-at-Law, at a meeting of Benchers of the Law Society of Upper Canada in Convocation, Osgoode Hall, Toronto, September 18, 1947. 13 p.
Location: WLMK Papers, J 5 Series, vol. 81, pp. 51382–51394.

F330 The Canadian Club of New York City, Presentation of Award and Medal, October 31, 1947, The Right Honourable Mackenzie King. 20 p.
Location: WLMK Papers, J 5 Series, vol. 102, pp. 65277–65296.

F331 The late Rt. Hon. Earl Baldwin of Bewdley. Tribute by the Prime Minister of Canada, Rt. Hon. W.L. Mackenzie King, Ottawa, December 14, 1947. 1 p.
Location: WLMK Papers, J 5 Series, vol. 81, p. 51639.

F332 [Statement made in the House of Commons, December 18, 1947, regarding trade and financial arrangements between United Kingdom and Canada]. 3 p.
Location: WLMK Papers, J 5 Series, vol. 103, pp. 65983–65986.

F333 Text of a statement made in the House of Commons by the Prime Minister, Mr Mackenzie King, December 18, 1947 [re United Kingdom mission coming to Canada to discuss trade and financial arrangements between the United Kingdom and Canada]. 4 p.
Location: WLMK Papers, J 5 Series, vol. 81, pp. 51648–51651.

F334 [Statement in the House of Commons, December 19, 1947 regarding civil service rates of pay]. 7 p. + tables (5 p.).
Location: WLMK Papers, J 5 Series, vol. 103, pp. 65991–66002.

F335 National Liberal Federation Dinner, Chateau Laurier, January 20, 1948. Section of speech by Prime Minister in relation to the problem of rising prices. 14 p.
Location: WLMK Papers, J 5 Series, vol. 104, pp. 66775–66793.

F336 Statement by the Prime Minister re Pensions and Student Veterans' Training Allowances, House of Commons, Monday, February 16, 1948. 3 p. + schedule (2 p.).
Location: WLMK Papers, J 5 Series, vol. 104, pp. 66396–66400.

F337 Statement by the Prime Minister to the House of Commons, Tuesday, February 24th, 1948, concerning the Hong Kong inquiry. 7 p.
Location: WLMK Papers, J 5 Series, vol. 82, pp. 52102–52108.

F338 Déclaration du premier ministre à la Chambre des communes, le mardi, 24 février 1948, au sujet de l'enquête relative à Hong-Kong. 5 p.
Location: WLMK Papers, J 5 Series, vol. 103, pp. 66198–66202.

F339 Statement by Prime Minister re Hong Kong inquiry, House of Commons, March 2, 1948. 1 p.
Location: WLMK Papers, J 5 Series, vol. 103, p. 66146.

F340 Convocation of the College of William and Mary in Virginia. Acknowledgement of honorary degree of Doctor of Laws by Rt. Hon. W.L. Mackenzie King, Prime Minister of Canada, April 2, 1948. 6 p.
Location: WLMK Papers, J 5 Series, vol. 82, pp. 52125–52130.

F341 Réunion du College of William and Mary de la Virginie. Remerciements du très honorable W.L. Mackenzie King, premier ministre du Canada, du titre honorifique de docteur en droit [le 2er avril 1948]. 6 p.
Location: WLMK Papers, J 5 Series, vol. 104, pp. 66978–66983.

F342 Statement by the Prime Minister on health services and health insurance, House of Commons, May 14, 1948. 16 p.
Location: WLMK Papers, J 5 Series, vol. 82, pp. 52269–52284.

F343 [Statement re] Flood conditions in the Fraser Valley [House of Commons], June 3, 1948. 1 p.
Location: WLMK Papers, J 5 Series, vol. 103, p. 66003.

F344 Statement by Prime Minister re Board of Transport Commissioners, House of Commons, June 8, 1948. 3 p.
Location: WLMK Papers, J 5 Series, vol. 82, pp. 52366–52368.

F345 Déclaration du premier ministre au sujet de la Commission de transports, Chambre des communes, le 8 juin 1948. 3 p.
Location: WLMK Papers, J 5 Series, vol. 103, pp. 66386–66388.

F346 Civic dinner tendered by the Mayor and Members of the Council of the City of Toronto, Royal York Hotel, June 12, 1948. Remarks by the Prime Minister. 17 p.
Location: WLMK Papers, J 5 Series, vol. 82, pp. 52976–52992.

F347 Official opening – Sunnybrook Hospital. Address by Right Honourable W.L. Mackenzie King, Prime Minister, Toronto, June 12, 1948. 8 p.
Location: WLMK Papers, J 5 Series, vol. 82, pp. 52967–52975.

F348 Civic dinner tendered by the Mayor and Members of the Council of the City of Toronto, Royal York Hotel, June 12, 1948. 17 p.
Location: WLMK Papers, J 5 Series, vol. 82, pp. 52950–52966.

F349 Déclaration du premier ministre sur le secours et le rétablissement de la vallée du Fraser, Chambre des communes, le 25 juin 1948. 4 p.

Location: WLMK Papers, J 5 Series, vol. 103, pp. 66019–66022.

F350 Statement by the Prime Minister on the relief and rehabilitation in the Fraser Valley, House of Commons, June 25, 1948. 4 p.
Location: WLMK Papers, J 5 Series, vol. 82, pp. 52431–52434.

F351 Address of welcome by the Rt. Hon. W.L. Mackenzie King, P.C., O.M., M.P., Prime Minister of Canada and Leader of the Liberal Party, Ottawa, August 5, 1948. 7 p.
Location: WLMK Papers, J 5 Series, vol. 104, pp. 66453–66459.

F352 Text of radio broadcast recorded by Rt. Hon. W.L. Mackenzie King, on November 15th, 1948, just before his resignation as Prime Minister of Canada was accepted. 2 p.
Location: WLMK Papers, J 5 Series, vol. 82, pp. 52791–52792.

F353 Remarks by Right Honourable W.L. Mackenzie King, Ottawa, June 20, 1949. 2 p. [On introducing Louis St Laurent at an election rally in Ottawa].
Location: WLMK Papers, J 5 Series, vol. 88, pp. 56626–56627.

The following texts of speeches were issued by the Office of the Director of Public Information:

F354 Address to be delivered by the Right Honourable W.L. Mackenzie King, Prime Minister of Canada, on the occasion of the ceremony commemorating the 50th anniversary of the death of Sir John A. Macdonald, Kingston, June 7th, 1941. 3 p. [Issued by the Office of Director of Public Information].
Location: OOE.

F355 Text of an address being delivered by the Prime Minister of Canada, the Right Honourable W.L. Mackenzie King, at Princeton University, June 17, 1941. 4 p. [Issued by the Office of Director of Public Information].
Location: WLMK Papers, J 5 Series, vol. 92, pp. 59145–59152.

The following texts of speeches were issued by the Department of External Affairs:

F356 Déclaration du premier ministre, le très honorable W.L. Mackenzie King, à l'Assemblée générale des Nations Unies, le 28 septembre

1948. (Ministère des affaires extérieures communiqué no. 77). 6 p.
Location: OOE.

F357 Statement by the Prime Minister, the Rt. Hon. W.L. Mackenzie King, at the United Nations General Assembly, September 28, 1948. (Department of External Affairs Press Release No. 77). 6 p.
Location: OOE.

The following texts of speeches were issued by the Canadian Information Service:

F358 Prime Minister King's speech at Dieppe. [August 19, 1946]. [Canadian Information Service Press Release]. 6 p.
Location: WLMK Papers, J 5 Series, vol. 100, pp. 64090–64095.

F359 Traduction du discours de M. Mackenzie King à Dieppe. [le 19 août 1946]. 6 p. [Service d'Information Canadien Communiqué de presse].
Location: WLMK Papers, J 5 Series, vol. 100, pp. 64108–64113.

The text of the following speech was issued by the United Nations Relief and Rehabilitation Administration:

F360 United Nations Relief and Rehabilitation Administration, Second Session of the Council. Address of welcome by the Rt. Hon. W.L. Mackenzie King, Prime Minister of Canáda, to the Second Session of the Council of the United Nations Relief and Rehabilitation Administration, Montreal, Monday, September 18th, 1944. 8 p.
Location: OOE.

Specially Bound Collections of Speeches

From time to time Mackenzie King had specially bound collections of his speeches prepared.

F361 War and peace: A series of addresses, 1936–38, on Canadian relations to the British Empire, the League of Nations and foreign countries, by Right Hon. W.L. Mackenzie King, Prime Minister and Secretary of State for External Affairs.

[The volume contains ten addresses covering the period from June 18, 1936, to August 18, 1938].
Location: OOP.

F362 Canada and the war: A series of addresses, 1939–1942 (Broadcast), by Right Hon. W.L. Mackenzie King, Prime Minister of Canada.
[The volume contains twenty-nine addresses covering the period from September 3, 1939, to December 16, 1942].
Twenty-five sets of this title were bound.
Location: OONL, OPET.

SECTION G

Compilations of Canadian Government Publications Containing Speeches and Other Documents Issued by Mackenzie King

House of Commons Debates

During his long political career, Mackenzie King represented five ridings in the House of Commons: Waterloo North (Ontario), 1908–1911, Prince (Prince Edward Island), 1919–1921, York North (Ontario), 1921–1925, Prince Albert (Saskatchewan), 1926–1945, and Glengarry (Ontario), 1945–1949.

Verbatim transcripts of all addresses delivered in the House of Commons are printed in:

G1 *Débats de la Chambre des communes, Compte rendu officiel.* 1907/08–1911, 1919–1949. [Ottawa: Imprimeur du Roi, 1908–1949]. 184 v.

G2 *House of Commons, Official Report, Debates.* 1907/08–1911, 1919–1949. [Ottawa: King's Printer, 1908–1949]. 184 v.

Documents on Canadian External Relations

G3 *Documents relatifs aux relations extérieures du Canada. Documents on Canadian external relations.* Volumes 3–13. [Ottawa: Information Canada and the Canadian Government Printing Centre, 1970–1993].

These volumes contain documents on all aspects of Canadian external relations ranging from the League of Nations and the United Nations to the Second World War, Imperial relations, the Paris

Peace Conference, and relations with individual countries. They contain numerous documents and statements by Mackenzie King as Secretary of State for External Affairs, a position which he also held from 1921 to 1930 and from 1935 to 1948.

Documents on Relations between Canada and Newfoundland

G4 *Documents on relations between Canada and Newfoundland. Documents relatifs aux relations entre le Canada et Terre-Neuve.* [Ottawa: Information Canada and the Canadian Government Publishing Centre, 1974–1984]. 3 v.

This collection of documents contains numerous letters and statements written and released by Mackenzie King during the period 1935 to 1948.

SECTION H

The William Lyon Mackenzie King Papers

The William Lyon Mackenzie King Papers[104] are located in the National Archives of Canada. The first section of the 232-metre collection was transferred by King to the National Archives in October 1946. On July 22, 1975, the twenty-fifth anniversary of his death, the ownership of the papers was transferred to the Crown. The King Papers are divided into public and personal sections.[105]

Jacqueline Neatby, who worked on the sorting and classifying of the King Papers for about fifteen years, has described the collection this way: 'Mr King's life is so richly documented that I think this collection is a unique phenomenon in the history of archives.'[106]

Public Papers

H1 Primary Series Correspondence, J 1 Series, 1889–1950. 44.7 m. [Volumes 1–447].

This series consists of a selection of the important correspondence from the Prime Minister's Office files and files from Laurier House.

104 This description of the Mackenzie King Papers is based on various finding aids, catalogue entries, and inventories produced by the staff of the National Archives of Canada.

105 For a description of the sorting and arranging of the King Papers, see Jean Dryden, 'The Mackenzie King Papers: An archival odyssey,' *Archivaria*, 6, Summer 1978, pp. 40–69.

106 NAC, WLMK Papers, MG 26, J 17 Series, Folder 1, Jacqueline Neatby, 'Memorandum re: W.L. Mackenzie King Papers, June 13, 1961,' p. 1.

The correspondence is arranged in alphabetical order by author within each year, with enclosures and replies kept together and numbered consecutively.

This series may be borrowed from the National Archives of Canada on microfilm.

Finding aid: Primary correspondence, Series J 1. 47 p.

The following indices are also available for the J 1 Series: a subject index is available for the period 1889 to 1921; computerized indices are available from 1921 to 1950 (correspondent index: 12,191 pages; subject index: 9,159 pages).

A card index containing a card for each correspondent and a list of letters within each year is available at the National Archives of Canada.

H2 Prime Minister's Office Correspondence, J 2 Series, 1922–1930, 1935–1948. 52 m. [Volumes 1–520].

This series consists of the routine correspondence that remained after the papers were selected for the Primary Series.

Finding aid: Public Archives of Canada. Manuscript [Division]. Archives publiques du Canada. [Division des] Manuscrits. W.L.M. King Papers, Prime Minister's Office Series, MG 26, J 2. Finding aid 502/Instrument de recherche 502. Prepared by Margaret Rowden in 1979. Préparé par Margaret Rowden en 1979. 487 p. [Contains a file listing of the 520 volumes].

H3 General Correspondence, J 3 Series, 1922–1950. 15.2 m. [Volumes 1–161].

This correspondence consists of the personal letters kept at Laurier House that remained after correspondence was selected for the Primary Series.

Finding aid: Public Archives Canada. Manuscript Division. Archives publiques du Canada. King, William Lyon Mackenzie, MG 26, J 3. Prepared in 1982 by P. DeLottinville of the Prime Ministers Archives. Préparé en 1982 par P. DeLottinville des Archives des premiers ministres. 7 p. [Contains a list of the first and last correspondents contained in each of the 161 volumes. A detailed finding aid, containing lists of each author within this series and the date of each letter, is available in the Prime Ministers Archives].

H4 Memoranda and Notes, J 4 Series, 1887–1950. 43.8 m. [Volumes 1–431].

This series is arranged in subject files within four chronological periods: 1887–1921, 1922–1932, 1933–1939, and 1940–1950. Memoranda that were enclosed in correspondence are found in the Primary Series. Several files are closed.

This series may be borrowed from the National Archives of Canada on microfilm.

Finding aid: Public Archives Canada. Manuscript Division. Archives publiques Canada. Division des manuscrits. King, W.L.M., MG 26, J 4 Series, Memoranda and notes/Memoires et notes. Finding aid no. 502/Instrument de recherche no 502. Prepared by Jean Dryden in 1974 and revised in June 1979. Further additions and revisions in 1982 and 1984. Préparé par Jean Dryden en 1974 et révisé en 1979. Révisions et renseignements supplémentares en 1982 et 1984. 124 p. [Contains a file listing of the contents of the 431 volumes].

H5 Speeches, J 5 Series, 1899–1950. 10.6 m. [Volumes 1–104].

This section is arranged in chronological order. It consists of various types of material: notes, drafts, printed copies, newspaper reports, and comments.

The speeches for the period 1899 to 1932 have been microfilmed. This series may be borrowed from the National Archives of Canada on microfilm.

Finding aid: Public Archives of Canada. Manuscript Division. Archives publiques du Canada. Division des manuscrits. W.L.M. King Papers, Speeches, MG 26, J 5. Finding aid 502/Instrument de recherche 502. Prepared by Jean Dryden in 1974. Préparé par Mlle Jean Dryden en 1974. 105 p. [Contains a listing of each speech delivered by King].

H6 Pamphlets and clippings, J 6 Series, 1891–1950. 42.1 m. [Volumes 1–245].

This series consists of clippings, pamphlets, and brochures.

Finding aid: Public Archives Canada. Manuscript Division. Archives publiques Canada. Division des manuscrits. King, William Lyon Mackenzie. Pamphlets and clippings series, MG 26, J 6. Finding aid 502/Instrument de recherche 502. Prepared by M. Hoogenraad and B. Lawson of Prime Ministers Archives in 1983. Préparé en 1983 par M. Hoogenraad et B. Lawson des Archives des premiers ministres. 134 p. [Contains a file listing of the 245 volumes].

Personal Papers

H7 Family Papers, J 7 Series, 1880–1950. 6.1 m. [Volumes 1–26].

This series consists of correspondence from members of the King family. The letters are arranged chronologically up to the end of 1917. After that date the arrangement is by the name of the correspondent.

This series may be borrowed from the National Archives of Canada on microfilm.

Finding aid: National Archives of Canada. Archives nationales du Canada. King, William Lyon Mackenzie. MG 26, J 7 Series. Family Papers. Finding aid no. 502. Instrument de recherche no 502. Revised by Maureen Hoogenraad in 1993. Révisé en 1993 par Maureen Hoogenraad. 71 p. [Contains a file listing of the 26 volumes].

H8 Personal Correspondence, J 8 Series, 1897–1950. 4 m. [Volumes 1–41].

This series contains correspondence not incorporated into the public series as it had been kept separate by Mackenzie King. Correspondence with Julia Grant (Princess Cantacuzene), volumes 10–14, is closed until 2001.

Finding aid: Public Archives of Canada. Manuscript Division. Archives publiques du Canada. Division des manuscrits. King, William Lyon Mackenzie. Personal Correspondence Series. MG 26, J 8. Finding aid no. 502/Instrument de recherche no 502. Prepared November 1978, Paulette Dozois, Prime Ministers Section. Préparé en novembre 1978, Paulette Dozois, Section des premiers ministres. 14 p. [Contains a file listing of the 41 volumes].

H9 Spiritualism, J 9 Series, 1919–1950. 1.4 m. [Volumes 1–7].

Correspondence, publications, and memoranda arranged in subject files. Closed to researchers until January 1, 2001.

H10 Laurier House and Kingsmere, J 10 Series, 1919–1950. 2.8 m. [Volumes 1–28].

Correspondence on plans, furniture, etc. Arranged in subject files. Files relating to staff members closed until January 1, 2001.

Finding aid: King, William Lyon Mackenzie. MG 26, J 10. Laurier House and Kingsmere. Prepared by Larry McNally. 1984. iii, 15 p.

H11 Finances, J 11 Series, 1907–1950. 1.6 m. [Volumes 1–16].

Consists of annual statements, material on investments, etc. Arranged in subject files. Closed to researchers until 2001.

H12 Personal, Miscellaneous, J 12 Series, 1905–1950. 2.1 m. [Volumes 1–21].

Consists of small subject files on personal matters. Some subjects are: cars, church, clubs, health, insurance, and staff. Staff files are closed to researchers until January 2001.

H13 Diaries and Diary Memoranda Books, J 13 Series, 1893–1950. 5.7 m.

Finding aid: Public Archives of Canada. Manuscript Division. Prime Ministers Section. Archives publiques du Canada. Division des manuscrits. Section des Archives des premiers ministres. King, William Lyon Mackenzie. MG 26, J 13. Diaries. Finding aid no 502/ Instrument de recherche no. 502. Prime Ministers Archives Section, 1981. Section des Archives des premiers ministres, 1981. 44 p.

H14 Papers of Members of the King Family, J 14 Series, 1840–1950. 2 m. [Volumes 1–20].

Consists of papers of John and Christina King, John King and Isabel King, Dr and Mrs Dougall Macdougall King, Mr and Mrs M. Lay, and the Lindsay family.

Finding aid: Public Archives of Canada. Manuscript Division. Archives publiques du Canada. Division des manuscrits. W.L.M. King Papers. King Family Papers. MG 26, J 14. Finding aid 502/ Instrument de recherche 502. Prepared by Jean Dryden in 1974. Préparé par Mlle Jean Dryden en 1974. 6 p.

H15 Souvenirs, J 15 Series, 1641, 1703, 1815–1950. 7.25 m. [Volumes 1–18].

This series contains a wide variety of material, including programs, historical documents, and memorabilia collected by King. It is organized by type of document.

Finding aid: Public Archives Canada. Manuscript Division. Archives publiques Canada. Division des manuscrits. King, William Lyon Mackenzie. MG 26, J 15. Finding aid no. 502/Instrument de recherche no 502. Revised by Prime Ministers Archives Section in 1983. Révisé par le personnel des Archives des premiers ministres en 1983. v, 26 p. 1983. [Contains a file listing of the 18 volumes].

H16 Election Campaign Posters, J 16 Series, 1940. 6 pages.

H17 Records of the Literary Executors, J 17 Series, 1938–1969. [Volumes 1–9].

Consists of correspondence of the literary executors, 1950–1958, relating to the writing of the official biography of Mackenzie King and the placement of the King Papers in the National Archives of Canada. Also included are financial records for the W.L. Mackenzie King memoir project, 1950–1957.

Finding aid: Public Archives of Canada. Manuscript Division. Archives publiques du Canada. Division des manuscrits. King, William Lyon Mackenzie. Records of the Literary Executors. MG 26, J 17. Finding aid no. 502/Instrument de recherche no 502. Prepared by the staff of the Prime Ministers Archives in 1981. Préparé en 1981 par le personnel des Archives des premiers ministres. [1981]. 11 p.

H18 McGregor, F.A., J 18 Series, 1950–1956. 10 cm. [1 volume].

Contains correspondence between F.A. McGregor, the literary executors, and others involved in the King estate and in the official biography of King, as well as some personal correspondence.

Finding aid: King, William Lyon Mackenzie. MG 26, J 18. Fred McGregor Papers. Prepared by Colleen Dempsey. 1980. 1 p.

H19 Royal Trust Company Estate Papers, 1950–1960. 160 m. [Volumes 1–2].

Consists of the Royal Trust Company files relating to the estate of Mackenzie King.

File list available.

SECTION I

Theses

Mackenzie King wrote two graduate theses: one for the Master of Arts degree at the University of Toronto in 1897 and the other for the Doctor of Philosophy degree at Harvard University in 1909.

I1 'The International Typographical Union.' [Master of Arts thesis, University of Toronto, 1897]. 45 p.
Unavailable for loan from the University of Toronto Archives.

I2 'Oriental immigration to Canada.' [Doctor of Philosophy thesis, Harvard University, 1909]. 79 p.
Unavailable for loan from the Harvard University Archives, but a photocopy may be purchased.

SECTION J

Sound Recordings

Recordings of over one hundred of Mackenzie King's speeches and statements have been preserved in sound archives. Most of the records are among the holdings of audiovisual materials at the National Archives of Canada. Copies of a few of them have been located in other repositories, including the British Broadcasting Corporation Sound Archives, the Milo Ryan Phonoarchive at the University of Washington, the Queen's University Archives, and the G. Robert Vincent National Voice Library.

The list of recordings has been arranged chronologically.

J1 Speech at the Montreal Forum during the 1925 federal election campaign, October 19, 1925.[107]
Location: National Archives of Canada, Audio-Visual Holdings.

J2 Address on the occasion of the Diamond Jubilee of Canadian Confederation, Parliament Hill, Ottawa, July 1, 1927.
Location: National Archives of Canada, Audio-Visual Holdings.

J3 Address of welcome in Quebec City for President Franklin D. Roosevelt, July 31, 1936.

107 It is interesting to note that this is the earliest surviving recording of a prime minister's voice. A recording of Lord Stanley, governor general (1888–1893), recorded in 1888, exists at the National Archives of Canada. See Rosemary Bergeron, 'Canadian Prime Ministers in the film and broadcasting age,' *The Archivist*, 20 (3), 1994, pp. 11–12.

Location: National Archives of Canada, Audio-Visual Holdings; British Broadcasting Corporation Sound Archives, 1149.

J4 Recorded message conveying the best wishes of Canada to South Africa on the occasion of the opening of the Empire Exhibition at Johannesburg, September 15, 1936.
Location: National Archives of Canada, Audio-Visual Holdings; British Broadcasting Corporation Sound Archives, 1174.

J5 Talk about King Edward VIII's abdication and its constitutional implications for Canada, December 11, 1936.
Location: National Archives of Canada, Audio-Visual Holdings.

J6 Reading of the proclamation of the accession of King George VI at ceremony in Ottawa, December 15, 1936.
Location: National Archives of Canada, Audio-Visual Holdings.

J7 Broadcast address on the occasion of the Coronation of King George VI, May 12, 1937.
Location: National Archives of Canada, Audio-Visual Holdings.

J8 Broadcast in 'Empire Homage' (BBC Coronation Program), May 12, 1937.
Location: British Broadcasting Corporation Sound Archives, 1145–9 and 1455.

J9 Radio broadcast on the Coronation, the Imperial Conference, and his visit to the Continent of Europe, July 19, 1937.
Location: National Archives of Canada, Audio-Visual Holdings.

J10 Talk during the International Symposium on World Economic Cooperation, sponsored by the National Peace Conference in the United States and the League of Nations Society of Canada, September 19, 1937.
Location: National Archives of Canada, Audio-Visual Holdings.

J11 Talk about Australia delivered on the occasion of Australia's 150th anniversary. [Broadcast by the Canadian Broadcasting Corporation], January 22, 1938.
Location: National Archives of Canada, Audio-Visual Holdings.

J12 Address to the Canadian Corps Reunion, Toronto, July 30, 1938.
Location: National Archives of Canada, Audio-Visual Holdings.

J13 Address at the opening of the Thousand Islands International

Bridge at Ivy Lea, Ontario, and Collins Landing, New York, August 18, 1938.
Location: CBC Radio Archives, Queen's University Archives.

J14 Address on Remembrance Day from Convocation Hall, University of Toronto, November 11, 1938.
Location: National Archives of Canada, Audio-Visual Holdings.

J15 Talk in the 'Government of Canada' series on the Canadian Broadcasting Corporation, January 23, 1939.
Location: National Archives of Canada, Audio-Visual Holdings.

J16 Address at state luncheon given in honour of King George VI and Queen Elizabeth at the Chateau Frontenac, Quebec City, May 17, 1939.
Location: National Archives of Canada, Audio-Visual Holdings.

J17 Introduction to speeches by King George VI and Queen Elizabeth before their departure from Halifax, June 15, 1939.
Location: British Broadcasting Corporation Sound Archives, 410–3.

J18 Radio speech on the declaration of a state of war between the United Kingdom and Germany, September 3, 1939.
Location: National Archives of Canada, Audio-Visual Holdings; British Broadcasting Corporation Sound Archives, 2287–2288.

J19 Broadcast from Ottawa on 'The issue in the present war,' October 27, 1939.
Location: National Archives of Canada, Audio-Visual Holdings.

J20 Broadcast from Ottawa on the organization of Canada's war effort, October 31, 1939.
Location: National Archives of Canada, Audio-Visual Holdings.

J21 Address announcing the British Commonwealth Air Training Plan, Ottawa, December 17, 1939.
Location: National Archives of Canada, Audio-Visual Holdings.

J22 Radio talk in the federal election campaign, February 23, 1940.
Location: National Archives of Canada, Audio-Visual Holdings.

J23 Radio talk in the federal election campaign, March 23, 1940.
Location: National Archives of Canada, Audio-Visual Holdings.

J24 Address on the war, June 7, 1940.
Location: National Archives of Canada, Audio-Visual Holdings.

J25 Address announcing Canada's declaration of war on Italy, June 10, 1940.
Location: National Archives of Canada, Audio-Visual Holdings.

J26 Talk in the Torch of Victory ceremony at the Parliament Buildings, Ottawa, June 11, 1941.
Location: National Archives of Canada, Audio-Visual Holdings.

J27 Remarks at the swearing in of the Earl of Athlone as Governor General in Ottawa, June 21, 1940.
Location: National Archives of Canada, Audio-Visual Holdings.

J28 Talk in the Canadian Broadcasting Corporation series 'Lets Face the Facts,' September 1, 1940.
Location: National Archives of Canada, Audio-Visual Holdings.

J29 Talk about the British Commonwealth Air Training Plan in BBC 'Wings of Empire' program, December 17, 1940.
Location: British Broadcasting Corporation Sound Archives, DX/10938–9.

J30 Broadcast containing New Year's Message, December 31, 1940.
Location: National Archives of Canada, Audio-Visual Holdings.

J31 Radio talk at the beginning of the War Savings Campaign, February 2, 1941.
Location: National Archives of Canada, Audio-Visual Holdings.

J32 Remarks containing thanks to Mayor Fiorello H. LaGuardia of New York City for his toast to England at the St George's Day Luncheon, Canadian Club, Ottawa, April 23, 1941.
Location: National Archives of Canada, Audio-Visual Holdings.

J33 Speech after reviewing troops on Parliament Hill, Ottawa, May 26, 1941.
Location: National Archives of Canada, Audio-Visual Holdings.

J34 Address to the people of the British Isles as the 1941 Victory Loan Campaign opens in Canada, May 30, 1941.
Location: National Archives of Canada, Audio-Visual Holdings.

J35 Address at ceremonies commemorating the fiftieth anniversary of

the death of Sir John A. Macdonald, Kingston, Ontario, June 6, 1941.
Location: National Archives of Canada, Audio-Visual Holdings.

J36 Speech at a dinner tendered in his honour by the Associated Canadian Organizations of New York City, New York, June 17, 1941.
Location: National Archives of Canada, Audio-Visual Holdings.

J37 Speech at an athletic competition for Canadian troops in England, August [23], 1941.
Location: National Archives of Canada, Audio-Visual Holdings.

J38 Address at the Lord Mayor's luncheon in his honour at the Mansion House, London, September 4, 1941.
Location: National Archives of Canada, Audio-Visual Holdings; British Broadcasting Corporation Sound Archives, 3232–3236.

J39 Talk on controlling the cost of living and the stabilization of prices and wages, October 18, 1941.
Location: National Archives of Canada, Audio-Visual Holdings.

J40 Talk announcing Canadian declaration of war against Japan following the Japanese attack on Pearl Harbor, December 8, 1941.
Location: National Archives of Canada, Audio-Visual Holdings.

J41 Introduction of Prime Minister Winston Churchill in an address before both Houses of Parliament, Parliament Buildings, Ottawa, December 30, 1941.
Location: National Archives of Canada, Audio-Visual Holdings.

J42 Talk to inaugurate the Victory Loan Drive, February 15, 1942.
Location: National Archives of Canada, Audio-Visual Holdings.

J43 Talk about the plebiscite to be held on April 27th on the Canadian Broadcasting Corporation, April 7, 1942.
Location: National Archives of Canada, Audio-Visual Holdings.

J44 Broadcast on the Canadian Broadcasting Corporation from Ottawa on the plebiscite to be held on April 27th, April 24, 1942.
Location: National Archives of Canada, Audio-Visual Holdings.

J45 Address at the Ottawa Air Training Conference, Ottawa, May 18, 1942.
Location: National Archives of Canada, Audio-Visual Holdings.

J46 Talk about the Dieppe raid, on the Canadian Broadcasting Corporation, August 19, 1942.
Location: Canadian Broadcasting Corporation.

J47 Broadcast entitled 'Three years of war' on the third anniversary of Canada's entry into the war, September 10, 1942.
Location: National Archives of Canada, Audio-Visual Holdings.

J48 Talk in 'Comrades in Arms,' a Canadian Armed Forces program, October 2, 1942.
Location: National Archives of Canada, Audio-Visual Holdings.

J49 Address to the sixty-second annual convention of the American Federation of Labor, at the Royal York Hotel, Toronto, October 9, 1942.
Location: National Archives of Canada, Audio-Visual Holdings.

J50 Address to the Pilgrims of the United States on Canada's war contribution to the war effort, New York City, December 2, 1942.
Location: National Archives of Canada, Audio-Visual Holdings; Milo Ryan Phonoarchive, University of Washington.

J51 Broadcast entitled 'Temperance and a total war effort' from Ottawa, December 16, 1942.
Location: National Archives of Canada, Audio-Visual Holdings.

J52 Talk for CBC 'Government of Canada' series, January 23, 1943.
Location: National Archives of Canada, Audio-Visual Holdings.

J53 Address to the Canadian Club, Royal York Hotel, Toronto, April 19, 1943.
Location: National Archives of Canada, Audio-Visual Holdings.

J54 Talk in the Fourth Victory Loan Campaign, May 21, 1943.
Location: National Archives of Canada, Audio-Visual Holdings.

J55 Remarks on welcoming Madame Chiang Kai-shek in the House of Commons, Ottawa, June 16, 1943.
Location: National Archives of Canada, Audio-Visual Holdings.

J56 Broadcast on the Sicilian campaign and the overthrow of Mussolini, August 2, 1943.
Location: National Archives of Canada, Audio-Visual Holdings.

J57 Broadcast on the landing of Canadian troops in the Aleutian Islands and the occupation of Kiska by Canadians, August 21, 1943.
Location: National Archives of Canada, Audio-Visual Holdings.

J58 Talk at the public reception to President Franklin D. Roosevelt on Parliament Hill, Ottawa, August 25, 1943.
Location: National Archives of Canada, Audio-Visual Holdings.

J59 Radio Talk about the surrender of Italy, on the Canadian Broadcasting Corporation, September 10, 1943.
Location: National Archives of Canada, Audio-Visual Holdings.

J60 Talk on the Canadian Broadcasting Corporation, December 4, 1943.
Location: National Archives of Canada, Audio-Visual Holdings.

J61 Broadcast to the British Broadcasting Corporation with his Christmas message to Canadian forces overseas, December 22, 1943.
Location: National Archives of Canada, Audio-Visual Holdings.

J62 Address of tribute to Sir William Mulock on the occasion of his one hundredth birthday, January 19, 1944.
Location: National Archives of Canada, Audio-Visual Holdings.

J63 Talk in London on the military collaboration between the Commonwealth nations and other free nations, May 12, 1944. [Broadcast on the British Broadcasting Corporation and the Canadian Broadcasting Corporation].
Location: National Archives of Canada, Audio-Visual Holdings.

J64 Address delivered before the joint Houses of Parliament of the United Kingdom, Westminster, London, May 11, 1944.
Location: National Archives of Canada, Audio-Visual Holdings; British Broadcasting Corporation Sound Archives, 7650–7654.

J65 Speech delivered at a civic reception sponsored by the City of Ottawa, May 25, 1944.
Location: National Archives of Canada, Audio-Visual Holdings.

J66 Remarks of introduction of John Curtin, Prime Minister of Australia, to both Houses of Parliament, Parliament Buildings, Ottawa, June 1, 1944.
Location: National Archives of Canada, Audio-Visual Holdings.

J67 Radio talk on the invasion of Western Europe by Allied Forces, June 6, 1944.
Location: National Archives of Canada, Audio-Visual Holdings.

J68 Remarks of introduction of Peter Fraser, Prime Minister of New Zealand, to both Houses of Parliament, Parliament Buildings, Ottawa, June 30, 1944.
Location: National Archives of Canada, Audio-Visual Holdings.

J69 Remarks of introduction of Charles de Gaulle on Parliament Hill, Ottawa, July 11, 1944.
Location: National Archives of Canada, Audio-Visual Holdings.

J70 Speech delivered at complimentary dinner held by the Liberal Party of Canada in honour of the 25th anniversary of his leadership of the Liberal Party, August 7, 1944.
Location: National Archives of Canada, Audio-Visual Holdings.

J71 Broadcast on the opening of the seventh Victory Loan Campaign, Ottawa, October 21, 1944.
Location: National Archives of Canada, Audio-Visual Holdings.

J72 Remarks at a ceremony on Parliament Hill, Ottawa, celebrating the launching of nine Canadian ships by nine repatriated servicemen in a program to promote the seventh Victory Loan Campaign, October 26, 1944.
Location: National Archives of Canada, Audio-Visual Holdings.

J73 Broadcast relating to Canada's support of the Army overseas from Ottawa, November 8, 1944.
Location: National Archives of Canada, Audio-Visual Holdings.

J74 Talk on 'Canada Calling,' a program to inaugurate the CBC International Service, February 25, 1945.
Location: National Archives of Canada, Audio-Visual Holdings.

J75 Talk on plans of Canadian government to postpone the next general election because of the end of the war, March 2, 1945.
Location: National Archives of Canada, Audio-Visual Holdings.

J76 Address delivered during the second plenary session of the United Nations Conference on International Organization, San Francisco, April 27, 1945.
Location: National Archives of Canada, Audio-Visual Holdings.

J77 Radio talk about the end of the war in Europe from San Francisco, May 8, 1945.
Location: National Archives of Canada, Audio-Visual Holdings; British Broadcasting Corporation Sound Archives, 8712.

J78 Speech delivered at a dinner held at the Macdonald Hotel, Edmonton, by the Alberta Liberal Association, during the federal election campaign, May 18, 1945.
Location: National Archives of Canada, Audio-Visual Holdings.

J79 Speech delivered at a public meeting in Prince Albert, Saskatchewan, during the federal election campaign, May 19, 1945.
Location: National Archives of Canada, Audio-Visual Holdings.

J80 Speech delivered at a public meeting held in the Civic Auditorium, Winnipeg, during the federal election campaign, May 24, 1945.
Location: National Archives of Canada, Audio-Visual Holdings.

J81 Talk in Winnipeg during the federal election campaign, May 30, 1945.
Location: National Archives of Canada, Audio-Visual Holdings.

J82 Speech on the results of the 1945 general election and the re-election of the Liberal Party, June 11, 1945.
Location: National Archives of Canada, Audio-Visual Holdings.

J83 Remarks recorded at the signing of the United Nations Charter, San Francisco, June 26, 1945.
Location: National Archives of Canada, Audio-Visual Holdings; G. Robert Vincent National Voice Library.

J84 Remarks on the end of the war in Japan, August 14, 1945.
Location: National Archives of Canada, Audio-Visual Holdings.

J85 Remarks on introduction of Clement Attlee, Prime Minister of the United Kingdom, before both Houses of the Canadian Parliament, Ottawa, November 19, 1945.
Location: National Archives of Canada, Audio-Visual Holdings.

J86 Remarks of introduction and welcome to Viscount Alexander of Tunis as he arrived in Canada to assume the governor generalship, Ottawa, April 12, 1946.
Location: National Archives of Canada, Audio-Visual Holdings.

J87 Address introducing Herbert Hoover at the Chateau Laurier, Ottawa, June 28, 1946.
Location: National Archives of Canada, Audio-Visual Holdings.

J88 Broadcast in 'The Nation's Business' series on the Canadian Broadcasting Corporation on the policies of the Liberal Party since the end of the war and plans for the postwar period, July 3, 1946.
Location: National Archives of Canada, Audio-Visual Holdings.

J89 Address to the Peace Conference at Paris, August 2, 1946.
Location: National Archives of Canada, Audio-Visual Holdings.

J90 Talk on the second anniversary of the landing of the Canadian troops at Dieppe during a visit to Dieppe, August 18, 1946.
Location: National Archives of Canada, Audio-Visual Holdings.

J91 Remarks at the National Citizenship ceremony in the Supreme Court Building, January 3, 1947.
Location: National Archives of Canada, Audio-Visual Holdings.

J92 Remarks on introducing President Harry S Truman at a session of both Houses of the Canadian Parliament, Ottawa, June 11, 1947.
Location: National Archives of Canada, Audio-Visual Holdings.

J93 Address at the opening of the Marian Congress, Ottawa, June 18, 1947.
Location: National Archives of Canada, Audio-Visual Holdings.

J94 Address of welcome to the Newfoundland delegation as discussions on union of Newfoundland with the Dominion opened in Ottawa, June 25, 1947.
Location: National Archives of Canada, Audio-Visual Holdings.

J95 Talk at the ceremony opening the British Section of the Canadian National Exhibition, Toronto, August 22, 1947.
Location: National Archives of Canada, Audio-Visual Holdings.

J96 Address at rural field day of Waterloo County Annual Civic Holiday, September 8, 1947.
Location: National Archives of Canada, Audio-Visual Holdings.

J97 Speech delivered at the Commonwealth Greetings Program held at the Canadian National Exhibition, Toronto, October 19, 1947. [Recorded message].
Location: National Archives of Canada, Audio-Visual Holdings.

J98 Interview on his arrival in Paris during a visit to England and the Continent, November 8, 1947.
Location: National Archives of Canada, Audio-Visual Holdings.

J99 Speech on the economic measures of the government to control the cost of living, November 17, 1947.
Location: National Archives of Canada, Audio-Visual Holdings.

J100 A message from our leader (1919–1948). 2 sides. 78 rpm. [1948].
This recording was distributed to delegates at the National Liberal Convention held in Ottawa in August 1948 to select a successor to Mackenzie King. The recording, which was contained in a red case, was accompanied by a pamphlet containing the text of the recorded message.
Location: National Archives of Canada, Audio-Visual Holdings.

J101 Speech to the National Liberal Convention following the election of Louis St Laurent as leader of the Liberal Party, August 7, 1948.
Location: National Archives of Canada, Audio-Visual Holdings.

J102 Address to the United Nations General Assembly, Paris, September 28, 1948.
Location: National Archives of Canada, Audio-Visual Holdings.

J103 Farewell address to the people of Canada on his retirement as Prime Minister, November 15, 1948.
Location: National Archives of Canada, Audio-Visual Holdings.

Commercially Released Recordings

J104 The message of the carillon, by the Right Honourable W.L. Mackenzie King, Prime Minister of Canada. HMV 216504–B. 78 rpm.
Actual moments during the playing of the carillon bell, Victory Tower, Ottawa, July 1, 1927. 'O Canada,' 'God Save the King.' Percival Price, Carillonneur. HMV 216504–A. 78 rpm.

SECTION K

Prefaces, Forewords, and Introductions by Mackenzie King

Mackenzie King wrote prefaces, forewords, and introductions for several books and publications during his lifetime.

The entries in this section have been arranged chronologically.

K1 KING, DOUGALL MACDOUGALL. *Nerves and personal power: Some principles of psychology as applied to conduct and health.* New York, Chicago, London, and Edinburgh: Fleming H. Revell Company, 1922. xiii, 311 p.
'Introduction': pp. i–x.

K2 DUNHAM, BERTHA MABEL. *The trail of the Conestoga.* Toronto: Macmillan Company of Canada, 1924. 342 p.
'Foreword': by W.L. Mackenzie King: p. [vii].

K3 CANADA. DEPARTMENT OF THE INTERIOR. *Prince Albert National Park,* by M.B. Williams. [Ottawa; King's Printer, 1930]. 24 p.
'Foreword': p. 4.

K4 QUEEN'S UNIVERSITY. *Queen's University in summer.* [Kingston: Queen's University, 1936?]. 8 p.
'The Premier's Message, The Rt. Hon. William Lyon Mackenzie King, P.C., C.M.G., M.P., LL.D., F.R.S.C., Prime Minister of Canada': p. [1].

K5 QUEEN'S UNIVERSITY. *Queen's: Our Alma Mater, 1841–1941. A statement to graduates and former students, from J.C. Macfarlane,*

Arts '11, Chairman, Endowment Committee. [Kingston: Queen's University, 1941]. 16 p.
[Message from] the Rt. Hon. W.L. Mackenzie King: p. [1].

K6 LEACOCK, STEPHEN, and LESLIE ROBERTS. *Canada's war at sea.* Montreal: Alvan M. Beatty Publications (1943) Limited. 2 v.
Volume 1: *Canada and the Sea,* by Stephen Leacock.
'Foreword by the Prime Minister': p. [5].

K7 Plan for the national capital. General report submitted to the National Capital Planning Committee. [Ottawa: King's Printer, 1950]. vi, 308 p.
'Foreword': p. iii.

K8 Projet d'aménagement de la capitale nationale. Rapport général soumis au Comité d'aménagement de la capitale nationale. [Ottawa: Imprimeur du Roi, 1950]. vi, 308 p.
'Avant-propos': p. iii.

SECTION L

Speeches and Letters Contained in Larger Works

A number of Mackenzie King's speeches and letters have been published in larger works. For the most part they have appeared only in the books and government publications listed below.

The entries in this section have been arranged chronologically, and the page references of the material by King have been listed unless there are too many items by King in a single document to provide detailed references to each King speech or letter.

L1 *Addresses delivered before the Canadian Club of Toronto, Season of 1912–1913.* Edited by the Literary Correspondent. Toronto: Warwick Bro's & Rutler, Limited, 1913. v, 279 p.
'Canada and the Navy' [March 10, 1913]: pp. 215–225.

L2 The Canadian Society of New York, *Year Book*, 1914. [New York, 1914]. 96 p.
[Address delivered at the annual dinner on December 10, 1913] William Lyon Mackenzie King: pp. 63–71.

L3 *The National Liberal Convention, Ottawa, August 5, 6, 7, 1919. The story of the convention and the report of its proceedings.* [Ottawa, 1919]. 214 p.
[Address on] 'Labor and Industrial Conditions': pp. 126–134.
[Address following election as Liberal Leader]: pp. 197–200.

L4 [ROSE, GEORGE M.] *In memory of the late Hon. William Costello Kennedy, P.C., M.P.* [Toronto: Hunter-Rose Co. Limited, 1923]. 44 p.
'Tributes in the House of Commons: Mr King': pp. 13–14.

L5 *Correspondence with the Canadian Government on the subject of the peace settlement with Turkey.* [British Parliamentary Papers, Cmd. 2146]. London: His Majesty's Stationery Office, 1924. 11 p.

L6 *British preference. Correspondence between the Prime Minister and members of the British Government.* Ottawa: King's Printer, 1924. 7 p. [Sessional Paper 111–1924].

L7 *The Department of Trade and Commerce, Canada. Report of proceedings of the Canada–West Indies Conference, 1925, with the Canada–British West Indies–Bermuda–British Guiana–British Honduras Trade Agreement, 1925.* Ottawa: King's Printer, 1925. 273 p.
[Address of William Lyon Mackenzie King, June 19, 1925]: pp. 2–5.

L8 *The ninetieth birthday of Charles William Elliot: Proceedings in Sanders Theatre and the Yard, March 20, 1924.* (Cambridge: Harvard University Press, 1925). 262 p.
[Telegram from] 'William Lyon Mackenzie King': p. 25.

L9 *Report of proceedings of the World's Poultry Congress, Ottawa, Canada, July 27 to August 4, Nineteen Hundred and Twenty-Seven, held under the distinguished patronage of His Excellency the Governor General of Canada.* [Ottawa, 1928]. xx, 538 p.
[Address by] Right Honourable W.L. Mackenzie King: pp. 3–5.

L10 *Rapport des délibérations du Congrès mondial d'aviculture, Ottawa, Canada, du 27 juillet au 4 août, dix-neuf cent vingt-sept. Tenu sous le haut patronage de son excellence le gouverneur-général du Canada.* [Ottawa: Mortimer Company Limited, 1928]. 582 p.
[Discours par] le très honorable W.L. Mackenzie King: pp. 3–5.

L11 *Report of the Executive Committee, National Diamond Jubilee of Confederation.* Ottawa: King's Printer, 1928. 122 p.
'Copy of message sent by the Prime Minister to the Premiers of the Canadian Provinces, June 30, 1927': p. 107.
[Address by the Right Honourable W.L. Mackenzie King at the laying of the cornerstone of the new departmental building, July 1, 1927]: pp. 76–77.
[Address by the Right Honourable W.L. Mackenzie King at the inauguration of the carillon, July 1, 1927]: pp. 77–81.
[Address by the Right Honourable W.L. Mackenzie King on Parliament Hill, July 1, 1927]: pp. 87–91.
[Address by the Right Honourable W.L. Mackenzie King at the

conclusion of the ceremony on Parliament Hill, July 1, 1927]: pp. 99–100.

[Address of welcome by the Right Honourable W.L. Mackenzie King to Colonel Charles Lindbergh, July 2, 1927]: pp. 100–101.

L12 *Twentieth Century Liberal Association of Canada. Report of Inaugural Meeting, Ottawa, March 19, 1930. Citizenship as politics, by Rt. Hon. W.L. Mackenzie King, M.P., Prime Minister of Canada. Hints on organization.* [Ottawa: Twentieth Century Liberal Association of Canada, 1930]. 31 p.

'Citizenship and politics: Address delivered by Right Hon. W.L. Mackenzie King, M.P., Prime Minister of Canada, at the Inaugural Banquet of the Twentieth Century Liberal Association of Canada': pp. 13–25.

L13 Martin, Chester, William Stewart Wallace, and T.C. Routley, eds. *The book of Canada. Published by the Canadian Medical Association on the occasion of the meeting of the British Medical Association in Winnipeg, August, 1930.* Toronto: Canadian Medical Assocation, 1930. xiii, 258 p.

'Message from the Prime Minister of Canada': p. xiii.

L14 *Correspondance relative à la rétrocession des ressources naturelle de l'Alberta. Session de 1930.* Ottawa: Imprimeur du Roi, 1931. 6 p.

[Lettre du premier ministre à l'honorable J.E. Brownlee, Premier ministre de l'Alberta, le 5 octobre 1929]: p. 4.

[Télégramme du prime ministre à l'honorable J.E. Brownlee, le 30 novembre 1929]: p. 6.

L15 *Return re transfer of Alberta natural resources, 1930 session.* Ottawa: King's Printer, 1931. 6 p.

[Letter from the prime minister to the Hon. J.E. Brownlee, Premier of Alberta, October 5, 1929]: p. 4.

[Telegram from the prime minister to the Hon. J.E. Brownlee, Premier of Alberta, November 30, 1929]: p. 6.

L16 *Correspondance relative à la rétrocession des ressources naturelles du Manitoba, Session de 1930.* Ottawa: Imprimeur du Roi, 1931. 6 p.

[Télégramme du le premier ministre à l'honorable John Bracken, le 12 juin 1929]: p. 3.

[Télégramme du premier ministre à l'honorable John Bracken, le 18 juin 1929]: p. 3.

[Lettre du premier ministre à l'honorable John Bracken, le 16 août 1929]: p. 6.

L17 *Return re transfer of Manitoba natural resources, 1930 session.* Ottawa: King's Printer, 1931. 6 p.

[Telegram from the prime minister to Hon. John Bracken, Premier of Manitoba, June 12, 1929]: p. 3.

[Telegram from the prime minister to the Hon. John Bracken, Premier of Manitoba, June 18, 1929]: p. 3.

[Letter from the prime minister to the Hon. John Bracken, Premier of Manitoba, August 16, 1929]: p. 6.

L18 *Correspondance relative à la rétrocession des ressources naturelle de la Saskatchewan, Session de 1930.* Ottawa: Imprimeur du Roi, 1931, 16 p.

[Lettre du premier ministre à l'honorable J.T.M. Anderson, premier ministre de la Saskatchewan, le 4 octobre 1929]: pp. 3–4.

[Télégramme du premier ministre à l'honorable J.T.M. Anderson, premier ministre de Saskatchewan, le 7 novembre 1929]: p. 5.

[Télégramme du premier ministre à l'honorable J.M. Anderson, le 31 décembre 1929]: pp. 7–8.

[Télégramme du premier ministre à l'honorable J.M. Anderson, le 31 décembre 1929]: p. 9.

L19 *Return re transfer of Saskatchewan natural resources, 1930 session.* Ottawa: King's Printer, 1931. 10 p.

[Letter from the prime minister to the Hon. J.T.M. Anderson, Premier of Saskatchewan, October 4, 1929]: pp. 3–4.

[Telegram from the prime minister to the Hon. J.T.M. Anderson, Premier of Saskatchewan, November 7, 1929]: p. 5.

[Letter from the prime minister to the Hon. J.T.M. Anderson, December 31, 1929]: pp. 8–9.

[Telegram from the prime minister to the Hon. J.T.M. Anderson, December 31, 1929]: p. 9.

L20 *The Liberal way: A record of opinion on Canadian problems as expressed and discussed at the first Liberal Summer Conference, Port Hope, September, 1933.* (Toronto and Vancouver: J.M. Dent & Sons Limited, 1933).

'The practice of Liberalism': pp. 269–287.

L21 *Documents relating to the Italo-Ethiopan conflict.* Ottawa: King's Printer, 1936. 182 p.
'Statement given to the press by the Secretary of State for External Affairs, October 29, 1935': pp. 165–166.

L22 *Dominion-Provincial Conference, 1935. Record of proceedings, Ottawa, December 9–13, 1935.* Ottawa: King's Printer, 1936. 74 p.

L23 *Imperial Conference, 1937. Summary of proceedings.* Ottawa: King's Printer, 1937. 73 p.
'[Opening] Statement by the Prime Minister of Canada': pp. 48–52.
'[Concluding] Statement of the Prime Minister of Canada': pp. 64–66.

L24 *Correspondence relating to the Kenogami River (Long Lake) Project and export of electrical power. (Supplement to publication tabled in the House of Commons, February 28, 1938, entitled 'Correspondence and documents relating to the St Lawrence Deep Waterway Treaty 1932, Niagara Convention 1929, and Ogoki River and Kenogami River (Long Lake) Projects and export of electrical power.').* Ottawa: King's Printer, 1938. 16 p.
'[Letter] From the Prime Minister of Canada to the Premier of Ontario, March 1, 1938': p. 8.
'[Letter] From the Prime Minister of Canada to the Premier of Ontario, March 21, 1938': p. 16.

L25 *Speeches by the King and Queen during Their Majesties' visit to Canada, 1939. Also speeches by the Right Honourable W.L. Mackenzie King, Prime Minister of Canada, the Honourable Senator Raoul Dandurand, Leader of the Government in the Senate, The Right Honourable Sir Frank Bowater, Lord Mayor of London (England). Discours du Roi et de la Reine au cours de la visite de Leurs Majestes au Canada, 1939. Ainsi que les discours, du très honorable W.L. Mackenzie King, premier ministre du Canada, de l'honorable sénateur Raoul Dandurand, représentant du Gouvernement au Sénat, du très honorable Sir Frank Bowater, lord-maire de Londres.* [Ottawa: King's Printer/Imprimeur du Roi, 1939]. 72 p.
'The speech of The Right Honourable W.L. Mackenzie King, Prime Minister of Canada, at the luncheon given by His Majesty's Government in Canada, welcoming King George VI and Queen Elizabeth on Their Majesties' arrival in Canada, at the Chateau Frontenac, Quebec, May 17th, 1939': pp. 3–6.

'The cablegram from The Right Honourable W.L. Mackenzie King, Prime Minister of Canada, to the Lord Mayor of London, read by the Lord Mayor at the Royal Luncheon at Guildhall upon Their Majesties' return from Canada and the United States of America, June 23rd, 1939': p. 34.

The French section of this publication contains the following:

'Traduction du discours du très honorable W.L. Mackenzie King, Premier ministre du Canada, pour souhaiter la bienvenue au Roi George VI et à la Reine Elizabeth, à l'occasion de l'arrivée de Leurs Majestés au Canada, au déjeuner offert par le gouvernement de Sa Majesté au Canada, au Château Frontenac, Quebec, le 17 mai 1939': pp. 39–42.

'Traduction du cablogramme du très honorable W.L. Mackenzie King, premier ministre du Canada, au lord-maire de Londres, lu par le lord-maire au déjeuner royal du Guildhall, au retour de Leurs Majestés du Canada et des États-Unis d'Amérique, le 23 juin 1939': p. 72.

L26 *Documents relating to the outbreak of war, September, 1939. A. Communications exchanged between His Majesty's Government in the United Kingdom and the Government of the Reich, between the 22nd of August and the 3rd of September, 1939, together with statements made in the House of Commons by the Prime Minister of the United Kingdom. B. Communciations addressed by the Prime Minister of Canada to the Heads of certain European States in August, 1939, and replies thereto.* [Ottawa: King's Printer, 1939]. 40 p.

'Telegram from the Prime Minister of Canada to the President of the Polish Republic, 25th August, 1939': p. 38.

'Telegram from the Prime Minister of Canada to the Chief of the Government of Italy, 25th August, 1939': p. 38

'Telegram from the Prime Minister of Canada to Herr Hitler, Reichsfuhrer, 25th August, 1939': p. 38.

L27 *Canada carries on. Review of the war effort of the Dominion as presented to the House of Commons, July 29–30, 1940.* [Ottawa, 1940]. 43 p.

'The Prime Minister [July 29, 1940]': pp. 3–6.

L28 *Le Canada en guerre. Une revue de l'effort de guerre de notre Dominion, telle que faite à la Chambre des communes, les 29 et 30 juillet 1940.* Ottawa: Service de l'Information, 1940. 46 p.

'Le premier ministre': pp. 3–7.

L29 *Correspondence and documents relating to the Great Lakes–St Lawrence Basin development, 1938–1941.* Ottawa: King's Printer, 1941. vi, 73 p.

L30 *Correspondance et documents relatifs à la canalisation du Bassin des Grands Lacs et du Saint-Laurent, 1938–1941.* Ottawa: Imprimeur du Roi, 1941. vi, 77 p.

L31 *Dominion–Provincial Conference, Tuesday, January 14, 1941 and Wednesday, January 15, 1941.* Ottawa: King's Printer, 1941. 100 p.

L32 *Canada carries on (No. 2). A review by Cabinet ministers ... taken from reports presented to the House of Commons, November–December, 1940.* [Ottawa: Director of Public Information, 1940]. 164 p.
'The Prime Minister, Rt. Hon. W.L. Mackenzie King, 12th November 1940': pp. 5–41.
'The Prime Minister, Rt. Hon. W.L. Mackenzie King, 2nd December 1940': pp. 153–164.

L33 *Le Canada en guerre (no. 2). Une revue de notre effort de guerre, d'après les déclarations faites à la Chambre des communes, à l'automne, 1940.* [Ottawa: Le Service de l'Information, 1940]. 169 p.
'Le premier ministre, le très hon. W.L. Mackenzie King, le 12 novembre 1940': pp. 4–41.
'Le premier ministre, le très hon. W.L. Mackenzie King, le 2 decembre 1940': pp. 157–169.

L34 *Christmas Day message from His Majesty King George VI to his people, broadcast from London, England, December 25th, 1940. Christmas Day message from Prime Minister Mackenzie King to the Canadian Army abroad and at home. Prime Minister Churchill's address to the Italian people, December 23rd, 1940.* [Winnipeg: Universal Life Assurance and Annuity Company, 1940?]. 16 p.
[Prime Minister King's message broadcast to the Armed Forces on Christmas Day]: pp. 6–7.

L35 *'Put your confidence in us. Give us your faith and your blessing, and under Providence all will be well.' Rt. Hon. Winston Churchill, P.C., C.H., M.P., Prime Minister of Great Britain. Message from the Prime Minister to the people of the British Empire and the United States, broadcast throughout the world from London, February 9th, 1941. 'There is only one way to meet total war and that is by total effort.' Rt. Hon. W.L. Mackenzie King, P.C., M.P., Prime Minister of Canada. Message from*

Prime Minister Mackenzie King to the people of Canada, broadcast from Ottawa, February 2nd, 1941. [Winnipeg: The Universal Life Assurance Company, 1941]. 32 p.
'"There is only way to meet total war and that is by total effort." The Canadian Prime Minister's address': pp. 19–28.

L36 *Commemoration service. Fiftieth anniversary of the death of Sir John A. Macdonald, June 6th, 1941. June 7th, 1941.* [Kingston? 1941?]. 25 p.
'Address by the Right Honourable W.L. Mackenzie King, P.C., LL.D., Prime Minister of Canada': pp. 9–12.

L37 BROADFOOT, S. RUPERT. *Holidaying in Canada on the Ottawa River.* [Ottawa, 1941]. 203 p.
'Canada speaks' [Message from Mackenzie King 'To the citizens of the United States,]: p. 6.

L38 *Canada and the war. An address to the Houses of Parliament, by the Right Honourable Winston Churchill, Prime Minister of Great Britain, and proceedings incidental thereto, December 30, 1941.* Ottawa: King's Printer, 1941. 11 p.
'Introduction by Right Hon. W.L. Mackenzie King, Prime Minister of Canada': pp. 3–4.

L39 *Ottawa Air Training Conference, May, 1942. Report of the Conference.* Ottawa: King's Printer, 1942. 25 p.
'Opening statement [by] the Prime Minister of Canada, the Right Honourable W.L. Mackenzie King': pp. 9–12.

L40 *Opportunity for youth! A report on the National Convention of Young Liberals, Fort Garry Hotel, Winnipeg, May 29–30, 1944.* [N.p., 1944]. 16 p.
'Greetings from the Prime Minister': p. 1.

L41 *Wartime economic stabilization to keep down the cost of living in Canada. What it is – how it works – Why it must be supported.* [Ottawa, 1944]. 16 p.
'We must hold the line' by W.L. Mackenzie King: [pp. 1–2].

L42 *La famille: allocations familiales.* Ottawa: La fédération Libérale nationale, 1944. 21 p.
[Excerpts from an address by Mackenzie King, July 25, 1944]: pp. 2–13.

L43 *Dominion–Provincial Conference (1945). Dominion and provincial submis-*

sions and plenary conference discussions. Ottawa: King's Printer, 1946. xi, 624 p.

L44 *Report on the United Nations Conference on International Organization, held at San Francisco, 25th April–26th June, 1945.* Ottawa: King's Printer, 1945. 138 p. (Department of External Affairs, Conference Series, 1945, No. 2).

[Address by the Prime Minister of Canada at the second plenary session of the Conference on April 27, 1945]: pp. 10–12.

L45 *Memorial ceremony in honor of Franklin Delano Roosevelt, Campobello, New Brunswick, August 1, 1946.* [Sackville: The Tribune Press, 1946]. 19 p.

'Prime Minister King's Message': pp. 9–14.

L46 *Dominion–Provincial Conference. Correspondence since the budget of 1946 on matters of substance regarding tax agreements with the Provinces.* Ottawa: King's Printer, 1947. 67 p.

Includes copies of correspondence between Prime Minister Mackenzie King and the provincial leaders.

L47 *Canada. Proposed arrangements for the entry of Newfoundland into Confederation. Terms believed to constitute a fair and equitable basis for union of Newfoundland with Canada should the people of Newfoundland desire to enter into Confederation. October 29, 1947.* Ottawa: King's Printer, 1948. 28 p.

'Letter from the Prime Minister of Canada to the Governor of Newfoundland': pp. 3–4.

'Speech by the Prime Minister of Canada, the Right Honourable W.L. Mackenzie King, at the first meeting between delegates from the National Convention of Newfoundland and representatives of the Government of Canada on June 25, 1947': pp. 23–25.

L48 *Report of the proceedings of the National Liberal Convention called by the National Liberal Federation of Canada at the request of Rt. Hon. W.L. Mackenzie King, P.C., O.M., M.P., Thursday, Friday, Saturday, August 5th, 6th, 7th, 1948, The Coliseum, Ottawa, Canada.* [Ottawa: National Liberal Federation of Canada, 1948]. 259 p.

'Call for a convention' [Speech of January 20, 1948, at a dinner of the National Liberal Federation of Canada]: pp. 5–13.

[Address of welcome to delegates and to declare the convention open]: pp. 49–51.

'Address to Convention': pp. 110–124.
[Address following the election of Louis St Laurent as leader of the Liberal Party]: pp. 232–234.

L49 OLLIVIER, MAURICE, compiler and editor. *The Colonial and Imperial Conferences from 1887 to 1937.* Volume 3. Ottawa: King's Printer, 1954.
This collection contains several speeches delivered by Mackenzie King at the Imperial Conferences of 1923, 1926, and 1937.

L50 *Report and documents relating to the negotiations for the union of Newfoundland with Canada.* Ottawa: King's Printer, 1956. 91 p. (Department of External Affairs, Conference Series, 1948, No. 2).
'Letter from the Prime Minister of Canada to the Governor of Newfoundland, dated October 2, 1947, submitting proposed arrangements for the entry of Newfoundland into Confederation': pp. 57–70.
'Statement issued by the Right Hon. W.L. Mackenzie King on July 30, 1948 [regarding the Second Poll of the National Referendum]': pp. 76–77.

L51 *Foreign relations of the United States, 1946, Volume III: Paris Peace Conference: Proceedings.* Washington: United States Government Printing Office, 1970. xl, 882 p.
[Address at the] Fifth Plenary Meeting, August 2, 1946: pp. 88–92.

L52 [Letter from William Lyon Mackenzie King to Jessie Low, March 28, 1921], 'Prime Ministers' Packet,' *Douglas Library Notes,* 9 (3), December 1960, p. 4.

SECTION M

Miscellaneous

A few items do not fit easily into any of the other sections of writings by Mackenzie King. Thus, they have been listed in this final section of Part 1. Entries are arranged chronologically.

M1 [University of Toronto]. *Students' handbook, '93–94. Presented by the Young Men's Christian Association of the University of Toronto.* [Toronto: Roswell & Hutchison, 1893]. 52 p.
Reference: Diary, September 7, 1893.

King noted in his diary that he aided in the preparation of this handbook. The fact that the John King Papers contains a copy of this handbook indicates that Mackenzie King contributed substantially to the compilation of this publication.

M2 *Report of hours and other conditions in the smaller mercantile establishment of Boston and vicinity: An investigation conducted for Consumer's League of Massachusetts.* [Boston, 1898]. 26 p. (Church social union Publication No. 53).

M3 *Industrial Disputes Investigation Act (1907).*[108] 20 p.

M4 *Loi des enquêtes en matière différends industriels, 1907.*[109] 16 p.

---

108 The full title of the statute is 'An Act to aid in the Prevention and Settlement of Strikes and Lockouts in mines and industries connected with Public Utilities.'

109 The full title is 'Loi ayant pour objet d'aider à prévenir et à régler les grèves et les contre-grèves dans les mines et dans les exploitations de services publics.'

Of this statute King wrote in his diary: 'God has given me the opportunity to frame this measure, & I have done it along lines & in a manner which I believe will further His will among men.'[110]

The bill received first reading in the House of Commons on December 17, 1906, King's birthday. Second and third readings took place on February 14 and March 19 respectively. It was passed in the Senate on March 21, 1907. It received royal assent on March 22, 1907.

For King's description of the enactment of this act, see *Industry and Humanity*, pp. 503–513.

M5 *An Act to prohibit the importation, manufacture and sale of opium for other than medicinal purposes.* 1 p.

M6 *Loi prohibant l'importation, la fabrication et la vente de l'opium à toutes fins autres que celles de la médecine.* 1 p.

The bill received first reading in the House of Commons on July 10, 1908. Second and third readings took place on July 13, 1908. It was passed in the Senate on July 17, 1908. It received royal assent on July 20, 1908.

Reference: Robert MacGregor Dawson, *William Lyon Mackenzie King: A political biography, 1874–1923*, p. 147.

M7 *What the Laurier Government has done for labour.* [Ottawa: Liberal Party, 1908]. 38 p.

Reference: King Diary, August 29, 1908.

In his diary, King noted that the pamphlet was to be entitled 'The Liberal Party and the working man.' However, the title appears to have been changed.

M8 *Proceedings of the Special Committee on Bill No. 21, 'An Act respecting hours of labour on public works,' comprising reports, evidence and correspondence, December 9, 1909–May 3, 1910.* Ottawa: King's Printer, 1910. 758 p. [Published as Appendix No. 4 to the House of Commons Journals, 1909–1910].

Mackenzie King was chairman of the committee.

M9 *61st Congress, 2d session. Senate Document No. 537. Wages and prices of commodities. Abstract from the proceedings of the [Canadian] House of*

110 King Diary, January 3, 1907.

Commons, April 12, 1910, relative to the 'Combines Investigation Act.' May 10, 1910. Referred to the Select Committee [of the United States Senate] to investigate wages and prices of commodities, and ordered to be printed. [Washington: Government Printing Office, 1910]. 61st Congress, 2d Session. Senate Documents, vol. 46. 45 p.

M10 *Letter from Mackenzie King to W.H.S. Cane, referred to in communication herewith to the men of North York overseas.* [Newmarket, November 8, 1917]. Newmarket: Era Print, 1917. 1 p.

M11 *Industry and humanity: A study in the principles underlying industrial reconstruction. Letter of transmittal to the trustees of the Rockefeller Foundation.* [Ottawa, 1918]. 8 p.

M12 *Correspondence with Governor General re dissolution of Parliament, 1926.* Ottawa: King's Printer, 1927. 6 p.

M13 'Department of Labour' [Chapter in William James Loudon, *Sir William Mulock: A short biography* (Toronto: Macmillan Company of Canada Limited, 1932), pp. 106–134].

In April 1931 Professor W.J. Loudon of the University of Toronto, who was writing a biography of Sir William Mulock, sent a two-page outline of a chapter on the Department of Labour, at Mulock's suggestion, to King, recommending that he write the chapter along the lines indicated and that he fill in certain dates as well.[111]

While King was too occupied with the parliamentary session to do any immediate work on the chapter, he agreed to write some material as soon as Parliament had adjourned.[112] It was not until September that King was able to proceed with the writing of the chapter. On September 7 he was able to make a beginning on the work at Kingswood, his home at Kingsmere during his days in the Department of Labour.[113] During the next two weeks King spent several hours a day on the chapter. During this period he read the House of Commons and Senate *Debates* for the early 1900s, the annual reports of the Department of Labour, and several of the reports relating to the early work of the department. Some of the material he read for

111 NAC, WLMK Papers, MG 26, J 1 Series, vol. 227, pp. 159024–159027, W.J. Loudon to William Lyon Mackenzie King, April 16, 1931.

112 Ibid., pp. 159035–159036, William Lyon Mackenzie King to W.J. Loudon, May 30, 1931.

113 King Diary, September 7, 1931.

the first time. 'It shows,' he wrote, 'how pressed I have been all along that this is the first time I have read the full debate – Commons and Senate which had to do with my own appointment to the Civil Service, the first step towards the premiership of Canada.[114]

At times he thought he was probably spending too much time on the chapter. He worried that he might have been putting too much about himself in the work and that he might be credited with being the author of the chapter.[115]

On September 24 he wrote: 'I cut out about ten pages of what I had written, or rather indicated where it could be cut out.'[116] He mailed the manuscript to Loudon on September 25. 'I think the concluding pages of it are effective and moving. I feel deeply moved as I read them over.'[117]

The completed chapter appears to have been fifty-seven pages in length.[118] A comparison of the draft with the published work shows that Loudon used most of the material in the final work.

King insisted that his name should not appear in any way as far as acknowledgments were concerned in the book. On November 6 he told Loudon: 'The mention in your letter that there has been any thought of crediting me with what was written on the Department of Labour has distressed me very much, for, as I have said, I can see wherein malicious persons would be only too ready to misrepresent the whole nature of the contribution.' He went on to say that if he did not receive definite assurance that his contribution was to be 'regarded solely as raw material' for Loudon to use and that it represented Mulock's understanding of the situation, he would request the return of the manuscript immediately for the purpose of revision.[119]

A week later he wrote again to Loudon: 'It is only upon the condition that I am to be kept out of the matter altogether that, in the circumstance, I could think of permitting any use of what I have, with a good deal of time and effort, but also with real plea-

114 King Diary, September 13, 1931.
115 King Diary, September 17 and 22, 1931.
116 King Diary, September 24, 1931.
117 King Diary, September 25, 1931.
118 NAC, WLMK Papers, MG 26, J 4 Series, vols. 457–458, pp. 51524–51580.
119 Ibid., p. 159057, William Lyon Mackenzie King to W.J. Loudon, November 6, 1931.

sure, supplied.'[120] Loudon agreed to leave King's name out of the Preface and promised to send King a copy of the proofs as soon as the chapter was set in type.[121] King was very pleased with this assurance, and the production of the book proceeded. On November 27 he wrote:

> To my joy, there came to hand yesterday, Loudon's Life of Sir William Mulock. It contains the story of the creation of the Department of Labour, & circumstance of my entrance into the public service of Canada – To have that story accurately told while Sir William is still alive, means very much. It is there now a part of history & a part of my own biography. The coming when it did, was like the assurance [?] & part fulfilment of the reward of 'the crown of glory' – an assurance that history wd. not fail to record the truth & give me my proper place in relation to the work I have done, & the motives that have been the actuating ones. In view of the significance of Labour discussion in our times, I am glad the story is of record in the form it is.[122]

Of the chapter he had written he noted: 'The chapter I wrote on the Dept. of Labour does more I think than any of the others to bring out Sir William's real contribution to his day & generation.' He added: 'He has been just in publishing the true account of our relations, and I am glad it is of [*sic*] while he is still alive.'[123]

In January 1935 King reread this chapter in Loudon's work. He recorded his reactions in his diary: 'It is excellent – and its bearing on the present situation could not possibly be better than it is. Being the literal truth and with Mulock still alive it is worth everything if properly used at the present time. It should be reprinted as a pamphlet by the Liberal Information Office.'[124]

M14 *Canadian Social Science Research Council. Correspondence with the Prime Minister concerning liberal arts courses in Canadian universities.* [Ottawa: The Canadian Social Science Research Council, 1943. 11 p.

120 Ibid., p. 159062, William Lyon Mackenzie King to W.J. Loudon, November 13, 1931.
121 Ibid., W.J. Loudon to William Lyon Mackenzie King, November 16, 1931.
122 King Diary, November 27, 1932.
123 King Diary, November 27, 1932.
124 King Diary, January 19, 1935.

M15 *Amendments to the Wartime Wages Control Order, 1943. (Effected by P.C. 1727 of March 13, 1944). Statement of the Prime Minister – Explanation of the changes.* Ottawa: King's Printer, 1944. 6 p.
Statement of the Prime Minister: pp. 1–2.

M16 *Correspondance entre le premier ministre et l'honorable J.L. Ralston, M.P., concernant le démission de M Ralston comme ministre de la Défense nationale, du 1er au 14 novembre 1944.* Ottawa: Imprimeur du Roi, 1944. 15 p.

M17 *Correspondence between the Prime Minister and the Honourable J.L. Ralston, M.P., relative to the resignation of Mr Ralston as Minister of National Defence, November 1st to November 14th, 1944.* Ottawa: King's Printer, 1944. 15 p.

M18 *What the Liberals stand for. A statement by the Rt. Hon. W.L. Mackenzie King, M.P., Prime Minister of Canada. As published by Maclean's Magazine, February 1st, 1945.* [Ottawa: National Liberal Federation, 1945]. 14 p.

M19 *Declaration on atomic energy made by the President of the United States of America, the Prime Minister of the United Kingdom and the Prime Minister of Canada, at Washington, November 15, 1945.* Ottawa: King's Printer, 1945. 4 p. (Canada. Department of External Affairs, Treaty Series, 1945, no. 13).

M20 *Déclaration sur l'énergie atomique faite par le President des Éats-Unis d'Amerique, le Premier Ministere du Royaume-Uni et le Premer Ministre du Canada, à Washington, le 15 novembre 1945.* Ottawa: Imprimeur du Roi, 1945. 5 p. (Canada. Ministre des affaires extérieures, Recueil des traites, no. 1945/13).

M21 *Déclaration concordante des gouvernements du Canada et des États-Unis d'Amérique concernant la collaboration en matière de défense entre les deux pays, faite à Ottawa et à Washington le 12 février 1947.* Ottawa: Imprimeur du Roi, 1951. 5 p. (Canada. Ministère des affaires extérieures, Recueil des traites, no. 1947/43).

M22 *Joint statement of the Governments of Canada and of the United States of America regarding defence cooperation between the two countries. Made in Ottawa and Washington on February 12, 1947.* Ottawa: King's Printer, 1951. 5 p. (Canada. Department of External Affairs, Treaty Series, 1947, no. 43).

M23 *Documents instructifs et inattaquables qu'il faut lire et faire lire: Texte de la correspondence échangée entre le premier ministre King et le premier ministre Duplessis au sujet de l'assurance-chômage et au sujet du sabotage de la Constitution canadienne à propos de la redistribution des comtés.* [N.p., n.d.] 31 p.

M24 *Mackenzie King on retirement.* [Ottawa: Canada Information Agency, 1950]. 3 p.
[Comments written by King in December 1949 at the time of his seventy-fifth birthday].
'The full text did not appear during his life is here published for the first time.'

M25 'Last will and testament of the Rt. Hon. W.L. Mackenzie King.' [February 28, 1950].
Text reprinted in *The Canadian Liberal,* 10 (3), September 1950, pp. 53–56. The complete text of the will was also printed in the Ottawa *Evening Citizen,* August 11, 1950, p. 9. A French translation of the will was printed in *La Presse,* 9 août 1950, p. 19.

M26 Canadian Jewish Congress. Central Region. *Toronto Jewry 60 years ago.* Toronto, 1958. 4 p.
Excerpts from an article by Mackenzie King entitled 'Foreigners who live in Toronto,' which was published in the Toronto *Mail and Empire,* September 25, 1897.

Part Two

WORKS ABOUT MACKENZIE KING

SECTION N

Books and Pamphlets about Mackenzie King and His Era

This section contains an alphabetical listing of all books and pamphlets on Mackenzie King. In addition, a substantial number of important books related to the Mackenzie King era have been included.

This section also includes a number of important reviews of books about Mackenzie King because in most cases they are significant contributions to the literature of King and his era in Canadian history.

N1 *An Act respecting Kingsmere Park.* Ottawa: King's Printer, 1951. 3 p. (15 George VI chap. 18).

N2 *An Act respecting Laurier House.* Ottawa: King's Printer, 1951. 4 p. (15 George VI chap. 19).

N3 ALLEN, RALPH. *Ordeal by fire: Canada, 1910–1945.* Toronto: Doubleday Canada Limited, 1961. ix, 492 p. (The Canadian History Series, vol. 5, edited by Thomas B. Costain).

N4 ANDREW, ARTHUR. *The rise and fall of a middle power: Canadian diplomacy from King to Mulroney.* Toronto: James Lorimer, 1994. 186 p.

N5 *Arrangements for the state funeral of the late Right Honourable W.L. Mackenzie King, P.C., O.M. Funeral service, Wednesday, July 26, 1950 at Ottawa. Internment, Thursday, July 27, 1950 at Toronto.* [Ottawa, 1950]. 24 p.

N6 *Beckles Willson and Mackenzie King: The modern Damon and Pythias.* [Ottawa? 1930?]. 8 p.

N7 BELOFF, MAX. *Imperial sunset: Volume 2: Dream of Commonwealth, 1921–42.* London: Macmillan Press, 1989. xiv, 412 p.

N8 'Bennett and King.' *The Canadian* [Published by the Liberal-Conservative Party], 1 (9), July 16, 1930. 32 p.

N9 BENSON, NATHANIEL ANKETELL. *'In Memoriam Principis': A memorial tribute to my honoured friend the Rt. Hon. W.L. Mackenzie King, O.M., P.C. (1874–1950) on the first anniversary of his death, July 22, 1951.* (Toronto: Privately printed, 1951). 6 p.
Only fifty copies of this pamphlet were printed.

N10 BOTHWELL, ROBERT, and NORMAN HILLMER, eds. *The in-between time: Canadian foreign policy in the 1930s.* Toronto: Copp Clark, 1975. 223 p. (Issues in Canadian History Series).

N11 BRENNAN, PATRICK HARVEY. *Reporting the nation's business: Press–government relations during the Liberal years, 1935–1957.* Toronto: University of Toronto Press, 1994. 250 p.

N12 BROCKINGTON, LEONARD WALTER. *Mr Mackenzie King's public bequests: A commentary on CBC National Network, August 8, 1950.* Ottawa: Trustees of the Estate of W.L. Mackenzie King, 1950. 7 p.

N13 BURNETT, ANDREW IAN. *The Right Honourable William Lyon Mackenzie King, P.C., O.M., December 17, 1874–July 22, 1950: Memorial addresses delivered at St Andrew's Church, Ottawa, Wednesday, July 26, 1950, Sunday, July 30, 1950.* [Ottawa, 1950]. 15 p.

N14 CANADA. ARCHIVES PUBLIQUES. *Maison Laurier – Ancienne résidence de deux Premiers ministres du Canada, Sir Wilfrid Laurier et le très honorable W.L. Mackenzie King.* [Ottawa: Imprimeur du Reine, 1961]. 15 p.

N15 CANADA. COMMISSION DE LA CAPITALE NATIONALE. *Le Domaine Mackenzie-King* [Ottawa: Commission de la Capitale nationale, n.d]. 20 p.

N16 CANADA. DEPARTMENT OF EXTERNAL AFFAIRS. *Statements in 1943 and 1944 on general international organization by the Rt. Hon. W.L. Mackenzie King, Prime Minister of Canada.* Department of External Affairs, Ottawa, January 15, 1945. Ottawa: King's Printer, 1945. 12 p.

N17 CANADA. DEPARTMENT OF NORTHERN AFFAIRS AND NATIONAL RESOURCES. NATIONAL PARKS BRANCH. *Woodside National Historic Park.* [Ottawa: Queen's Printer, 1964]. 15 p.

N18 CANADA. NATIONAL CAPITAL COMMISSION. *The Mackenzie King Estate.* [Ottawa: National Capital Commission, n.d.]. 20 p.

N19 CANADA. NATIONAL HISTORIC SITES SERVICE. *Woodside National Historic Park.* Ottawa: Queen's Printer, 1971. 12 p.

N20 CANADA. PUBLIC ARCHIVES. *Laurier House – Former residence of two Prime Ministers of Canada, Sir Wilfrid Laurier and the Rt. Hon. W.L. Mackenzie King.* [Ottawa: Queen's Printer, 1961]. 15 p.

N21 – *Laurier House – Former residence of two Canadian Prime Ministers, Sir Wilfrid Laurier, Rt. Hon. William Lyon Mackenzie King, P.C., O.M.: Historical background and information for the guidance of visitors.* [Ottawa, 197?]. 8 p.

N22 *Canada's century: Sir Wilfrid Laurier to W.L. Mackenzie King.* (Montreal: Monotto Publishing Company, 1945). 16 p.

N23 *Chambre des communes, Ottawa. Dévoilements des portraits des premiers ministres canadiens en fonctions au cours des deux guerres mondiales, feu le très honorable Sir Robert L. Borden et le très honorable W.L. Mackenzie King, le 10 juin, 1947.* Ottawa: Imprimeur du Roi, 1947. 7 p.

N24 CLICHE, LOUIS-PHILIPPE. *Mackenzie King. Texte d'une causerie prononcée à la radio au poste CHLT, juin 1945.* [N.p., n.d.] 6 p.

N25 COLOMBO, JOHN ROBERT. *Mackenzie King's ghost, and other personal accounts of Canadian hauntings.* Willowdale, Ontario: Hounslow Press, 1991. 190 p.

N26 CONN, STETSON, and BYRON FAIRCHILD. *The framework of Hemispheric defence.* Washington: Office of the Chief of Military History, Department of the Army, 1960. xv, 470 p. (United States Army in World War II: Special Studies).

N27 COOK, RAMSAY. *The regenerators: Social criticism in late Victorian Canada.* Toronto: University of Toronto Press, 1985. x, 291 p.

N28 COOK, RAMSAY, ed. *The Dafoe–Sifton correspondence, 1919–1927.* Winnipeg: Manitoba Record Society, 1966. xxiii, 310 p. (Manitoba Record Society Papers, vol. 2).

N29 CRAVEN, PAUL. *'An impartial umpire': Industrial relations and the Canadian state, 1900–1911.* Toronto: University of Toronto Press, 1980. x, 386 p. (The state and economic life, 3).

N30 CREIGHTON, DONALD GRANT. *The forked road, Canada, 1939–1957.* Toronto: McClelland and Stewart, 1976. xii, 319 p. (The Canadian Centenary Series, vol. 18).

N31 DAWSON, ROBERT MacGREGOR. *Canada in world affairs: Two years of war, 1939–1941.* London, Toronto, and New York: Oxford University Press, 1943. viii, 342 p. (vol. 2).

N32 – *The Conscription Crisis of 1944.* Toronto: University of Toronto Press, 1961. 136 p.

N33 – *William Lyon Mackenzie King: A political biography, 1874–1921.* Toronto: University of Toronto Press, 1958. xiii, 521 p. [vol. 1 of the official biography].

Kingsmere Edition:

N34 *William Lyon Mackenzie King: A political biography, vol. I, 1874–1923.* By Robert MacGregor Dawson.

Super Royal Octavo format, text printed on Cortlea White with special endpapers. Pp. 536 + 18 coated inserts (including a special series printed in this edition only).

Quarter-bound by hand in green morocco leather and heavy buckram, gold leaf stamped on front and spine, gilted top, head- and tail-bands.

Three hundred and fifty hand-numbered copies of this limited edition were issued.

N35 *Le demi-successeur de Laurier: l'honorable William-Lyon Mackenzie King – ce qu'il est, ce qu'il n'est pas.* [N.p., 1925]. 2 p.

N36 DILKS, DAVID N. *Britain and Canada in the age of Mackenzie King. Part II: Britain, Canada and the wider world.* London: Canadian High Commission, 1978. 20 p. (Canada House Lecture Series Number 4).

N37 DUNSMORE, SPENCER. *Wings for victory: The British Commonwealth Air Training Plan.* Toronto: McClelland and Stewart, 1994. 399 p.

N38 DZIUBAN, STANLEY W. *Military relations between the United States and Canada, 1939–1945.* Washington: Office of the Chief of

Military History, Department of the Army, 1959. xv, 432 p. (United States Army in World War II: Special Studies).

N39 EAYRS, JAMES GEORGE. *The art of the possible: Government and foreign policy in Canada.* Toronto: University of Toronto Press, 1961. 232 p.

N40 – *In defence of Canada.* Toronto: University of Toronto Press, 1965–1973. 3 v. (Studies in the structure of power: Decision-making in Canada).

N41 ENGLISH, JOHN, and JOHN O. STUBBS, eds. *Mackenzie King: Widening the debate.* Toronto: Macmillan, 1978. ix, 253 p.

N42 ESBEREY, JOY ELAINE. *Knight of the Holy Spirit: A study of William Lyon Mackenzie King.* Toronto: University of Toronto Press, 1980. viii, 245 p.

N43 FARRIS, JOHN WALLACE DE BEQUE. *Mackenzie King – The true successor to Sir Wilfrid Laurier.* Victoria: Clarke and Stuart Company Limited, 1926. 20 p.

N44 FERNS, HENRY STANLEY, and BERNARD OSTRY. *The age of Mackenzie King: The rise of the leader.* Toronto: British Book Service, 1955. 356 p.

N45 – *The age of Mackenzie King: The rise of the leader.* Toronto: J. Lorimer, 1976. xviii, 356 p.

N46 FORSEY, EUGENE ALFRED. 'Mr Mackenzie King and the Constitution.' [Paper delivered to a joint meeting of the Canadian Historical Association and the Canadian Political Science Association, Montreal, June 6, 1951]. 21 p.

N47 FORTMANN, MICHEL. *La politique de la défense canadienne de Mackenzie King à Trudeau, 1945–1979.* Montréal: Dept. de sciences politiques, Université de Montréal, 1988. 90 p.

N48 FOSDICK, RAYMOND B. *John D. Rockefeller, Jr: A portrait* (New York: Harper and Brothers, 1956). ix, 477 p.

N49 FRASER, BLAIR. *'Here is the man who is most likely, I think, to go down in history as our greatest Prime Minister.' – Blair Fraser. Mr King. 'An intimate, revealing pen-portrait of Mr King,' by Blair Fraser, Maclean's Ottawa editor. Published by Maclean's Magazine, February 1st, 1945.* [Ottawa: National Liberal Federation, 1945]. 14 p.

N50 – *The search for identity, Canada, 1945–1967.* Toronto: Doubleday Canada Limited, and Garden City, New York: Doubleday and Company, Inc., 1967. viii, 325 p. (The Canadian History Series, vol. 6, edited by Thomas B. Costain).

N51 [GIBBONS, J.J.] *Reprint of open letters no. 1 to no. 20 to W.L. Mackenzie King.* Winnipeg: J. J. Gibbons Ltd., 1925. 20 p.

N52 GIBSON, FREDERICK WELLINGTON, and BARBARA ROBERTSON, eds. *War at Ottawa: The Grant Dexter memoranda, 1939–1945.* (Winnipeg: Manitoba Record Society, 1994). xxviii, 513 p. (Manitoba Record Society Papers, vol. 11).

N53 GITELMAN, HOWARD M. *Legacy of the Ludlow Massacre: A chapter in American industrial relations.* Philadelphia: University of Pennsylvania Press, 1988. xv, 355 p.

N54 GRAHAM, WILLIAM ROGER, ed. *The King–Byng Affair, 1926: A question of responsible government.* Toronto: Copp Clark, 1967. 140 p. (Issues in Canadian History Series).

N55 GRANATSTEIN, JACK LAWRENCE. *Canada's war: The politics of the Mackenzie King government, 1939–1945.* Toronto: Oxford University Press, 1975. 436 p.

N56 – *Conscription in the Second World War, 1939–1945: A study in political management.* Toronto: Ryerson Press, 1969. 85 p. (The Frontenac Library).

N57 – *Mackenzie King: His life and world.* Toronto and New York: McGraw-Hill Ryerson, 1977. 202 p.

N58 – *W.L. Mackenzie King.* Toronto: Fitzhenry and Whiteside, 1976. 62 p. (The Canadians).

N59 – *W.L. Mackenzie King.* Longueuil, Québec: Éditions Julienne, 1978. 62 p. (Célébrités canadiennes).
Translated by George Bryns.

N60 – and J. MACKAY HITSMAN. *Broken promises: A history of conscription in Canada.* Toronto: University of Toronto Press, 1977. 281 p.

N61 GRAY, CHARLOTTE. *Mrs King: The life and times of Isabel Mackenzie King.* Toronto: Viking, 1997. xiv, 386 p.

N62 GRIERSON, FRANK. *William Lyon Mackenzie King: A memoir for the earnest consideration of all patriotic Canadians.* Ottawa, 1952. 110 p.

N63 GROOME, AGNES JEAN. *C.C.F. foreign policy as a factor in Mackenzie King's entry into World War II.* Ottawa: Canadian Historical Association, 1974. 49 p.

N64 HARDY, HENRY REGINALD. *Mackenzie King of Canada: A biography.* Toronto: Oxford University Press, 1949. xii, 390 p.

N65 – *Mackenzie King of Canada: A biography.* Westport, Conn.: Greenwood Press, 1970. xii, 390 p.

N66 HAYDON, ANDREW. *Mackenzie King and the Liberal Party.* Toronto: Thomas Allen, 1930. 54 p.

N67 *Heroism: A collection of essays by students of Pickering College, Newmarket, based on the book, 'The Secret of Heroism' by the Right Honourable William Lyon Mackenzie King.* Newmarket, 1939. 31 p.

N68 HILLIKER, JOHN. *Canada's Department of External Affairs, vol. 1: The Early Years, 1909–45.* (Montreal and Kingston: McGill-Queen's University Press, 1990). 480 p.

N69 HILLMER, NORMAN. *Britain and Canada in the age of Mackenzie King: Part 1: The outstanding imperialist.* London: Canadian High Commission, 1978. 13 p. (Canada House Lecture Series, No. 4).

N70 *Historical background and information for the guidance of visitors. Laurier House, former residence of two Prime Ministers, Sir Wilfrid Laurier, Rt. Hon. William Lyon Mackenzie King, P.C., O.M.* [Ottawa, 1951?]. 8 p.

N71 HOLMES, JOHN WENDELL. *The shaping of peace: Canada and the search for world order, 1943–1957.* (Toronto, Buffalo, and London: University of Toronto Press, 1979–1982). 2 v.

N72 *Houses of Parliament, Ottawa. Unveiling of portraits of Canada's Prime Ministers in two world wars, the late Right Hon. Sir Robert L. Borden and the Right Hon. W.L. Mackenzie King, June 10, 1947.* Ottawa: King's Printer, 1947. 7 p.

N73 HUTCHISON, BRUCE. *The incredible Canadian: A candid portrait of Mackenzie King, his works, his times and his nation.* Toronto: Longmans, Green, 1952. 454 p.

N74 – *The incredible Canadian: A candid portrait of Mackenzie King, his works, his times and his nation.* New York: Longmans, Green, 1955. 454 p.

N75 – *The incredible Canadian: A candid portrait of Mackenzie King, his works, his times and his nation.* Toronto: Longmans, Green, 1970. x, 454 p. (A Windjammer Book). [Paperback edition].

N76 IRVINE, WILLIAM. *Political servants of capitalism: Answering Lawson and Mackenzie King.* Ottawa: Labour Publishing Company, 1933. 112 p.

N77 JONES, RICHARD. *Vers une hégémonie libérale: Aperçu de la politique canadienne de Laurier à King.* Québec: Les Presses de l'université Laval, 1980. 256 p. (Cahiers d'histoire politique, 1).

N78 *King's message to the people of Montreal.* [Montreal, n.d.]. 3 p.

N79 LA FÉDÉRATION LIBÉRALE NATIONALE. *Complot et crise.* Ottawa: La Fédération Libérale Nationale, 1944. 27 p.

N80 – *King et Québec.* Ottawa: La Fédération Libérale Nationale, 1944. 20 p.

N81 – *Mackenzie King, le 7 août 1944.* [Montréal, 1944]. 31 p.

N82 LAURENDEAU, ANDRE. *La crise de la conscription.* Montreal: Éditions du jours, 1962. 158 p.

N83 *La résidence où le très hon. W.L. Mackenzie King a vécu de 1901 à 1910. The residence where the Rt. Hon. W.L. Mackenzie King lived from 1901 to 1910.* [Ottawa, n.d.]. 3 p.

N84 LE GRIS, CLAUDE. *L'entrée du Canada sur la scène internationale (1919–1927).* Paris: Presses universitaires de France, 1966. xi, 93 p.

N85 *The life story of Mackenzie King.* [Montreal: Montreal World Publishing Company Limited, 1926]. 16 p.

N86 *Le vrai Canadien, W.L. Mackenzie King.* Montréal: Lithographie canadienne Limitée, 1945. 7 p.
Reprinted from articles appearing in 'Le Canada,' August 10, 1943, December 18, 1944, and May 1, 1945.

N87 LEWIS, JOHN. *Mackenzie King, prémier ministre du Canada: L'homme et ses idées.* Montréal: Chez les Éditeurs, 1929. 191 p.

N88 – *Mackenzie King, the man: His achievements.* Toronto: Morang, 1925. 136 p.

Limited Edition:

N89 *Mackenzie King, the man: His achievements.* Toronto: Morang, 1925. 136 p. By John Lewis.

Morang and Company of Toronto brought out this limited, de luxe edition in 1925. The title page is in two colours, red and black, and contains a vignetted portrait of King done by an artist specially commissioned for the work. The edition was limited to five hundred copies, and they were signed by Mackenzie King. Printed on Strathmore Alexandra Japan antique paper, it was bound in full maroon Australian lambskin with decorations in gold. It was printed in Scottish face 12-point type extended.[125]

N90 LINGARD, CHARLES CECIL, and REGINALD GEORGE TROTTER. *Canada in world affairs: September 1941 to May 1944.* Toronto: Oxford University Press, 1950. xii, 320 p. (vol. 3).

N91 LOCHHEAD, DOUGLAS. *Three 20th-century Canadian diarists: W.L. Mackenzie King, Charles Ritchie, Robertson Davies.* London: Canadian High Commission, 1985. 16 p. (Canada House Lecture Series No. 24).

N92 *Loi concernant la maison Laurier (Laurier House).* Ottawa: Imprimeur du Roi, 1951. 4 p. (15 George VI chap. 19).

N93 *Loi concernant le parc de Kingsmere.* Ottawa: Imprimeur du Roi, 1951. 3 p. (15 George VI chap. 18).

N94 [LUCAS, WILLIAM THOMAS].[126] *A former Progressive exposes King.* [Ottawa: National Liberal Conservative Organization, 1926]. 4 p.

N95 LUDWIG, EMIL. *Mackenzie King: A portrait sketch.* Toronto: Macmillan, 1944. 62 p.

N96 – *Mackenzie King: Esquisse d'un portrait.* Montréal: Editions de l'Arbre, 1944. 95 p.
Translated by Andre Champroux.

---

125 The de luxe edition was described in a circular issued by the publisher: *Mackenzie King, the man: His achievements, by John Lewis* [Toronto, 1925]. 2 p.

126 The Library of Parliament catalogue lists Lucas as author of the pamphlet.

N97 – *Ritratto di Mackenzie King.* Roma: E.O.T.-Edizioni del Secolo, 1946. 101 p.
Translated by Giorgia de Cousandier.

N98 *Mackenzie King.* Ottawa: National Liberal Committee, 1930. 4 p. (National Liberal Committee Publication No. 1).

N99 *Mackenzie King. Chanson de politique avec deux chansons. En vente partout.* [Montréal?: Imprimerie Pigeon, Ltée., 1935?]. 4 p. [Song sheet].

N100 *Mackenzie King: A personal view.* Waterloo, Ont.: Association for Canadian Studies, 1977. 71 p. (Canadian issues, vol. 1, No. 2).

N101 'Mackenzie King Memorial Edition.' *Canadian Liberal,* 3 (3), September 1950. 68 p.

N102 *A man of many roles. Mr King as champion of Empire.* [Ottawa: Runge Press Limited, 1930]. 4 p. [From the *Ottawa Journal,* July 22, 1930].

N103 MARTIN, PAUL. *A lifetime of public service: A brief biographical sketch of Mackenzie King.* Ottawa: Mortimer, 1945. 47 p.

N104 – *A very public life.* Ottawa: Deneau, 1983–1985. 2 v.

N105 McGILLICUDDY, OWEN ERNEST. *The making of a Premier: An outline of the life story of the Rt. Hon. W.L. Mackenzie King, C.M.G..* Toronto: Musson, 1922. 97 p.

N106 McGOVERN, GEORGE STANLEY, and LEONARD F. GUTTRIDGE. *The great coalfield war.* Boston: Houghton, 1972. 383 p.

N107 McGREGOR, FRED ALEXANDER. *The fall and rise of Mackenzie King, 1911–1919.* Toronto: Macmillan, 1962. 358 p.

N108 [McKAY, JOE?]. *'The Interpreter's House': A few classic examples of the literary style of Rt. Hon. W.L. Mackenzie King which reveal his philosophy* [N.p., 1945]. 4 p.

N109 MONET, JACQUES. *William Lyon Mackenzie King.* 25 mai 1982. Montréal: Services des transcriptions et dérivés de la radio, Maison de Radio-Canada, 1982. [Transciption d'une émission de radio]. 10 p. (Portraits des premiers ministres du Québec et du Canada, cahier no. 33).

N110 MOORE, WILLIAM HENRY. *Mackenzie King: The obstinate idealist.* Ottawa: National Liberal Federation, 1935. 8 p. [Reprinted from *Public Life*].

N111 – *Mackenzie King and the wage earner.* Ottawa: National Liberal Federation, 1935. 8 p. [Reprinted from *Public Life*].

N112 *Mr King's excuses answered.* Montreal: Liberal-Conservative Party, 1926. 4 p.

N113 *Mr Mackenzie King and his anti-Catholic alliances.* [Ottawa, 1927]. 12 p.

N114 NATIONAL LIBERAL FEDERATION. *Industry and humanity; Mackenzie King and a new social order. A comparison and contrast with principles and policies underlying the National Recovery Program in the United States.* Ottawa: National Liberal Federation, 1934. 10 p. [Reprinted from the *Toronto Daily Star*, January 10 and 12, 1934].

N115 – *Mackenzie King: The man who understood.* [N.p., 1926]. 8 p.

N116 NATIONAL LIBERAL FEDERATION OF CANADA. *Mackenzie King, August 7, 1944.* [Ottawa: National Liberal Federation of Canada, 1944]. 32 p.

N117 – *Who is this man King?* Ottawa, 1935? 7 p.

N118 NEATBY, HERBERT BLAIR. *La grande dépression des années '30.* Montréal: La Presse, 1975. 202 p. [Translation of *The politics of chaos*]. [Translated by Lucien Parizeau].

N119 – *Mackenzie King, the lonely heights, 1924– 1932.* Toronto: University of Toronto Press, 1963. xii, 452 p. [vol. 2 of the official biography].

Kingsmere Edition:

N120 *William Lyon Mackenzie King, vol. II, 1924–1932: The lonely heights.* By H. Blair Neatby.

Super Royal Octavo format, text printed on Cortlea White with special endpapers. Pp. 468 + 14 coated inserts (including a special series of photographs in this edition only).

Quarter-bound by hand in green morocco leather and heavy buckram, gold leaf stamped on front and spine, gilted top, head- and tail-bands.

Three hundred and fifty hand-numbered copies of this limited edition were issued.

N121 *Mackenzie King, the prism of unity, 1932–1939.* Toronto: University of Toronto Press, 1976. x, 366 p. [vol. 3 of the official biography].
This volume of the official biography was not issued in the Kingsmere Edition.

N122 – *The politics of chaos: Canada in the thirties.* Toronto: Macmillan, 1972. 196 p.

N123 NICHOLSON, MURRAY WILLIAM. *Woodside and the Victorian family of John King.* Ottawa: Parks Canada, 1984. 117 p.

N124 – *Woodside et la famille victorienne de John King.* Ottawa: Parcs Canada, 1984. 128 p.

N125 NOLAN, BRIAN. *King's war: Mackenzie King and the politics of war, 1939–1945.* Toronto: Random House, 1988. 188 p.

N126 – *King's war: Mackenzie King and the politics of war, 1939–1945.* Toronto: Fawcett Crest, 1988. x, 205 p. [Paper cover edition].

N127 *Ordannance des funérailles d'état de feu le très honorable William Lyon Mackenzie King, C.P., P.M. Service funèbre, mercredi 26 juillet 1950, à Ottawa. Inhumation, jeudi 27 juillet 1950, à Toronto.* [Ottawa, 1950]. 13 p.

N128 PAINCHAUD, PAUL, ed. *De Mackenzie King à Pierre Trudeau: Quarante ans de diplomatie canadienne. From Mackenzie King to Pierre Trudeau: Forty years of Canadian diplomacy, 1945–1985.* (Ste Foy, Québec: Laval University/Les presses de l'université Laval, 1990). ix, 748 p.

N129 PHILIP, PERCY JAMES. '*Fantasio.*' [Broadcast on the Canadian Broadcasting Corporation, September 1954]. [Ottawa: Canadian Broadcasting Corporation, 1954]. 8 p.

N130 PICKERSGILL, JOHN WHITNEY. *The Liberal Party.* Toronto: McClelland and Stewart Limited, 1962. xiii, 146 p.

N131 – *Le parti libéral.* Montréal: Éditions du Jour, 1963. 124 p.

N132 – *Political leadership and the parliamentary system illustrated from the career of Mackenzie King. Address to the History Club of the University of Western Ontario, by Hon. J.W. Pickersgill, London, Ontario, Monday, October 3, 1966.* [Ottawa, 1966]. 15 p.

N133 – *Seeing Canada whole: A memoir.* Toronto: Fitzhenry and Whiteside, 1994. 858 p.

N134 PICKERSGILL, JOHN WHITNEY, and DONALD FREDERICK FORSTER, eds. *The Mackenzie King record.* Toronto: University of Toronto Press, 1960–1970. 4 v.

N135 The University of Toronto Press issued the four volumes in a de luxe red leather set with gold letters with gilt top.
The Mackenzie King Record was also issued in a four- volume boxed set.

N136 THE PILGRIMS. Speeches at a dinner in honor of the Right Honourable W.L. Mackenzie King, P.C., M.P., Prime Minister of Canada, The Hotel Plaza, Wednesday, Second December, Nineteen Forty-Two. [New York: The Pilgrims, 1943?]. 40 p.

N137 *Planning for victory: The Quebec Conference, 1943.* [Ottawa: National Film Board of Canada, 1943]. 48 p.

N138 *Politique instable: Les contractions de M. King et de ses amis.* [N.p., n.d.] 2 p.

N139 PRESS GALLERY, OTTAWA. *Moody and Sankey's hymnal by Tory and Grit, Press Gallery, Ottawa, May 4, Nineteen Twenty Nine.* Ottawa: F.A. Acland, 1929. 17 p.

N140 *Right Honourable W.L. Mackenzie King, Prime Minister of Canada. Speech by the Right Honourable Ernest Lapointe. (Delivered at the Royal York Hotel, Toronto, August 8, 1939). On the occasion of the complimentary banquet tendered Mr King by the Liberal Party of Canada, on the completion of his 20 years of leadership of the party.* [Ottawa, 1939]. 7 p.

N141 ROGERS, NORMAN McLEOD. *Mackenzie King.* A revised and extended edition of a biographical sketch by John Lewis. Toronto: G.N. Morang, 1935. 212 p.

N142 ROME, DAVID, compiler. *On Mackenzie King and Jewish sweating labor.* Montreal: Canadian Jewish Congress, National Archives, 1979. 2 v. (Canadian Jewish Archives, New Series, Nos. 12 and 13).

N143 ROSE, BERNARD. *Industry and humanity: An outstanding contribution to the understanding of industrial relations and the need for economic justice. Analysis and re-evaluation.* [Montreal, 1933]. 32 p. [Reprinted from the *Labor World,* Montreal].

N144 RUMILLY, ROBERT. *La guerre de 1939–1945: Ernest Lapointe.* Montréal and Paris: Fides, 1968. 318 p. (*Histoire de la Province de Québec,* 38).

N145 – *La guerre de 1939–1945: La plébiscite.* Montréal and Paris: Fides, 1969. 295 p. (*Histoire de la Province de Québec*, 39).

N146 – *Mackenzie King.* Montréal: Éditions Bernard Valiquette, 1944. 151 p.

N147 SAINT-AUBIN, BERNARD. *King et son époque.* Montréal: Les Éditions de la presse, Ltée., 1982. 409 p.

N148 ST JOHN, PETER, ed. *Mackenzie King to the philosopher king: Canadian foreign policy in the 20th century.* Winnipeg: St John's College, 1984. 472 p.

N149 SHIELDS, T.T. *Hepburn, Drew, King, Manion: What shall we do with them: An address.* Toronto: Jarvis Street Baptist Church, 1940. 29 p.

N150 – *Premier King's Plebiscite speech analyzed. A respectful and urgent appeal to clergymen and churches, lodges and other organizations and everybody, to unite in an endeavour to dissuade the government from the execution of its fatally disruptive proposal.* [N.p., 1942]. 32 p.
Address delivered in Jarvis Street Baptist Church, Toronto, February 2, 1942.

N151 *Some appreciative reviews of the secret of heroism, a memoir of Henry Albert Harper, by W.L. Mackenzie King.* New York: Fleming H. Revell, 1919. 15 p.

N152 SOWARD, FREDERIC HUBERT, JOSEPH FREDERICK PARKINSON, NORMAN ARCHIBALD MACRAE MACKENZIE, and TERENCE WILLIAM LEIGHTON MACDERMOT. *Canada in world affairs: The pre-war years.* Toronto: Oxford University Press, 1941. xiii, 343 p. (vol. 1).

N153 – *Canada in world affairs: From Normandy to Paris, 1944–1946.* London, Toronto, and New York: Oxford University Press, 1950. xi, 359 p. (vol. 4).

N154 SPENCER, ROBERT ALLAN. *Canada in world affairs: From UN to NATO, 1946–1949.* Toronto: Oxford University Press, 1959. xi, 447 p. (vol. 5).

N155 STACEY, CHARLES PERRY. *Arms, men and governments: The war policies of Canada, 1939–1945.* Ottawa: Queen's Printer, 1970. 681 p.

N156 – *Armes, hommes et gouvernements: Les politiques de guerre du Canada, 1939–1945.* Ottawa: Imprimeur de la Reine, 1970. 747 p.

N157 – *Canada and the age of conflict: A history of Canadian external relations.* Toronto, Buffalo, and London: University of Toronto Press, 1981. Vol. 2: 1921–1948: The Mackenzie King era. x, 491 p.

N158 – *Mackenzie King and the Atlantic Triangle.* Toronto: Macmillan of Canada, 1976. xv, 74 p. (The Joanne Goodman Memorial Lectures, 1976).

N159 – *La vie doublement secrète de Mackenzie King.* Traduit de anglais par René Chicoine. Montréal: P. Tisseyre, 1979. 287 p.

N160 – *A very double life: The private world of Mackenzie King.* Toronto: Macmillan of Canada, 1976. 256 p.

N161 – *A very double life: The private life of Mackenzie King.* Halifax: Goodread Biographies, 1985. 227 p. [Paperback edition].

N162 TEATERO, WILLIAM ROY. *Mackenzie King: A man of mission.* Don Mills: T. Nelson and Sons (Canada), 1978. 192 p.

N163 THOMPSON, JOHN HERD (with ALLEN SEAGER). *Canada, 1922–1939: Decades of discord.* Toronto: McClelland and Stewart, 1985. xiv, 438 p. (Canadian Centenary Series, vol. 15).

N164 *À travers le discours de l'honorable M King sur le budget le 30 avril 1925.* Montréal: Imprimeur populaire, 1925. 7 p.

N165 UNIVERSITY OF TORONTO PRESS. *New publications on Canada's most enigmatic public figure from University of Toronto Press.* [Toronto: University of Toronto Press, 1980]. 8 p.

N166 VEATCH, RICHARD. *Canada and the League of Nations.* Toronto: University of Toronto Press, 1975. xi, 224 p.

N167 VON BAEYER, EDWINNA. *Garden of dreams: Kingsmere and Mackenzie King.* Toronto and Oxford: Dundurn Press, 1990. 232 p.

N168 WARD, NORMAN McQUEEN, ed. *A party politician: The memoirs of Chubby Power.* Toronto: Macmillan of Canada, 1966. x, 419 p.

N169 *Westminster Abbey. The order of service in memory of the Right Honourable William Lyon Mackenzie King, O.M., sometime Prime Minister of Canada, on Friday, July 28, 1950, at 12.30 P.M.* [London, 1950]. 6 p.

N170 WHALEN, DWIGHT. *Mackenzie King's Christmas letter to a little girl.* Niagara Falls: Horseshoe Press, 1992. 10 p.
Limited edition of one hundred numbered copies.

N171 WHITAKER, REGINALD. *The government party: Organizing and financing the Liberal Party of Canada, 1930–58.* Toronto and Buffalo: University of Toronto Press, 1977. xxiv, 507 p.

N172 WIGLEY, PHILIP G. *Canada and the transition to Commonwealth: British–Canadian relations, 1917–1926.* Cambridge, London, New York, and Melbourne: Cambridge University Press, 1977. x, 294 p.

N173 WILTON, JAMES W. *Power at any price* [The book of the chronicles of Wilfrid and Wilyonus, Kings of Canada]. [Winnipeg: Print Shop, c. 1930]. 175 p. [A satire on Sir Wilfrid Laurier and Mackenzie King].

SECTION O

Articles about Mackenzie King

This section contains an alphabetical listing of periodical and newspaper articles about Mackenzie King, as well as a selection of articles relating to important aspects of the King era. A subtantial number of reviews of books about King are also included.

A bibliographer always has a difficult decision to make regarding newspaper articles. A significant number of articles about King, most of which appeared after his death, are presented here. It is felt that some of these articles contribute to a better understanding of Mackenzie King and his times; they – and sometimes even their titles alone – offer insight into the popular image of the man. In addition, many provide significant facts about King's life that have not been adequately dealt with by his biographers. Some articles suggest areas of his life that require further research.

O1 ABBOTT, DOUGLAS. 'The farther back you get, the better he looks.' *The Telegraph-Journal* [St John, N.B.], December 16, 1974, p. 5.

O2 'The abdication of Mr King.' *Round Table*, 38 (5), 1948, p. 708.

O3 ABERDEEN, MARCHIONESS OF. 'A Prime Minister in quest of the homes of his ancestors.' *Deeside Field*, 8, 1938, pp. 61–63.

O4 ACLAND, FREDERICK ALBERT. 'Canadian Industrial Disputes Investigation Act.' *Annals of the American Academy of Political and Social Sciences*, 32, September 1910, pp. 419–437.

O5 – 'Canadian legislation concerning industrial disputes.' *Canadian Law Times*, 36 (3), March 1916, pp. 207–222.

O6 – 'Mackenzie King comes back.' *Current History*, 43, December 1935, pp. 249–252.

O7 ALEXANDER, FRED. 'Canadian Liberal leader.' *Australian Outlook*, 14 (1), April 1960, pp. 90–96. [Review of Dawson, *William Lyon Mackenzie King: A political biography, 1874–1923*, vol. 1].

O8 ALWAY, RICHARD MARTIN HOLDEN. 'Hepburn, King, and the Rowell-Sirois Commission.' *Canadian Historical Review*, 48 (2), June 1967, pp. 113–141.

O9 ANGERS, FRANCOIS-ALBERT. 'Pourquoi M King n'est pas délié.' *L'Action Nationale*, 19 (5), mai 1942, pp. 251–262.

O10 ANGLIN, DOUGLAS GEORGE. 'The rise of Mackenzie King and the decline of the Conservative Party.' *Political Studies*, 4 (3), October 1956, pp. 307–310. [Review of Ferns and Ostry, *The age of Mackenzie King: The rise of the leader*, and John R. Williams, *The Conservative Party of Canada, 1920–1949*].

O11 ARCHER, FRED. 'Mackenzie King sought spirit aid in state affairs.' *Psychic News* [London], no. 950, August 19, 1950, p. 1.

O12 – 'WLMK: Spiritualist.' *Ottawa Evening Citizen*, October 10, 1950, p. 32. [This article was from the *Psychic News*].

O13 ARGUS, 'Le spiritisme de Mackenzie King.' *Le Devoir*, 17 décembre 1951, p. 4.

O14 ARNELL, J.C. 'The development of joint North American defence.' *Queen's Quarterly*, 72 (2), Summer 1970, pp. 190–204.

O15 'Backstage at Ottawa: He left the back door open.' *Maclean's Magazine*, 61 (5), March 1, 1948, p. 15.

O16 BAIN, GEORGE. 'Louis St Laurent: The conscription issue.' *The Globe Magazine*, April 21, 1962, pp. 8–11.

O17 BAKER, WILLIAM M. 'The miners and the mediator: the 1906 Lethbridge strike and Mackenzie King.' *Le Travailleur/Labour*, no. 11, Spring/Printemps 1983, pp. 89–117.

O18 BALDWIN, JIM. 'The King Chronicle misunderstands a master of evasion.' *Toronto Star*, March 26, 1988, p. J3. [Relates to 'The King Chronicle' shown on CBC-TV, March 27–March 29, 1988].

O19 BALDWIN, ROBERT WARREN. 'Mr King's drama.' *Saturday Night*, 53 (49), October 8, 1938, p. 5.

O20 BALDWIN, WARREN. 'His anniversary phobia may also decide date to resign premiership.' *The Globe and Mail*, August 2, 1948, p. 15.

O21 'Bassett didn't use diaries.' *Leader-Post* [Regina], January 7, 1975, p. 19.

O22 BENSON, NATHANIEL. 'The community must come first!: An interview with Mackenzie King.' *Forbes Magazine of Business*, 49 (11), June 1, 1947, pp. 14–15, 28–29.

O23 BIRCHALL, FREDERICK T. 'War leader of Canada.' *New York Times Magazine*, April 7, 1940, pp. 7, 18.

O24 BIRD, JOHN. 'Hilarious episode in Truman's last visit.' *Ottawa Citizen*, November 11, 1953, p. 7. [Relates to the visit of President Harry S Truman to Ottawa in June 1947 and King's marking of 7,305 days in office].

O25 – 'Quick changeover for PM: No twilight interregnum like King's, this time.' *Financial Post*, February 3, 1968, p. 10. [Relates to the period from the election of Louis St Laurent as Liberal leader and the resignation of Mackenzie King].

O26 BISHOP, CHARLES LAWRENCE. 'Fifty years recalled.' *Ottawa Evening Citizen*, July 24, 1950, pp. 3, 8.

O27 – 'Mr King: Political marvel.' *Montreal Daily Star*, July 24, 1950, p. 11.

O28 – 'Years around Parliament: Thoughts, men, memories: Rt. Hon. Mackenzie King.' *Ottawa Citizen*, January 12, 1946, pp. 1, 3.

O29 BISHOP, LESLIE. 'Canada's Mackenzie King.' *Fortnightly*, 174, December 1950, pp. 374–378.

O30 BLACK, BARBARA. 'Montreal spy connection adds spice to the latest Mackenzie King novel.' *Montreal Gazette*, April 11, 1987, p. G6.

O31 BLACKBURN, CLYDE ROBERT. 'Biography reveals romance in Mackenzie King's life; might have wed nurse.' *The Globe and Mail*, November 17, 1958, p. 10.

O32 – 'The many phases in the public and private life of Mackenzie King are revealed in new biography.' *Ottawa Citizen*, November 17, 1958, p. 9.

O33 – 'While shy of the press, he was an ex-reporter.' *Winnipeg Free Press*, July 24, 1950, p. 13.

O34 [BLOOM, CHESTER ABBOTT?] 'The contrasts.' *Winnipeg Free Press*, July 24, 1950, p. 12.

O35 BLADEN, VINCENT WHEELER. 'The Lemieux Act.' *Canadian Forum*, 5 (54), March 1925, pp. 168–170.

O36 BLAKE, RAYMOND B. 'William Lyon Mackenzie King's attitude towards Newfoundland's entry into Confederation.' *Newfoundland Quarterly*, 82 (4), Spring 1987, pp. 26–37.

O37 BLAKELY, ARTHUR. 'Among the one-eyed.' *Montreal Gazette*, January 16, 1954, p. 2.

O38 – 'The great enigma of Canadian politics.' *Montreal Star*, November 22, 1958, p. 35. [Review of Dawson, *William Lyon Mackenzie King: A political biography, 1874–1923*, vol. 1].

O39 – 'The heir apparent.' *Montreal Gazette*, November 18, 1958, p. 8. [Review of Dawson, *William Lyon Mackenzie King: A political biography, 1874–1923*, vol. 1].

O40 – 'The helping hand.' *Montreal Gazette*, December 11, 1958, p. 8. [Review of Dawson, *William Lyon Mackenzie King: A political biography, 1874–1923*, vol. 1].

O41 – 'The other worldliness of Mr King.' *Montreal Gazette*, November 17, 1958, p. 8. [Review of Dawson, *William Lyon Mackenzie King: A political biography, 1874–1923*, vol. 1].

O42 – 'Out of thin air.' *Montreal Gazette*, November 16, 1956, p. 8. [Relates to the death of Percy Phillips and his talk with Mackenzie King at Kingsmere in 1954].

O43 – 'In pastures green.' *Montreal Gazette*, December 27, 1955, p. 6. [Review of Ferns and Ostry, *The age of Mackenzie King: The rise of the leader*].

O44 BOONE, MIKE. 'Britain's King comes to TV: The chronicle of a prime minister.' *Montreal Gazette*, March 26, 1988, p. 1. [Review of 'The King Chronicle' shown on CBC-TV, March 27–March 29, 1988].

O45 – 'Engrossing tale of the prime minister who would be King.' *Mont-*

real Gazette, March 27, 1988, p. F-6. [Review of 'The King Chronicle' shown on CBC-TV, March 27–March 29, 1988].

O46 BORDEN, HENRY. 'Footnote on Dawson's King.' *Canadian Historical Review*, 43 (3), September 1962, p. 275.

O47 BOTHWELL, ROBERT, and JOHN ENGLISH. '"Dirty work at the crossroads": New perspectives on the Riddell incident.' Canadian Historical Association, *Historical Papers*, 1972, pp. 265–281.

O48 BOURINOT, ARTHUR STANLEY. 'Kingsmere: Where two premiers tramped the woods.' *Saturday Night*, 42 (45), September 24, 1927, p. 5.

O49 – 'Kingsmere's associations.' *Saturday Night*, 65 (43), August 1, 1950, p. 20.

O50 BOWMAN, CHARLES A. 'Mackenzie King and the purloined lamb.' *Maclean's Magazine*, 68 (20), October 1, 1955, p. 20.

O51 – 'Mr King's domestic side little known to public.' *Ottawa Citizen*, August 26, 1949, p. 5.

O52 BRADY, ALEXANDER. 'Turning new leaves.' *Canadian Forum*, 35 (422), March 1956, pp. 283–284. [Review of Ferns and Ostry, *The age of Mackenzie King: The rise of the leader*].

O53 BRAITHWAITE, DENNIS. 'Pat on back for "Close-up" courage.' *Toronto Daily Star*, March 18, 1960, p. 20.

O54 BREHL, JACK. 'Portrait of mother inspired King's career.' *Toronto Daily Star*, July 24, 1950, p. 17.

O55 'British historian: "King exercised the decisive influence on the C'wealth."' *Ottawa Journal*, January 30, 1969, p. 46.

O56 BROWN, EDWARD KILLORAN. 'Mackenzie King of Canada.' *Harper's Magazine*, 186 (1112), January 1943, pp. 192–200.
Reprinted in Malcolm Ross, ed., *Our sense of identity: A book of Canadian essays* (Toronto: Ryerson Press, 1954), pp. 177–191.

O57 BRUNT, STEPHEN. 'Book reveals Mackenzie King's power ploys.' *The Globe and Mail*, October 20, 1984, pp. 1–2. [Review of Richard S. Malone, *A world in flames, 1944–1945*].

O58 BURNETT, ANDREW IAN. 'Mackenzie King's hidden strength found in religious convictions.' *Star Weekly*, September 9, 1950, p. 12.

O59 BUXTON, WILLIAM. 'The making of Mackenzie King.' *Canadian Forum*, 71 (809), May 1992, pp. 32–34. [Review of Howard M. Gitelman, *Legacy of the Ludlow Massacre: A chapter in American industrial history*].

O60 BYERS, DANIEL. 'Mobilizing Canada: The National Resources Mobilization Act, the Department of National Defence, and compulsory military service in Canada, 1940–1945.' *Journal of the Canadian Historical Association/Revue de la Société historique du Canada*, 7, 1996, pp. 175–203.

O61 'The Byng–King correspondence.' *Canadian Annual Review*, 1926–27, pp. 69–74.

O62 'The Byng–King correspondence: Some secret history.' *Ottawa Journal*, February 16, 1927, p. 6.

O63 CAHILL, JACK. 'King chroniclers rate the King Chronicle.' *Toronto Star*, March 31, 1988, p. A24.

O64 CAMERON, ADAM KIRK, 'Questions for the shade of Mr Mackenzie King.' [Letter to the ed.]. *Montreal Gazette*, September 29, 1954, p. 8.

O65 CAMPBELL, MURRAY. 'History shifted in a railway car as PM agreed to defence board: Ogdensburg Declaration: Canada's future changed in 1940 during a 15-minute meeting between Mackenzie King and Roosevelt.' *The Globe and Mail*, August 17, 1990, p. A13.

O66 'Canada: The general election.' *Round Table*, 20 (80) September 1930, pp. 837–856.

O67 'Canada's quiet Mackenzie King quietly breaks an old record.' *Life*, 24 (16), April 16, 1948, p. 59.

O68 CARMICHAEL, DAVID. 'Mackenzie King's spooky ruins.' *Star Weekly*, July 24, 1971, pp. 14–17.

O69 CARNEGIE, R.K. 'Daniel Surely, counsellor-at-large declares Mackenzie King greatest Prime Minister.' *Ottawa Citizen*, June 22, 1949, p. 3.

O70 – 'Great his faith: Eulogy touches throng at King's funeral in St Andrew's.' *Ottawa Citizen*, July 27, 1950, p. 36.

O71 – 'King may have written some 50,000 letters.' *Ottawa Citizen*, December 27, 1950, p. 4.

O72 – 'Sidelights of a great man.' *Ottawa Citizen*, July 24, 1950, p. 36.

O73 CARSON, NEIL. 'Forgotten hero [Henry Albert Harper].' *The Globe and Mail*, August 16, 1962, p. 7.

O74 CARTER, JOHN. 'The reciprocity election of 1911: Waterloo North, A case study.' *Waterloo Historical Society [Proceedings]*, 62, 1974, pp. 77–87.

O75 CAYGEON, ROBERT. 'Mackenzie King – an old-fashioned Liberal.' *Saturday Night*, 48 (41), August 19, 1933, p. 3.

O76 CHAMPOUX, ROGER. 'Derniers regards du peuple qu'il a servi.' *La Presse*, 24 juillet 1950, pp. 1, 24.

O77 – 'L'ultime hommage rendu au T.H.M. King.' *La Presse*, 27 juillet 1950, p. 1.

O78 CHECKLAND, SYDNEY G. 'Innocence and anxiety: Canada between the wars.' *Bulletin of Canadian Studies*, 5 (2), October 1981, pp. 25–37.

O79 CHEVRIER, BERNARD. 'Mackenzie King seeks election in Glengarry.' *Viewpoint Canada*, 1 (2), April–May 1981, pp. 31–32.

O80 CHISHOLM, ELSPETH. 'Never: Ernest Lapointe and conscription, 1935–1944.' *Canada: An historical magazine*, 3 (3), March 1976, pp. 2–21; 3 (4), June 1976, pp. 40–53.

O81 CLARE, JOHN. 'Backstage with the King biography/a true or false picture.' *Maclean's Magazine*, 72 (1), January 3, 1959, p. 3.

O82 CLARK, GREGORY. 'He was a romantic.' *The Standard* [Montreal], August 12, 1950, p. 27.

O83 – 'Mr King on post-war Canada.' *Toronto Star*, August 14, 1943, p. 3.

O84 – 'Unpurchasable patriot.' *Star Weekly*, August 5, 1939, pp. 5, 10.

O85 – 'Un patriot incorruptible.' *Le Canada – Montréal*, 7 août 1939, p. 5.

O86 – 'With the Prime Minister in Britain.' Empire Club of Canada, *Addresses*, 1941–42, pp. 39–53.

O87 CLARK, JAMES B.M. 'The Canadian election.' *Nineteenth Century*, 108, September 1930, pp. 334–344.

O88 'Conservatives were shocked by King's wartime ploy: book.' *Montreal Gazette*, October 23, 1984, p. 9. [Review of Richard S. Malone, *A world in flames, 1944–1945*]. [Canadian Press dispatch].

O89 'Continuity of Mackenzie King's career so marked as to look like destiny.' *Toronto Star*, December 17, 1921, p. 16.

O90 COOK, RAMSAY. 'The age of Mackenzie King.' *The Globe and Mail*, January 22, 1977, p. 39. [Review of Ferns and Ostry, *The age of Mackenzie King: The rise of the leader*].

O91 – 'J.W. Dafoe at the Imperial Conference, 1923.' *Canadian Historical Review*, 41 (1), March 1960, pp. 14–40.

O92 COPPS, EDWIN. 'A distorted image of Mackenzie King.' *Saturday Night*, 75 (8), April 16, 1960, pp. 27–28.

O93 'A corrective needed to distorted biography.' *Montreal Star*, December 13, 1955, p. 10.

O94 COURTNEY, JOHN CHILDS. 'Prime Ministerial character: An examination of Mackenzie King's political leadership.' *Canadian Journal of Political Science*, 9 (1), March 1976, pp. 77–100.

O95 – 'Mackenzie King and Prince Albert constituency: The 1933 redistribution.' *Saskatchewan History*, 29 (1), Winter 1976, pp. 1–13.

O96 COUSINEAU, LOUISE. 'Mackenzie King parlait à l'esprit de son chien.' *La Presse*, 26 mars 1988, p. E-2.

O97 CRAVEN, PAUL. 'King and content: A reply to Whitaker.' [Article entitled 'The Liberal corporatist ideas of Mackenzie King']. *Labour/Le Travailleur*, 4 (4), 1979, pp. 165–185.

O98 CREIGHTON, DONALD GRANT. 'Young Mackenzie King.' *University of Toronto Quarterly*, 38 (2), January 1959, pp. 197–200. [Review of Dawson, *William Lyon Mackenzie King: A political biography, 1874–1923*, vol. 1].

O99 CRERAR, THOMAS ALEXANDER. 'Incredible Canadian: An evaluation.' *International Journal*, 8 (3), Summer 1953, pp. 151–156. [Review of Bruce Hutchison, *The incredible Canadian*].

O100 CROSS, AUSTIN FLETCHER. 'The age of Mackenzie King.' *Ottawa Citizen*, December 24, 1955, p. 27. [Review of Ferns and Ostry, *The age of Mackenzie King: The rise of the leader*].

O101 – 'Compare funerals of Sir Wilfrid, Mr King.' *Ottawa Citizen*, July 27, 1950, p. 19.

O102 – 'Eulogy moves congregation. Mr King's empty pew draped in black crepe.' *Ottawa Citizen*, July 26, 1950, pp. 1, 18.

O103 – 'Mr King's papers.' *The National Magazine*, September 1950, p. 11.

O104 – 'Political patriarch.' *Canadian Business*, 19 (5), May 1946, pp. 46, 108, 110.

O105 – 'Startling revelations promised in vol. 3.' *Ottawa Citizen*, July 7, 1956, p. 2. [Relates to future volume of biography by H.S. Ferns and Bernard Ostry].

O106 CROWLEY, TERENCE ALLAN. 'Mackenzie King and the 1911 election.' *Ontario History*, 61 (4), December 1969, pp. 181–196.

O107 'A crown of laurel for Mackenzie King from the grave of his beloved mother.' *Toronto Daily Star*, December 17, 1921, p. 1.

O108 CUFF, JOHN HASLETT. 'Portrait captures King's enigma.' *The Globe and Mail*, March 26, 1988, p. C3. [Relates to the 'The King Chronicle' shown on CBC-TV, March 27–March 29, 1988].

O109 CUFF, ROBERT D., and JACK LAWRENCE GRANATSTEIN. 'The rise and fall of Canadian–American free trade, 1947–48.' *Canadian Historical Review*, 58 (4), December 1977, pp. 459–482.

O110 DE BRISAY, RICHARD. 'Liberals on the wrong road.' *Canadian Forum*, 10 (116), May 1930, pp. 271–273.

O111 – 'Mr King's platform.' *Canadian Forum*, 10 (117), June 1930, pp. 311–313.

O112 – 'The new Liberal policy.' *Canadian Forum*, 10 (111), December 1929, pp. 75–77.

O113 'A delicate subject.' *The Archivist*, 2 (2), March–April 1975, pp. 2–3.

O114 DEMPSON, PETER. 'Preoccupations of Mr King stay writing of memoirs.' *Toronto Telegram*, July 18, 1949, p. 6.

O115 DENISON, MERRILL. 'Fireworks coming in Canada.' *Harper's Magazine*, 190 (1135), December 1944, pp. 62–73.

O116 DESBARATS, LILIAN SCOTT. 'Recollections of Laurier House.' *Ottawa Journal*, June 25, 1951, p. 21.

O117 DEXTER, GRANT. 'Distorted image.' *Winnipeg Free Press*, January 14, 1956, p. 28. [Review of Ferns and Ostry, *The age of Mackenzie King: The rise of the leader*].

O118 – 'Interviewing Mr King.' *Winnipeg Free Press*, September 12, 1935, p. 11.

O119 – 'Life of Mackenzie King.' *Winnipeg Free Press*, December 31, 1949, p. 16. [Review of H. Reginald Hardy, *Mackenzie King of Canada*].

O120 – 'Mr King – It will be recovery before reform.' *Maclean's Magazine*, 48 (21), November 15, 1935, pp. 19, 39–40.

O121 – 'Mackenzie King: The war years.' *Winnipeg Free Press*, November 12, 1960, p. 22. [Review of J.W. Pickersgill, ed., *The Mackenzie King record*, vol. 1].

O122 – 'Off-the-record with Mr King.' *The Beaver*, 72 (6), December 1992–January 1993, pp. 21–23.

O123 – 'This man Mackenzie King.' *Saturday Night*, 50 (46), September 21, 1935, pp. 5, 8.

O124 DEY DAUNT, ELIZABETH. 'Ottawa's Laurier House is real treasure trove.' *Daily Standard Freeholder* [Cornwall], April 25, 1953, p. 13.

O125 'Diefenbaker doesn't like publication of King diaries.' *Leader-Post* [Regina], January 14, 1975, p. 7.

O126 DiMANNO, ROSIE. 'Donald Brittain reincarnates Mackenzie King.' *Toronto Daily Star*, March 26, 1988, p. J1.

O127 DINGMAN, HAROLD. 'Mackenzie King won early fame as conciliator and author of labor laws.' *The Globe and Mail*, July 24, 1950, p. 8.

O128 – 'Mackenzie King sums up.' *New Liberty*, 25 (5), July 1948, pp. 7–10.

O129 – 'Wartime conscription crisis of 1944 greatest crisis in King's career.' *The Globe and Mail*, July 24, 1950, p. 10.

O130 – 'Who will be King's successor?' *New Liberty*, 24 (11), March 15, 1947, pp. 8–9, 39–41.

O131 'La discipline de parti et la convention de confiance: Une perspective historique.' *Revue parlementaire canadienne*, 16 (2), Eté 1993, pp. 12–19.

O132 'Disponibilité des papiers King de 1947.' *L'Archiviste*, 4 (6), novembre–décembre 1977, p. 14.

O133 'Does history belong to the men who made it?' *Maclean's Magazine*, 71 (26), December 20, 1958, p. 4.

O134 'A dog adored a Prime Minister.' *Living Tissue*, 27 (3), January, 1943, pp. 6–7.

O135 DONALD, MARGOT. 'A prime minister at home.' *Toronto Star*, July 4, 1929, p. 4.

O136 DOWNEY, TERRENCE J. 'An appreciation of a great Canadian. Considerable achievements of Mackenzie King.' *Leader-Post* [Regina], July 22, 1975, p. 29.

O137 DOWNTON, ERIC. 'Battle over the bier.' *Vancouver Sun*, July 22, 1985, p. A5. [Discusses Canadian policy regarding the Korean War and a discussion held on the train by federal cabinet ministers on the way to the funeral of Mackenzie King].

O138 DRINKWATER, WILLIAM S. 'Historique de la Gazette du travail.' *Le Gazette du travail*, 75 (9), septembre 1975, pp. 536–539.

O139 – 'The story of the Labour Gazette.' *Labour Gazette*, 75 (9), September 1975, pp. 587–590.

O140 DRYDEN, JEAN E. 'The Mackenzie King Papers: An archival odyssey.' *Archivaria*, 6, Summer 1978, pp. 40–69.

O141 DUNNELL, MILT. 'Mr Hewitt told Mackenzie King he was fired.' *Toronto Daily Star*, December 9, 1953, p. 19. [An account of an incident when King was reporter for the *Toronto News*].

O142 DUROCHER, RENÉ. 'The odd man in: Mackenzie King.' *Horizon Canada*, 9 (105), pp. 2497–2503.

O143 DURRANCE, THOMAS DRAKE. 'Top man of Canada.' *Coronet*, 22 (1), May 1947, pp. 114–118.

O144 EAYRS, JAMES GEORGE. 'Decision of Times recalls Mackenzie King's campaign.' *Ottawa Journal*, February 23, 1970, p. 7. [Relates to the appointment of John A. Stevenson as Ottawa correspondent of the London *Times*].

O145 – 'Oedipus Rex.' *Canadian Forum*, 56 (662), June–July 1976, pp. 30–35. [Review of C.P. Stacey, *A very double life*.]

O146 – 'Pickersgill is still King's backroom boy.' *Toronto Daily Star*, August 25, 1970, p. 6

O147 – 'War didn't change King's prejudices.' *Toronto Daily Star*, August 27, 1970, p. 6.

O148 – 'Will Mackenzie King attend his 100th anniversary?' *Toronto Star*, December 14, 1974, p. B6.

O149 EDGAR, WILLIAM WILKIE. 'The settlement of industrial disputes in Canada.' *Journal of Political Economy*, 16 (2), February 1908, pp. 88–93.

O150 EDINBOROUGH, ARNOLD. 'Did King sell out Canada to U.S.? Creighton says "yes."' *Financial Post*, August 5, 1972, p. 12.

O151 EGGLESTON, WILFRID. 'Canadian politics: The old era and the new.' *Queen's Quarterly*, 60 (4), Winter 1948–1949, pp. 476–488.

O152 – 'Mackenzie King.' *Winnipeg Free Press*, November 22, 1958, p. 23. [Review of Dawson, *William Lyon Mackenzie King: A political biography, 1874–1923*, vol. 1].

O153 – 'Mackenzie King's era.' *Saturday Night*, 64 (7), November 20, 1948, p. 4.

O154 – 'Record career of Mackenzie King had turning point as newsman.' *Saturday Night*, 61 (40), June 8, 1946, p. 8.

O155 – 'The stature of Mackenzie King.' *Saturday Night*, 64 (44), August 8, 1950, p. 3.

O156 – 'The tribute to Mackenzie King: An inspiring pilgrimage.' *Winnipeg Free Press*, July 28, 1950, p. 19.

O157 ESBEREY, JOY ELAINE. 'Personality and politics: A new look at the King–Byng dispute.' *Canadian Journal of Political Science*, 6 (1), March 1973, pp. 37–55.

O158 – 'Prime Ministerial character: An alternative view.' *Canadian Journal of Political Science*, 9 (1), March 1976, pp. 101–106.

O159 'Excitable letter-writer.' *Winnipeg Free Press*, June 12, 1943, p. 17. [Relates to the King–Byng affair of 1926].

O160 'Family prevented King's marriage.' *Winnipeg Free Press*, November 18, 1958, p. 9. [Canadian Press dispatch].

O161 FARQUHARSON, DUART. 'Mackenzie King: Labor's friend or foe?' *Winnipeg Tribune*, July 29, 1972, p. 16. [Review of George S. McGovern and Leonard F. Guttridge, *The great coalfield war*].

O162 FELTEAU, CYRILLE. 'Mackenzie King a marqué la politique canadienne pendant un quart de siècle.' *La Presse*, 16 décembre 1974, p. A-5.

O163 FERGUSON, GEORGE VICTOR. 'Flies did not settle easily on Mr King.' *Montreal Star*, November 9, 1963, Entertainment Section, p. 5. [Review of Neatby, *William Lyon Mackenzie King: The lonely heights, 1924–1932*].

O164 FERNS, HENRY STANLEY. 'History and Mr Mackenzie King's diary.' *The Globe and Mail*, January 5, 1959, p. 6.

O165 – 'The ideas of Mackenzie King.' *Manitoba Arts Review*, 6 (2/3), Spring 1949, pp. 4–11.

O166 – 'Mackenzie King: Foreign policy.' *Ottawa Citizen*, August 4, 1944, p. 20.

O167 – 'Mackenzie King: Nation builder.' *Ottawa Citizen*, August 7, 1944, p. 12.

O168 – 'Mackenzie King: Social reformer.' *Ottawa Citizen*, August 2, 1944, p. 18.

O169 – 'Mackenzie King and self-government for India, 1947.' *British Journal of Canadian Studies*, 2 (1), June 1987, pp. 110–121.

O170 – 'Mackenzie King of Canada.' *Canadian Forum*, 27 (334), November 1948, pp. 174–177; 27 (335), December 1948, pp. 200–201; 27 (336), January 1949, pp. 226–228.

O171 – 'Mackenzie King on television.' *British Journal of Canadian Studies*, 3 (2), 1988, pp. 308–312.

O172 – 'Prime Minister King's life.' *The Globe and Mail*, November 22, 1958, p. 16. [Review of Dawson, *William Lyon Mackenzie King: A political biography, 1874–1923*, vol. 1].

O173 – 'Taking charge of Canada.' *Times Literary Supplement*, June 12, 1981, p. 674. [Review of Joy E. Esberey, *Knight of the Holy Spirit*].

O174 – 'William Lyon Mackenzie King.' *Chamber's Encyclopedia*, 8, pp. 229–230.

O175 – 'William Lyon Mackenzie King.' *Collier's Encyclopedia* [1981 Edition], pp. 91–92.

O176 – and BERNARD OSTRY. 'Mackenzie King and the First World War.' *Canadian Historical Review*, 36 (2), June 1955, pp. 93–112.

O177 – and EDGAR McINNIS. 'Mackenzie King: Two views.' *Canadian Historical Review*, 40 (1), March 1959, pp. 51–59. [Review of Dawson, *William Lyon Mackenzie King: A political biography, 1874–1923*, vol. 1].

O178 FERRIS, BOB. 'Laurier House – a unique educational resource.' *The Archivist*, 11 (3), May–June 1984, pp. 17–18.

O179 – 'La maison Laurier.' *L'Archiviste*, 11 (3), mai–juin 1984, pp. 17–18.

O180 FERRIS, ELMER ELLSWORTH. 'Mackenzie King and Canadian labour troubles.' *Outlook*, 96 (1), October 29, 1910, pp. 507–510.

O181 FISHER, DOUGLAS. 'Weird Willie: A PM to remember.' *Executive*, 26 (2), February 1984, pp. 47–48.

O182 FLANAGAN, THOMAS E. 'Problems of psychobiography.' *Queen's Quarterly*, 89 (3), Autumn 1982, pp. 596–610.

O183 FLEMING, R.B. 'Hostess to a nation: Nellie King ruled Ottawa society and once helped rescue a tottering government.' *The Beaver*, 77 (4), August/September 1997, pp. 7–14.

O184 'For Mr King's monument, look at Canada, 1950.' *Maclean's Magazine*, 63 (17), September 1, 1950, p. 1.

O185 FORD, ARTHUR RUTHERFORD. 'King reminisces on way to "Frisco."' *London Free Press*, April 24, 1945, pp. 1–2.

O186 – 'Senator Crerar evaluates Mackenzie King in political life of Canada.' *London Free Press*, July 11, 1953, p. 6.

O187 FORSEY, EUGENE ALFRED. 'A gamble and the constitution: A new telling of the King–Byng story.' *Saturday Night*, 68 (13), January 3, 1953, pp. 9, 19, 34.

O188 – 'The incredible Mr Hutchison.' *Ottawa Citizen*, December 6, 1952, p. 38. [Review of Bruce Hutchison, *The incredible Canadian*].

O189 – 'Meet Mackenzie King.' *Saskatchewan Commonwealth*, 9 (2), June 6, 1945, pp. 4–5.

O190 – 'Mr Forsey offers replies to Free Press criticism.' [Letter to the Ed.]. *Winnipeg Free Press*, June 12, 1943, p. 22. [Relates to the King–Byng affair of 1926].

O191 – 'Mr King and the government's labour policy.' *Canadian Forum*, 21 (250), November 1941, pp. 231–232.

O192 – 'Mr King and the government's labour policy.' *Canadian Forum*, 21 (252), January 1942, pp. 296–298.

O193 – 'Mr King and parliamentary government.' *Canadian Journal of Economics and Political Science*, 17 (4), November 1951, pp. 451–467.

O194 – 'Parliament is endangered by Mr King's principle.' *Saturday Night*, 64 (1), October 9, 1948, pp. 10–11.

O195 FRANCIS, DANIEL. 'King vs. revisionist: It took five court cases before young Willie was able to suppress a heretical biography about his rebel grandfather.' *Books in Canada*, 8 (3), March 1979, pp. 4–7.

O196 FRASER, BLAIR. 'Mackenzie King as I knew him.' *Maclean's Magazine*, 63 (17), September 1, 1950, pp. 7–9, 52–54.

O197 – 'Mr King.' *Maclean's Magazine*, 58 (3), February 1, 1945, pp. 10, 45, 47–48.

O198 – 'The Prime Minister.' *Maclean's Magazine,* 59 (11), June 1, 1946, pp. 7–8, 79–81.

O199 – 'The PM who talked with the dead.' *Maclean's,* 108 (26), June 26, 1995, p. 41. [Excerpts from Fraser's article, which was first published in *Maclean's Magazine* on December 15, 1951].

O200 – 'The secret life of Mackenzie King, spiritualist.' *Maclean's Magazine,* 64 (24), December 15, 1951, pp. 7–9, 60–61.
Reprinted in H. Gordon Green and Guy Sylvestre, eds., *A century of Canadian literature / Un siècle de literature canadienne* (Toronto: Ryerson Press, and Montreal: Editions HMH, 1967), pp. 295–302.

O201 – 'Should they censor the King papers?' *Maclean's Magazine,* 68 (11), May 28, 1955, pp. 6, 61–62.

O202 – 'Why the CBC shunned the King story.' *Maclean's Magazine,* 69 (7), March 31, 1956, pp. 5, 58–59.

O203 [FREEDMAN, MAX?]. 'Indiscretions of Mr King.' *Winnipeg Free Press,* July 13, 1956, p. 19. [Signed 'M.F.'].

O204 – 'Mr Mackenzie King.' *Winnipeg Free Press,* December 20, 1952, p. 14. [Review of Bruce Hutchison, *The incredible Canadian*].

O205 FREEMAN, ALAN. 'Dec. 17: Centenary of Mackenzie King.' *The Whig-Standard* [Kingston], December 10, 1974, p. 7. [Canadian Press article].

O206 – 'Mackenzie King's writings opened to public. Wartime Prime Minister's diaries reveal problems.' *Leader-Post* [Regina], January 3, 1975, p. 8. [Canadian Press dispatch].

O207 FRENCH, GOLDWIN. 'Some comments on the "Incredible Canadian."' *Waterloo Review,* Summer 1959, pp. 37–40.

O208 FRENCH, WILLIAM. 'Sex and all, he's still an enigma.' *The Globe and Mail,* April 8, 1976, p. 15. [Review of C.P. Stacey, *A very double life: The private world of Mackenzie King*].

O209 FULFORD, ROBERT. 'Mackenzie King left literary monument.' *Toronto Daily Star,* August 30, 1980, p. H5.

O210 GALT, GINNY. 'Mackenzie King was hard-boiled, but not crackpot.' *Leader-Post* [Regina], January 8, 1975, p. 12.

O211 GARDNER, RAY. 'When Mackenzie King inspected opium factories.' *Maclean's Magazine*, 73 (19), September 10, 1960, p. 72.

O212 GESSELL, PAUL. 'The King–King wingding.' *Toronto Star*, April 25, 1992, p. B5. [Description of an incident between the Canadian and British governments following the engagement of Princess Elizabeth and Prince Philip in July 1947 regarding formal approval by the two governments].

O213 – 'Mrs King unveiled: Biography probe, life of Mackenzie King's beloved mother.' *Ottawa Citizen*, August 19, 1997, p. B9.

O214 GIBSON, JAMES ALEXANDER. 'At first hand: Recollections of a Prime Minister.' *Queen's Quarterly*, 61 (1), Spring 1954, pp. 13–20.

O215 – 'Mr Mackenzie King and Canadian autonomy, 1921–1946.' Canadian Historical Association *Annual Report*, 1951, pp. 1–10.

O216 – 'Mr Mackenzie King and the blunt pencil: Some marginalia of Canadian foreign policy.' *Dalhousie Review*, 32 (1), Spring 1952, pp. 19–24.

O217 – 'Root and branch in Canadian foreign policy, 1938–1947.' *Bulletin of Canadian Studies*, 5 (2), October 1981, pp. 48–62.

O218 GIDDENS, FRANCIS W. 'The notebook of a secretary.' *Ottawa Journal*, April 22, 1939, p. 8. [Giddens was King's former secretary].

O219 – 'The Prime Minister on horseback.' *Ottawa Journal*, September 10, 1941, p. 8.

O220 'God told King to resign – diary.' *Montreal Gazette*, January 3, 1979, p. 1. [Canadian Press–United Press International dispatches].

O221 GOLD, WILLIAM F. 'Comparaison reveals common interests [between Brian Mulroney and Mackenzie King.]' *Calgary Herald*, January 3, 1988, p. B1.

O222 – 'Mulroney imitates crafty King on abortion issue.' *Calgary Herald*, July 14, 1989, p. A5.

O223 GOLDENBURG, HYMAN CARL. 'Canada's Prime Minister.' *Fortnightly*, no. 829, January 1936, pp. 71–78.

O224 GRAHAM, WILLIAM ROGER. 'King, Byng and Mr Meighen.' *Horizon Canada*, 8 (94), pp. 2233–2239.

O225 – 'Some comments on a credible Canadian.' *Canadian Historical Review*, 39 (4), December 1958, pp. 296–311.

O226 GRANATSTEIN, JACK LAWRENCE. 'King and country.' *International Journal*, 24 (2), Spring 1969, pp. 374–377. [Review of J.W. Pickersgill and Donald F. Forster, eds., *The Mackenzie King record*, vol. 2].

O227 – 'Mackenzie King and the turn to social welfare.' *Quarterly of Canadian Studies for the Secondary School*, 2 (1), Spring 1972, pp. 13–22.

O228 – 'The Mackenzie Kingdom: Review article.' *Canadian Forum*, 50 (598–599), November–December 1970, pp. 273–275. [Review of J.W. Pickersgill and Donald F. Forster, eds., *The Mackenzie King record*, vols. 3–4].

O229 – 'Poets, novelists and politicians: The case of Mackenzie King.' *Tamarack Review*, no. 65, March 1975, pp. 30–38.

O230 – 'Le Québec et le plébiscite de 1942 sur la conscription.' *Revue d'histoire de l'Amérique français*, 27 (1), juin 1973, pp. 43–62.

O231 – 'That cursed question: Conscription in the two world wars.' *Quarterly of Canadian Studies for the Secondary School*, 5 (1), 1978, pp. 16–22.

O232 – 'Was King really bribed? Diaries cast doubt on it.' *The Globe and Mail*, January 18, 1977, p. 7.

O233 – 'The York South by-election of 1942: A turning point in Canadian history.' *Canadian Historical Review*, 48 (2), June 1967, pp. 142–158.

O234 – and ROBERT BOTHWELL. 'A self-evident national duty, 1935–1939.' *Journal of Imperial and Commonwealth History*, 3 (2), January 1975, pp. 212–233.

O235 – and ROBERT D. CUFF. 'The Hyde Park Declaration, 1941: Origins and significance.' *Canadian Historical Review*, 55 (1), March 1974, pp. 59–80.

O236 GRAY, CHARLOTTE. 'Crazy like a fox. All we ever hear about is Mackenzie King's "Kookiness." It's time we admitted he's easily the best prime minister Canada ever had.' *Saturday Night*, 112 (8), October 1997, pp. 42–46, 48, 50, 94.

O237 GRAY, JOHN. 'Diary's release would horrify King, executor says.' *The Globe and Mail,* January 7, 1981, p. 8.

O238 GRAY, WALTER. 'At Laurier House: Mr Diefenbaker plays host to two Liberal ghosts.' *The Globe and Mail,* July 19, 1960, p. 7.

O239 GREER, HAROLD. 'King and the Korean war: A warning from the dead?' *The Whig-Standard* [Kingston], January 3, 1974, p. 6.

O240 GRIFFIN, FREDERICK. 'King – The defender.' *Star Weekly,* March 16, 1940, pp. 3, 5.

O241 – 'Kingsmere.' *Toronto Star Weekly,* February 4, 1928, p. 17.

O242 GWYN, RICHARD. 'Party deposited $25,000 in King's bank account.' *Ottawa Journal,* January 6, 1977, pp. 1–2.

O243 HALL, H. DUNCAN. 'The genesis of the Balfour declaration of 1926.' *Journal of Commonwealth Political Studies,* 1, 1961–1963, pp. 169–193.

O244 HAMBLETON, GEORGE. 'The Mackenzie King diaries.' *Ottawa Evening Citizen,* August 14, 1950, p. 32.

O245 HAMILTON, LILLIAN N. 'Commends Mr King for his faith.' [Letter to the Editor]. *The Globe and Mail,* November 18, 1950, p. 6.

O246 HARBOUR, FRANCES VRYLING. 'Conscription and socialization: Four Canadian ministers [Mackenzie King, Charles G. Power, James Layton Ralston, and Thomas Alexander Crerar].' *Armed Forces and Society,* 15 (2), Winter 1989, pp. 227–247.

O247 HARDY, HENRY REGINALD. 'King chosen leader after three ballots.' *Ottawa Citizen,* August 4, 1948, p. 2.

O248 – 'King's stock soared after effective speech.' *Ottawa Citizen,* August 3, 1948, p. 11.

O249 – 'The Kingsmere estate.' *Ottawa Evening Citizen,* August 9, 1950, p. 32.

O250 – 'Liberal platforms of 1919 and 1948 compared.' *Ottawa Citizen,* August 9, 1948, p. 11.

O251 – 'Our fantastic legacy from Mackenzie King.' *Maclean's Magazine,* 64 (14), July 15, 1951, pp. 7–9, 38–39.

O252 HARKNESS, ROSS. 'The Byng incident: Is our governor-general a figurehead or safeguard of the electors' rights?' *Toronto Daily Star*, April 10, 1963, p. 7.

O253 HARRIS, WALTER. 'How my Auntie communed with the ghost of Mackenzie King.' *New Liberty*, 35 (8), November 1959, pp. 35, 42, 48–49.

O254 HART, MICHAEL. 'Almost but not quite: The 1947–48 bilateral Canada–U.S. negotiations.' *American Review of Canadian Studies*, 19 (1), Spring 1989, pp. 25–58.

O255 HEENEY, ARNOLD DANFORTH PATRICK. 'Mackenzie King and the Cabinet Secretariat.' *Canadian Public Administration*, 10 (3), September 1967, pp. 366–375.

O256 HENDERSON, GEORGE FLETCHER. 'Archives display of Mackenzie King letters.' *Factotum* [Monthly Bulletin of the Douglas Library, Queen's University], 10 (12), December 1974, pp. 10–11.

O257 – 'Mackenzie King and Queen's University, 1893–1950.' *Historic Kingston*, 39, 1991, pp. 62–79.

O258 – 'Mackenzie King and the stone angels of Moorside.' *Up the Gatineau*, 18, 1992, pp. 1–4.

O259 – 'Mackenzie King the farmer.' *Up the Gatineau*, 20, 1994, pp. 15–21.

O260 – 'Mackenzie King's first visit to Kingsmere.' *Up the Gatineau*, 19, 1993, pp. 8–11.

O261 – 'Strange Mackenzie King remains a mystery still.' *The Whig-Standard* [Kingston], July 6, 1976, p. 7. [Review of C.P. Stacey, *A very double life: The private world of Mackenzie King*.]

O262 HERCHAK, GAYLE. 'Souls of indiscretion.' *Alberta Report*, 10 (49), November 28, 1983, p. 8.

O263 HIGH, STANLEY. 'Canada's Mackenzie King.' *Reader's Digest*, 47 (281), September 1945, pp. 70–73.

O264 HILLMER, NORMAN. 'The incredible Canadian: Mackenzie King and the Commonwealth.' *University of Leeds Review*, 22, 1979, pp. 77–85.

O265 – 'O.D. Skelton: The scholar who set a future pattern.' *International Perspectives,* September–October 1973, pp. 46–49.

O266 – and JACK LAWRENCE GRANATSTEIN. 'Historians rank the best and worst prime ministers.' *Maclean's,* 110 (16), April 21, 1997, pp. 34–39. [Mackenzie King was ranked as Canada's greatest prime minister, followed by Sir John A. Macdonald and Sir Wilfrid Laurier].

O267 HOLMES, JOHN W. 'How Canada made its groping way into world affairs.' *The Globe and Mail,* April 28, 1962, p. 26. [Review of Walter A. Riddell, ed., *Documents on Canadian foreign policy,* vol. 1].

O268 HOOGENRAAD, MAUREEN. 'Mackenzie King à Berlin.' *L'Archiviste,* 20 (3), 1994, pp. 19–21.

O269 – 'Mackenzie King in Berlin.' *The Archivist,* 20 (3), 1994, pp. 19–21.

O270 HOW, DOUGLAS. 'Mackenzie King: The man nobody knew.' *Reader's Digest,* 113 (678), October 1978, pp. 205–210, 212, 214, 216, 220–222, 224–226, 228, 230, 232, 234, 236, 238, 242, 244, 246, 248, 251–252, 254.

O271 – 'Mackenzie King a lone ranger says caretaker at Kingsmere.' *Montreal Gazette,* July 24, 1950, p. 5.

O272 – 'Mr King and the people: Few knew him; he knew Canada.' *The Globe and Mail,* July 24, 1950, p. 19.

O273 HUME, J.A. 'King's diary: The mirror of a man.' *Ottawa Citizen,* November 9, 1963, p. 14. [Review of Neatby, *William Lyon Mackenzie King: The lonely heights, 1924–1932*].

O274 – 'Paint box of King diary used in a new portrayal.' *Ottawa Citizen,* December 8, 1962, p. 41. [Review of F.A. McGregor, *The fall and rise of Mackenzie King, 1911–1919*].

O275 HUMPHRIES, CHARLES WALTER. 'Mackenzie King looks at two 1911 elections.' *Ontario History,* 66 (3), September 1964, pp. 203–206.

O276 HUSTAK, ALAN. 'Ghost of Mackenzie King lives at Kingsmere: PM of 21 years remains a mystery 40 years after his death.' *Montreal Gazette,* July 29, 1990, section D, p. 5.

O277 HUTCHISON, BRUCE. 'Canadian finishes a job.' *Christian Science Monitor Magazine*, March 13, 1948, p. 7.

O278 – 'The causerie.' *Winnipeg Free Press*, July 30, 1950, p. 19. [Relates to the King memoirs].

O279 – 'How Mackenzie King won his greatest gamble.' *Maclean's Magazine*, 65 (21), November 1, 1952, pp. 16–17, 37–48.

O280 – 'King: The complicated man.' *Ottawa Citizen*, December 5, 1958, p. 6.

O281 – 'King as a great leader.' *Ottawa Citizen*, December 15, 1958, p. 6.

O282 – 'Mackenzie King: A strange legend and unknown man.' *The Globe and Mail*, December 17, 1974, p. 7.

O283 – 'Mackenzie King and the "revolt" of the Army: A postscript.' *Maclean's Magazine*, 66 (10), May 15, 1953, pp. 20, 57–58.

O284 – 'Mackenzie King between two worlds.' *Christian Science Monitor*, April 6, 1940, p. 6.

O285 – 'Mackenzie King of Canada.' *American Mercury*, 63 (276), December 1946, pp. 661–668.

O286 – 'Prime Minister! most vigorous man in cabinet.' *Vancouver Sun*, December 17, 1943, pp. 14–15.

O287 – 'Prime Ministers' diaries valuable historic records.' *Leader-Post* [Regina], January 31, 1959, p. 14.

O288 – 'Seven Mackenzie Kings Canadians never knew.' *Maclean's*, 77 (19), October 3, 1964, pp. 12–13, 28, 30, 32–35.

O289 – 'Thoughts on Mackenzie King.' *Maclean's Magazine*, 65 (22), November 15, 1952, pp. 30–31, 70–73.

O290 HYATT, ALBERT MARK JOHN. 'The King–Byng episode: A footnote to history.' *Dalhousie Review*, 43 (4), Winter 1963–1964, pp. 469–473.

O291 'Il voyait sa mère et ses chiens dans sa crème à barbe.' *La Presse*, 3 janvier 1979, p. A-4.

O292 INGLIS, A.I. 'Loring C. Christie and the imperial idea, 1919–1926.' *Journal of Canadian Studies*, 7 (2), May 1972, pp. 19–27.

O293 JENNINGS, SARAH. 'The ruins at Kingsmere: Former Prime Minister William Lyon Mackenzie King's folly in the Gatineau Hills.' *City & Country Home,* 13 (5), October 1994, pp. 30–33.

O294 KARSH, YOUSUF. 'Premier King in color.' *Maclean's Magazine,* 60 (19), October 1, 1947, pp. 24–25, 73.

O295 KATZ, SIDNEY. 'The "devil" in Mackenzie King.' *The Globe and Mail,* October 18, 1984, p. L11.

O296 KEENLEYSIDE, HUGH LLEWELLYN. 'The Canadian election of 1925.' *Current History,* 23 (4), January 1926, pp. 508–511.

O297 KERR, AINSLIE. 'Clothes closet phone for the young WLMK.' *Ottawa Citizen,* June 27, 1951, p. 3. [Description of 331 Somerset Street where King had rooms from 1901 to 1910].

O298 KEYSERLINGK, R.H. 'Mackenzie King's spiritualism and his view of Hitler in 1939.' *Journal of Canadian Studies,* 20, Winter 1985/86, pp. 26–44.

O299 KING, JOHN, MARY TRUMAN, and HUGH WINSOR. 'Papers show King was given $25,000 by party fundraisers.' *The Globe and Mail,* January 16, 1977, pp. 1–2.

O300 'King admirant la patineuse Scott mais craignait devoir l'embrasser.' *La Presse,* 4 janvier 1979, p. A-6.

O301 'King avait plus de difficultés à administrer sa maison qu'il en avait eues à diriger le pays.' *La Presse,* 3 janvier 1980, p. A-2.

O302 'The King–Byng correspondence: Some secret history.' *Ottawa Journal,* February 16, 1927, p. 6.

O303 'King craignait une 3e guerre mondiale.' *La Presse,* 3 janvier 1979, p. A-4.

O304 'King diaries are spirited.' *Leader-Post* [Regina], January 3, 1975, p. 19.

O305 'King diaries open to all.' *Leader-Post* [Regina], January 3, 1975, p. 8. [Canadian Press dispatch].

O306 'King ingurgitait des potions allant de la morphine à la vitamine E.' *La Presse,* 3 janvier 1981, p. B-10.

O307 'King n'aimait pas les conférences de presse.' *La Presse,* 4 janvier 1979, p. A-6.

O308 'King no crackpot, former secretary [Walter Turnbull] says.' *The Globe and Mail,* January 7, 1975, p. 3.

O309 'King of Canada: Mackenzie King, Prime Minister of Canada, heads Uncle Sam's nearest neighbour nation to the north.' *True Comics,* no. 12, 1942, pp. 1–6.

O310 'King Papers to Archives in 1975. Diaries to be kept as well.' *Leader-Post* [Regina], May 24, 1955, p. 11.

O311 'King s'est cru inspiré de Dieu.' *La Presse,* 3 janvier 1979, p. A-4.

O312 'King's spiritual beliefs downgraded achievements.' *Leader-Post* [Regina], December 17, 1974, p. 45.

O313 'King's spiritual friends did not affect policies.' *Leader-Post* [Regina], February 18, 1975, p. 5. [Summary of C.P. Stacey lecture at the University of British Columbia, February 14, 1975].

O314 'Kissing – and a film star – caused King agony.' *Montreal Gazette,* January 4, 1979, p. 1. [Canadian Press dispatch].

O315 KNOWLES, R.E. 'Revisiting boyhood scenes ex-Premier's greatest joy.' *Toronto Star,* September 28, 1932, pp. 1, 3.

O316 KRITZWISER, KAY. 'Laurier House, Mackenzie King's old home.' *The Globe and Mail,* March 27, 1976, p. 42.

O317 LABRECHE, JULIANNE. 'Once and future king.' *Maclean's,* 92 (3), January 15, 1979, pp. 15–17.

O318 LAMBERT, NORMAN PLATT. 'In August 1939 Mackenzie King envisaged outbreak of World War II.' *Ottawa Journal,* September 4, 1959, p. 6.

O319 LANCTOT, GUSTAVE. 'Mackenzie King d'après ses memoires.' *Revue de l'Université Laval,* 13 (9), mai 1959, pp. 826–829. [Review of Dawson, *William Lyon Mackenzie King: A political biography, 1874–1923,* vol. 1].

O320 LANGLOIS, GEORGES. 'Laurier et Lincoln modèles de M King.' *La Presse,* 16 décembre 1944, pp. 31–32.

O321 – 'M King, membre à vie de la galerie de la presse.' *La Presse,* 16 décembre 1944, pp. 31–32.

O322 – 'M King a recherché avant tout la paix.' *La Presse,* 26 juillet 1950, pp. 1, 24.

O323 LANGTON, HUGH HORNBY. 'Mackenzie King, William Mulock, James Mavor and the University of Toronto students revolt of 1895.' *Canadian Historical Review*, 69 (4), December 1988, pp. 490–503.

O324 LAPOINTE, HUGHES, and DOUGLAS ABBOTT. 'Complex, charming, tough, dominating.' *Chronicle-Herald* [Halifax], December 14, 1974, p. 10.

O325 LAPOINTE, KIRK. 'He lived in a world of constant self-delusion.' *TV Guide*, 12 (13), March 26, 1988, pp. 4–5, 9, 11. [Relates to 'The King Chronicle' shown on CBC-TV, March 27–March 29, 1988].

O326 LAURENDEAU, ARTHUR. 'La collusion King–Meighen–Tim Buck.' *Action nationale*, 19 (4), avril 1942, pp. 170–171.

O327 LAVOIE, MICHAEL. 'Canadian civil war loomed over conscription.' *Leader-Post* [Regina], January 3, 1976, p. 10. [Canadian Press dispatch].

O328 LEDERLE, JOHN WILLIAM. 'The Liberal Convention of 1919 and the selection of Mackenzie King.' *Dalhousie Review*, 27 (1), April 1947, pp. 85–92.

O329 LEITERMAN, DOUGLAS. 'The King nobody knew.' *CBC Times*, 12 (35), March 5–11, 1960, pp. 4–5, 18. [Relates to the CBC-TV programs in the 'Close-up' series, which were telecast on March 10 and March 17, 1960].

O330 LEMIEUX, EDMOND. '"La conscription si": "Une poulet à la King" (Notes en marge du dernier débat).' *Action nationale*, 19 (7), juillet 1942, pp. 393–413.

O331 'Les papiers King de 1948.' *L'Archiviste*, 5 (6), novembre–décembre 1978, p. 8.

O332 LEVINE, ALLAN. 'A gentleman of the fourth estate: Grant Dexter on Parliament Hill.' *The Beaver*, 72 (6), December 1992–January 1993, pp. 17–20.

O333 LEWIS, DAVID. 'His privy parts: On perusing the diaries of Mackenzie King, self-appointed leader and most peculiar man.' *Books in Canada*, 5 (6), June 1976, pp. 3–4. [Review of C.P. Stacey, *A very double life: The private world of Mackenzie King*].

O334 LEWIS, JOHN. 'New Liberal leader in Canada.' *World's Work*, 39 (4), February 1920, pp. 346–351.

O335 'The Liberal Convention of 1919: Mackenzie King as party leader.' *Canadian Annual Review*, 1919, pp. 603–610.

O336 LOGAN, JOHN DANIEL. 'The Prime Minister as a man of letters.' *Canadian Magazine*, 61 (3), July 1923, pp. 211–217.

O337 'Look calls on Canada's war chief.' *Look Magazine*, January 13, 1942, pp. 54–55.

O338 LOWER, ARTHUR REGINALD MARSDEN. 'The King who stood before kings.' *Winnipeg Free Press*, October 17, 1970, p. 21. [Review of J.W. Pickersgill and Donald F. Forster, eds., *The Mackenzie King record*, vols. 3–4].

O339 – 'Mackenzie King through his diaries.' *Queen's Quarterly*, 68 (1), Spring 1961–1962, pp. 169–173. [Review of J.W. Pickersgill, ed., *The Mackenzie King record*, vol. 1].

O340 – 'Mr King.' *Canadian Banker*, 57 (3), Autumn 1950, pp. 46–55.

O341 – 'Monument among the tombstones: Dawson's Mackenzie King.' *Queen's Quarterly*, 66 (1), Spring 1959, pp. 146–150. [Review of Dawson, *William Lyon Mackenzie King: A political biography, 1874–1923*, vol. 1].

O342 LUDWIG, EMIL. 'Mackenzie King.' *Contemporary Review*, 174, September 1948, pp. 151–154.

O343 LYNCH, CHARLES. 'Mackenzie King's carpet hid Canada's problems.' *Ottawa Citizen*, December 18, 1974, p. 7.

O344 LYON, GEORGE H. 'Canadian Prime Minister as seen by U.S. newsmen.' *Ottawa Citizen*, April 28, 1941, p. 3.

O345 – 'Close-up of Premier King in his house of memories.' *Ottawa Citizen*, April 29, 1941, p. 7.

O346 – 'Mackenzie King lives in a house of memories.' *New York PM*, May 12, 1941, p. 5.

O347 – 'Meet Mackenzie King, head man of Canada at war.' *New York PM*, May 11, 1941, p. 5.

O348 'Lyon Mackenzie King au bord de la guerre civile.' *La Presse*, 2 janvier 1976, pp. A-1, A-6.

O349 MacCORMAC, JOHN. 'A Gladstonian Liberal steers Canada.' *New York Times*, December 1, 1935, pp. 3, 21.

O350 MacEWEN, GWENDOLYN. 'Kingsmere.' *The Tamarack Review*, no. 57, Second Quarter, 1971, pp. 41–43.

O351 MacFARLANE, JOHN. 'Mr Lapointe, Mr King, Quebec and conscription.' *The Beaver*, 75 (2), April/May 1995, pp. 26–31.

O352 MacINDOE, J.J. 'McKenzie [*sic*] King a spiritualist.' [Letter]. *Two Worlds*, 1951.

O353 MACKAY, ROBERT ALEXANDER. 'The political ideas of William Lyon Mackenzie King.' *Canadian Journal of Political and Economic Science*, 3 (1), February 1937, pp. 1–22.

O354 – 'The Mackenzie King saga.' *Dalhousie Review*, 51 (2), 1971, pp. 257–263. [Review of J.W. Pickersgill and Donald F. Forster, eds., *The Mackenzie King record*, vols. 3–4].

O355 'Mackenzie King, architect of Canadian sovereignty.' *Round Table*, 40 (106), September 1950, pp. 304–307.

O356 'Mackenzie King, step by step.' *New World Illustrated*, 1 (1), March 1940, pp. 3–6, 49.

O357 'Mackenzie King diary.' *Leader-Post* [Regina], December 18, 1974, p. 10.

O358 'Mackenzie King paid a great tribute to famous medium.' *Psychic News*, no. 16, September 21, 1950, p. 2.

O359 'Mackenzie King Papers of 1948.' *The Archivist*, 5 (6), November–December 1978, p. 10.

O360 'Mackenzie King riddle: How he hid bizarre belief.' *Toronto Star*, January 3, 1979, p. 10.

O361 'Mackenzie King will great human document, names the people his heirs.' *Ottawa Journal*, August 9, 1950, p. 23.

O362 'Mackenzie King's romance.' *Toronto Telegram*, November 18, 1958, p. 6.

O363 MacLENNAN, HUGH. 'Canada hypnotized by King.' *The Globe and Mail*, January 16, 1978, p. 16. [Excerpt from address by Hugh MacLennan to Canadian Club of Toronto].

O364 – 'Culture, Canadian style.' *Saturday Review of Literature,* 25 (13), March 28, 1942, pp. 3–4, 18–20.

O365 – 'The ghost that haunts us.' *The Montrealer,* 24 (4), April 1953, pp. 54, 56. [Review of Bruce Hutchison, *The incredible Canadian*].
Reprinted in Dorothy Duncan, ed., *Thirty and three* (Toronto: Macmillan, 1954), pp. 104–111.

O366 – 'The psychology of Canadian nationalism.' *Foreign Affairs,* 27 (3), April 1949, pp. 413–425.

O367 – 'The ten greatest Canadians.' *New Liberty,* 26 (90), November 1949, p. 13.[127]

O368 MacNEILL, ALEXANDER [FRED A. McGREGOR].[128] 'Is Mackenzie King responsible for a new note in Rockefeller Jr.'s relations with labour?' *Star Weekly* [Toronto], January 29, 1916, p. 12.

O369 MacSWEENY, JOSEPH. 'Colloquium delves into life of Mackenzie King.' *Ottawa Citizen,* December 17, 1974, p. 35.

O370 – 'King "linked" to Rockefellers.' *Ottawa Citizen,* December 18, 1974, p. 71.

O371 – 'King needed a wife to ease loneliness: Casgrain.' *Ottawa Citizen,* December 19, 1974, p. 62.

O372 – 'Senator [Eugene Forsey] rips into King.' *Leader-Post* [Regina], December 18, 1974, p. 10. [Canadian Press dispatch].

O373 MacTAVISH, NEWTON McFAUL. 'The King family in literature.' *Maclean's Magazine,* 49 (6), March 15, 1936, p. 22.

O374 – 'W.L. Mackenzie King, the new leader of the Liberal Party in Canada.' *Canadian Magazine,* 54 (1), November 1919, pp. 71–74.

O375 – 'The vision of immortality: A reconsideration of the Rt. Hon. Mackenzie King's remarkable book, "The Secret of Heroism."' *Canadian Magazine,* 64 (3), April 1925, pp. 70–71, 85.

---

127 MacLennan named Samuel de Champlain, Count Frontenac, Joseph Howe, Donald MacKay, Sir John A. Macdonald, Sir William Osler, Sir Wilfrid Laurier, Tom Thompson, Sir Frederick Banting, and Mackenzie King as the ten greatest Canadians.

128 A footnote reference in Dawson, *William Lyon Mackenzie King: A political biography, 1874–1923,* p. 491, identifies McGregor as the author of this article.

O376 MALLORY, JAMES. 'A note on the King era.' *Canadian Forum*, 30 (357), October 1950, p. 152.

O377 MALLORY, JAMES RUSSELL. 'The appointment of the Governor General: Responsible government, autonomy and the Royal prerogative.' *Canadian Journal of Economics and Political Science*, 36 (1), February 1960, pp. 96–107.

O378 – 'Mackenzie King.' *Political Studies*, 8 (1), February 1960, pp. 78–80. [Review of Dawson, *William Lyon Mackenzie King: A political biography, 1874–1923*, vol. 1].

O379 – 'Mackenzie King and the origins of the Cabinet Secretariat.' *Canadian Public Administration*, 19 (2), Summer 1976, pp. 254–266.

O380 'A man and a dog.' *Star Weekly*, October 19, 1940, p. 19.

O381 'A man in Canada's image.' *The Globe and Mail*, January 6, 1977, p. 6.

O382 MANSERGH, NICHOLAS. 'Dominions autonomous or independent? The Mackenzie King view, 1926 and 1947.' *Bulletin of Canadian Studies*, 6 (2), Autumn 1983, pp. 11–15.

O383 – 'Prime Ministers' Prime Minister.' *International Journal*, 16 (4), Autumn 1961, pp. 523–529. [Review of J.W. Pickersgill, ed., *The Mackenzie King record*, vol. 1].

O384 MARKHAM, VIOLET. 'Mackenzie King.' *Westminster Gazette*, December 8, 1921.

O385 MARTIN, GED. 'Mackenzie King, the medium and the messages.' *British Journal of Canadian Studies*, 4 (1), 1989, pp. 109–135.

O386 – 'Mackenzie King and the hymnbook.' *British Journal of Canadian Studies*, 3 (2), 1988, pp. 389–390.

O387 MARTIN, JOE. 'William Lyon Mackenzie King: Canada's first management consultant?' *Business Quarterly*, 56 (1), Summer 1991, pp. 31–36.

O388 MARTIN, ROBERT. 'Laurier House: History haunts Ottawa landmark.' *The Globe and Mail*, April 19, 1980, Travel Section, p. 4.

O389 – 'Mackenzie King: Stuffy home left imprint for life.' *The Globe and Mail*, November 3, 1979, p. T3.

O390 McAREE, JOHN VERNER. 'More light on Mr King.' *Montreal Gazette*, October 1, 1955, p. 6. [Review of Ferns and Ostry, *The age of Mackenzie King: The rise of the leader*].

O391 – 'Mr King and spiritism.' *The Globe and Mail*, September 23, 1953, p. 6.

O392 – 'Mr King and spirits.' *The Globe and Mail*, September 14, 1953, p. 6.

O393 – 'New light on Mr King.' *The Globe and Mail*, November 10, 1950, p. 6.

O394 – 'Questions for a ghost.' *The Globe and Mail*, October 26, 1954, p. 6.

O395 McCOOK, JAMES. 'Hands of clock had strange message for Mackenzie King.' *Ottawa Journal*, November 17, 1958, p. 7. [Review of Dawson, *William Lyon Mackenzie King: A political biography, 1874–1923*, vol. 1].

O396 – 'Heaven helps Mr King.' *Ottawa Journal*, November 5, 1963, p. 6. [Review of Neatby, *William Lyon Mackenzie King: The lonely heights, 1924–1932*].

O397 – 'Remembered others even in last hour.' *Ottawa Journal*, July 24, 1950, pp. 1, 16.

O398 McDONALD, ROBERT. 'Mackenzie King wrote to actress over 3 decades.' *Sunday Star*, December 7, 1986, p. B4.

O399 McDOUGALD, J.B. 'Rt. Hon. W.L. Mackenzie King.' *The Gazette* [Montreal], July 25, 1950, p. 6.

O400 McGEACHY, JAMES BURNS. 'Canada's mystical Prime Minister.' *Financial Post*, 52 (47), November 22, 1958, p. 7. [Review of Dawson, *William Lyon Mackenzie King: A political biography, 1874–1923*, vol. 1].

O401 McGUIGAN, MICHAEL. 'Neighbour King – his is a hands-across-the-border policy.' *Who*, June 1941, pp. 15–17, 58.

O402 McINTYRE, LYNN, and JOEL J. JEFFRIES. 'William Lyon Mackenzie King: The defense mechanisms of a social reformer.' *University of Toronto Medical Quarterly*, 56, April 1979, pp. 136–140.

O403 McKECHNIE, L.M. 'Must Mackenzie King's diary be burned?' *The Telegram* [Toronto], November 17, 1958, p. 7. [Review of Dawson, *William Lyon Mackenzie King: A political biography, 1874–1923*, vol. 1].

O404 McKEOWN, ROBERT. 'Mackenzie's private life with the occult.' *Montreal Star*, December 14, 1974, p. B-5.

O405 – 'Mackenzie King's "ruins" become the framework for a festival.' *Weekend Magazine*, 5 (28), July 9, 1955, pp. 8–9.

O406 McNAUGHT, KENNETH W. 'Canadian foreign policy and the Whig interpretation, 1936–1939.' Canadian Historical Association *Report*, 1957, pp. 43–54.

O407 – 'National affairs.' *Saturday Night*, 81 (2), February 1966, pp. 9–10. [Review of James Eayrs, *In defence of Canada: Appeasement and rearmament*].

O408 – 'A private diary and a public document.' *Dalhousie Review*, 39, Summer 1959, pp. 90–95. [Review of Dawson, *William Lyon Mackenzie King: A political biography, 1874–1923*, vol. 1].

O409 'McNaughton image remained untarnished despite loss of command of overseas army.' *The Whig-Standard* [Kingston], December 16, 1963, pp. 19–20. [Canadian Press dispatch].

O410 MEARS, F.C. 'Anglo-American agent.' *Canadian Business*, 12 (2), February 1939, pp. 20–23.

O411 'Memories of Yuletide, politician long past.' *The Whig-Standard* [Kingston], December 22, 1992, p. 5. [Canadian Press dispatch]. [Relates to the correspondence between King and Marilyn Kilbasco, a young girl the prime minister met at Woodside during a visit there in the autumn of 1947].

O412 MILNES, ARTHUR H. 'Mackenzie King: Le jeune journaliste.' *Revue parliamentaire canadienne*, 15 (3), automne 1992, pp. 14–15.

O413 – 'Mackenzie King: The young journalist.' *Canadian Parliamentary Review*, 15 (3), Autumn 1992, pp. 14–15.

O414 MOHER, MARK. 'The "biography" in politics: Mackenzie King in 1935.' *Canadian Historical Review*, 55 (2), June 1974, pp. 238–248.

O415 MOIR, JOHN SARGENT. 'William Lyon Mackenzie King.' *Encyclopedia Americana*, 1988 edition, 16, pp. 452–453.

O416 MORTON, JAMES. 'Unfailing thoughtfulness of others one of Mr King's first attributes.' *Vancouver Sun*, July 26, 1950, p. 4.

O417 'Mr King and the nation.' *Saturday Night*, 65 (43), August 1, 1950, p. 6.

O418 'Mr King in 1895.' *Saturday Night*, 64 (10), December 11, 1948, p. 5.

O419 'Mr King was unable to subscribe [to the purchase of the home of William Lyon Mackenzie, 82 Bond Street, Toronto].' *York Pioneer*, 1959, pp. 16–18.

O420 'Mr King's memoirs.' *Saturday Night*, 65 (2988), August l, 1950, p. 2.

O421 MUNRO, JOHN ALEXANDER. 'Loring Christie and Canadian external relations, 1935–1939.' *Journal of Canadian Studies*, 7 (2), May 1972, pp. 28–35.

O422 – 'Neatby's Mackenzie King a fascinating account.' *International Perspectives*, March–April 1979, pp. 26–28. [Review of Neatby, *William Lyon Mackenzie King: The prism of unity, 1932–39*].

O423 – 'Nouvel examen de l'affaire Riddell.' *Affaires extérieures*, 21 (10), octobre 1969, pp. 384–395.

O424 – 'Récit fasinant sur Mackenzie King.' *Perspectives internationales*, mars–avril 1977, pp. 27–29. [Review of Neatby, *William Lyon Mackenzie King: The prism of unity, 1932–39*].

O425 – 'The Riddell affair reconsidered.' *External Affairs*, 21 (10), October 1969, pp. 361–375.

O426 MUNRO, J.K. 'Why King won Laurier's mantle.' *Maclean's Magazine*, 32 (9), September 1919, pp. 35–37, 39.

O427 MURPHY, BRIAN. 'Les papiers King: Un héritage irremplaçable.' *L'Archiviste*, 14 (3), mai–juin 1987, pp. 8–9.

O428 – 'The Mackenzie King Papers: An irreplaceable heritage.' *The Archivist*, 14 (3), May–June 1987, pp. 8–9.

O429 MURRAY, GLADSTONE. 'Mr Mackenzie King succeeds Mr Bennett.' *Ottawa Citizen*, December 18, 1935, p. 22.

O430 NEATBY, HERBERT BLAIR. 'Henry Albert Harper.' *Dictionnaire biographique du Canada*, 13, pp. 482–483.

O431 – 'Henry Albert Harper.' *Dictionary of Canadian Biography*, 13, p. 445.

O432 – 'Knight of the Holy Spirit: Mackenzie King insisted his motives were unselfish and pure. But he was not the man he thought he was.' *The Globe and Mail*, January 3, 1981, p. 13. [Review of Joy E. Esberry, *Knight of the Holy Spirit*].

O433 – 'Mackenzie King and French Canada.' *Journal of Canadian Studies*, 11 (1), February 1976, pp. 3–13.

O434 – 'Mackenzie King and psycho-biography.' *Social Sciences in Canada*, 3 (3), 1975, pp. 15–16.

O435 – 'Mackenzie King and the depression: The reluctant reformer.' *Canadian Issues/Themes canadiens*, 3, 1987, pp. 39–49.

O436 – 'Mackenzie King and the national identity.' Historical and Scientific Society of Manitoba, *Papers*, Third Series, 24, 1968, pp. 77–87.

O437 – 'Mackenzie King's record of his interview with Adolf Hitler, 29 June 1937.' *Zeitschrift der Gesellschaft fur Kanada-Studien*, 6 Jahrgang/Nr. 1, pp. 117–125.

O438 – 'William Lyon Mackenzie King.' *The Canadian Encylopedia*, 3, pp. 940–941.

O439 – 'William Lyon Mackenzie King.' *Encylopedia Britannica*, 13, pp. 359–360.

O440 – 'William Lyon Mackenzie King.' *L'Encyclopedie du Canada*, 2, pp. 1046–1047.

O441 NELSON, JAMES. 'Royal meeting was big issue.' *Leader-Post* [Regina], January 3, 1975, p. 18. [Relates to the meeting of King George VI at Quebec City in May 1939].

O442 – 'Sleepless time after dismisal.' *Leader-Post* [Regina], January 3, 1975, p. 18. [Relates to the Conscription Crisis of November 1944].

O443 NESMITH, THOMAS. 'What did Mackenzie King tell Shirley Temple?' *Communique* [Association for Manitoba Archives], 14 (3), Summer 1994, p. 1.

O444 'New book describes Mackenzie King as a ladies' man.' *Toronto Star,* March 5, 1976, p. 1.

O445 NEWMAN, PETER C. '"Check with Jack" Ottawa era ends.' *Toronto Daily Star,* September 20, 1967, p. 7.

O446 – 'The nobility of Sailor Jack's last career – literary chamberlain, history's guardian.' *The Globe and Mail,* January 17, 1976, p. 37.

O447 '1947 Mackenzie King Papers opened.' *The Archivist,* 4 (6), November–December 1977, p. 13.

O448 NOWLAN, A. '"Age of Mackenzie King" well worth the reprinting.' *Atlantic Advocate,* 67, February 1977, p. 63.

O449 O'CONNOR, MURRAY. 'Laurier House.' *The Canadian Liberal,* 3 (4), December 1950, pp. 41–44.

O450 O'HARA, KATHLEEN. 'Kingsmere is among Canada's national treasures.' *The Toronto Star,* August 30, 1997, p. G14.

O451 O'LEARY, MICHAEL GRATTAN. 'An historic letter: Bared in new King biography.' *Ottawa Journal,* December 5, 1955, p. 6. [Review of Ferns and Ostry, *The age of Mackenzie King: The rise of the leader*].

O452 – 'The once and future King.' *The Canadian,* May 14, 1977, pp. 4–6, 8, 10. [Excerpt from *Grattan O'Leary: Recollections of people, press and politics*].

O453 – 'The riddle of King's war leadership.' *Liberty,* 18 (44), November 1, 1941, pp. 14–16.

O454 O'MALLEY, MICHAEL. 'Mackenzie King dreamed of "The most beautiful capital in the world."' *Canadian Heritage,* 12 (1), February–March 1986, pp. 35–37.

O455 O'NEILL, JULIET. 'King still intriging to Canadian public years after death.' *Vancouver Sun,* July 26, 1980, p. H6.

O456 'Old King pictures in Quebec homes.' *The Gazette* [Montreal], July 25, 1950, p. 12.

O457 'Old straw threshed anew.' *Winnipeg Free Press,* May 11, 1943, p. 13. [Account of the King–Byng affair of 1926].

O458 'On bench at Kingsmere: Noted newsman says he talked with late Mackenzie King 3 months ago.' *Ottawa Citizen,* September 25,

1954, p. 2. [Canadian Press dispatch]. [Account of Percy James Philip's conversation with Mackenzie King at Kingsmere].

O459 ORMSBY, MARGARET ANCHORETTA. 'T. Dufferin Pattullo and the little new deal.' *Canadian Historical Review*, 43 (4), December 1962, pp. 277–297.

O460 'The other Mr King.' *Ottawa Citizen*, May 21, 1948, p. 32.

O461 OWEN, IRIS M. 'Mr King and the problem of survival.' *New Horizons: Journal of the New Horizons Research Foundation*, 2 (2), Part 4, September 1978, pp. 7–17.

O462 'Party discipline and the confidence convention: An historical perspective.' *Canadian Parliamentary Review*, 16 (2), Summer 1993, pp. 13–20.

O463 PEARSON, LESTER BOWLES. 'Reflections on inter-war Canadian foreign policy.' *Journal of Canadian Studies*, 7 (2), May 1972, pp. 36–42.

O464 PENNAMEN, GARY. 'Battles of the titans: Mitchell Hepburn, Mackenzie King, Franklin Roosevelt, and the St Lawrence Seaway.' *Ontario History*, 89 (1), March 1997, pp. 1–21.

O465 PHILIP, PERCY JAMES. 'My conversation with Mackenzie King's ghost.' *Liberty*, 31 (11), January 1955, pp. 17, 58–59.

O466 PHILLIPS, ROBERT ARTHUR JOHN. 'King of the Gatineau.' *Up the Gatineau*, 11, 1985, pp. 2–9.

O467 – 'Kingsmere: A Prime Minister's gift to his people.' *Review* [Imperial Oil], no. 382, 1986, pp. 21–25.

O468 – 'Kingsmere revisited.' *Ottawa Magazine*, 5 (3), June 1985, pp. 32–33, 44, 46–47.

O469 PHILPOTT, ELMORE. 'Mr King passes.' *Vancouver Sun*, July 24, 1950, p. 4.

O470 PICKERSGILL, JOHN WHITNEY. 'Bureaucrats and policitians.' *Canadian Public Administration*, 15 (3), Fall 1972, pp. 410–425.

O471 – 'I knew the real Mackenzie King.' *Weekend Magazine*, 10 (10), October 1, 1960, pp. 2–4, 6, 46.

O472 – 'Mackenzie King diaries.' *Canadian Historical Review*, 53 (1), March 1972, p. 112.

O473 – 'Mackenzie King en vedette.' '*Dialogue*,' 3 (3), mars 1977, pp. 3, 14.

O474 – 'The Mackenzie King industry.' '*Dialogue*,' 3 (3), March 1977, pp. 3, 14.

O475 – 'Mackenzie King spurned Rockefeller for an uncertain career in politics.' *The Globe and Mail*, December 15, 1962, p. 22. [Review of F.A. McGregor, *The fall and rise of Mackenzie King, 1911–1919*].

O476 – 'Mackenzie King's speeches.' *Queen's Quarterly*, 57 (3), Autumn 1950, pp. 304–311.

O477 – 'Mr Mackenzie King and the development of the Commonwealth.' *The Canadian Liberal*, 6 (4), Winter 1953–1954, pp. 225–232.

Also printed in the Empire Club of Canada, *Addresses*, 1953–1954, pp. 118–130.

O478 – W.L. Mackenzie King.' *The New Encyclopedia Britannica*, 15th edition, 10, pp. 473–474.

O479 PICTON, JOHN. 'The mystery of a PM's missing diary.' *Sunday Star*, December 30, 1984, p. 10.

O480 PRANG, MARGARET. 'Mackenzie King woos Ontario, 1919–1921.' *Ontario History*, 58 (1), March 1966, pp. 1–20.

O481 PREBBLE, JOHN. 'The queer story of Mackenzie King: Crystal-gazing premier. Believed in supernatural – and "read" tea-leaves. Believed he made contact with dead pet dog.' *Sunday Dispatch*, June 7, 1953.

O482 – 'The queer story of Mackenzie King: Dead mother warned him about his health. Duchess declared he was "guided" on world affairs.' *Sunday Dispatch*, June 14, 1953.

O483 – 'The queer story of Mackenzie King: Roosevelt "message" warned him about trouble in the Far East.' *Sunday Dispatch*, June 21, 1953.

O484 PRESTON, ADRIAN W. 'Canada and the higher direction of the Second World War, 1939–1945.' *Royal United Service Institution Journal*, 110 (657), February 1965, pp. 28–44.

O485 'Prime Minister: King pin.' *Newsweek*, 27 (24), June 17, 1946, p. 54.

O486 'Prime Minister King and his "official family."' *Monetary Times*, 113 (8), August 1945, pp. 32–35, 64.

O487 'Prime Minister Mackenzie King, his country has come of age.' *Time*, 47 (1), January 7, 1946, pp. 22–24. [Includes cover portrait of Mackenzie King].

O488 PROCTOR, VALERIE. 'Laurier House: A history.' *The Archivist*, 8 (4), July–August 1981, pp. 8–11.

O489 – 'La maison Laurier: Pages d'histoire.' *L'Archiviste*, 8 (4), juillet–août 1981, pp. 8–11.

O490 'Question of Mr King's private diary.' *Ottawa Journal*, April 1, 1950, p. 6.

O491 QUIGLEY, MAURICE. 'Mackenzie King – warts and all.' *TV Times*, March 26, 1988, p. 8. [Relates to 'The King Chronicle' shown on CBC-TV, March 27–March 29, 1988].

O492 REA, JAMES EDGAR. 'Clay from feet to forehead: The Mackenzie King controversy.' *The Beaver*, 73 (21), April–May 1993, pp. 27–34.

O493 – 'The Conscription Crisis: What really happened?' *The Beaver*, 74 (2), April–May 1994, pp. 10–19.

O494 REGENSTREIF, SAMUEL PETER. 'A threat to leadership: C.A. Dunning and Mackenzie King.' *Dalhousie Review*, 44, Autumn 1964, pp. 272–289.

O495 'The retiring Mr King.' *Maclean's Magazine*, 54 (8), April 15, 1941, p. 12.

O496 REID, COLIN, and DONALD FORSTER. '"Opera Bouffe": Mackenzie King, Mitch Hepburn, the appointment of the Lieutenant-Governor and the closing of Government House, Toronto, 1937.' *Ontario History*, 69 (4), December 1977, pp. 239–256.

O497 REID, ESCOTT. 'Canada and the threat of war: A discussion of Mr Mackenzie King's foreign policy.' *University of Toronto Quarterly*, 6 (2), January 1937, pp. 242–253.

O498 – 'The Canadian election of 1935 and after.' *American Political Science Review*, 30 (1), February 1936, pp. 111–121.

O499 – 'Did Mr King flout Parliament?' *Canadian Forum*, 15 (181), February 1936, pp. 11–12.

O500 – 'Mr Mackenzie King's foreign policy, 1935–36.' *Canadian Journal of Economics and Political Science*, 3 (1), February 1937, pp. 86–97.

O501 REID, TIM. 'Ever absorbing, not so complete.' *The Globe Magazine*, November 23, 1968, p. 19. [Review of J.W. Pickersgill and Donald F. Forster, eds., *The Mackenzie King record*, vol. 2].

O502 'Restoring the ruins of a wall on Mackenzie King's estate.' *Toronto Daily Star*, December 26, 1988, p. A33.

O503 RICHARDSON, BURTON TAYLOR. 'The career of Mackenzie King.' *Ottawa Citizen*, July 24, 1950, p. 36.

O504 – 'Meet the Prime Minister.' *Winnipeg Free Press*, October 10, 1940, p. 15.

O505 RICHER, LEOPOLD. 'L'énigme de M Mackenzie King.' *Le Devoir*, 11 janvier 1943, p. 1.

O506 RISTECHUBER, RENE. 'Mackenzie King et la France.' *Revue des deux mondes*, fasc. 2/1–3, 1954, pp. 116–136, 287–305, 459–473.

O507 – 'W.L. Mackenzie King, Premier ministre du Canada.' *France Amérique: Revue mensuelle des nations Américanes*, Numéro spécial de Noël, 1946, pp. 603–606.

O508 RITCHIE, CHARLES. 'Founding the United Nations: Some diary notes: At the San Francisco Conference, 1945.' *International Perspectives*, September–October 1985, pp. 7–14.

O509 ROBERTS, LESLIE. 'The crisis that shook Canada.' *New Liberty*, 27 (2), February 1950, pp. 15–19.

O510 ROBERTS, LLOYD. 'Mackenzie King: The man.' *Christian Science Monitor*, December 4, 1935, p. 5.

O511 ROBERTSON, HEATHER. 'Ever hear a ouija rattle, watch a scholar shake in fear, see an archive disappear? It's the unseen hand of Wm. Lyon you-know-who.' *Saturday Night*, 91 (8), November 1976, pp. 39–40.

O512 – 'Kingsmere: Retreat for an eccentric.' *Reader's Digest*, 130 (778), February 1987, pp. 47–50.

O513 – 'Kingsmere, Quebec: Of gargoyles, ghosts and gardens.' *Equinox*, 5 (28), July–August 1986, pp. 93, 95, 97–98, 100–103.

O514 – 'Was Willie King off his rocker? Prime Minister certainly was peculiar.' *Vancouver Sun*, September 3, 1983, p. G8.

O515 ROBERTSON, PETER. '"En pleine forme": Mackenzie King traverse l'Atlantique en 1934.' *L'Archiviste*, 17 (4), juillet–août 1990, pp. 12–13.

O516 – '"Feeling like a fighting cock": Mackenzie King at sea, 1934.' *The Archivist*, 17 (4), July–August 1990, pp. 17, 20.

O517 ROOSEVELT, ELEANOR. 'Mrs Roosevelt looks forward to visits of Canada's premier.' *Ottawa Journal*, December 21, 1943, p. 10. (In her 'My Day' column).

O518 ROSS, VAL. 'Restoration of a tarnished King. In the anti-charisma nineties, the strange and stodgy Mackenzie King has been rediscovered as the perfect hero. Leaders take note.' *The Globe and Mail*, May 31, 1997, pp. C1, C3.

O519 ROTHNEY, GORDON OLIVER. 'A Liberal decade.' *Canadian Forum*, 25 (229), December 1945, pp. 203–204.

O520 – 'Quebec saves our King.' *Canadian Forum*, 25 (299), July 1945, pp. 83–84.

O521 'Rt. Hon. William Lyon Mackenzie King, O.M., C.M.G., LL.D.' *Labour Gazette*, 50 (9), September 1950, pp. 1289–1291.

O522 RUDIN, BRADLEY. 'Mackenzie King and the writing of Canada's anti-labour laws.' *Canadian Dimension*, 8 (4–5), January 1972, pp. 42–48.

O523 'Ruins Mackenzie King built to undergo restoration to original ruinous state.' *Montreal Gazette*, December 8, 1987, p. B6.

O524 'Ruins rebuilt by Mr King on Gatineau estate.' *The Globe and Mail*, May 31, 1951, p. 17.

O525 SALMON, M. STEPHEN. 'Fool propositions: Mackenzie King, the Dominion Marine Association and the Inland Water Freight Rates Act of 1923.' *Fresh Water*, 2 (1), Summer 1987, pp. 8–19.

O526 SANDERSON, G.F. 'L'austégrité fait une victime: La Gazette du travail – 1900–1978.' *La Gazette du travail*, 77 (11/12), novembre–decembre 1978, pp. 470–471.

O527 – 'Victim of austerity: The Labour Gazette, 1900–1978.' *Labour Gazette*, 77 (11/12), November–December 1978, pp. 482–483.

O528 SANDWELL, BERNARD KEBLE. 'His monument is a free nation.' *New York Times*, February 22, 1953, section 7, pp. 1, 26. [Review of Bruce Hutchison, *The incredible Canadian*].

O529 – 'How Mr King kept power.' *Saturday Night*, 65 (43), August 1, 1950, pp. 12, 34.

O530 – 'Mr Forsey and Mr King are not so far apart.' *Saturday Night*, 58 (42), June 26, 1943, pp. 10–11.

O531 – 'Mr King and Mr Meighen. What did we vote for in 1926?' *Saturday Night*, 67 (7), November 24, 1951, pp. 4–5.

O532 – 'Mr King: Politician vs. human being.' *Saturday Night*, 65 (7), November 22, 1949, p. 13. [Review of H. Reginald Hardy, *Mackenzie King of Canada*].

O533 – 'Mr King and what to do about him.' *Saturday Night*, 56 (35), May 3, 1941, p. 12.

O534 – 'The Prime Ministership has become a vast power in Mr King's hands.' *Saturday Night*, 64 (6), November 13, 1948, pp. 10, 48.

O535 – 'What did we vote for in 1926?' *Saturday Night*, 67 (7), November 24, 1951, pp. 4–5.

O536 – 'William Lyon Mackenzie King, 1874–1950.' *Dictionary of National Biography*, 1941–1950, pp. 457–462.

O537 SANGSTER, JOAN. 'The 1907 Bell Telephone Strike: Organizing women workers.' *Labour/Le Travailleur*, 3, 1978, pp. 109–130.

O538 SAYWELL, JOHN. 'The man behind the Prime Minister felt the hand of God at his shoulder.' *Toronto Daily Star*, November 22, 1958, p. 34. [Review of Dawson, *William Lyon Mackenzie King: A political biography, 1874–1923*, vol. 1].

O539 SCHMIDT, GRACE. 'Mackenzie King Centennial Colloquium.' *Waterloo Historical Society [Proceedings]*, 62, 1974, p. 76.

O540 SCOTT, FRANCIS REGINALD. 'Mr King and the king makers.' *Canadian Forum*, 30 (359), December 1950, pp. 197–199.

Reprinted in Jack Lawrence Granatstein and Peter Stevens, eds., *Forum: Canadian life and letters: Selections from the Canadian Forum, 1920–70* (Toronto: University of Toronto Press, 1972), pp. 268–270.

O541 'Secret King diary on Gouzenko affair among key missing documents.' *The Globe and Mail*, January 2, 1976, p. 8.

O542 SENESE, DONALD. 'Willie and Felix: ill-matched acquaintances.' *Ontario History*, 84 (2), June 1992, pp. 141–148.

O543 SERVICE, J.D. 'Mackenzie King: Varsity student and alumnus.' *University of Toronto Alumni Bulletin*, February 1951, pp. 1, 18–19.

O544 SHARP, WALTER R. 'The Canadian election of 1926.' *American Political Science Review*, 21 (1), February 1927, pp. 101–113.

O545 – 'The Canadian election of 1925.' *American Political Science Review*, 20 (1), February 1926, pp. 107–117.

O546 SHORTT, ADAM. 'Canadian Industrial Disputes Investigation Act.' *American Economic Association Quarterly*, Third Series, 10, April 1909, pp. 158–179.

O547 SKELTON, OSCAR DOUGLAS. 'The Imperial Conference of 1923.' *Journal of the Canadian Bankers Association*, 31 (2), January 1924, pp. 153–162.

O548 SMALL, DOUG. 'Latest King diary offers some hints PM was gay.' *Winnipeg Free Press*, January 3, 1980, p. 5. [In his 'Capital Talk' column].

O549 SMITH, BEVERLY. 'King of Canada.' *American Magazine*, 131, January 1941, pp. 14–15.

O550 SMITH, IRVING NORMAN. 'How Mackenzie King fought the war.' *Saturday Night*, 75 (21), October 15, 1960, pp. 25–26. [Review of J.W. Pickersgill, ed., *The Mackenzie King record*, vol. 1].

O551 – 'In L.B. Pearson's autobiography some hard words for W.L. Mackenzie King.' *Ottawa Journal*, October 17, 1972, p. 6. [Review of Lester B. Pearson, *Mike*, vol. 1].

O552 – 'Lord Byng's letter to George V on row with Mackenzie King.' *Ottawa Journal*, September 27, 1952, p. 6. [Review of Harold G. Nicolson, *King George the Fifth: His life and reign*].

O553 – 'Mackenzie King abroad: A Journal reporter's picture.' *Ottawa Journal*, July 25, 1950, p. 6.

O554 – 'Mr King in his study: An exclusive interview on 25th anniversary.' *Ottawa Journal*, August 5, 1944, p. 8.

O555 – 'Must history be dull? Mr King made it lively.' *Ottawa Journal*, March 21, 1959, p. 6. [Review of Dawson, *William Lyon Mackenzie King: A political biography, 1874–1923*, vol. 1].

O556 – 'A reporter's farewell with affectionate respect.' *Ottawa Journal*, July 24, 1950, p. 6.

O557 – 'The truly incredible Canadian.' *Ottawa Journal*, December 1, 1962, p. 6. [Review of F.A. McGregor, *The fall and rise of Mackenzie King, 1911–1919*].

O558 – 'What a Christmas Day: De Gaulle took Miquelon, Mr King took Washington.' *Ottawa Journal*, July 11, 1956, p. 6. [Account of Christmas Day, 1941].

O559 SMITH, WILLIAM A., and PAULETTE DOZOIS. 'Les papiers de William Lyon Mackenzie King – 1949.' *L'Archiviste*, 7 (2), mars–avril 1980, pp. 6–9.

O560 – 'William Lyon Mackenzie King Papers – 1949.' *The Archivist*, 7 (2), March–April 1980, pp. 6–9.

O561 'Sought limit on Commowealth's monarchy links: Diary reveals King's "get tough" strategy with Crown.' *Winnipeg Free Press*, January 5, 1979, p. 8. [Canadian Press dispatch].

O562 SOWARD, FREDERIC HUBERT. 'The descent from the lonely heights.' *International Journal*, 26, Winter 1970/71, pp. 194–201. [Review of J.W. Pickersgill and Donald Forster, eds., *The Mackenzie King record*, vols. 3–4].

O563 SPAULDING, WILLIAM BRAY. 'Why Rockefeller supported medical education in Canada: The William Lyon Mackenzie King connection.' *Canadian Bulletin of Medical History/Bulletin canadien d'histoire de la médecine*, 10 (1), 1993, pp. 67–76.

O564 SPRY, GRAHAM. 'Creators of the contemporary Commonwealth: Jan C. Smuts and W.L. Mackenzie King.' *English-Speaking World*, 32 (6), November 1950, pp. 29–32.

O565 ST LAURENT, LOUIS STEPHEN. 'St Laurent persuaded Mackenzie King not to resign after 1947 Korean incident.' *The Globe and Mail,* October 14, 1961, p. 17. [Review of James Eayrs, *The art of the possible: Government and foreign policy in Canada*].

O566 STACEY, CHARLES PERRY. 'Canadian leaders of the Second World War.' *Canadian Historical Review,* 66 (1), March 1985, pp. 64–72.

O567 – 'The Divine mission: Mackenzie King and Hitler.' *Canadian Historical Review,* 61 (4), December 1980, pp. 502–512.

O568 – '"A dream of my youth": Mackenzie King in North York.' *Ontario History,* 76 (3), September 1984, pp. 273–286.

O569 – 'From Meighen to King: The reversal of Canadian external policies, 1921–1923.' *Transactions of the Royal Society of Canada,* Series 4, 7, 1969, pp. 223–246.

O570 – 'The love affair that nearly drove King mad.' *Toronto Star,* March 8, 1976, p. C-3. [Excerpt from his *A very double life: The private world of Mackenzie King*].

O571 – 'Mackenzie King and the clergyman's wife.' *Toronto Star,* March 10, 1976, p. B3. [Excerpt from his *A very double life: The private world of Mackenzie King*].

O572 – 'Mackenzie King and the monarchy.' *Monarchy Canada,* May 1978, pp. 6–8. [Edited transcript of a talk given to the Toronto Branch of the Monarchist League of Canada].

O573 – 'Mackenzie King diaries, 1893–1931.' *Canadian Historical Review,* 58 (2), June 1977, pp. 234–236.

O574 – 'Mackenzie King saw his mother as link to destiny.' *Toronto Star,* March 9, 1976, p. B2. [Excerpt from his *A very double life: The private world of Mackenzie King*].

O575 – 'Mackenzie King's diary reveals his "dark side."' *Toronto Star,* March 6, 1976, p. B1. [Excerpt from his *A very double life: The private world of Mackenzie King*].

O576 – 'Spirit messages reassured King: "You are wise."' *Toronto Star,* March 11, 1976, p. B3. [Excerpt from his *A very double life: The private world of Mackenzie King*].

O577 – 'The turning-point: Canadian–American relations during the Roosevelt–King era.' *Canada: An historical magazine*, 1 (1), Autumn 1973, pp. 1–9.

O578 STAEBLER, H.L. 'Mackenzie King.' Waterloo Historical Society, *Annual Report*, 38, 1950, pp. 10–13.

O579 STEPLER, JACK. 'See King's ruins as link in his spiritualistic ventures.' *Ottawa Citizen*, October 4, 1952, p. 17.

O580 STEVENS, GEOFFREY. 'The old ghost writer.' *The Globe and Mail*, January 8, 1975, p. 6. [Relates to the 1935 biography of King].

O581 STEVENSON, JOHN ALEXANDER. 'The Canadian elections and after.' *Empire Review*, 44 (311), December 1926, pp. 509–518.

O582 – 'The career of Mackenzie King.' *Political Quarterly*, 21 (4), October–December 1950, pp. 395–410.

O583 – 'Distinguished visitors and apparitions.' *Saturday Night*, 70 (2), October 16, 1954, pp. 16–17.

O584 – 'The general election in Canada.' *Fortnightly*, 147, May 1940, pp. 512–521.

O585 – 'New era in Canada.' *Foreign Affairs*, 26 (3), April 1948, pp. 515–527.

O586 STUCHEN, PHILIP. 'A visit to Laurier House.' *Queen's Review*, 24 (7), October 1950, pp. 200–202.

O587 SWAINSON, DONALD WAYNE. 'Neurosis and causality in Canadian history.' *Queen's Quarterly*, 89 (3), Autumn 1982, pp. 611–616.

O588 – 'Trends in Canadian biography: Recent historical writing.' *Queen's Quarterly*, 87 (3), Autumn 1980, pp. 413–429.

O589 SWANSON, FRANK. 'He had the run of Mr King's mind.' *Ottawa Citizen*, September 28, 1960, p. 1. [A summary of J.W. Pickersgill's work for Mackenzie King].

O590 'Tallulah Bankhead avait charmé Mackenzie King par s façon désinvolte de boire du champagne.' *La Presse*, 5 janvier 1977, p. A-6.

O591 TAYLOR, ROBERT. 'Few Canadians ever knew real warmth of Mr King.' *Toronto Daily Star*, July 24, 1950, p. 17.

O592 – 'His social reforms great humanitarian's legacy to Canadians.' *Toronto Daily Star,* July 24, 1950, p. 17.

O593 TEMPLETON, CHARLES. 'Survey disagrees with Close-up.' *Toronto Daily Star,* March 11, 1960, p. 21. [Relates to the CBC-TV programs in the 'Close-up' series, which were telecast on March 10 and March 17, 1960].

O594 TENNYSON, BRIAN D. 'Mackenzie King and patronage in the public service: An historical footnote.' *Journal of Canadian Studies,* 6 (1), February 1971, pp. 56–60.

O595 TESSARO, ANNAMARIA. 'Mackenzie King in North Waterloo.' *Waterloo Historical Society [Proceedings],* 66, 1978, pp. 18–40.

O596 THOMAS, JOHN KEMPSTER. 'Mackenzie King at 70: The paradox of the Prime Minister.' *New World Illustrated,* 5 (10), December 1944, pp. 9–13.

O597 THOMPSON, JOHN HERD. '"Writing history with lightning": Mackenzie King's television biography.' *Canadian Historical Review,* 69 (4), December 1988, pp. 503–510. [Discussion of 'The King Chronicle' shown on CBC-TV, March 27–March 29, 1988].

O598 THORNTON, MARTIN. 'President Truman and Canada in 1947: The "Truman Travelling Troupe."' *British Journal of Canadian Studies,* 9 (1), 1994, pp. 72–86.

O599 TOUSHER, GARY. 'King's Divine mission is anything but dull.' *Broadcast Week Magazine* in *The Globe and Mail,* March 26, 1988, p. 9. [Discussion of 'The King Chronicle' shown on CBC-TV, March 27–March 29, 1988].

O600 TRUMAN, MARY. 'An abundance of women in a bachelor PM's life.' *The Globe and Mail,* January 5, 1977, p. 1.

O601 – 'King feared lonely poverty out of office, diaries show.' *The Globe and Mail,* January 3, 1979, p. 3.

O602 – 'Pills, potions and wealth plagued aging King.' *The Globe and Mail,* January 3, 1980, p. 9.

O603 TUCKER, ALBERT. 'Historian's biography.' *Canadian Literature,* no. 21, Summer 1964, pp. 58–60. [Review of Neatby, *William Lyon Mackenzie King: The lonely heights, 1924–1932*].

O604 'Two grandfathers.' *Saturday Night*, 53 (34), June 25, 1938, p. 1.

O605 UHL, ALEXANDER. 'Canada's Mackenzie King brings unity in war effort.' *New York PM*, November 5, 1940, p. 5.

O606 'Un p'tit gars de St-Zotique aurait bien voulu adopter le chien de Mackenzie King.' *La Presse*, 5 janvier 1980, p. C-17.

O607 'Un sujet délicat.' *L'Archiviste*, 2 (2), mars–avril 1975, pp. 2–3.

O608 UNDERHILL, FRANK HAWKINS. 'The Canadian version of "The Prince."' *Canadian Forum*, 41 (1), April 1961, pp. 1–3. [Review of J.W. Pickersgill, ed., *The Mackenzie King record*, vol. 1, and Roger Graham, *Arthur Meighen: The door of opportunity*].

O609 – 'The close of an era: Twenty-five years of Mr Mackenzie King.' *Canadian Forum*, 24 (284), September 1944, pp. 124–125.
Reprinted in Frank Hawkins Underhill, *In search of Canadian Liberalism* (Toronto: Macmillian Company of Canada, 1960), pp. 114–119.

O610 – 'Concerning Mr King.' *Canadian Forum*, 30 (356), September 1950, pp. 121–122, 125–127.
Reprinted in Frank Hawkins Underhill, *In search of Canadian Liberalism* (Toronto: Macmillan Company of Canada, 1960), pp. 133–140.

O611 – 'The Dawson biography of Mackenzie King.' *Canadian Forum*, 39 (463), August 1959, pp. 102–103.

O612 – 'The Divine Right of a Canadian Prince.' *Ottawa Citizen*, December 28, 1968, p. 30. [Review of J.W. Pickersgill, ed., *The Mackenzie King record*, vol. 2].

O613 – 'The end of the King era in Canada.' *Canadian Forum*, 28 (331), August 1948, pp. 97–98; 28 (332), September 1948, pp. 121–122, 126–127.
Reprinted in Frank Hawkins Underhill, *In search of Canadian Liberalism* (Toronto: Macmillan Company o Canada, 1960), pp. 126–133.

O614 – 'Liberalism à la King.' *Canadian Forum*, 28 (325), February 1948, pp. 257–258.
Reprinted in Frank Hawkins Underhill, *In search of Canadian Liberalism* (Toronto: Macmillan Company of Canada, 1960), pp. 123–126,

and Jack Lawrence Granatstein and Peter Stevens, eds., *Forum: Canadian life and letters: Selections from the Canadian Forum, 1920–70* (Toronto: University of Toronto Press, 1972), pp. 248–250.

O615 – 'Mr King's foreign policy.' *Canadian Forum*, 18 (210), July 1938, pp. 104–105.

O616 – 'The sad case of Tweedledum and Tweedledee again.' *Saskatoon Daily Star*, October 28, 1925, p. 4.

O617 – 'Tweedledum King and Tweedledee Meighen.' *Saskatoon Daily Star*, October 22, 1925, p. 4.

O618 – 'Twenty years as Prime Minister.' *Canadian Forum*, 26 (306), July 1946, pp. 77–78.

Reprinted in Frank Hawkins Underhill, *In search of Canadian Liberalism* (Toronto: Macmillan Company of Canada, 1960), pp. 119–126.

O619 – 'Was King innocent or statesman?' *The Globe Magazine*, January 1, 1966, p. 13. [Review of James Eayrs, *In defence of Canada, volume 2: Appeasement and rearmament*].

O620 – 'William Lyon Mackenzie King.' *Encyclopedia Canadiana*, 1960 edition, 5, 405–409.

O621 VIGEANT, PIERRE. 'W.L. Mackenzie King: L'homme énigmatique qui a dominè la politique canadienne pendant un quart de siècle.' *Le Devoir*, 24 juillet 1950, p. 4.

O622 'Vindicating Col. Ralston: More about truth in history.' *Ottawa Journal*, January 7, 1950, p. 6.

O623 W. [initial only], F.B. 'The man from Kingsmere.' *Winnipeg Free Press*, July 24, 1950, p. 17.

O624 WAITE, PETER BUSBY. 'Debauching the archanges: Canada's political leaders.' *The Beaver*, 76 (6), December 1994/January 1995, pp. 17–28.

O625 – 'Late harvest: Mackenzie King and the Italian lady.' *The Beaver*, 75 (6), December 1995/January 1996, pp. 4–10.

O626 – 'Les grands hommes de nos billets de banque.' *Sélection du Reader's Digest (Canada)*, 91 (541), juillet 1992, pp. 78–83.

O627 – 'Mr King and Lady Byng.' *The Beaver*, 67 (2), April/May 1997, pp. 24–30.

O628 – 'The men on our money.' *Reader's Digest (Canada)*, 141 (843), July 1992, pp. 84–90. [Brief biographical sketches of the four prime ministers on our paper money – Sir John A. Macdonald, Sir Wilfrid Laurier, Sir Robert Borden, and Mackenzie King].

O629 – 'W.L. Mackenzie King.' *Academic American Encyclopedia*, 12, pp. 81–82.

O630 WALKER, HARRY J. 'Sir Galahad memorial enshrines self-sacrifice of Henry Harper.' *The Journal* [Ottawa], December 4, 1943, p. 14.

O631 WALKER, HARRY JAMES WILLIAM. 'Odyssey of a government ed.: W.L. Mackenzie King.' *Trades and Labour Congress Journal*, 26 (2), February 1947, pp. 18–20.

O632 – 'Prairie assignment.' *Labour Gazette*, 50 (9), September 1950, pp. 1488–1493.

O633 WALTER, FELIX. 'Mr King of Canada.' *Time and Tide*, July 29, 1950, p. 748.

O634 WARD, NORMAN McQUEEN. 'Dawson on King.' *Canadian Forum*, 38 (457), February 1959, pp. 251–252. [Review of Dawson, *William Lyon Mackenzie King: A political biography, 1874–1923*, vol. 1].

O635 – 'What happens when a Governor General governs?' *Quarterly of Canadian Studies for the Secondary School*, 3 (1), pp. 3–13.

O636 WARDHAUGH, ROBERT ALEXANDER. 'Awaiting the return of commonsense: Mackenzie King and Alberta.' *National History: A Canadian Journal of Enquiry and Opinion*, 1 (3), Summer 1997.

O637 – 'Cogs in the machine: The Charles Dunning–Jimmy Gardiner feud.' *Saskatchewan History*, 48 (1), Spring 1996, pp. 20–29.

O638 – 'A marriage of convenience?: Mackenzie King and Prince Albert constituency.' *Prairie Forum*, 11 (2), Fall 1996, pp. 177–200.

O639 – 'Region and nation: The politics of Jimmy Gardiner.' *Saskatchewan History*, 45 (2), Fall 1993, pp. 24–36.

O640 – 'The "Impartial Umpire" views the West: Mackenzie King and the search for the New Jerusalem.' *Manitoba History*, Spring 1995, pp. 11–22.

O641 WEBB, JONATHAN. 'The unexpected innocence of Mackenzie King.' *Canadian Review*, 3 (4), September 1976, pp. 24–25, 39–40.

O642 WELLES, SAM. 'Statesman's other side.' *Life Magazine*, 34, (12), March 23, 1953, pp. 109–116, 118.

O643 WERIER, VAL. 'Mackenzie King's secret: Newly discovered letters reveal "spiritual" link.' *Winnipeg Tribune*, December 14, 1951, pp. 1, 3, 8.

O644 WEST, BRUCE. 'King remembered.' *The Globe and Mail*, July 3, 1968, p. 21.

O645 WHALEN, DWIGHT. 'Christmas '47: King comforts a hurting child.' *Toronto Star*, December 22, 1991, p. D1.

O646 WHITAKER, REGINALD. 'The Liberal corporatist ideas of Mackenzie King.' *Labour/Le travailleur*, 2, 1977, pp. 137–169.

O647 – 'Mackenzie King in the dominion of the dead.' *Canadian Forum*, 55 (658), February 1976, pp. 6–11.

O648 – 'Political thought and political action in Mackenzie King.' *Journal of Canadian Studies*, 13 (4), Winter 1978–79, pp. 40–60.

O649 WHITE, JEAN. 'Statesman's romance.' [Letter to the ed.]. *Ottawa Citizen*, November 26, 1958, p. 6.

O650 WHITEWAY, DOUG. 'Robertson blends fact, fiction.' *Winnipeg Free Press*, October 20, 1986, p. 16. [Review of Heather Robertson, *Lily: A rhapsody in red*].

O651 WHITTON, CHARLOTTE. 'In the first ministry.' *Evening Citizen*, July 27, 1950, p. 3.

O652 'Who will succeed Mr King?' *Monetary Times*, 116 (8), August 1948, pp. 23–28.

O653 WIGLEY, PHILIP. 'Whitehall and the 1923 Imperial Conference.' *Journal of Imperial and Commonwealth Relations*, 1 (2), 1973, pp. 223–235.

O654 WILGRESS, LEOLYN DANA. 'Mr Mackenzie King, 1874–1950.' *Listener*, 44 (1122), July 27, 1950, pp. 117–118.

O655 'William Lyon Mackenzie King.' *Current Biography*, 1940, pp. 457–459.

O656 WILLIAMS, FRED. 'Canada's Mackenzie King went on strike to defend freedom of speech.' *The Globe and Mail*, February 15, 1940, p. 6.

O657 WILLS, TERRANCE. 'Kinky or not, King diaries are a national treasure.' *Montreal Gazette*, January 3, 1981, p. 8.

O658 'Woman in Ontario sought estate as King's wife, lawyer's files show.' *The Globe and Mail*, January 4, 1980, p. 2.

O659 WOODCOCK, GEORGE. 'Historians and biographers.' *Canadian Literature*, no. 70, Autumn, 1976, pp. 3–4. [Editorial relating to C.P. Stacey, *A very double life: The private world of Mackenzie King*].

O660 WRENCH, SIR EVELYN. 'Memories of Mackenzie King.' *Spectator*, 185 (6370), July 28, 1950, p. 108.

O661 ZOLF, LARRY. 'Let's be fair to the old codger.' *Telegraph-Herald* [Halifax], December 16, 1974, p. 5.

SECTION P

Books with Sections Relating to Mackenzie King

This section contains an alphabetical listing of books containing chapters or significant sections relating to Mackenzie King.

P1 ARCHIVES NATIONALES DU CANADA. 'Le journal de William Lyon Mackenzie King' in *Trésors des Archives du Canada* (Toronto, Buffalo, and London: University of Toronto Press, 1992), pp. 220–221.

P2 – 'Le très honorable William Lyon Mackenzie King' in *Les premiers ministres du Canada, 1867–1994. Présenté par la Chambre des communes et les Archives nationales du Canada* (Ottawa: Archives nationales du Canada, 1994), p. 10.

P3 BALDWIN, JOHN. 'King as administrator' in *Mackenzie King: A personal view*, Canadian Issues, 1 (2), Spring 1977, pp. 57–61.

P4 BEAVERBROOK, LORD. 'Bennett and Mackenzie King' in his *Friends: Sixty years of intimate personal relations with Richard Bedford Bennett, PC, KC, JP, LLB, Hon. LLD, FRSC, Viscount Bennett of Mickleham, Surrey, and of Calgary and Hopewell, Canada, one-time Prime Minister of Canada: A personal memoir with an appendix of letters* (London and Melbourne: Heinemann, 1959), pp. 133–134.

P5 BELOFF, MAX. 'Britain and Canada between the two world wars: A British view' in Peter Lyon, ed., *Britain and Canada: Survey of a changing relationship* (London: Frank Cass, 1976), pp. 50–60.

P6 BENSON, NATHANIEL ANKETELL. 'The passing of a leader' in his *None of it came easy: The story of James Garfield Gardiner* (Toronto: Burns and MacEachern, 1955), pp. 212–219.

P7 BERTON, PIERRE. 'Mother's boy' in his *The great depression* (Toronto: McClelland and Stewart, 1990), pp. 54–62.

P8 – '"Not a five cent piece!"' in his *The great depression* (Toronto: McClelland and Stewart, 1990), pp. 47–54.

P9 – 'The Prime Minister and the dictator' in his *The great depression* (Toronto: McClelland and Stewart, 1990), pp. 411–418.

P10 BLISS, MICHAEL. 'King: Dividing us least' in *Right Honourable Men: The descent of Canadian politics from Macdonald to Mulroney* (Toronto: HarperCollins Publishers, 1994), pp. 122–151.

P11 – 'King: Welfare Liberalism' in his *Right Honourable Men: The descent of Canadian politics from Macdonald to Mulroney* (Toronto: HarperCollins Publishers, 1994), pp. 152–183.

P12 BOSC, MARC. 'William Lyon Mackenzie King' in his *The Broadview book of Canadian parliamentary anecdotes* (Peterborough: Broadview Press, 1988), pp. 117–154.

P13 BOTHWELL, ROBERT SELKIRK. 'The health of the common people' in John English and John O. Stubbs, eds., *Mackenzie King: Widening the debate* (Toronto: Macmillan of Canada, 1977), pp. 191–220.

P14 BOTHWELL, ROBERT SELKIRK, IAN DRUMMOND, and JOHN ENGLISH. 'The end of Mackenzie King, 1945–8' in their *Canada since 1945: Power, politics, and provincialism* (Toronto, Buffalo, and London: University of Toronto Press, 1981), pp. 57–127.

P15 BRAGDON, CHANDLER. 'Reactions to the Canadian–American rapprochement of 1935–1939: A summary' in *Reflections on Canada and on the Canada/United States relationship* (Plattsburgh: State University of New York, Center for the Study of Canada, 1991), pp. 64–69. (Focus Canada, vol. 1).

P16 CANADA. CENTENNIAL COMMISSION. COMMISSION DU CENTENAIRE. 'Rt. Honourable William Lyon Mackenzie King/ Le très honorable William Lyon Mackenzie King' in *The founders and the guardians: Fathers of Confederation, Governors General, Prime*

Ministers: A collection of biographical sketches and portraits. Fondateurs et gardiens: Pères de la Confédération, Gouverneurs généraux, Premiers ministres: Un recueil de notes biographiques et de portraits (Ottawa: Queen's Printer/Imprimeur de la Reine, 1968), pp. 138–139.

P17 CANADA. NATIONAL CAPITAL COMMISSION. 'William Lyon Mackenzie King (1874–1950)' in *Statues of Parliament Hill/Statues de la Colline du Parlement* (Ottawa: National Capital Commission, 1986), pp. 111–121.

P18 CARLAND, JOHM M. 'Shadow and substance: Mackenzie King's perception of British intentions at the 1923 Imperial Conference' in Gordon Martel, ed., *Studies in British imperial history: Essays in honour of A.P. Thornton* (London: Macmillan, 1986), pp. 178–200.

P19 CASSIDY, KEITH. 'Mackenzie King and American Progressivism' in John English and John O. Stubbs, eds., *Mackenzie King: Widening the debate* (Toronto: Macmillan of Canada, 1977), pp. 105–129.

P20 COLLARD, EDGAR ANDREW. 'W.L. Mackenzie King' in his *Les premiers ministres du Canada, 1867–1967* (Montréal: La Texaco Canada Limitée, 1967?), pp. [21–22].

P21 – 'W.L. Mackenzie King' in his *The Prime Ministers of Canada* (Montreal: Texaco Canada Limited, 1967?), pp. [21–22].

P22 COLOMBO, JOHN ROBERT. 'Laurier House, house of spirits' in his *Mysterious Canada: Strange sights, extraordinary events and peculiar places* (Toronto: Doubleday Canada, 1988), pp. 199–201.

P23 – 'Vision of the chapel' in his *Mysterious Canada: Strange sights, extraordinary events, and peculiar places* (Toronto: Doubleday Canada, 1988), pp. 205–206.

P24 COOK, RAMSAY. 'The modernist pilgrim's progress [Part I]' in his *The regenerators: Social criticism in late Victorian English Canada* (Toronto, Buffalo, and London: University of Toronto Press, 1985), pp. 196–213.

P25 CORBETT, RON. 'King of Kingswood'/'Un certain M King' in Ron Corbett and Malak, *The Gatineau/La Gatineau* (Erin: Stoddart, 1994), pp. 51–60.

P26 COUCILL, IRMA. 'Rt. Honourable William Lyon Mackenize King' in her *Founders and guardians* (Toronto: John Wiley and Sons, 1982), pp. 148–149.

P27 COURTNEY, JOHN CHILDS. 'Prime-Ministerial character: An examination of Mackenzie King's political leadership' in John English and John O. Stubbs, eds., *Mackenzie King: Widening the debate* (Toronto: Macmillan of Canada, 1977), pp. 55–88.

P28 CROSBIE, JOHN S. 'Mackenzie King' in his *Canada and its leaders* (Toronto, New York, and London: Baxter Publishing, 1968), pp. 107–115.

P29 CROSS, AUSTIN FLETCHER. 'Mackenzie the first' in his *The people's mouths* (Toronto: Macmillan, 1943), pp. 17–36.

P30 CUFF, ROBERT D., and JACK LAWRENCE GRANATSTEIN. 'The abortive customs union, Winter, 1947/48' in their *American dollars – Canadian prosperity: Canadian–American economic relations, 1945–1950* (Toronto and Sarasota: Samuel Stevens, 1978), pp. 64–82.

P31 – 'Getting on with the Americans: Canadian perceptions of the United States, 1939–1945' in their *Ties that bind: Canadian–American relations in wartime from the Great War to the Cold War* (Toronto and Sarasota: Samuel Stevens and Hakkert and Company, 1977), pp. 93–112.

P32 – 'The Hyde Park declaration, 1941: Origins and significance' in their *Ties that bind: Canadian–American relations in wartime from the Great War to the Cold War* (Toronto and Sarasota: Samuel Stevens and Hakkert and Company, 1977), pp. 69–92.

P33 CUMMINS, GERALDINE. 'Reminiscences of a British Commonwealth statesman' [Appendix 2] in her *Unseen adventures: An autobiography covering thirty-four years of work in the psychical research* (London, New York, Melbourne, Sydney, and Cape Town: Rider and Company, 1951), pp. 176–181.

P34 DAFOE, JOHN WESLEY. 'Mr King at Geneva' [from the *Winnipeg Free Press*, October 1, 1936] in Lucien Brault, Jean-Louis Gagnon, Wilfred Kesterton, Duncan C. McArthur, Frank Hawkins Underhill, and Christopher Young, eds., *A century of reporting: The National Press Club anthology/Un siècle de reportage: Anthologie du*

Cercle National des Journalistes (Toronto and Vancouver: Clarke, Irwin and Company, 1967), pp. 201–203.

P35 – 'Ogdensburg, August 17, 1940' in his *Canada fights: An American democracy at war* (New York and Toronto: Farrar and Rinehart, 1941), pp. 1–14.

P36 DANDO, JOHN. 'Man of judgment' in his *Forward with Canada: Builders of a nation* [N.p., Northern Electric Company Limited, 1949], pp. 20–24.

P37 DAWSON, ROBERT McGREGOR. 'King, Meighen and approaches to political leadership' in Thomas Alexander Hockin, ed., *Apex of power: The Prime Minister and political leadership in Canada* (Scarborough, Ont.: Prentice-Hall, 1971), pp. 92–95.

P38 – 'Mackenzie King as leader' in Hugh Garnet Thorburn, ed., *Party politics in Canada* (Toronto: Prentice-Hall of Canada, 1967), pp. 124–129.

P39 DOMINO [Augustus Bridle]. 'The grandson of a patriot: Hon. W.L. Mackenzie King' in his *The masques of Ottawa* (Toronto: Macmillan, 1921), pp. 52–64.

P40 DONALDSON, GORDON. 'God and King' in his *Eighteen men: The Prime Ministers of Canada* (Toronto: Doubleday Canada, and Garden City, N.Y.: Doubleday and Company, 1985), pp. 115–130.

P41 – 'Riddle of the ruins' in his *Eighteen men: The Prime Ministers of Canada* (Toronto: Doubleday Canada, and Garden City, N.Y.: Doubleday and Company, 1985), pp. 149–163.

P42 DUHAIME, LLOYD. 'Arthur Meighen's gamble' in his *Hear! Hear! 125 years of debate in Canada's House of Commons* (Toronto: Stoddart, 1993), pp. 104–112.

P43 – 'The King–Byng thing' in his *Hear! Hear! 125 years of debate in Canada's House of Commons* (Toronto: Stoddart, 1993), pp. 101–104.

P44 – 'Send for my honourable friend' in his *Hear! Hear! 125 years of debate in Canada's House of Commons* (Toronto: Stoddart, 1993), pp. 112–113.

P45 DUNTON, ARNOLD DAVIDSON. 'King as administrator' in *Mackenzie King: A personal view*, Canadian Issues, 1 (2), Spring 1977, pp. 49–51.

P46 – 'Reminiscences' in *Mackenzie King: A personal view,* Canadian Issues, 1 (2), Spring 1977, pp. 23–29.

P47 EAYRS, JAMES GEORGE. 'Clio and Jack' in his *Greenpeace and her enemies* (Toronto: Anansi, 1973), pp. 230–241.

P48 – 'King and the historians' in *Mackenzie King: A personal view,* Canadian Issues, 1 (2), Spring 1977, pp. 65–67.

P49 – '"A low dishonest decade": Aspects of Canadian external policy, 1931–1939' in Hugh Keenleyside, ed., *The growth of Canadian policies in external affairs* (Durham, N.C.: Duke University Press), 1960, pp. 59–80.

P50 EBON, MARTIN. 'W.L. Mackenzie King: The Prime Minister was discreet' in his *They knew the unknown* (New York: The New American Library, 1971), pp. 193–199.

P51 ESTORICK, ERIC. 'W.L. Mackenzie King' in his *Changing Empire: Churchill to Nehru* (New York: Duell, Sloan and Pearce, 1950), pp. 130–169.

P52 FERNS, HENRY STANLEY. 'Bernie, King, and I: Writing *The Age of Mackenzie King*' in his *Reading from left to right: One man's political history* (Toronto, Buffalo, and London: University of Toronto Press, 1983), pp. 297–310.

P53 FORD, ARTHUR RUTHERFORD. 'Crisis over conscription – Retirement of Ralston and appointment of McNaughton – King executes a somersault' in his *As the world wags on* (Toronto: Ryerson Press, 1980), pp. 181–185.

P54 – 'King a political enigma – Shrewdness in picking lieutenants – His political philosophy – Not a good source of news – His sentimental side – His last appearance' in his *As the world wags on* (Toronto: Ryerson Press, 1980), pp. 173–180.

P55 FORSEY, EUGENE ALFRED. 'The Canadian constitutional crisis of 1926' in his *The royal power of dissolution of Parliament in the British Commonwealth* (Toronto: Oxford University Press, 1968), pp. 131–250.

P56 – 'Constitutional annus mirabilis' and 'Mr King and Parliamentary Government' in his *Freedom and order: Collected essays* (Toronto: McClelland and Stewart, 1974), pp. 84–109.

P57 – 'Mr King and parliamentary government' in his *Freedom and order: Collected essays* (Toronto: McClelland and Stewart, 1974), pp. 87–100.

P58 FORSEY, EUGENE, JAMES RUSSELL MALLORY, and JOHN WHITNEY PICKERSGILL. 'Mackenzie King: A conversation piece' in J.G. Greenslade, ed., *Canadian politics: Speeches by F.M. Watkins, Stanley Knowles, J.R. Mallory and H.D. Hicks, delivered at the Mount Allison Summer Institute, August 13–15, 1959* (Sackville: Mount Allison University, [1959]), pp. 64–67.

P59 FRASER, BLAIR. 'Mackenzie King: A tribute' in John Fraser and Graham Fraser, eds., *Blair Fraser reports: Selections, 1944–1969* (Toronto: Macmillan of Canada, 1969), pp. 33–42.

P60 FRENCH, DORIS. 'The third man' in her *Faith, sweat and politics: The early trade union years in Canada* (Toronto: McClelland and Stewart, 1962), pp. 132–143.

P61 FURTADO, R. DE L., and BRONWEN STANLEY-JONES. 'William Lyon Mackenzie King' in their *Prime Ministers of Canada, 1867–1980* (Markham, Ont.: Law and Business Publications (Canada) Inc., 1980), pp. 62–66.

P62 GARNER OF CHIDDINGLY, LORD. 'Britain and Canada in the 1940s and 1950s' in Peter Lyon, ed., *Britain and Canada: Survey of a changing relationship* (London: Frank Cass, 1976), pp. 85–104.

P63 GIBSON, FREDERICK WELLINGTON. 'The Cabinet of 1921' in Frederick W. Gibson, ed., *Cabinet formation and bicultural relations: Seven case studies* (Ottawa: Queen's Printer, 1970), pp. 63–104.

P64 – 'The Cabinet of 1935' in Frederick W. Gibson, ed., *Cabinet formation and bicultural relations: Seven case studies* (Ottawa: Queen's Printer, 1970), pp. 105–141.

P65 – 'Le ministère Mackenzie King de 1921' in Frederick W. Gibson, ed., *La formation du ministère et les relations biculturelles: Études de sept cabinets* (Ottawa: Imprimeur de la Reine, 1970), pp. 67–110.

P66 – 'Le ministère Mackenzie King de 1935' in Frederick W. Gibson, ed., *La formation du ministère et les relations biculturelles: Études de sept cabinets* (Ottawa: Imprimeur de la Reine, 1970), pp. 111–148.

P67 GIBSON, JAMES ALEXANDER. 'Reminiscences' in *Mackenzie King: A political view*, Canadian Issues, 1 (2), Spring 1977, pp. 37–45.

P68 GRANATSTEIN, JACK LAWRENCE. 'Financing the Liberal Party, 1935–1945' in Michael Cross and Robert Bothwell, eds., *Policy by other means: Essays in honour of C.P. Stacey* (Toronto and Vancouver: Clarke, Irwin & Company, 1972), pp. 179–199.

P69 – 'King and his cabinet: The war years' in John English and John O. Stubbs, eds., *Mackenzie King: Widening the debate* (Toronto: Macmillan of Canada, 1977), pp. 173–190.

P70 GRANATSTEIN, JACK LAWRENCE, and NORMAN HILLMER. 'The best of neighbours, 1935–1939' in their *For better or for worse: Canada and the United States to the 1990s* (Toronto: Copp Clark Pitman, 1991), pp. 103–131.

P71 – 'Cold war and warm hearts, 1945–1957' in their *For better or for worse: Canada and the United States to the 1990s* (Ottawa: Copp Clark Pitman, 1991), pp. 163–191.

P72 – 'Forged in war, 1939–1945' in their *For better or for worse: Canada and the United States to the 1990s* (Toronto: Copp Clark Pitman, 1991), pp. 133–162.

P73 – 'The sting of competition, 1919–1935' in their *For better or for worse: Canada and the United States to the 1990s* (Toronto: Copp Clark Pitman, 1991), pp. 71–102.

P74 GRANATSTEIN, JACK LAWRENCE, and DESMOND MORTON. 'Mr King and Mr Roosevelt' in their *A nation forged in fire: Canadians and the Second World War, 1939–1945* (Toronto: Lester and Orpen Dennys, 1989), pp. 31–35.

P75 GRANATSTEIN, JACK LAWRENCE, IRVING M. ABELLA, DAVID J. BERCUSON, R. CRAIG BROWN, and HERBERT BLAIR NEATBY. '1919–1939: The years of boom and bust' in their *Twentieth century Canada* (Toronto: McGraw-Hill Ryerson, 1983), pp. 179–231.

P76 – '1939–1957: The Liberal ascendancy' in their *Twentieth century Canada* (Toronto: McGraw-Hill Ryerson, 1983), pp. 265–312.

P77 GRANT, MADELINE. 'William Lyon Mackenzie King: A bibliography' in John English and John O. Stubbs, eds., *Mackenzie King:*

Widening the debate (Toronto: Macmillan of Canada, 1977), pp. 221–253.

P78 GRAVEL, JEAN-YVES. 'Le Québec militaire, 1939–1945' in his *Le Québec et la guerre* (Montréal: Éditions du Boréal Express, 1974), pp. 77–108.

P79 GRIFFIN, FREDERICK. 'Mackenzie King' in Lawrence A. Fernsworth, ed., *Dictators and democrats* (New York: Robert M. McBridge, 1941), pp. 325–337.

P80 HAMILTON, ROBERT MORRIS, compiler. 'William Lyon Mackenzie King' in his *Canadian quotations and phrases: Literary and historical* (Toronto: McClelland and Stewart, 1956), p. 112.

P81 – and DOROTHY SHIELDS, compilers. 'William Lyon Mackenzie King' in their *The dictionary of Canadian quotations and phrases* (Toronto: McClelland and Stewart, 1979), pp. 493–497.

P82 HEENEY, ARNOLD. 'The Anglo-Canadian neurosis: The case of O.D. Skelton' in Peter Lyon, ed., *Britain and Canada: Survey of a changing relationship* (London: Frank Cass, 1976), pp. 61–84.

P83 – 'Last years with Mackenzie King' in his *The things that are Caesar's: Memoirs of a public servant* (Toronto: University of Toronto Press, 1972), pp. 82–95.

P84 – 'Principal secretary to Mackenzie King' in his *The things that are Caesar's: Memoirs of a public servant* (Toronto: University of Toronto Press, 1972), pp. 327–353.

P85 – 'Secretary to the Cabinet' in his *The things that are Caesar's: Memoirs of a public servant* (Toronto: University of Toronto Press, 1972), pp. 73–81.

P86 – 'War years' in his *The things that are Caesar's: Memoirs of a public servant* (Toronto: University of Toronto Press, 1972), pp. 54–72.

P87 HENRY, LORNE J. 'William Lyon Mackenzie King' in his *Canadians: A book of biographies* (Toronto: Longmans, Green and Company, 1950), pp. 98–106.

P88 HILLMER, NORMAN. 'The pursuit of peace: Mackenzie King and the 1937 Imperial Conference' in John English and John O. Stubbs, eds., *Mackenzie King: Widening the debate* (Toronto: Macmillan of Canada, 1977), pp. 149–172.

P89 HUTCHISON, BRUCE. 'The baited trap' in his *Mr Prime Minister, 1867–1964* (Toronto: Longmans Canada, 1964), pp. 221–236.

P90 – 'The fighting man' in his *Mr Prime Minister, 1867–1964* (Toronto: Longmans Canada, 1964), pp. 257–284.

P91 – 'The Gothic Hill' in his *The far side of the street* (Toronto: Macmillan of Canada, 1976), pp. 64–76.

P92 – 'The scoop and the yawn' in his *The far side of the street* (Toronto: Macmillan of Canada, 1976), pp. 219–232.

P93 – 'The unseen hand' in his *Mr Prime Minister, 1867–1964* (Toronto: Longmans Canada, 1964), pp. 202–236.

P94 JONES, DONALD. 'Why Mackenzie King built a replica of Pasteur's tomb in Toronto' in his *Fifty tales of Toronto* (Toronto, Buffalo, and London: University of Toronto Press, 1992), pp. 105–108.

P95 KARSH, YOUSUF. 'William Lyon Mackenzie King' in his *Karsh Canadians* (Toronto, Buffalo, and London: University of Toronto Press, 1978), pp. 90–91.

P96 LEVINE, ALLAN. 'Managing the war' in his *Scrum wars: The prime ministers and the media* (Toronto: Dundurn Press, 1993), pp. 175–184.

P97 – 'The trials of Mackenzie King' in his *Scrum wars: The prime ministers and the media* (Toronto: Dundurn Press, 1993), pp. 124–150.

P98 LOCKE, GEORGE HERBERT. 'William Lyon Mackenzie King' in his *Builders of the Canadian commonwealth* (Toronto: Ryerson Press, 1923), pp. 285–286.

P99 LOTZ, JIM. 'The incredible Canadian: The Rt. Hon. William Lyon Mackenzie King' in his *Prime Ministers of Canada* (London: Bison Books, 1987), pp. 74–91.

P100 LYNCH, CHARLES. 'My own Canadian home' in his *You can't print that: Memoirs of a political voyeur* (Edmonton: Hurtig Publishers, 1983), pp. 124–134.

P101 McANDREW, WILLIAM JAMES. 'Mackenzie King, Roosevelt, and the New Deal: The ambivalence of reform' in John English and John O. Stubbs, eds., *Mackenzie King: Widening the debate* (Toronto: Macmillan of Canada, 1977), pp. 130–148.

P102 MACDONALD, MALCOLM J. 'King: The view from London' in John English and John O. Stubbs, eds., *Mackenzie King: Widening the debate* (Toronto: Macmillan of Canada, 1977), pp. 40–54.

P103 MacEWEN, GWENDOLYN. 'Kingsmere' in her *Noman* (Ottawa: Oberon Press, 1972), pp. 52–54.

P104 McLEOD, JACK, and CYNTHIA M. SMITH. 'Mackenzie King (I)' in their *The Oxford book of Canadian political anecdotes* (Toronto, Oxford, and New York: Oxford University Press, 1988), pp. 95–98.

P105 – 'Mackenzie King (II)' in their *The Oxford book of Canadian political anecdotes* (Toronto, Oxford, and New York: Oxford University Press, 1988), pp. 116–123.

P106 MALONE, RICHARD SANKEY. 'Conscription crisis and Ralston's resignation' in his *A world in flames, 1944–1945: A portrait of war, Part Two* (Toronto: Collins, 1984), pp. 139–159.

P107 – 'The general's revolt' in his *A world in flames, 1944–1945: A portrait of war, Part Two* (Toronto: Collins, 1984), pp. 288–296.

P108 – 'Ralston's resignation' in his *Missing from the record* (Toronto: Collins, 1946), pp. 149–160.

P109 MANSERGH, NICHOLAS. 'Men of Commonwealth: Smuts, Mackenzie King and Nehru' in his *The Commonwealth experience* (London: Weidenfeld and Nicolson, 1969), pp. 369–397.

P110 MARKHAM, VIOLET. 'William Lyon Mackenzie King' in her *Friendship Harvest* (London: Max Reinhardt, 1956), pp. 143–167.

P111 MARTIN, LAWRENCE. 'The best bilateral years: Franklin Roosevelt and Mackenzie King' and 'Life with Harry' in his *The Presidents and the Prime Ministers: Washington and Ottawa face to face: The myth of bilateral bliss, 1867–1982* (Toronto and Garden City: Doubleday, 1982), pp. 111–163.

P112 MARTIN, PAUL. 'King: The view from the backbench and the Cabinet table ' in John English and John O. Stubbs, eds., *Mackenzie King: Widening the debate* (Toronto: Macmillan of Canada, 1977), pp. 30–39.

P113 – 'Reminiscences' in *Mackenzie King: A personal view,* Canadian Issues, 1 (2), Spring 1977, pp. 9–14.

P114 MATHESON, JOHN ROSS. 'Mackenzie King and the flag, 1925' in his *Canada's flag: A search for a country* (Belleville: Mika Publishing Company, 1986), pp. 24–37.

P115 – 'Mackenzie King and the flag, 1945–1946' in his *Canada's flag: A search for a country* (Belleville: Mika Publishing Company, 1986), pp. 38–64.

P116 MYERS, ARTHUR. 'Mackenzie King, Canada's famed Prime Minister, or, how to run a country and still have time for the next world' in his *Ghosts of the rich and famous* (Chicago and New York: Contemporary Books, 1988), pp. 146–161.

P117 NATIONAL ARCHIVES OF CANADA. 'The diary of William Lyon Mackenzie King' in *Treasures of the National Archives of Canada* (Toronto, Buffalo, and London: University of Toronto Press, 1992), pp. 220–221.

P118 – 'The Right Honourable William Lyon Mackenzie King' in *The Prime Ministers of Canada, 1867–1994. Presented by the House of Commons and the National Archives of Canada* (Ottawa: National Archives of Canada, 1994), p. 10.

P119 NEATBY, HERBERT BLAIR. 'The Liberal way: Fiscal and monetary policy in the 1930s' in Victor Hoar, ed., *The great depression* (Toronto: Copp Clark, 1975), pp. 84–114.

P120 – 'Mackenzie King and the historians' in John English and John O. Stubbs, eds., *Mackenzie King: Widening the debate* (Toronto: Macmillan of Canada, 1977), pp. 1–14.

P121 – 'Mackenzie King and the historians' in Barry M. Gough, ed., *In search of the visible past: History lectures at Wilfrid Laurier University, 1973–4* (Waterloo: Wilfrid Laurier University Press, 1975), pp. 77–89.

P122 – 'Mackenzie King and national unity' in Harvey L. Dyck and H. Peter Krosby, eds., *Empire and Nation: Essays in honour of Frederic H. Soward* (Toronto: University of Toronto Press, 1969), pp. 54–70.

P123 – 'The political ideas of William Lyon Mackenzie King' in Marcel Hamelin, ed., *Les idées publiques des premiers ministres du Canada/ The political ideas of the Prime Ministers of Canada* (Ottawa: Les Éditions de l'Université d'Ottawa, 1969), pp. 121–137.

P124 – 'William Lyon Mackenzie King' in Robert L. McDougall, ed., *Canada past and present: A dialogue: Our living tradition*, Fifth Series (Toronto: University of Toronto Press, in association with Carleton University, 1965), pp. 1–20.

P125 – 'William Lyon Mackenzie King: The conciliator' in his *The politics of chaos: Canada in the thirties* (Toronto: Macmillan of Canada, 1972), pp. 72–87.

P126 NORTHERN ELECTRIC COMPANY LIMITED. 'The rebel's grandson' in *Forward with Canada* (N.p., 1951), pp. 6–9.

P127 O'LEARY, MICHAEL GRATTAN. 'A closer look at King' in his *Recollections of people, press, and politics* (Toronto: Macmillan of Canada, 1977), pp. 81–96.

P128 – 'Hon. W.L. Mackenzie King chosen leader in spirited contest' [from the *Ottawa Journal*, August 8, 1919] in Lucien Brault, Jean-Louis Gagnon, Wilfred Kesterton, Duncan C. McArthur, Frank Hawkins Underhill, and Christopher Young, eds., *A century of reporting: The National Press Club anthology/Une siècle de reportage: Anthologie du Cercle Nationale des Journalistes* (Toronto and Vancouver: Clarke, Irwin and Company, 1967), pp. 166–167.

P129 – 'King, Byng, and Meighen' in his *Recollections of people, press, and politics* (Toronto: Macmillan of Canada, 1977), pp. 54–67.

P130 ONDAATJE, CHRISTOPHER. 'The Rt. Hon. William Lyon Mackenzie King' in his *The Prime Ministers of Canada: Macdonald to Mulroney, 1867–1985* (Toronto: Pagurian Press, 1985), pp. 85–94.

P131 ONDAATJE, CHRISTOPHER, and ROBERT CATHERWOOD. 'The Rt. Hon. William Lyon Mackenzie King' in their *The Prime Ministers of Canada, 1867–1967* (Toronto: Canyon Press, 1967), pp. 103–112.

P132 ONDAATJE, CHRISTOPHER, and DONALD SWAINSON. 'The Rt. Hon. William Lyon Mackenzie King' in their *The Prime Ministers of Canada* (Toronto: Pagurian Press, 1975), pp. 103–110.

P133 PICKERSGILL, JOHN WHITNEY. 'The death of Mackenzie King' in his *My years with Louis St Laurent: A political memoir* (Toronto and Buffalo: University of Toronto Press, 1975), pp. 121–122.

P134 – 'Mackenzie King's political attitudes and public policies: A personal impression' in John English and John O. Stubbs, eds., *Mackenzie King: Widening the debate* (Toronto: Macmillan of Canada, 1977), pp. 15–29.

P135 – 'Reminscences' in *Mackenzie King: A personal view*, Canadian Issues, 1 (2), Spring 1977, pp. 15–22.

P136 READER'S DIGEST ASSOCIATION (CANADA) LIMITED. 'The interpreter: Mackenzie King serves as a link between Churchill and Roosevelt' in their *The Canadians at war, 1939/45* (Montreal: Reader's Digest, 1969), vol. 1, pp. 52–63.

P137 – 'Showdown: The toll of battle finally forces the conscription crisis Mackenzie King had avoided for five years' in their *The Canadians at war, 1939/45* (Montreal: Reader's Digest, 1969), vol. 2, pp. 559–567.

P138 RICHER, LEOPOLD. 'M Mackenzie King' in his *Nos chefs à Ottawa* (Montréal: Éditions Albert Levesque, 1935), pp. 24–31.

P139 RITCHIE, CHARLES. 'Reminiscences' in *Mackenzie King: A personal view*, Canadian Issues, 1 (2), Spring 1977, pp. 31–35.

P140 ROBERTS, LESLIE. 'The Prime Minister' in his *These be your gods* (Toronto: Musson Book Company, 1929), pp. 40–54.

P141 ROBERTSON, GORDON. 'King as administrator' in *Mackenzie King: A personal view*, Canadian Issues, 1 (2), Spring 1977, pp. 53–56.

P142 ROBERTSON, HEATHER. 'Other men's wives: Mrs King and Mrs Patteson' in her *More than a rose: Prime Ministers, wives and other women* (Toronto: McClelland–Bantam, Inc., 1991), pp. 175–196.

P143 – 'Other men's wives: Mrs King and Mrs Patteson' in her *More than a rose: Prime Ministers, wives and other women* (Toronto: McClelland–Bantam, Inc. and Seal Books), pp. 194–216. [Seal Paperback edition].

P144 ROBINSON, JUDITH. 'Crystal ball' in her *This is on the house* (Toronto: McClelland and Stewart, 1957), pp. 29–31.

P145 SANGER, CLYDE. 'Mackenzie King and the conscription crisis, 1942–44' in his *Malcolm MacDonald: Bringing an end to Empire* (Montreal, Kingston, London, and Buffalo: McGill-Queen's University Press, 1995), pp. 214–230.

P146 SARTY, ROGER. 'Mr King and the Armed Forces' in Norman Hillmer, Robert Bothwell, Roger Sarty, and Claude Beauregard, eds., *A country of limitations: Canada and the world in 1939/Un pays dans la gêne: le Canada et le monde en 1939* ([Ottawa]: Canadian Committee for the History of the Second World War/Comité canadien d'Histoire de la Deuxième Guerre mondiale, 1996), pp. 217–246.

P147 SAUER, ANGELIKA. 'Goodwill and profit: Mackenzie King and Canadian appeasement' in Norman Hillmer, Robert Bothwell, Roger Sarty, and Claude Beauregard, eds., *A country of limitations: Canada and the world in 1939/Un pays dans la gêne: le Canada et le monde en 1939* ([Ottawa]: Canadian Committee for the History of the Second World War/Comité canadien d'Histoire de la Deuxième Guerre mondiale, 1996), pp. 247–269.

P148 SAWATSKY, JOHN. 'Did Mackenzie King fumble when Gouzenko defected? [Appendix B]' in his *Gouzenko: The untold story* (Toronto: Macmillan of Canada, 1984), pp. 273–275.

P149 SAYWELL, JOHN TUPPER. 'Mitch Hepburn and Willie King's War' in Norman Hillmer, Robert Bothwell, Roger Sarty, and Claude Beauregard, eds., *A country of limitations: Canada and the world in 1939/Un pays dans la gêne: le Canada et le monde en 1939* ([Ottawa]: Canadian Committee for the History of the Second Woarld War/ Comité canadien d'Histoire de la Deuxième Guerre mondiale, 1996), pp. 120–137.

P150 SCHEINBERG, STEPHEN J. 'Rockefeller and King: The capitalist and the reformer' in John English and John O. Stubbs, eds., *Mackenzie King: Widening the debate* (Toronto: Macmillan of Canada, 1977), pp. 89–104.

P151 SIME, JESSICA GEORGINA, and FRANK NICHOLSON. 'Three meetings with Mr Mackenzie King' in their *Brave spirits* (London: The Authors, 1952), pp. 157–165.

P152 SMITH, IRVING NORMAN. 'Mr King in his study' in his *A reporter reports* (Toronto: Ryerson Press, 1954), pp. 5–13.

P153 – A reporter's farewell to Mr King' in his *A reporter reports* (Toronto: Ryerson Press, 1954), pp. 24–29.

P154 STACEY, CHARLES PERRY. 'Swanning with Rex' in his *A date with* *history: Memoirs of a Canadian historian* (Ottawa: Deneau Publishers, 1982), pp. 181–192.

P155 STRATFORD, PHILIP. 'The conscription crisis, 1942' in his *André Laurendeau: Witness for Quebec* (Toronto: Macmillan of Canada, 1973), pp. 1–121.

P156 SWETTENHAM, JOHN. 'The conscription crisis' in his *McNaughton, vol. 3, 1944–1946* (Toronto, Winnipeg, and Vancouver: Ryerson Press, 1969), pp. 20–68.

P157 SWINTON, EARL OF. 'Canada's famous leaders' in his *Sixty years of power; Some memories of the men who wielded it* (London: Hutchinson, 1966), pp. 213–216.

P158 UNDERHILL, FRANK HAWKINS. 'William Lyon Mackenzie King' in ENCYCLOPEDIA CANADIANA, *Men of destiny: Canada's Governors General and Prime Ministers* (Ottawa, 1958), pp. 29–32.

P159 VINING, CHARLES [ARTHUR McLAREN]. 'Mr King' in his *Bigwigs: Canadian wise and otherwise* (Toronto: Macmillan Company, 1935), pp. 82–85.

P160 WILLIAMS, JEFFERY. 'King and constitution' in his *Byng of Vimy: General and Governor General* (London: Leo Cooper and Secker & Warburg Ltd., 1983), pp. 301–324.

P161 WRIGHT, GERALD C.V. 'Mackenzie King: Power over the political executive' in Thomas Alexander Hockin, ed., *Apex of power: the Prime Minister and political leadership in Canada* (Scarborough: Prentice-Hall, 1971), pp. 200–208.

SECTION Q

Mackenzie King in Fiction

Mackenzie King appears as a fictionalized character in several books. The listing of these titles is arranged alphabetically by author.

Q1 BURKE, STANLEY, and ROY PETERSON. *Swamp song.* Vancouver: Douglas and McIntyre, 1978. 44 p.

Q2 DAVIES, ROBERTSON. *High spirits.* Harmondsworth, Middlesex, England; New York, N.Y.: Penguin Books, 1982.
'Conversations with the little table': pp. 139–149.

Q3 MacLENNAN, HUGH. *Two solitudes.* Toronto: Collins, 1945. 370 p.
MacLennan's biographer, Elspeth Cameron, writes:

> As many readers at once recognized, [Huntley] McQueen was a caricature of William Lyon Mackenzie King, Prime Minister of Canada; his name is an amalgam of elements from King's, with 'King' changed to 'Queen' and the 'Mac' transposed. Both are bachelors who work in the upper floor stories at night; both men revere their dead mothers and 'commune' with portraits of them for advice. Each wears and adjusts his pince-nez in a ponderous style; each actively dislikes air-conditioned railway cars and planes.[129]

---

129 Elspeth Cameron, *Hugh MacLennan: A writer's life* (Toronto and Buffalo: University of Toronto Press, 1981), pp. 180–181.

Cameron also writes: 'MacLennan was amused that the cover for Macmillan's Laurentian Library paperback edition of *Two Solitudes* showed McQueen with the features of Mackenzie King.'[130] MacLennan mentioned the subject of McQueen in a letter to Dorothy Dumbrille in 1946:

> McQueen in a sense does bear a few outward resemblances to the P.M., but otherwise not. The P.M. in my opinion is a genius and a great statesman. Without the genius he might have been like McQueen, but there's quite a difference. Someone else must have had the same idea, for the character in the Stage '47 production[131] talked exactly like the P.M.[132]

It is interesting to note that MacLennan received a suggestion to write a biography of Mackenzie King.[133] MacLennan's name came up in discussions of the literary executors when they were selecting the official biographer.[134]

MacLennan once wrote this summary of King:

> Mackenzie King has never been an easy man to know. He was the most reserved of our prime ministers. It is therefore no more than a personal opinion which prompts me to claim that he has been the only one of our statesmen who can rightly be called a genius, a term which I define as a man whose subsconscious enables him to travel by a single leap to insights which other men seldom attain unaided. In politics, it is the rarest of qualities.[135]

Q4 ROBERTSON, HEATHER. *Willie: A romance. Volume 1: The King years.* Toronto: James Lorimer, 1983. 359 p.

Q5 – *Willie: A romance. Volume 1: The King years.* Toronto: General Paperbacks, 1983. 464 p.
[Paperback edition].

---

130 Ibid., p. 391.

131 Originally broadcast on the Canadian Broadcasting Corporation on December 15, 1946, the Stage '47 production of *Two Solitudes* was adapted by Hugh Kemp.

132 QUA, Dorothy Dumbrille Papers, Box 1, Hugh MacLennan to Dorothy Dumbrille, January 2, 1946 [i.e., 1947].

133 Ibid., p. xi.

134 NAC, MG 26, J 18 Series, Folder 1, F.A. McGregor to John W. Gray, November 16, 1950.

135 Hugh MacLennan, 'The ten greatest Canadians,' *New Liberty*, 26 (9), November 1949, p. 13.

Q6 – *L'homme qui se croyait aimé ou, La vie secrète d'un premier ministre.* Montréal: Boréal, 1987. 475 p. [Traduction de *Willie*].

Q7 – *Lily: A rhapsody in red.* Toronto: James Lorimer, 1986. 327 p.

Q8 – *Lily: A rhapsody in red. Volume 2: The King years.* Toronto: General Paperbacks, 1986. 327 p.
[Paperback edition].

Q9 – *Igor: A novel of intrigue.* Toronto: James Lorimer, 1989. 250 p.

Q10 WARD, MRS HUMPHRY. *Canadian born.* London: J. Murray, 1910. 346 p.

American Edition:

Q11 – *Lady Merton, colonist.* New York: Doubleday, 1910. 350 p.

Some believe that King appears as George Anderson in this novel. Robert MacGregor Dawson, King's official biographer, wrote: 'King was popularly supposed to have furnished the model for her hero, an engineer and budding public figure, whose entry into Parliament was greatly aided by his success in settling labour disputes.'[136]

In 1935 King makes reference to the book. In his diary he wrote: 'There I read the account of the day in spring in the park at Vancouver, which seemed to relate to Eleanor Grenough's walk and mine together it had to do with flowers, nature & spring.'[137]

The book was published in 1910, two years after Mrs Ward visited Canada. The book is dedicated 'To Canada in memory of a happy journey, May–June, 1908.'

Q12 WHEATLEY, PATIENCE. 'Mr Mackenzie King' in *The Fiddlehead*, no. 115, Fall 1977, pp. 106–113.
Reprinted in Roger Ploude and Michael Taylor, eds. *Fiddlehead greens: Stories from the Fiddlehead.* Ottawa: Oberon Press, 1979, pp. 163–175.

136 Dawson, *William Lyon Mackenzie King: A political biography, 1874–1923*, p. 210.
137 King Diary, April 17, 1935.

SECTION R

Theses and Dissertations about Mackenzie King and His Era

This section contains an alphabetical listing of theses and dissertations about Mackenzie King as well as several significant aspects of the Mackenzie King era. If a major part of the thesis has been published, a note with a cross-reference to the book has been provided.

Information about the availability of the theses for purchase and borrowing by interlibrary loan has been provided. All theses with a 'TC,' 'TH,' or 'TJ' number may be purchased from Micromedia Limited, Toronto.

R1 ADAMS, RONALD A. 'Mackenzie King and the Soviet Trade Mission to Canada, 1924–1927.' [University of Ottawa: Master of Arts Thesis, 1970]. vi, 155 leaves.
Available on interlibrary loan from the Library, University of Western Ontario.

R2 ANDERSON, JOHN C. 'Mackenzie King and collective security: The League of Nations and the United Nations.' [University of Alberta: Master of Arts Thesis, 1977]. vii, 160 leaves.
TC-34279.
Available on interlibrary loan from the National Library of Canada.

R3 ATHERTON, JAMES J. 'The Department of Labour and industrial relations, 1900–1911.' [Carleton University: Master of Arts Thesis, 1972]. viii, 411 leaves.
TC-10933.
Available on interlibrary loan from the National Library of Canada.

R4 BAGLEY, JOHN FRANCIS. 'The first Quebec Conference, August 14–24, 1943: Decision at the crossroads.' [Georgetown University: Doctor of Philosophy Thesis, 1973]. viii, 317 leaves.
Available on interlibrary loan from the Library, Georgetown University.

R5 BALLARD, ELIZABETH JEAN. 'Characteristics of Canadian Prime Ministers: Ratings by historians and political scientists.' [University of British Columbia: Master of Arts Thesis, 1984]. vi, 103 leaves.
TC-59159.
Available on interlibrary loan from the National Library of Canada.

R6 BOYLE, PATRICK JOHN. 'The National Liberal Federation of Canada: Antecedents and formative years, 1920–1940.' [Queen's University: Master of Arts Thesis, 1975]. vi, 192 leaves.
TC-24804.
Available on interlibrary loan from the National Library of Canada.

R7 BRENNAN, PATRICK HARVEY. 'A responsible civilized relationship: Reporting the nation's business, 1935–1957.' [York University: Doctor of Philosophy Thesis, 1989]. x, 428 p.
TH-49627-4.
Available on interlibrary loan from the National Library of Canada.
For a published version see N11.

R8 BURNS, ROBERT JOSEPH. 'The co-operative efforts of William Lyon Mackenzie King and Franklin Delano Roosevelt: A study in Canadian–American relations.' [University of Western Ontario: Master of Arts Thesis, 1969]. iv, 247 leaves.
Available on interlibrary loan from the Library, University of Western Ontario.

R9 BYCHOK, PAUL. '"La muraille qui vous protège": Ernest Lapointe and French Canada, 1935–41.' [Queen's University: Master of Arts Thesis, 1984]. v, 307 leaves.
TH-26596-5.
Available on interlibrary loan from the National Library of Canada.

R10 CRAVEN, PAUL. 'An impartial umpire: Industrial relations and the Canadian state, 1900–11.' [University of Toronto: Doctor of Philosophy Thesis, 1978]. vi, 621 leaves.
TC-43628.

Available on interlibrary loan from the National Library of Canada.
For a published version see N29.

R11 CRESSY, ARTHUR CHEEVER. 'Canadian–American relations in World War II.' [Tufts University: Doctor of Philosophy Thesis, 1952]. 316 leaves.
Available on interlibrary loan from the Library, Tufts University.

R12 DZIUBAN, STANLEY W. 'United States military collaboration with Canada in World War II.' [Columbia University: Doctor of Philosophy Thesis, 1955]. xiii, 830 leaves.
Available on interlibrary loan from the Library, Columbia University.

R13 ESBEREY, JOY ELAINE. 'Personality and politics: A study of William Lyon Mackenzie King.' [University of Toronto: Doctor of Philosophy Thesis, 1974]. 2 v.
Available on interlibrary loan from the Library, University of British Columbia.
For a published version see N42.

R14 FROHN-NIELSEN, THOR ERIK. 'Canada's Foreign Enlistment Act: Mackenzie King's expedient response to the Spanish Civil War.' [University of British Columbia: Master of Arts Thesis, 1982]. vi, 104 leaves.
TC-59180.
Available on interlibrary loan from the National Library of Canada.

R15 HARBOUR, FRANCES VRYLING. 'Conscription and schemata: The lessons of history and four Canadian ministers in World War II.' [Columbia University: Doctor of Philosophy Thesis, 1986]. 2 v.
Available on interlibrary loan from the Library, Columbia University.

R16 HART, JOHN FREDERIC VINCENT. 'The political and legal uses of reference cases of the Mackenzie King government, 1935–1940.' [University of British Columbia: Master of Arts Thesis, 1987]. vi, 165 leaves.
Available on interlibrary loan from the Library, University of British Columbia.

R17 JOYNT, CAREY BONTHRON. 'Canadian foreign policy, 1919–1939.' [Clark University: Doctor of Philosophy Thesis, 1951]. 313 leaves.
Available on interlibrary loan from the Library, Clark University.

R18 KOTTMAN, RICHARD NORMAN. 'The diplomatic relations of the United States and Canada, 1927–1941.' [Vanderbilt University: Doctor of Philosophy Thesis, 1958]. 526 leaves.
Available on interlibrary loan from the Library, Vanderbilt University.

R19 LeBLANC, BERNARD CHARLES. 'A reluctant recruit: Angus L. Macdonald and conscription, 1940–1945.' [Queen's University: Master of Arts Thesis, 1987]. iv, 118 leaves.
TH-38568-5.
Available on interlibrary loan from the National Library of Canada.

R20 LUBIN, MARTIN. 'Conscription, the national identity enigma and the politics of enthno-cultural cleavage in Canada during World War II.' [University of Illinois: Doctor of Philosophy Thesis, 1973]. vii, 714 leaves.
Available on interlibrary loan from the Library, University of Illinois.

R21 MacLEOD, KEVIN. 'Mackenzie King and the emergence of the new Commonwealth status (1948).' [Carleton University: Master of Arts Thesis, 1984]. iv, 118 leaves.
Available on interlibrary loan from the Library, Carleton University.

R22 MAHOOD, ROBERT FISHER. 'Ideology in the work of Mackenzie King.' [University of Saskatchewan: Master of Arts Thesis, 1972]. vii, 200 leaves.
TC-14818.
Available on interlibrary loan from the National Library of Canada.

R23 MATSON, WILLIAM LAWRENCE. 'William Lyon Mackenzie King and Franklin Delano Roosevelt, their effect on Canadian–American relations, 1935–1939.' [University of Maine: Doctor of Philosophy Thesis, 1973]. 287 leaves.
Available on interlibrary loan from the Library, University of Maine.

R24 MERRICK, JOHN ROBERT. 'Canada and the origin of the United Nations, 1941–1945.' [Queen's University: Master of Arts Thesis, 1974]. ix, 251 leaves.
Available on interlibrary loan from the Library, Queen's University.

R25 MULLER, STEVEN. 'The Canadian Prime Ministers, 1867–1948: An essay on democratic leadership.' [Cornell University: Doctor of Philosophy Thesis, 1958]. 2 v.
Available on interlibrary loan from the Library, Cornell University.

R26 ROPEL-MORSKI, HERMINA P. 'William Lyon Mackenzie King: The corporate man.' [McMaster University: Master of Arts Thesis, 1978]. xii, 151 leaves.
TC-39978.
Available on interlibrary loan from the National Library of Canada.

R27 ROSKIES, ETHEL. 'The Liberalism of William Lyon Mackenzie King.' [McGill University: Master of Arts Thesis, 1960]. 2 v.
Available on interlibrary loan from the Library, McGill University.

R28 ST JEAN, SYLVAIN. 'Leadership et développement psychodynamique étude d'un cas: William Lyon Mackenzie King.' [Université de Montréal: Master of Science Thesis, 1988].
Available from the Library, Université de Montréal.

R29 SLOBODIN, THOMAS BRENT. 'A tangled web: The relationship between Mackenzie King's foreign policy and national unity.' [Queen's University: Doctor of Philosophy Thesis, 1986]. xviii, 512 leaves.
TH-32085-0.
Available on interlibrary loan from the National Library of Canada.

R30 STEWART, JOHN BENJAMIN. 'Parliament and executive in wartime Canada, 1939–1945.' [Columbia University: Doctor of Philosophy Thesis, 1953]. 275 leaves.
Available on interlibrary loan from the Library, Columbia University.

R31 WARDHAUGH, ROBERT ALEXANDER. 'James G. Gardiner, land policy and Dominion–Provincial relations.' [University of Saskatchewan: Master of Arts Thesis, 1990]. v, 162 leaves.
Available on interlibrary loan from the Library, University of Saskatchewan.

R32 – 'Mackenzie King and the Prairie West.' [University of Manitoba: Doctor of Philosophy Thesis, 1995]. viii, 530 p.
TJ-13554.
Available on interlibrary loan from the National Library of Canada.

R33 WILCOX, VICTORIA MARGARET. 'Prime Minister and Governor-General: Mackenzie King and Lord Tweedsmuir, 1935–1940.' [Queen's University: Master of Arts Thesis, 1976]. iv, 201 leaves.
TC-32694.
Available on interlibrary loan from the National Library of Canada.

SECTION S

Newsreels with Material Relating to Mackenzie King

More than one hundred incidents in Mackenzie King's life have been preserved on motion picture film in newsreels. The newsreels date from the early 1920s to King's funeral on July 26, 1950. The material in this section is listed chronologically. The newsreels are on file at the National Archives of Canada and the United States National Archives.

Information about four videocassettes and educational kits has also been included at the end of this section.

S1 Mackenzie King on a visit to his riding at Newmarket, Ontario [July 27, 1921?].
Location: National Archives of Canada, NFA 7710 and NFA 7712.

S2 Mackenzie King shown at Union Station, Ottawa and Parliament Hill as Lord Byng of Vimy arrives to assume governor generalship of Canada, August 12, 1921.
Location: National Archives of Canada, NFA 7706 1021 and 1022.

S3 Mackenzie King and Sir Robert Borden are shown in Ottawa as Lord Byng leaves Canada at the end of his term as Governor General of Canada, September 27, 1926. [National Film Board].
Location: National Archives of Canada, NFA 7706 1008 to 1010.

S4 Mackenzie King at Prime Ministers' Conference, London, 1926.
Location: National Archives of Canada, NFA 76-7-29.

S5 Mackenzie King at Toronto Garrison Parade, May 22, 1927.
Location: National Archives of Canada, NFA 7704 349 and 350.

S6 Mackenzie King greets William Phillips, first American envoy to confer directly with the Canadian government, as he arrives in Ottawa, June 2, 1927. [Fox Movietone News].
Location: National Archives of Canada, NFA 7709 813.

S7 Mackenzie King at the dedication of the Peace Tower Carillon, Parliament Buildings, Ottawa, July 1, 1927.
Location: National Archives of Canada, NFA 3075, 3079, 3085, 3087.

S8 Mackenzie King and Prime Minister Stanley Baldwin during the visit of the Prince of Wales to Canada, August 2, 1927.
Location: National Archives of Canada, NFA 7710 245-246.

S9 Mackenzie King and Charles Lindbergh in Ottawa, August 1927. [National Film Board].
Location: National Archives of Canada, NFA T(CBC 975A and 975B) and NFA 7710 243 and 244.

S10 Mackenzie King on visit to Ottawa Ski Club, Pointe Fortune, Quebec, March 3, 1929.
Location: National Archives of Canada, NFA 8800 9231, 13-0192, and O1V1CV 8307 086-7.

S11 Mackenzie King speaks to tariff protestors on steps of Parliament Hill, Ottawa [1920s]. [Fox Movietone News].
Location: National Archives of Canada, NFA 1609-15 and NFA 1606-15.

S12 Mackenzie King as he presents a cane to Sir Baden-Powell during a visit to Toronto, 1920s.
Location: National Archives of Canada, NFA 9081.

S13 Mackenzie King inspects Boy Scouts on Parliament Hill, Ottawa, on their way to the Empire Jamboree in England [1920s].
Location: National Archives of Canada, NFA 76-6-114, 76-7-32.

S14 Mackenzie King shown on a visit to Barrie and poses with his sister, Jennie, and her family. [Undated].
Location: National Archives of Canada, O1V1CV 8110 030-2.

S15 Mackenzie King shown on Parliament Hill as Governor General Lord Willingdon arrives to open a session of Parliament [1926–1931].
Location: National Archives of Canada, NFA 7710 167 and 168.

S16 Mackenzie King speaking at Kingsmere with a series of short talks for several movie companies, 1930. [Hearst Movietone News].
Location: National Archives of Canada, NFA 7807 204.

S17 Mackenzie King attends dog races on Parliament Hill, Ottawa, 1930.
Location: National Archives of Canada, O1V1CV 022-5.

S18 Mackenzie King shown at the opening of the David Dunlop Observatory, May 31, 1935. [J.J. Burns Collection].
Location: National Archives of Canada, F2AC 8305 097.

S19 Mackenzie King and the provincial premiers at the Dominion–Provincial Conference, Ottawa, December 1935.
Location: National Archives of Canada, O1V1CV 8110 030-2.

S20 Mackenzie King speaks about the League of Nations, 1936.
Location: National Archives of Canada, NFA 8922.

S21 Mackenzie King speaks about the abdication of King Edward VIII, December 1936.
Location: National Archives of Canada, NFA 9050.

S22 Mackenzie King arrives in Washington where he is greeted by U.S. Secretary of State Cordell Hull, March 5, 1937.
Location: National Archives of Canada, NFA 9160, 9238.

S23 Mackenzie King speaks at the opening of Fort Henry, Kingston, Ontario, August 1, 1938.
Location: Queen's University Archives, A. ARCH mi 6.

S24 Mackenzie King and President Franklin D. Roosevelt at the dedication of the Thousand Islands International Bridge, Ivy Lea, Ontario, and Collins Landing, New York, August 18, 1938.
Location: United States National Archives, United Newsreel, 695.

S25 Mackenzie King receiving a bouquet from a young girl, 1938.
Location: National Archives of Canada, F2AC 8305 089.

S26 Mackenzie King welcomes Cordell Hull, U.S. Secretary of State, on a visit to Ottawa, 1938.
Location: National Archives of Canada, O1V1CV 8110 030-2.

S27 Visit of King George VI and Queen Elizabeth to Canada and the United States. Contains numerous shots of Mackenzie King with Their Majesties during their thirty-day tour of Canada and the United States, May 17–June 15, 1939. [Castle Films].
Location: National Archives of Canada, NFA 79-9-248 to 250, NFA 7301 2737.

[National Film Board] footage:
Location: National Archives of Canada, NFA 10-0397, 13-0398, 1530-H, V4-10 and V4-11.

Associated Screen News footage:
Location: National Archives of Canada, NFA 4561 and NFA 76-9-311.

S28 Mackenzie King and Governor General Lord Tweedsmuir at the entrance to the Parliament Buildings as Canada enters the war, September 1939. [Fox Movietone News].
Location: National Archives of Canada, NFA 8778.

S29 Mackenzie King talks about what World War II will mean to Canada, September 28, 1939.
Location: National Archives of Canada, NFA 9155.

S30 Mackenzie King lays a wreath at the National War Memorial, Ottawa, November 11, 1939.
Location: National Archives of Canada, NFA 8970.

S31 Mackenzie King with Lord Riverdale and the British Mission when he announces the creation of the British Commonwealth Air Training Plan, Ottawa, December 1939.
Location: National Archives of Canada, O1V1CV 8110 030-2.

S32 Mackenzie King signs the National Registration Act, 1940.
Location: National Archives of Canada, O1V1CV 8110 030-2.

S33 Mackenzie King on election day, March 26, 1940.
Location: National Archives of Canada, NFA 8973 and O1V1CU 8406 054-1.

S34 Mackenzie King on a tour of the Warm Springs Foundation grounds with President Franklin D. Roosevelt, April 1940.
Location: United States National Archives, Motion Picture Collection, Universal Newsreel, 1903.

S35 Mackenzie King about to enter the Parliament Buildings on the day of the opening of a new session of Parliament, May 18, 1940. [Fox Movietone News].
Location: National Archives of Canada, NFA 7808 354.

S36 Mackenzie King greets the Earl of Athlone and the Countess of Athlone in Ottawa, June 21, 1940.
Location: National Archives of Canada, NFA 7808 351.

S37 Mackenzie King and President Franklin D. Roosevelt at Ogdensburg, New York, August 1940.
Location: United States National Archives, Motion Picture Collection, Universal Newsreel, 903.

S38 Mackenzie King conferring with President Franklin D. Roosevelt and U.S. Secretary of State Henry Stimson at Norwood, New Jersey, August 1940. [Paramount News, vol. 40, no. 102].
Location: United States National Archives, Motion Picture Collection, 200 PN 2.102.

S39 Mackenzie King with President Roosevelt and U.S. Secretary of State Henry Stimson inspecting U.S. Army troops near Canadian border in New York State, August 1940. [Movietone News].
Location: United States National Archives, Motion Picture Collection, 200 I 43.

S40 Mackenzie King speaking on the Canadian war effort, 1940. [March of Time, vol. 6, no. 8].
Location: United States National Archives, Motion Picture Collection, 200 MT 6.8.

S41 Mackenzie King meeting with members of the Canadian–American Joint Defence Board, Ottawa, August 1940. [United News].
Location: United States National Archives, Motion Picture Collection, 208 UN.1002.

S42 Mackenzie King shown as he talks with Fiorello La Guardia, mayor of New York City, as Canadian–American Defence Board meets in Ottawa [August 27, 1940?].
Location: National Archives of Canada, NFA 7808 324.

S43 Mackenzie King at airport before departure from Europe [with C.D. Howe and General Georges P. Vanier], 1940s. [Fox Movietone News].
Location: National Archives of Canada, NFA 9205.

S44 Mackenzie King introduces provincial premiers at Conference, 1940s. [Fox Movietone News].
Location: National Archives of Canada, NFA 4143.

S45 Mackenzie King speaks and hints at conscription [1940?]. [National Film Board 'Canada at War' series].
Location: National Archives of Canada, NFA 7705 483.

S46 Mackenzie King and Norman Rogers at Canadian Legion War Services Campaign, 1940.
Location: National Archives of Canada, NFA 2718-1 to 2721.

S47 Mackenzie King visits troops at air training school, Boundary Bay, British Columbia [1941?].
Location: National Archives of Canada, O1V1CV 8110 030-2.

S48 Mackenzie King sees famous regiment depart [1941?]. [N. Gunn Collection].
Location: National Archives of Canada, NFA 3300-00, 3300-01, 3300-02, and 3300-03.

S49 Mackenzie King takes salute of a military regiment in Calgary, 1941.
Location: National Archives of Canada, O1V1CV 8110 030-2.

S50 Mackenzie King shown as he signed the Seaway Agreement for Canada, March 18, 1941. [Fox Movietone News].
Location: National Archives of Canada, NFA 9156.

S51 Mackenzie King cuts ribbon at ceremony to open a new road built by Canadian troops in Britain and inspects guard of honour before the ceremony, 1941. [Fox Movietone News].
Location: National Archives of Canada, NFA 7906 1234.

S52 Mackenzie King booed at Aldershot, 1941. [National Film Board 'Canada at War' series].
Location: National Archives of Canada, NFB 116B0162033, O1V2CV 8205 0137, and NFA 7705 484.

S53 Mackenzie King laying a wreath at the National War Memorial, Ottawa, September 10, 1941. [Paramount News, vol. 1, no. 8].
Location: United States National Archives, Motion Picture Collection, 200 PN 1.8.

S54 Mackenzie King at Queen's University centennial dinner, Kingston, Ontario, October 18, 1941.
Location: National Archives of Canada, NFA 7906 1146.

S55 Mackenzie King and Pilot Officer Paul Emile Morin at Uplands Airport, Ottawa, where Governor General Earl of Athlone presents wings to graduates of the British Commonwealth Air Training Plan, 1941. [Fox Movietone News].
Location: National Archives of Canada, NFA 7904 146.

S56 Mackenzie King arriving in the United Kingdom, 1941 or 1944. [Canadian Army Film Unit Collection].
Location: National Archives of Canada, NFA 1450; 13-0145.

S57 Mackenzie King at news conference in London, England, 1941 or 1944. [Fox Movietone News].
Location: National Archives of Canada, NFA 7906 1138.

S58 Mackenzie King at the unveiling of a plaque at the birthplace of Sir Wilfrid Laurier at St Lin, Quebec, November 20, 1941.
Location: National Archives of Canada, O1V1CV 8110 030-2.

S59 Mackenzie King shown at press conference held by Winston Churchill at Rideau Hall, Ottawa, December 1941.
Location: National Archives of Canada, O1V1CV 8110 030-2.

S60 Mackenzie King at train station in Ottawa as he bids farewell to Prime Minister Winston Churchill, December 31, 1941. [Fox Movietone News].
Location: National Archives of Canada, NFA 7906 1211.

S61 Mackenzie King wearing a fur hat that was presented to him by the Parliamentary Press Gallery, Ottawa, late 1941 or early 1942.
Location: National Archives of Canada, O1V1CV 8110 030-2.

S62 Mackenzie King and Governor General Earl of Athlone and Princess Alice entering the Parliament Buildings as a new session of Parliament opens, January 24, 1942. [Fox Movietone News].
Location: National Archives of Canada, NFA 7906 1246.

S63 Mackenzie King at United Nations Day ceremony on Parliament Hill, Ottawa, 1940s.
Location: National Archives of Canada, O1V1CV 8110 030–2.

S64 Mackenzie King at the time of the conscription plebiscite, April 1942. [Paramount News, vol. 1, no. 71].
Location: United States National Archives, Motion Picture Collection, 200 PN 1.71.

S65 Mackenzie King speaks at the opening of the Air Conference in Ottawa before an audience of air force representatives from Czechoslovakia, China, Poland, Greece, British Commonwealth countries, Belgium, the Netherlands, Norway, Yugoslavia, and the United States, May 18, 1942. [Fox Movietone News].
Location: National Archives of Canada, IDC ISN 23648.

S66 Mackenzie King speaks at ceremony welcoming two airmen, Pilot Officer Paul Emile Morin, Distinguished Flying Medal, and Pilot Officer Larry Robillard, Distinguished Flying Medal, F.M. in Ottawa, June 5, 1942. [Associated Screen News].
Location: National Archives of Canada, NFA 7904 114, 147, and 150.

S67 Mackenzie King speaks at ceremony welcoming Buzz Beurling to Ottawa at Rockcliffe Airport, November 10, 1942. [Fox Movietone News].
Location: National Archives of Canada 01V1CV 8401 004-7.

S68 Mackenzie King at cabinet meeting, 1942. [National Film Board].
Location: National Archives of Canada O1V1CU 8010 087-10.

S69 Mackenzie King at funeral of Sir Edward Beatty, March 23, 1943. [Fox Movietone News].
Location: National Archives of Canada, 7301 8961.

S70 Mackenzie King is shown as he delivers a radio broadcast on the landing of the Canadian troops in Sicily, July 10, 1943.
Location: National Archives of Canada, 01C2CU 8007 248.

S71 Mackenzie King shaking hands with Prime Minister Winston Churchill after his arrival in Quebec City for the Quebec Conference, August 1943.
Location: United States National Archives, Motion Picture Collection, 200 PH 2.102.

S72 First Quebec Conference, August 14–24, 1943, attended by Prime Minister Winston Churchill, Prime Minister Mackenzie King, and President Franklin Roosevelt, 1943.
Location: National Archives of Canada, NFA 3053, 3065, 3075, 3079, and 3087.

S73 Mackenzie King and President Franklin D. Roosevelt visit an air base, 1943. [March of Times, vol. 9 no. 7].

Location: United States National Archives, Motion Picture Collection, 200 MT 9.7.

S74 Mackenzie King greets successful Canadian bomber crew at Ottawa, September 4, 1943.
Location: National Archives of Canada, NFA 7906 1247.

S75 Mackenzie King talks about the Canadian war effort, 1943. [Associated Screen News].
Location: United States National Archives, Motion Picture Collection, 200, 245.

S76 Mackenzie King after his arrival in London for the Prime Ministers' Conference, May 1944. [Paramount News, vol. 3, no. 75].
Location: United States National Archives, Motion Picture Collection, 200 PN 3.75.

S77 Mackenzie King arriving in London for Commonwealth Prime Ministers' Conference, May 1944. [Canadian Army Newsreel].
Location: National Archives of Canada, O1V1CU 8010 087.

S78 Mackenzie King shown at Commonwealth Prime Ministers' Conference in London, May 1944. [National Film Board 'Canada at War' series].
Location: National Archives of Canada, NFA 7705 489.

S79 Mackenzie King at D-Day briefings, 1944.
Location: National Archives of Canada, NFA 4082 and 4083.

S80 Mackenzie King speaks to the British press at a news conference in England [1944?].
Location: National Archives of Canada, NFA 7906 1138.

S81 Mackenzie King speaking at ceremony greeting Prime Minister Curtin of Australia in Ottawa, June 1, 1944. [Canadian Paramount News].
Location: National Archives of Canada, NFA 1168, 13-0202.

S82 Mackenzie King speaking at dinner held by the Liberal Party of Canada in honour of the 25th anniversary of his leadership of the party, August 7, 1944. [Fox Movietone News].
Location: National Archives of Canada, NFA 8946.

S83 Second Quebec Conference, September 10–15, 1944, attended by

Prime Minister Churchill, Prime Minister King, and President Roosevelt.
Location: National Archives of Canada, NFA 4620.

S84 Mackenzie King addresses UNRRA meeting in Montreal, September 18, 1944. [United News].
Location: United States National Archives, Motion Picture Collection, 208 UN.122.

S85 Mackenzie King arriving at Parliament Buildings as Canadian Parliament called to deal with conscription issue meets, 1944. [Fox Movietone News].
Location: National Archives of Canada, NFA 8947.

S86 Mackenzie King at the San Francisco United Nations Conference, April–June 1945. [United News].
Location: United States National Archives, Motion Picture Collection, 208 UN.155; 208 UN.161.

S87 Mackenzie King speaking during the election campaign and after results showed the Liberals had won the election (including footage as he made a radio address to the nation), May–June 1945. [Canadian Army Film Unit].
Location: National Archives of Canada, O1V1CU 8303 029-12 and O1V1CU 8406 008-19.

S88 Mackenzie King at cabinet meeting, 1945.
Location: National Archives of Canada, NFA8309 2725-2727.

S89 Mackenzie King at ceremony as General Crerar returns home and attends official welcome in Ottawa, August 7, 1945.
Location: National Archives of Canada, O1V1CU 8406 008-19.

S90 Mackenzie King after his arrival in Washington, D.C., for talks with Prime Minister Clement Attlee and President Harry S Truman, November 1945. [Paramount News, vol. 5, no. 23].
Location: United States National Archives, Motion Picture Collection, 200 PN 5.23.

S91 Mackenzie King at conference with Prime Minister Clement Attlee and President Harry S Truman at Washington, D.C., November 1945. [United News].
Location: United States National Archives, Motion Picture Collection, 208 UN.182.

S92 Mackenzie King, President Harry S Truman, and Prime Minister Clement Attlee at meeting in Washington, D.C., November 1945. [Paramount News, vol. 5, no. 24].
Location: United States National Archives, Motion Picture Collection, 200 PN 5.24.

S93 Mackenzie King shown as he bids farewell to Lord and Lady Athlone as they leave Canada, Ottawa, March 16, 1946.
Location: National Archives of Canada, O1V1CV 8110 030-2.

S94 Mackenzie King shown as he greets Viscount and Lady Alexander as they arrive in Ottawa, April 12, 1946.
Location: National Archives of Canada, O1V1CV 8110 030-2.

S95 Mackenzie King at the Victory Parade, London, England, June 9, 1946.
Location: United States National Archives, Motion Picture Collection, RG 111, ADC 6056-2.

S96 Mackenzie King arriving in Paris [1946]. [Fox News].
Location: National Archives of Canada, NFA 76-5-189.

S97 Mackenzie King on his arrival at Nuremberg, Germany, August 21, 1946.
Location: United States National Archives, Motion Picture Collection, RG 111, ADC 6176-1.

S98 Mackenzie King shown on visit to Dieppe military cemetery, where he inspects honour guard, unveils plaque, and lays wreath, October 1946. [Fox Movietone News].
Location: National Archives of Canada, NFA 8997.

S99 Mackenzie King at the United Nations General Assembly meeting at Flushing, New York, 1946. [Paramount News, vol. 6, no. 18].
Location: United States National Archives, Motion Picture Collection, 200 PN 6.18.

S100 Mackenzie King is shown in a winter coat and also seated at his desk, Winter 1946.
Location: National Archives of Canada, NFA 7707 148-1.

S101 Mackenzie King receiving Canadian citizenship papers at the Supreme Court Building and making an address on the occasion, January 3, 1947. [Fox Movietone News].
Location: National Archives of Canada, NFA 9041, 9065.

S102 Mackenzie King greeting President Harry S Truman, Mrs Truman, and their daughter Margaret, after their arrival in Ottawa, June 10, 1947. [Paramount News, vol. 6, no. 84].
Location: United States National Archives, Motion Picture Collection, 200 PN 6.84.

S103 Mackenzie King speaks at the opening of the Canadian National Exhibition, Toronto, August 22, 1947. [Associated Screen News].
Location: National Archives of Canadas, NFA 13-0405 and NFA 4108.

S104 Mackenzie King arrives in Paris and is greeted at la Gare du Nord by Georges P. Vanier, Canadian ambassador to France, November 8, 1947. [Fox Movietone News].
Location: National Archives of Canada, NFA 9116.

S105 Mackenzie King addresses Dutch Parliament, November 13, 1947. [Paramount News].
Location: National Archives of Canada, NFA 2114.

S106 Mackenzie King at the wedding of Princess Elizabeth and Prince Philip at Westminster Abbey, November 20, 1947. [Paramount News, vol. 7, no. 27].
Location: United States National Archives, Motion Picture Collection, 200 PN 7.27.

S107 Mackenzie King at the opening of Parliament, Ottawa [December 5, 1947?]. [Paramount News, vol. 8, no. 47].
Location: United States National Archives, Motion Picture Collection, 200 PH 8.65.

S108 Mackenzie King with Mary Pickford in Ottawa, January 12, 1948. [Fox Movietone News].
Location: National Archives of Canada, NFA 9030.

S109 Mackenzie King greets Barbara Ann Scott at Ottawa, March 9, 1948. [Paramount News, vol. 7, no. 58].
Location: United States National Archives, Motion Picture Collection, 200 PN 7.58.

S110 Mackenzie King receiving a degree at William and Mary College, Williamsburg, Virginia, April 2, 1948. [Paramount News, vol. 17, no. 65].

Location: United States National Archives, Motion Picture Collection, 200 PN 7.65.

S111 Mackenzie King addressing the National Liberal Party Convention as he retired from the leadership of the party after twenty-one years; poses with his successor, Louis St Laurent, August 1948. [Paramount News, vol. 7, no. 101] and [National Film Board of Canada, Eye Witness, no. 6, and Coup d'oeil, no. 6].
Location: United States National Archives, Motion Picture Collection, 200 PN 7.101; National Archives of Canada, National Film Board of Canada, 1985-0189.

S112 Mackenzie King poses with his successor as prime minister and leader of the Liberal Party, Louis St Laurent, and the governor general, Lord Alexander, at Government House, following King's resignation, November 15, 1948. [Paramount News, vol. 8, no. 26] and [National Film Board of Canada, Eye Witness, no. 9, and Coup d'oeil, no. 9].
Location: United States National Archives, Motion Picture Collection, 200 PN 8.26; National Archives of Canada, National Film Board of Canada, 1985-0258.

S113 Mackenzie King shown at the opening of Parliament, Ottawa, January 26, 1949.
Location: National Archives of Canada, NFA 7708 706.

S114 Mackenzie King at ceremonies on the occasion of Newfoundland's entry into Confederation, Ottawa, April 1, 1949. [Paramount News, vol. 8, no. 65].
Location: United States National Archives, Motion Picture Collection, 200 PN 8.65.

S115 Funeral of Mackenzie King in Ottawa, July 26, 1950. [Associated Screen News].
Location: National Archives of Canada, O1V1CU 8110 030-1.

Audiovisual Educational Kits

S116 *As friend and foe.*
Videocassette. National Film Board of Canada. [1980].
Direction: Laszlo Barna and Laura Alper.
Production: Mark Zannis and Peter Katadotis.

The early history of the labour movement in Canada is described in this videocassette. It examines Mackenzie King's role in developing solutions to labour conflicts in Canada and the United States.

S117 *The life of Mackenzie King. 1. The formative years, 1874–1930. 2. The final years, 1930–1950.* Toronto: Prentice-Hall Media, 1977. (See Hear Now series). Includes two filmstrips and two audiocassettes. Written by Gary Smith. John Ford, Producer. Murray Westgate, Mavor Moore (King), and Anne Butler, Narrators.

S118 *Mackenzie King and the conscription crisis.* National Film Board of Canada, c. 1991. [Videorecording].
Written and directed by Erna Buffie.

S119 *Canada at War* series (*Le Canada en guerre*).
13 videocassettes. National Film Board of Canada. [1962].
Newsreel footage of Mackenzie King is featured prominently in the following series:

1. Dusk [1936–March 1940].
2. Blitzkrieg [April–November 1940].
3. Year of Siege [September 1940–October 1941].
4. Days of Infamy [December 1941–June 1942].
5. Ebbtide [July–September 1942].
6. Turn of the Tide [October 1942–July 1943].
7. Road to Ortona [July 1943–January 1944].
8. Directions [December 1943–June 1944].
9. The Norman Summer [June–September 1944].
10. Cinderella on the Left [June–December 1944].
11. Crisis on the Hill [September 1944–March 1945].
12. V was for Victory [April–August 1945].
13. The Clouded Dawn [August 1945–1946].

The series is also available in French:

1. L'Itinéraire de la ligne Siegfried.
2. Blitzkrieg.
3. Tenir.
4. Dieppe ou 'la Générale.'
5. Profil du combattant.
6. La Maîtrise des airs et des mers.

7. La Calvaire d'Ortona.
8. Visiter l'Italie.
9. Un matin calme.
10. Le Rivage de l'enfer.
11. L'Aube a éclatаté.
12. D plus 333.
13. Le Malaise de la paix.

Produced by Stanley Clish, Peter Jones, and Donald Brittain.

SECTION T

Sound Recordings Relating to Mackenzie King

Several recordings of interviews relating to Mackenzie King or 'talking-book' editions of books about King are available in Canadian archives and libraries. These recordings are listed alphabetically by the name of the author or interviewee.

T1 BROCKINGTON, LEONARD WALTER. Broadcast on the Canadian Broadcasting Corporation on the terms of the will of Mackenzie King, August 8, 1950.
Location: National Archives of Canada, Audio-Visual Holdings.

T2 CANADIAN BROADCASTING CORPORATION. Funeral service of Mackenzie King, St Andrew's Prebysterian Church, Ottawa, July 26, 1950.
Location: National Archives of Canada, Audio-Visual Holdings.

T3 COLDWELL, MAJOR JAMES WILLIAM. [Tribute to Mackenzie King, July 1950].
Location: National Archives of Canada, T1980-138/1.

T4 DREW, GEORGE ALEXANDER. [Tribute to Mackenzie King, July 1950].
Location: National Archives of Canada, 500723-2 D.

T5 DRYDEN, JEAN. Interviews relating to the Mackenzie King Papers in the National Archives of Canada. Includes interviews with Frederick W. Gibson and Jacqueline Neatby.
Location: National Archives of Canada, Audio-Visual Holdings.

T6 ESBERERY, JOY ELAINE. *Knight of the Holy Spirit: A study of William Lyon Mackenzie King.* Nine sound cassette tapes.
Location: University of British Columbia Library, Special Collections Department.

T7 GIBSON, FREDERICK WELLINGTON. [Interview with Douglas Leiterman for a two-part television program on Mackenzie King ['Close-up'] entitled 'The King Nobody Knew']. [1959].
Location: National Archives of Canada, T1974-50/7.

T8 HUTCHISON, BRUCE. *The incredible Canadian: A candid portrait of Mackenzie King, his works, his times and his nation.* Fifteen sound cassette tapes.
Location: University of British Columbia Library, Special Collections Department.

T9 LAMB, WILLIAM KAYE. 'Mackenzie King and history: Use and abuse of his diaries.' Fifteen sound cassette tapes.
Location: University of British Columbia, Special Collections Department.

T10 LOW, SOLON. [Tribute to Mackenzie King, July 1950].
Location: National Archives of Canada, T1980–138/1.

T11 STACEY, CHARLES PERRY. *A very double life: The private world of Mackenzie King.* [Toronto: Canadian National Institute for the Blind, 1976?]. 3 tape reels.

SECTION U

The Mackenzie King Photograph Collection in the National Archives of Canada

The Mackenzie King Photograph Collection at the National Archives of Canada contains approximately 25,000 photographs. This collection documents the life and career of Mackenzie King from his days as a university student to his death in 1950. The collection contains extensive coverage of his work as Deputy Minister of Labour (1900–1908), Minister of Labour (1909–1911), consultant for the Rockefeller Foundation (1914–1917), and Prime Minister of Canada (1921–1926, 1926–1930, and 1935–1948).

In addition, there is a substantial collection of photographs of John and Isabel King and other members of the King family. There is also a large collection of photographs of Mackenzie King's friends.

There is no complete index to the collection.

As copies of photographs from the collection are ordered, prints of the photographs are added to the card index.

SECTION V

Books Dedicated to Mackenzie King

During his lifetime several books were dedicated to Mackenzie King. In this section the list of these books is arranged chronologically.

V1 CAMPBELL, WILFRED. *Poetical tragedies.* Toronto: William Briggs, 1908. 309 p.

Dedicated
TO
MY FRIENDS
W. L. MACKENZIE KING
AND
F. A. ACLAND

William Wilfred Campbell (1861–1918) was a well-known Canadian poet. King and Campbell were intimate friends for many years. Campbell visited King at Kingsmere, and it is said that one of his best-known poems was written there, on the veranda of King's cottage. After Campbell's death King and some friends paid for a monument over his grave in Beechwood Cemetery, Ottawa. They also arranged to have a medallion by Robert Tait McKenzie placed on the monument.

V2 KING, JOHN. *McCaul, Croft, Forneri: Personalities of early university days.* Toronto: Macmillan, 1914. 256 p.

TO
My Sons
IN TOKEN OF
OUR COMMON ALMA MATER

John King (1843–1916) was the father of Mackenzie King. He was educated at the University of Toronto (Bachelor of Arts, 1864, and Master of Arts, 1865). After being called to the bar of Ontario in 1869, he practised law in Berlin (now Kitchener) until 1893. In that year he was appointed as a lecturer at Osgoode Hall, a position he held until 1914. In Toronto he practised law in the firm of King and Sinclair. In 1872 he married Isabel Grace Mackenzie, daughter of William Lyon Mackenzie. In addition to the above book, John King was the author of *The Other Side of the Story* (Toronto, 1886), *A Decade in the History of Newspaper Libel* (Woodstock, 1892), and *The Law of Defamation* (Toronto, 1907).

V3 KING, DOUGALL MACDOUGALL. *The battle with tuberculosis and how to win it; a book for the patient and his friends.* Philadelphia and London: J.B. Lippincott Company, 1917. 258 p.

GRATEFULLY AND AFFECTIONATELY DEDICATED
TO MY WIFE
AND
TO MY BROTHER

Dougall Macdougall King (1878–1922) was the brother of Mackenzie King. Following his graduation from the University of Toronto with a Bachelor of Medicine degree in 1902, he practised medicine in Ottawa until 1913. After that date he lived in Colorado, where he had moved because of ill-health. In addition to *The Battle with Tuberculosis and How to Win It* he was also author of *Nerves and Personal Power* (Toronto, 1922).

V4 LANCTOT, GUSTAVE. *Francois Xavier Garneau.* Toronto: Ryerson Press, [1926?]. 197 p. (Makers of Canadian literature series).

AU TRÈS HONORABLE
WILLIAM LYON MACKENZIE KING
PREMIER MINISTRE DU CANADA

Gustave Lanctot (1883–1975) was Dominion Archivist from 1937 to 1948. King and Lanctot were friends for many years. During Lanctot's term as archivist, King transferred the first of his massive collection of private papers to the Public Archives of Canada.

V5 WILLSON, BECKLES. *From Quebec to Picadilly and other places, some Anglo-Canadian memories.* London: Jonathan Cape, 1929. 366 p.

TO
MY DISTINGUISHED FRIEND
AND FELLOW-COUNTRYMAN
THE RIGHT HONOURABLE
WILLIAM LYON MACKENZIE KING
WHOSE YOUTHFUL IDEAS
HAVE NOT BEEN DEGRADED NOR
HIS HUMAN SYMPATHIES
SEALED BY SUCCESS

Beckles Willson (1869–1942) was a well-known journalist and author. Born at Montreal, Willson worked for several American newspapers before joining the staff of the London *Daily Mail.* He was the author of many books, including *The Life of Lord Strathcona and Mount Royal* (1915) and *The Romance of Canada* (1907).

It is uncertain when King and Willson first met. However, the first letter in the King–Willson correspondence is dated 1923.

The dedication by Willson caused King a great deal of worry. In February 1930 he described the book by Willson with 'its dedication to me & which more or less insults the memory of Sir Wilfrid & others ... This thing is certain to be used widely in Quebec & elsewhere as a part of an appeal to prejudice which is the essence of Toryism. It was part of infernal impertinence on Wilson [*sic*] part to dedicate the book to me, especially without asking my permission. I had no knowledge of its existence or that it was even in contemplation until I received a copy.' He added: 'It is things like this which make public life so hard & which keep many of the best men out of it.'[138]

On March 13, 1930, the subject of the book was raised in the House of Commons. In his reply to a question by George Parent, the Conservative member for Quebec West, King made it clear that he had no knowledge that Willson proposed to dedicate the book to

138 King Diary, February 16, 1930.

him. King added: 'Unfortunately he has, but I wish he had dedicated it to someone else.'[139]

A few months later an anonymous pamphlet entitled *Beckles Willson and Mackenzie King: The Modern Damon and Pythias* was published in 1930.

V6 BUCHAN, JOHN. *Augustus.* London: Hodder and Stoughton Ltd., 1937. 356 p.

TO MY FRIEND
WILLIAM LYON MACKENZIE KING
FOUR TIMES PRIME MINISTER OF CANADA

John Buchan (1873–1940) was Governor General of Canada from 1935 to 1940. Buchan and King, who first met in England in 1919, were close friends from that date. Buchan visited Mackenzie King at his Kingsmere estate frequently during his governor generalship. Buchan is best known for his many novels, which include *Thirty-Nine Steps, The House of the Four Winds,* and *Greenmantle.*

V7 CLEMENS, CRYRIL CONISTON. *Mark Twain and Franklin D. Roosevelt.* Webster Groves, Missouri: International Mark Twain Society, 1949. 20 p.

Dedicated to
RT. HON. W. L. MACKENZIE KING
For twenty-one years Prime Minister of Canada
Devoted Friend of Franklin D. Roosevelt
and
Lifelong Admirer of Mark Twain

Cyril Coniston Clemens was the president of the International Mark Twain Society for many years. It is unclear when King and Clemens first became acquainted. However, they carried on an extensive correspondence from 1937 until King's death in 1950.

139 House of Commons, *Debates,* March 13, 1930, p. 549.

SECTION W

Poems Relating to Mackenzie King

Throughout the years a number of poems about Mackenzie King have been published. Entries in this section are arranged alphabetically by author.

W1 FORAN, MICHAEL. 'Mackenzie King.' *Toronto Daily Star,* July 26, 1950, p. 6.

W2 INKSTER, TOM. 'The ruins at Kingsmere.' *Alive Magazine,* no. 40, 1974, p. 8.

W3 LEE, DENNIS. 'William Lyon Mackenzie King.' *Alligator Pie* (Toronto: Macmillan of Canada, 1974), p. 28.

W4 MAITLAND, G.H. 'Great, wise and good. In memoriam W.L.M. King.' *Toronto Daily Star,* July 24, 1950, p. 6.

W5 MATHEWS, ROBIN. 'When you see him on the frontispiece.' *This Magazine,* 9 (1), March–April 1975, p. 23.

W6 NAUSE, JOHN. 'Meditations on the Moorside ruins' in Frank M. Tierney, ed., *Poets of the capital* (Ottawa: Borealis Press, 1973), pp. 113–115.

W7 SCOTT, FRANCIS REGINALD. 'W.L.M.K.' *The eye of the needle: Satires, sorties and sundries* (Montreal: Contact Press, 1957), pp. 21–22.
Also printed in George Parker, ed., *The evolution of Canadian literature in English, 1914–1945* (Toronto: Holt, Rinehart and Winston, 1973), pp. 162–163.

Also published in Keith Wilson and Elva Motheral, eds., *The poets' record: Verses on Canadian history* (Winnipeg: Peguis Publishers, 1975), pp. 92–93.

W8 SOUSTER, RAYMOND. 'Willie the Lion' in Keith Wilson and Elva Motheral, eds., *The poets' record: Verses on Canadian history* (Winnipeg: Peguis Publishers, 1975), p. 90.

W9 THERSITES. 'Father William.' *Canadian Forum*, 27, December 1947, p. 199.

SECTION X

Plays Relating to Mackenzie King

In recent years at least three plays about Mackenzie King have been written. All of them have been performed in Toronto. They are arranged here alphabetically by author.

X1 GOURLAY, ELIZABETH. *Isabel: The continuous dream of the former Prime Minister: A play in three acts.* Toronto: Playwrights Co-op, 1979. 50 p.

X2 HOLLINGSWORTH, MICHAEL. *The life and times of Mackenzie King.* [Toronto, 1993?]. 110 p.

X3 STRATTON, ALLAN. *Rexy: A play.* Toronto: Playwrights Canada, 1981. 58 p.

Reprinted in Allan Stratton, *2 plays. A Flush of Tories & Rexy* (Montreal: Nuage Editions, 1991), pp. 94–171.

SECTION Y

Radio and Television Programs Relating to Mackenzie King

Since 1948 a number of radio and television programs about Mackenzie King have been broadcast. In this section the programs are arranged chronologically. Details about the programs, including the persons being interviewed, are provided. Locations of recordings or videotapes are also listed.

Radio Programs

Y1 April 23, 1948. 'Salute to Prime Minister Mackenzie King'
Canadian Broadcasting Corporation.
Includes excerpts from radio speeches by Mackenzie King – September 1, 1940, May 8, 1945, and August 1946.
Broadcast by the International Service of the Canadian Broadcasting Corporation in the 'Canadian Chronicle' series.
Location of recording: National Archives of Canada.

Y2 July 24, 1950. [Tribute to Mackenzie King]
British Broadcasting Corporation.
The program includes tributes by King George VI, Prime Minister Daniel F. Malan of South Africa, Prime Minister Liaquit Ali Khan of Pakistan, Prime Minister Sidney Holland of New Zealand, Prime Minister Jawaharlal Nehru of India, Lewis W. Douglas, the U.S. Ambassador to Great Britain, and Prime Minister Clement R. Attlee of Great Britain. Several journalists give accounts of King's life and career.
Location of recording: National Archives of Canada, 820409-9(7).

Y3 December 6, 1957. 'Assignment'
Canadian Broadcasting Corporation.
Discusses Mackenzie King during the Second World War. Dennis Sweeting describes the incident at a sports day in Borden, England, when King was booed by enlisted men.
Location of recording: National Archives of Canada, 8206d22-9(1).

Y4 January 19, 1961. 'FM News'
Contains the first of a three-part interview of J.W. Pickersgill by Tom Earle. During the interview they discuss the book *The Mackenzie King record*, edited by Pickersgill.
Location of recording: CBC Radio Archives.

Y5 January 20, 1961. 'FM News'
Contains the second of a three-part interview of J.W. Pickersgill by Tom Earle. They continue to discuss Pickersgill's book *The Mackenzie King record* and the career of Mackenzie King.
Location of recording: CBC Radio Archives.

Y6 January 2, 1975. 'As It Happens'
Canadian Broadcasting Corporation.
Robert McKeown discusses the recently opened section of the Mackenzie King diaries.
Location of recording: CBC Radio Archives.

Y7 October 28, 1976. 'Morningside'
Canadian Broadcasting Corporation.
Bernard Ostry, co-author of *The age of Mackenzie King*, discusses the book. Bernard Trotter and Davidson Dunton comment on the CBC's cancellation of a program about the book.
Location of recording: CBC Radio Archives.

Y8 January 9, 1977. 'Sunday Magazine'
Canadian Broadcasting Corporation.
Bernard Ostry, Blair Neatby, Bruce Hutchison, J.W. Pickersgill, and C.P. Stacey discuss King as a man and a politician. Also they talk about recently opened King diaries.
Location of recording: CBC Radio Archives.

Y9 March 3, 1977. 'Morningside'
Canadian Broadcasting Corporation.

Includes a report by Elizabeth Gray on the attempt by 'Sunday Morning' to contact the spirit of Mackenzie King in a seance at Laurier House. The seance was attended by a number of journalists from CBC programs and Ottawa newspapers.
Location of recording: CBC Radio Archives.

Y10 March 6, 1977. 'Sunday Morning'
Canadian Broadcasting Corporation.
Includes a report on a seance held at Laurier House in which an attempt to contact the spirit of Mackenzie King was made.
Location of recording: CBC Radio Archives.

Y11 January 7, 1979. 'Sunday Morning'
Canadian Broadcasting Corporation.
The program includes a discussion of the 1948 Mackenzie King diaries, which had just been opened at the Public Archives of Canada. C.P. Stacey comments on the diaries. Chris Wiggins reads excerpts from them.
Location of recording: CBC Radio Archives.

Y12 January 7, 1979. 'Sunday Magazine'
Canadian Broadcasting Corporation.
The program includes an interview with Blair Neatby by Bob Oxley about the 1948 King diaries, which had just been released to the public.
Location of recording: CBC Radio Archives.

Television Programs

Y13 CLOSE-UP. 'The King Nobody Knew'
Canadian Broadcasting Corporation.
Part 1: March 10, 1960
The program opens with on-the-street interviews to determine how much the people remember about Mackenzie King. Much of the remainder of the program consists of a series of interviews between Douglas Leiterman and a number of King's old colleagues, staff, and friends – including Charles G. Power, Miss L.F. Zavitske, J.W. Pickersgill, Julia Grant, Mrs H.O. McCurry, Lester B. Pearson, Frederick W. Gibson, M.G. Coldwell, W.J. Turnbull, F.A. McGregor, J.E. Handy, John A. Stevenson, Bruce Hutchison, General H.D.G. Crerar, and James Sinclair.

Part 2: March 17, 1960

A substantial portion of the second program consists of a discussion of King's interest in spiritualism and his personal life. Douglas Leiterman interviews two of the mediums in Great Britain who helped King to communicate with members of his family and friends – Geraldine Cummins and Helen Hughes. The two spiritualists describe some of the seances and the use of automatic writing. Others interviewed about his personal life and career are Frederick W. Gibson, Lester B. Pearson, A.R.M. Lower, John Diefenbaker, C.D. Howe, Eugene Forsey, Bruce Hutchison, M.G. Coldwell, W.J. Turnbull, J. Edouard Handy, and F.A. McGregor.

Produced and edited by Ross McLean and Patrick Watson. J. Frank Willis is the announcer.

Location of print: National Archives of Canada, Audio-Visual Holdings.

Y14 THE DAYS BEFORE YESTERDAY: STRUGGLE FOR NATIONHOOD.

(a) 'King or chaos (1935–1939).' November 25, 1973.

Brian Nolan, Director.

Documentary on the history of Canada during the Great Depression, during the tenures of R.B. Bennett and Mackenzie King. Discusses the effect of the Depression on Canadian society.

The days before yesterday: Struggle for nationhood series, Part 4.

(b) 'For King and country.' December 2, 1973.

Munroe Scott, Director.

Documentary on Canada during the Second World War and the effect of the war on the economy. Discusses the Conscription Crisis and its effect on Canadian politics.

The days before yesterday: Struggle for nationhood series, Part 5.

(c) 'King of Canada (1945–1948).' December 9, 1973.

Munroe Scott, Director.

Discusses postwar Canada with an analysis of postwar reconstruction and expansion. In this portrait of King's last years as prime minister, there is also a detailed examination of his personal life.

The days before yesterday: Struggle for nationhood series, Part 6.

Y15 TAKE 30. March 14, 1976. 'A True and Faithful Account'

Canadian Broadcasting Corporation.

C.P. Stacey discusses Mackenzie King and his recently published book *A very double life: The private world of Mackenzie King.* The program includes discussions of King's mother, Joan Patteson, and his interest in spiritualism. It includes newsreel footage of events in King's life. Film footage of Laurier House and King's estate at Kingsmere is included. Excerpts from the King diary were also read.

Location of videotape: National Archives of Canada, NFA, VI7905-007.

Y16 THE KING CHRONICLE.

Part 1: 'Mackenzie King and the Unseen Hand'

March 27, 1988. Canadian Broadcasting Corporation.

This program covers King's life from his days as a student at the University of Toronto to the beginning of the King–Byng Crisis in 1926. Major episodes in the story include his romance with Matilda Grossert, the 1919 Liberal convention, his friendship with Joan and Godfroy Patteson, the Imperial Conference of 1923, the Customs Scandal of 1926, and his relations with Lord and Lady Byng.

Part 2: 'Mackenzie King and the Great Beyond'

March 28, 1988. Canadian Broadcasting Corporation.

This program covers the period 1926 to 1941, and deals with the story of the King–Byng affair, the election of 1930, the outbreak of the Second World War, the invasion of Hong Kong, King's spiritualist activities, and the visit of Winston Churchill to Canada in 1941.

Part 3: 'Mackenzie King and the Zombie Army'

March 29, 1988. Canadian Broadcasting Corporation.

The last eight years of King's life are covered in the third episode of this series. It describes the national plebiscite in 1942, the Conscription Crisis of 1944, King's last years in office, his retirement, and his death in 1950.

Written and directed by Donald Brittain. Produced by Adam Symansky. Co-produced by the Canadian Broadcasting Corporation and the National Film Board. Mackenzie King is played by Sean McCann.

Location of prints: National Film Board of Canada.

SECTION Z

Unpublished Material Relating to Mackenzie King

A number of unpublished items about Mackenzie King have been located. In this section the material is arranged alphabetically by the author's name. The location of a copy of each item is also provided.

Z1 BURKHOLDER, EDGAR LEROY, JR. 'A bibliography about William Lyon Mackenzie King.' [Montreal: McGill University Library School, 1954]. 9 l.
Location: McGill University Library School.

Z2 CRAIG, SHEILA ELIZABETH DOUGLAS. 'Mackenzie King as a war minister: A bibliography of monographs and periodical articles, dealing with the activities of William Lyon Mackenzie King during World War II.' [Toronto: University of Toronto Library School, 1965]. iv, 16 l.
Location: University of Toronto Library School.

Z3 DE CARAFFE, MARC, and JANET WRIGHT. 'Le domaine Mackenzie-King, Kingsmere, Québec.' [Ottawa: National Capital Commission, 1984]. 20 p. [Agenda paper].
Location: National Capital Commission Library.

Z4 DIEFENBAKER, JOHN GEORGE. 'Notes for a speech by the Right Honourable John G. Diefenbaker, P.C., Q.C., Prime Minister of Canada, at the unveiling of National Historic Plaque at Laurier House, July 19, 1960.' 5 p.
Location: John George Diefenbaker Centre, Saskatoon.

Z5 FERGUSON, GEORGE VICTOR. [Radio talk on Mackenzie King on the Canadian Broadcasting Corporation, November 20, 1948]. 6 p.
Location: NAC, WLMK Papers, MG 26, J 3 Series, vol. 43, Folder 3.

Z6 FERGUSON, MAUD. 'Laurier House: Talk by Maud Ferguson, August 1, 1951, 10.35–10.45 am EDT.' 6 p.
Location: NAC, WLMK Papers, MG 26, J 17 Series, vol. 3, Folder 6.

Z7 – 'Laurier House: Talk by Maud Ferguson, August 8, 1951, 10.35–10.45 am EDT.' 6 p.
Location: NAC, WLMK Papers, MG 26, J 17 Series, vol. 3, Folder 6.

Z8 GIBSON, FREDERICK WELLINGTON. 'Queen's University. School of Graduate Studies. History 837: Canada in the era of Mackenzie King. 1973–74 Academic Session: Professor F.W. Gibson.' [1973]. 30 p.
Location: QUA, Frederick Wellington Gibson Papers.

Z9 GOUIN, LEON MERCIER. 'Mackenzie King – Homme d'état et socioloque.' [1944]. 42 p.
Location: NAC, WLMK Papers, J 1 Series, vol. 305, pp. 258039–258080.

Z10 GRANT, MADELINE. 'Preliminary edition. William Lyon Mackenzie King: A bibliography. Compiled by Madeline Grant, with the assistance of Professor John R. English.' [University of Waterloo, 1974]. 30 p.
Location: Library of Parliament.

Z11 LOVE, J.D. 'Colorado and Mackenzie King.' [1952/53]. [Used in a seminar on Mackenzie King during the winter of 1952/53]. 11 p.
Location: NAC, MG 30, D240, Frank Hawkins Underhill Papers, Box 35, Folder 194c.

Z12 LOWER, ARTHUR REGINALD MARSDEN. 'Mackenzie King and recent Canadian politics.' [Notes for an address at St Lawrence University, Canton, New York, August 9, 1950]. 3 p.
Location: QUA, Arthur Reginald Marsden Lower Papers, Box 22, Folder 623.1.

Z13 MORGAN, JUDITH. 'A bibliography of printed materials concerning Mackenzie King's external policy, 1939–1945.' [Toronto: University of Toronto Library School, 1967]. iv, 12 p.
Location: University of Toronto Library School.

Z14 POWER, CHARLES GAVAN. 'Mackenzie King's life – comments.' [Interview between Power and A.F.C. Fraser, June 30, 1966]. 38 p.
Location: QUA, Charles Gavan Power Papers, Box 87.

Z15 SMYTHE, ROBERT. 'King of Kingsmere: A selection of diary entries, correspondence and photographs from the W.L.M. King papers and collections.' [Ottawa: National Capital Commission, 1981]. 222 p.
Location: National Capital Commission Library.

Z16 STEVENSON, JOHN ALEXANDER. [Unpublished biography of William Lyon Mackenzie King]. 99 p.
Location: QUA, John Alexander Stevenson Papers, Box 1.

Z17 UNDERHILL, FRANK HAWKINS. Talk in Symposium on Robert MacGregor Dawson's *William Lyon Mackenzie King: A political biography*, Canadian Historical Association, June 6, 1959. 9 p.
Location: NAC, MG 30, D204, Frank Hawkins Underhill Papers, Box 35, Folder 194c.

APPENDICES

SECTION AA

Appendix 1: Article by Mackenzie King about His Work as a Reporter for *The Globe*

During 1895 and 1896 Mackenzie King worked as reporter for *The Globe.*[140] In 1934[141] he wrote an article for *The Globe and Mail* in which he described his work as a reporter:

> My period of association with The Globe was so brief and inconspicuous that I doubt if it merits any mention in a history of that paper. I became associated with The Globe at the time the evening edition was established preparatory to the elections of 1896. The men taken on at that time included H.A. Livingston, Lawrence Lyon, Wilson Blue, M.O. Hammond and myself. We were under the special direction of T.D.S. Moore. I had miscellaneous assignments, but, among other things, for a time did the round of the Police Court, fire halls, hospitals, etc. I recall reporting special noon day services at the cathedral, many lectures and a prize fight, for which I was given some extra remuneration by Mr Acland for an outside news service. I also wrote a number of articles on special subjects, among the number the first article, I think, which appeared on the X-ray experiments being made at the School of Science in Toronto. I also wrote up feature articles, such as accounts of the Salvation Army social work, foreign colonies, etc.
>
> *When Hyams Skipped*
> I think I was on The Globe at the time of the famous Hyams twins trial and was

---

140 King also wrote a few articles for *The Globe* in 1894 during his third year as a student at the University of Toronto.

141 *The Globe and Mail*, March 28, 1934, p. 15.

the one who received from E.F.B. Johnston, their lawyer, the word of their having skipped bail. I did a great deal of work for the morning edition as well as the evening edition.

My salary, I think, was $5 a week at the outset, and I believe it was increased to $8 before I left. What I appreciated was Willison's kindness in allowing me to draw my two weeks' vacation salary after I had left The Globe to go to Chicago to pursue postgraduate studies there.

I graduated in Arts from the University of Toronto in 1895, and while engaged in journalism completed a university course in law and received the degree of LL.B. I was associated with the Mail for a short time and later with the News before going to The Globe. It was from the News that I went to The Globe.

Launched Labor Department

Having received a fellowship in political economy in the University of Chicago in 1897, I stayed with The Globe until the courses commenced at the university and then went on to pursue my studies there. From Chicago I went to Harvard and from Harvard abroad. I then came back to Ottawa to edit the Labor Gazette and to start the Department of Labor. While with the Mail and Empire I wrote a series of articles on the housing of the working people, the sweating system, foreign colonies in the cities, all of which were in the nature of studies of social and industrial problems. I did something of the same kind of work on The Globe, but did not to the same extent. I left The Globe for Chicago in September, 1896.

Early Meeting with Laurier

In view of the subsequent developments it might be of interest to readers of The Globe to know that I had to do with the reporting of the meeting held by Sir Wilfrid Laurier in North York in 1896, when Sir William Mulock was a candidate. I stayed the night at Sir William's home, and Sir Wilfrid was also a guest.

Little did I then believe that I would be one of Sir William's successors as member in North York constituency, much less did I dream of ever being Sir Wilfrid's successor in the leadership of the Liberal Party and Premiership of the Dominion. I recall, on the night of the Liberal victory, announcing the returns from the office of The Globe to the crowds beneath. I believe I was chosen for that job as possessing at that time, one of the strongest voices.

Election Festivities

I recall a supper of sandwiches which some of us had in company with the men who worked the presses and others of The Globe staff at the time of that memorable victory.

It is interesting to recall that among those who were on the staff of The Globe at the time were our friends, J.E. Atkinson and F.A. Acland. Acland became Secretary of the Department of Labor and later Deputy Minister. He was my choice for these positions; also R.H. Coats came from The Globe staff to be H.A. Harper's successor as Assistant Editor of the Labor Gazette, after Harper's death. Atkinson has always been a very good friend and supporter both of the party and myself. John Lewis was one of the editors in my day.

Among other pleasures I have derived in public life was that of recommending his appointment to the Senate of Canada, in recognition of his service to Liberalism, which has been very great indeed. Sir John Willison, while differing politically after his association with the News was always a personal friend of my father and myself. At the time of my father's death he was one of the pall-bearers, as was also Atkinson.

SECTION BB

Appendix 2: Mackenzie King's Proposed Books

During his lifetime King considered writing books on a number of subjects. However, the pressure of his work as a civil servant and political leader prevented him from undertaking most of the books he had considered. The following is a description of some of the works that he proposed during his lifetime.

BB1 'In the sight of Almighty God'

As King returned to Boston on the train for the second term at Harvard, he thought of 'a good title for a book which I would like to write – "In the sight of Almighty God" – a revelation of things as they are.' He added: 'I said to myself I would write it.'[142]

BB2 An economic history of Canada

On January 21, 1898, he wrote: 'I was thinking again today of an economic history of Canada.'[143]

BB3 A sketch of Arnold Toynbee's life

On May 8, 1898, King told Harper of his 'intention to write a little sketch of Toynbee's life.' He told Harper that he would dedicate the

142 King Diary, January 4, 1898.
143 King Diary, January 21, 1898.

book to him.[144] A few weeks later he noted in his diary that 'Toynbee has been a great influence in my life.'[145] There is no evidence that King did any work on this projected book.

BB4 A novel based on his own life

In the middle of his love affair with Matilda Grossert, King considered a novel based on his own life. Of the proposed book he wrote: 'I thought this afternoon of writing it all up as a romance, ended by making it an incident in present war, make myself go to Cuba, [A] nurse there etc, but this I will consider. I may hope for a better ending.'[146]

BB5 Book on sweating and the clothing trade

After having written several newspaper articles on 'sweating,' King, while at Harvard University, hoped to write a book on the subject. Writing to his father and mother on October 9, 1898, he said: 'I shall go on with my book on Sweating & the Clothing Industry which I hope to advance considerably this year. I will try a race with father & his work on libel.'[147]

BB6 A constitutional history of Canada

In the 1890s Mackenzie King considered writing a constitutional history of Canada. On June 14, 1896, he wrote: 'I have long felt a great desire to write a Constitutional History of this country.'[148] He was so anxious to do this work that he considered applying to the University of Toronto for a fellowship instead of accepting the fellowship offered to him by the University of Chicago. However, he withdrew his application in favour of the one from the University of Chicago.

In June 1897 John King proposed that he and Mackenzie King write a constitutional history of Canada together. 'There is nothing,' Mackenzie King wrote, 'I wd. like to do more.'[149]

A few months later he wrote:

144 King Diary, May 8, 1898.

145 King Diary, June 13, 1898.

146 King Diary, May 17, 1898.

147 NAC, WLMK Papers, MG 26, J 7 Series, vol. 3, p. 426, William Lyon Mackenzie King to his father and mother, October 9, 1898.

148 King Diary, June 14, 1896.

149 King Diary, June 2, 1897.

I would like to write an economic, a constitutional and political history of Canada. I see a fine field to work in, and the soil has scarcely a furrow in it. A financial history might be also good, but what are the chances. I question however if a history of labor in America is not the better than all, and it may be to this that I will turn my attention more particularly as soon as I get my Ph.D. degree.[150]

BB7 Biography of William Lyon Mackenzie

Since his days as a university student King was deeply influenced by the life and work of his maternal grandfather, William Lyon Mackenzie. In 1895 while he was reading Lindsey's biography of Mackenzie, King wrote: 'Last night I read more of Mackenzie's life & felt more deeply inspired I could not get to sleep for an hour or two after going to bed.'[151] A few days later he wrote:

> Reading the life of dear grandfather I have become a greater admirer of his than ever prouder of my own mother and the race from which I am sprung. Many of his principles I pray I have inherited. I feel I understand perfectly the feeling that prompted his actions I can feel his inner life in myself. I have greater desire to carry on the work he endeavored to perform, to better the condition of the poor, denounce corruption, the tyranny of abused power and uphold right and honorable principles.[152]

A few days later he noted that he had inherited the name of his grandfather and remarked: 'Surely I have some great work to accomplish before I die.'[153]

There is evidence that King may have decided to write a biography of Mackenzie as early as 1904. At that time he was making an abstract of his life based on the notes taken during the reading of the Lindsey biography.[154]

On January 12, 1906, King discussed with William Wilfred Campbell their writing together a biography of Mackenzie. 'I believe,' he wrote in his diary, 'together we might produce a most valuable vol-

150 NAC, WLMK Papers, MG 26, J 7 Series, vol. 3, p. 548, William Lyon Mackenzie King to his father and mother, November 13, 1898.

151 King Diary, June 19, 1895.

152 King Diary, June 22, 1895.

153 King Diary, July 16, 1895.

154 King Diary, March 2, 1904.

ume, treating the whole subject from a point of view of psychological forces, inner vision, belief etc.'[155]

During the same year William Dawson LeSueur began work on a biography of William Lyon Mackenzie. From the outset King was displeased with LeSueur as the biographer of his grandfather because he believed that LeSueur would not write a sympathetic account.[156] On January 6, 1906, King wrote: 'He is certainly not the man to do justice to grandfather in any volume he may write.'[157]

In May 1908, however, the LeSueur manuscript was rejected by George W. Morang, the publisher. A long legal battled follow when Morang refused to return the manuscript. While LeSueur eventually obtained the manuscript, another trial followed when the heirs of the Mackenzie family sought to prevent LeSueur from publishing the book with another company and from making any use of the notes taken when he did research on the book from the Mackenzie Papers in the hands of the Lindsey family.[158]

Over the years King devoted a great deal of attention to the biography of Mackenzie. In July 1934 he mentioned that he hoped to be able to write the life of Mackenzie,[159] and in June 1935 he wrote that he still considered the possibility. At that time he told Norah Storey of the Public Archives that he 'had a strong personal desire to attempt the life of Mackenzie myself, and some day might, if she were agreeable, wish to have her as a collaborator in the work.'[160]

By 1944 King was in touch with an English writer, Catherine Macdonald Maclean. At that time he mentioned the possibility, some day, of having her write his grandfather's life.[161] Maclean, who was

155 King Diary, January 12, 1906.

156 King Diary, January 3, 1906.

157 King Diary, January 6, 1906.

158 These events have been described by several writers in detail. See Alexander Brian McKillop, ed., *A critical spirit: The thought of William Dawson LeSueur* (Toronto: McClelland and Stewart, 1977), pp. 273–282; Alexander Brian McKillop, ed., *William Lyon Mackenzie: A reinterpretation, by William Dawson LeSueur* (Toronto: Macmillan of Canada, 1979), pp. viii–xi; Daniel Francis, 'King vs. revisionist: It took five court cases before young Willie was able to suppress a heretical biography about his rebel grandfather,' *Books in Canada*, 8 (3), March 1979, pp. 4–7.

159 King Diary, July 7, 1934.

160 King Diary, June 25, 1935.

161 NAC, WLMK Papers, MG 26, J 17 Series, vol. 1, Folder 22, William Lyon Mackenzie King to Catherine Macdonald Maclean, July 4, 1944.

born in Scotland, was author of biographies of William Hazlitt and of Dorothy and William Wordsworth. King and Maclean had met during the 1930s and had remained in correspondence over the years.

During the winter of 1949 King mentioned to John Gray, president of the Macmillan Company of Canada Limited, that he had Maclean in mind to write the biography.[162] Extensive correspondence took place between King and Gray throughout the remainder of 1949 and into the spring of 1950.

The Mackenzie biography occupied a great deal of King's time during the last few months of his life. By June 1950 the agreement for Maclean to write the book had been drafted. King was to pay Maclean $4,000 a year for two years and travelling expenses from England to write the book.[163]

On July 19 Fred McGregor wrote to Gray regarding the biography. McGregor told Gray that King was interested in the size and general style of the book. For example, he wanted some idea of the general layout of the book and whether it would contain appropriate illustrations.[164]

The King Papers contain a memorandum dated July 20, the day King became unconscious and two days before his death. In it King inquired as to whether Maclean had received a copy of Leonard W. Brockington's address at the opening of the Mackenzie House at 82 Bond Street in Toronto on May 9 and a copy of King's address in Toronto in 1934.[165]

Mackenzie King saw the Mackenzie biography 'as an endeavour to "round out" that part of my life's purposes.'[166] On July 18, 1950, only four days before his death, he discussed the writing of the biography by Catherine Maclean with Fred McGregor, who was to write to Macmillan regarding the work.[167] King had agreed to spend the $4,000 a year for two years to engage Miss Maclean for the work.

---

162 NAC, WLMK Papers, MG 26, J 17 Series, vol. 1, Folder 23, William Lyon Mackenzie King to John Gray, March 15, 1949.

163 Ibid., June 1, 1950.

164 Ibid., Fred A. McGregor to John Gray, July 19, 1950.

165 Ibid., Fred A. McGregor to William Lyon Mackenzie King, July 20, 1950.

166 King Diary, April 21, 1949.

167 King Diary, July 18, 1950.

King's will contained the following clause relating to the Mackenzie biography: 'I authorize my Literary Executors to complete any arrangements which may be necessary with Miss Catherine Macdonald Maclean, of London, England, for the writing of a biography of my grandfather, William Lyon Mackenzie. I direct my Trustees to make whatever payments are approved by my Literary Executors for the writing and publication of this biography.'[168]

The project was never completed. Miss Maclean died on January 9, 1960, before the manuscript was finished.[169]

BB8 Book on the fair wages movement

In the spring of 1901 Mackenzie King started work on the topic of the fair wages movement. He hoped to write first an article, then a thesis on the topic, and later a book. On March 26 he began sorting his clippings on the subject.[170] The following day he described further his plans for the book: 'My plan is to run the series of articles in the [Labour] Gazette first, then to make my report to the Govt., and then to have each published in book form (if a publisher can be found). This will kill 3 birds with one stone. – I forgot – send in my thesis at Harvard for Ph.D. – which makes 4 birds.'[171] By the following day he was dictating work on the movement to the stenographer at the *Labour Gazette* office.[172] A few weeks later King visited Boston and had a talk with Professor F.W. Taussig about the proposed book. Taussig told him that it was likely that either Macmillan or Longmans would publish the book.[173]

In October King discussed the book with Sir William Mulock, the postmaster general who was also in charge of labour matters. Mulock urged King to write a book or two in the labour area.[174]

Work on the book was interrupted by King's visit to western Canada and the death of Harper in December 1901. Early in 1902 he

168 NAC, WLMK Papers, MG 26, J 17 Series, vol. 2, Folder 1, 'Last will and testament of William Lyon Mackenzie King, February 28, 1950.'

169 NAC, WLMK Papers, MG 26, J 17 Series, Box 1, Folder 21, 'Correspondence re: Dr C.M. Maclean contract, 1953–1957.'

170 King Diary, March 26, 1901.

171 King Diary, March 27, 1901.

172 King Diary, March 28, 1901.

173 King Diary, April 5, 1901.

174 King Diary, October 1, 1901.

wrote: 'I must get out a book on Labour Legislation in Canada – this part of poor Bert's incompleted task, a good article on Trade Unionism in Canada, my book on the Fair Wages & Public Contracts Movement, and Bert's writing and letters. This is a sufficient task for a year. I have hardly hopes of completing the two tasks, but will endeavour hard to do so.'[175]

King proceeded with the book on Harper, which was published in 1906 as *The Secret of Heroism.* As late as July 1902 King still hoped to write a thesis on the sweating system and the fair wages movement. While he completed his thesis at Harvard seven years later, it was not on this topic, and the other books were never written.[176]

BB9 Biography of his mother

On December 21, 1937, during a conversation with Lord Tweedsmuir, King mentioned that he would like to write something about his mother. 'I told him,' he notes in his diary, 'then that if I ever did, I would seek to write it from the point of view that what a man is, he owes it not to himself but to his parents who have made sacrifices for him, and all that is in the way of progress is the result of seeming sacrifices along the way of life.'[177] No further references to this project have been located.

BB10 Study of the opium trade

In 1908 King wrote a report on the need for suppression of the opium trade in Canada.[178] By early 1909 King had proposed that he might write a book on the topic. In February George H. Doran of George H. Doran Company, a New York publishing company, was in touch with him encouraging him to undertake the work.[179]

BB11 'A newspaper for the poor'

During his days as a reporter for *The Globe* Mackenzie King consid-

---

175 King Diary, January 15, 1902.

176 King Diary, July 4, 1902.

177 King Diary, December 21, 1937.

178 *Report by W.L. Mackenzie King, C.M.G., Deputy Minister of Labour, on the need for the suppression of the opium trade in Canada.* Ottawa: King's Printer, 1908. 13 p. A French translation of the report was also published.

179 NAC, WLMK Papers, MG 26, J 1 Series, vol. 11, p. 10282, George H. Doran to William Lyon Mackenzie King, February 18, 1909.

ered a 'newspaper for the poor.' 'I would like to see it given a trial,' he wrote, '& may be the one to start it.'[180] A few days later he spent some time drafting an article on this newspaper. 'The idea seems to me,' he wrote, 'a very good & practical one.'[181] On the following day he continued to work on his idea for the newspaper. However, soon he had received his fellowship at the University of Chicago, and his work with *The Globe* ended.

BB12 Biography of Sir Wilfrid Laurier

In 1911 King mentioned the writing of a biography of Sir Wilfrid Laurier. 'My idea,' he told Violet Markham, 'is not to bring out Sir Wilfrid's life just now.' He added: 'The work would be undertaken with the understanding that it would not be made public until after his death.'[182] In this letter to Miss Markham, King described the proposed Laurier biography in some detail. He proposed to analyse the political history of the past twenty-five years. 'The life and times' of Sir Wilfrid Laurier, as he proposed it to be, would be based on Laurier's correspondence and on personal interviews with the former prime minister.[183]

In September 1911 King discussed the idea of the biography with Laurier. He told Laurier that he would be prepared to spend the next year or two on the biography. Laurier told King that 'there was no one whom he would rather have do it.' King's diary provides us with these comments concerning his own feelings about writing the biography: 'I can hardly express the delight I feel in this opportunity ... It is truly the opportunity of a life time, & come what may I must bend to the tasks, as a serious part of my life work ... I will give my whole time to the task.'[184]

A month later King had a long talk with Laurier in his library at Laurier House. King told Laurier that he was prepared to spend the winter on the biography. He suggested that he would begin the writing with the latter part of his career. Laurier suggested the conven-

180 King Diary, June 17, 1896.

181 King Diary, June 19, 1896.

182 NAC, WLMK Papers, MG 26, J 1 Series, vol. 18, pp. 16461–16465, William Lyon Mackenzie King to Violet Markham, December 17, 1911.

183 Ibid.

184 King Diary, September 25, 1911.

tion of 1893 at which he was elected leader as the place to begin the writing. King told Laurier that he 'wanted to make it a work which wd. influence men in all countries, & be a contribution to liberalism.' As the two men discussed the project King asked Laurier to make notes of books or documents that he should read. He proposed spending evenings reading the books that Laurier had read 'to get the thought that had influenced him.' Laurier suggested that Sydney Fisher might be willing to help King with the work. Laurier commented again on King's attributes for the work – the writing of good English and his enthusiasm for the work.[185]

King continued work on the biography during the remainder of 1911 and the beginning of 1912. He read the Willison biography of Laurier.[186] He had had several discussions with Laurier about the work. He turned down an offer from George Atkinson to write special articles for the *Toronto Star.* King began to keep a 'special vol. devoted to Sir W. interviews.'[187]

King used every opportunity for long conversations with Laurier. For example, he had a long talk with him on a train trip to Eganville in February 1912. The two men discussed the greatest achievements of his career, the books that had influenced him, English politicians, a meeting with Louis Riel, and the preparation of his speeches.

During the first week of March 1912 King was working for as much as four to five hours a day on the biography. On March 15, however, he confided to his diary: 'I have made little headway with Sir Wilfrid's life, and feel it in a way that perhaps it is a mistake to work too exclusively on it.'[188] King, however, continued to mention the biography as late as February 1913. At that time he told Laurier that he 'regretted not getting on with his biography.' Laurier told King that he 'better wait till I am dead.' He promised, however, to look up documents for King as soon as the parliamentary session was over.[189]

185 King Diary, October 23, 1911.

186 Sir John Stephen Willison, *Sir Wilfrid Laurier and the Liberal Party* (Toronto: Morang, 1903). 2 v.

187 King Diary, January 10, 1912.

188 King Diary, March 15, 1912.

189 King Diary, February 14, 1913.

In 1919 a publisher heard that King was writing a biography of Laurier and indicated his desire to talk with him about the book.[190] King replied:

> As to the life of Sir Wilfrid Laurier, it is true that I commenced a work of the kind, but I was obliged to abandon it on account of my studies for the Rockefeller Foundation. What may be possible in the near future will depend on how events stage themselves. I am still not without hope of being able to make some contribution to the political history of Canada, through what I know of the policies of the Liberal Party during recent years and the sources of their inspiration.[191]

Three weeks later King was elected leader of the Liberal Party, and he had no further time to devote to the biography of his predecessor.

After Laurier's death in 1919, Oscar Douglas Skelton, professor of political and economic science at Queen's University, wrote a biography of the former prime minister. The two-volume work *The Life and Letters of Sir Wilfrid Laurier* was published in 1921.[192] There is no evidence that Mackenzie King assisted with this work by providing access to his files of research notes.

It is interesting to note that as late as July 1934 King mentioned in his diary that he still hoped to write a biography of Laurier.[193] As the sorting of his papers proceeded during the last few months of his life, King had Frederick Gibson make photostats of some of his correspondence. Of the material photostated he wrote: 'It included several letters between Sir Wilfrid & myself & :a very important memo I had written on my talks with Sir Wilfrid. How it got among the papers I don't know, but it reveals the importance of losing no time on this work.'[194]

BB13 Biography of Andrew Carnegie

At the beginning of 1919 King gave some thought to writing a biography of Andrew Carnegie. The project would have involved the

---

190 NAC, WLMK Papers, MG 26, J 1 Series, vol. 42, p. 36997, Thomas Allen to William Lyon Mackenzie King, June 16, 1919.

191 Ibid., p. 37001, William Lyon Mackenzie King to Thomas Allen, July 15, 1919.

192 Oscar Douglas Skelton, *The life and letters of Sir Wilfrid Laurier* (Toronto: Gundy, 1921). 2 v.

193 King Diary, July 17, 1934.

194 King Diary, December 8, 1949.

revising of Carnegie's reminiscences and the writing of his life. At the same time he was offered the position of director of the Carnegie Foundation of New York. 'Tho' not definitely expressed,' King wrote, 'I know that were I to offer to do this work [that is, the biography], it would be entrusted to me, and that I could have a sum of $100,000 for the doing of it, if desired.'[195]

The matter of the Carnegie biography arose again in May 1919. At that time John A. Poynton, Carnegie's secretary, said that the Corporation would be guided by anyone King was to suggest as a biographer. King stated that he would prefer not to suggest anyone until he discussed it with friends in England during his visit, which was to take place within a few months.[196] King left Ottawa for England on May 12. Immediately upon his return to Ottawa he was elected leader of the Liberal Party.

A biography of Carnegie was eventually written by Burton Jesse Henrick in 1932.[197]

BB14 'Foundation Stones'

In the spring of 1934 King thought about another book he might like to write, to be called 'Foundation Stones.' It would 'include the address on grandfather given the other night [March 6] – which would relate to municipal affairs, the one at the University, (educational) – one to the Women's Liberal Association – political & social – (one perhaps later – re St Andrew's Church – give these & others as a memorial of the 100th anniversary of Toronto, as I did the Message of the Carillon, for the 60th anniversary of Canada.' He added: 'I would like to do this – a reference to Gladstone in a speech re Lord Aberdeen put the title into my mind – the speech was made at the time of presentation of his bust a month or two ago to the city of Aberdeen – the thought has just come to me – the city of my father's father. –'[198]

There is no evidence that King gave any further thought to this book.

---

195 King Diary, January 1–14, 1919.

196 King Diary, May 15, 1919.

197 Burton Jesse Hendrick, *The life of Andrew Carnegie* (Garden City, N.Y.: Doubleday, 1932). 2 v.

198 King Diary, March 18, 1934.

BB15 Memoirs

King summarized the plans for his memoirs with these words:

> What if at all possible, I am most anxious to accomplish is to make the work the story of the development of Canada as a nation in what, undoubtedly, were the most significant years of our country's history, and, in so doing, to afford some insight into the nature and the problem of government and public affairs as gained by personal knowledge and experience. I would seek to illustrate or substantiate what is set forth by events and documents recorded, and to give to the whole an inspirational note which I would hope the personal and biographical material might afford.[199]

King planned to write four volumes of memoirs. By February 1949 he had decided on the following working titles for them:

Volume 1, The prepatory years
Volume 2, Between the wars
Volume 3, World War II
Volume 4, Fulfilment of a policy[200]

The work would have included letters and documents. He hoped to publish about ten additional volumes of state papers.

The former prime minister planned to select a number of major subjects, such as his relations with royalty, his election as leader, the famous constitutional crisis of 1926, and the development of Dominion status. He proposed to dictate from memory, without consulting documents. He would pass this memorandum to the person who was assisting him with the memoirs, who would then add details to the memorandum based on documents in his papers. King would then produce a final draft of each chapter.[201]

As early as 1944 publishers were writing to King to express their interest in publishing his memoirs. The King Papers contain many letters from publishers in Canada, Britain, and the United States indicating an interest in King's autobiography.

---

199 NAC, WLMK Papers, MG 26, J 17 Series, vol. 4, Folder 9, William Lyon Mackenzie King to C.I. Bernard, president of the Rockefeller Foundation, March 14, 1949.

200 NAC, WLMK Papers, MG 26, J 17 Series, vol. 4, Folder 19 [Notes relating to the memoirs].

201 QUA, Grant Dexter Papers [Additions], Box 1, Memorandum by Max Freedman, July 1949.

Two years before his retirement, King began the first step toward the writing of his memoirs. In September 1946 he appointed Frederick W. Gibson of Queen's University to begin sorting his personal papers. Gibson was joined in this work by Jacqueline Côté, a graduate of Queen's University. They worked on the papers as they were transferred to the Public Archives from Laurier House.

In 1949 the Rockefeller Foundation made a grant of $100,000 to King to undertake work on his memoirs. The grant was to be administered by McGill University. In January 1950, only seven months before his death, King hired Fred McGregor, who had first worked with King in 1914, to assist him with his memoirs. In addition, King considered having a journalist help him with the work. Several men including B.K. Sandwell, Max Freedman, and Alexander Inglis discussed the work with King. He did not reach the stage of hiring anyone other than McGregor to assist him.

King, unfortunately, made little progress with the memoirs beyond making some notes to help with the actual writing. Four main reasons account for his failure to progress with what he hoped to be the last major work of his life. First, his health declined rapidly in the months following his retirement. Second, the sheer mass of his personal papers was so large that the sorting would have taken years to complete. Third, King attempted to carry on extensive correspondence with his intimate friends. Finally, he spent a substantial portion of his last few months working on his will.

After King's death, his literary executors decided that an official biography making use of his extensive papers would be written. Professor Robert MacGregor Dawson of the University of Toronto was chosen as the official biographer. By 1958 he had completed the first volume and a small volume on the 1944 Conscription Crisis. In July 1958 Dawson died. Professor H. Blair Neatby of the University of British Columbia was selected to complete the biography covering material to the outbreak of the Second World War. The period from 1939 to King's retirement in 1948 was covered by *The Mackenzie King Record*, an edited version of the diaries by J.W. Pickersgill and Donald F. Forster.

SECTION CC

Appendix 3: The Serialized Articles and Biography by Reginald Hardy

In July 1948 a series of twenty articles by Reginald Hardy, the well-known Canadian newspaperman, was serialized in Canadian newspapers by the Southam Company. Entitled 'Mr Canada,' the series was expanded into a manuscript later to be published by Oxford University Press as *Mackenzie King of Canada: A Biography.*[202] While the series was published in newspapers across Canada, the example for this work was taken from the Ottawa *Evening Citizen.* The titles of the individual articles varied from newspaper to newspaper.

With the exception of the first article which King did not like, he was generally pleased with the series of newspaper articles. For example, of the ninth article on Woodside he wrote: 'I liked it very much. That part is well written.'[203] On the following day when another article dealt with his childhood home, King wrote that it 'was really quite beautifully written.'[204] Two days later he confided to his diary: 'I read another of Hardy's articles – rather nicely written.'[205] He summarized his feelings about the series, on July 26, after reading the last of the series: 'The article itself I thought very kind and nice, as indeed the whole series as a whole has been.'[206] He was relieved, however, when the series was concluded. 'I am indeed grateful,'

202 Henry Reginald Hardy, *Mackenzie King of Canada: A biography* (Toronto and London: Oxford University Press, 1949). xii, 390 p.

203 King Diary, July 13, 1948.

204 King Diary, July 14, 1948.

205 King Diary, July 16, 1948.

206 King Diary, July 26, 1948.

he wrote, 'that they are at an end. What I disliked is not so much the articles but attempting to tell the people too much about one's affairs.'[207]

Hardy then proceeded to expand the articles into a full-length book. On December 22, 1948, Hardy send a copy of the manuscript to King. He asked King to read it and to let him know about any points on which he disagreed and suggested that they might be able to discuss them later.[208] King did not begin to read Hardy's manuscript until January 5. At first he was not impressed. It was, he said, 'made up largely of stories gathered from people in Berlin [Kitchener] who have still "recollections."'[209]

Two days later, as he continued reading the manuscript, King expressed concern about several personal references – his spiritualist activities, the fact that Laurier House had been left to the Liberal Party, and his friendship with Joan Patteson 'to exclusion of all others.' 'It does seem most unfair,' he wrote, 'that one cannot enjoy one's own privacy, or some privacy, when out of public life, but this is an age of sensation and vulgarity.'[210] 'These things,' he confided to his diary, 'that are all matters of one's private life, & entitled to be treated with reserve.'[211] He was very pleased, however, with Hardy's account of the First World War – 'delighted at the fairness of the account.' He added: 'I had forgotten much that is there recorded, and marvellous in places how well it had been done.' 'On the whole,' he concluded, ' very good where on public issues. I do not like the personal incident side.'[212] As he read the Hardy manuscript he realized the need to make progress with his memoirs: 'It made me see however the need to get on with my own Memoirs.'[213]

By mid-January King had several long talks with Hardy about the manuscript and changes that King desired to see made in it. It appears that Hardy agreed to delete references to the gift of Laurier House to the party, spiritualism, and his friendship with Joan Patteson. On January 21 he wrote: 'On revision of his [Hardy] MSS got some important changes made.'[214]

207 King Diary, July 27, 1948.

208 NAC, WLMK Papers, MG 26, J 1 Series, vol. 438, p. 399465, H.R. Hardy to William Lyon Mackenzie King, December 22, 1948.

209 King Diary, January 5, 1949.

210 King Diary, January 7, 1949.

211 King Diary, January 8, 1949.

212 King Diary, January 9, 1949.

213 King Diary, January 11, 1949.

214 King Diary, January 21, 1949.

Mr King was, however, very troubled with the suggested title of the book – 'Mr Canada.' Hardy told King that the Canadian publisher desired this title while the English publisher did not favour it. Instead of this title, King suggested 'under 5 sovereigns' or '50 years of public service.'[215] On April 22 he told Hardy that if the book were published under the title it 'would be certain to create a false impression, one which in the mind of the public generally would create a bitter prejudice toward myself and toward the party of which, for neary 30 years, I was leader.' 'So deeply do I feel on this matter,' he told Hardy, 'that unless this can be arranged I shall find it necessary to seek legal advice as to the means to be taken to prevent the publication, under the title "Mr Canada" of any book purporting to be a biography of myself.'[216] Eight days later he was relieved to learn that the title 'Mr Canada' would not be used.[217]

When the book was published in October 1949 it appeared under the title *Mackenzie King of Canada: A Biography.* His general acceptance of the book can be gauged by the fact that he sent copies to many of his friends as gifts at Christmas, 1949.

The series was published in newspapers across Canada. In this work the listing was taken from the Ottawa *Evening Citizen.*

CC1 Chapter 1. 'Mackenzie King jig-saw puzzle.' *Evening Citizen* [Ottawa], July 3, 1948, p. 15.

CC2 Chapter 2. 'Made political economy basis of his education.' Ibid., July 5, 1948, p. 3.

CC3 Chapter 3. 'Had many girl friends but never fell in love.' Ibid., July 6, 1948, p. 3.

CC4 Chapter 4. 'Happy, memorable years at University of Toronto.' Ibid., July 7, 1948, p. 3.

CC5 Chapter 5. 'Journalism proved aid to career's development.' Ibid., July 8, 1948, p. 3.

215 King Diary, January 22, 1949.

216 NAC, WLMK Papers, MG 26, J 1 Series, vol. 444, pp. 406703–406704, William Lyon Mackenzie King to H.R. Hardy, April 14, 1949.

217 King Diary, April 22, 1949.

CC6 Chapter 6. 'Made first-hand study of labor conditions.' Ibid., July 9, 1948, p. 3.

CC7 Chapter 7. 'Defeat in home riding was regarded as affront.' Ibid., July 10, 1948, p. 3.

CC8 Chapter 8. 'Worked far into night on reports of speeches.' Ibid., July 12, 1948, p. 3.

CC9 Chapter 9. 'Memories of childhood are revived during visit.' Ibid., July 13, 1948, p. 3.

CC10 Chapter 10. 'Tenant describes visit of King to old home.' Ibid., July 14, 1948, p. 3.

CC11 Chapter 11. 'Tender episodes found in his correspondence.' Ibid., July 15, 1948, p. 3.

CC12 Chapter 12. 'Kilbasco letters show warmth and humanity.' Ibid., July 16, 1948, p. 3.

CC13 Chapter 13. 'Temperance is means of safeguarding health.' Ibid., July 17, 1948, p. 3.

CC14 Chapter 14. 'Son of Billy's teacher made clerk of Senate.' Ibid., July 19, 1948, p. 3.

CC15 Chapter 15. 'Innocent abroad paid for music in Paris.' Ibid., July 20, 1948, p. 3.

CC16 Chapter 16. '"Pat" fulfilled need for faithful companion.' Ibid., July 21, 1948, p. 3.

CC17 Chapter 17. 'Told Hitler Canada was on Britain's side.' Ibid., July 22, 1948, p. 3.

CC18 Chapter 18. 'Manpower stand basis for endless argument.' Ibid., July 23, 1948, p. 3.

CC19 Chapter 19. 'Has taxpaying trouble like everyone else.' Ibid., July 24, 1948, p. 3.

CC20 Chapter 20. 'Many interpretations of title "The Old Man."' Ibid., July 26, 1948, p. 3.

SECTION DD

Appendix 4: The Official Biography

Following King's death in July 1950 the literary executors of his estate, William Kaye Lamb, J.W. Pickersgill, Norman Robertson, and Fred McGregor, decided to appoint an official biographer to write his biography. Late in the year they chose Professor Robert MacGregor Dawson of the Department of Political Economy, University of Toronto, to hold this position. His appointment was conditional upon the agreement of the Rockefeller Foundation to make available the funds granted to McGill University in 1949 to enable King to prepare his memoirs.

Early in 1951 the Rockefeller Foundation agreed that its original grant could be used for the writing of the official biography. On February 8 the Board of Governors of McGill University and the literary executors of the King estate announced the appointment of Dawson.[218]

From 1951 to 1958 Dawson worked on the biography. He decided to make extensive use of a series of memoranda prepared by a number of researchers (including Frederick W. Gibson, Jacqueline (Côté) Neatby, Fred McGregor, James Eayrs, Alex Lane, and Harry James Walker). The extent of the King Papers made it virtually impossible for a single individual to read all of them.

When Dawson realized that it would be years before he reached the period of the 1944 Conscription Crisis and that several of the participants might be dead by that time, he decided to proceed with writing that sec-

218 *Montreal Gazette*, 'Biographer named of Mackenzie King,' February 8, 1951, p. 15.

tion before continuing chronologically with the biography.[219] By proceeding in this way Dawson was able to interview several of the men most involved with the events of 1944, including Angus L. Macdonald, C.G. Power, and Thomas A. Crerar. Dawson completed a book-length volume entitled *The Conscription Crisis of 1944.*

Professor Dawson died on July 16, 1958. By this time, volume one had been completed and was ready for the printer. It was published on November 17, 1958. Professor H. Blair Neatby of the Department of History at the University of British Columbia was chosen to replace Dawson as the official biographer. Volumes two and three, which were written by Neatby, were published in 1963 and 1976 respectively.

It was decided that the official biography would end with the outbreak of the Second World War in September 1939. The years 1939 to 1948, the year of King's retirement, were covered by the published volumes of *The Mackenzie King Record.* Published by the University of Toronto Press in four volumes from 1960 to 1970, this publication contains over 1,500 pages of edited diaries.[220]

The official biography was serialized in the *Weekend Magazine.*[221]

Volume One:

DD1 [Part 1] 'Willie.' *Weekend Magazine,* 8 (45), November 8, 1958, pp. 2–4, 62–64, 66.

DD2 [Part 2] 'The young reformer.' Ibid., 8 (46), November 15, 1958, pp. 32–36.

DD3 [Part 3] 'The party leader.' Ibid., 8 (47), November 22, 1958, pp. 32–34, 36, 38–39.

DD4 [Part 4] 'The Canadian.' Ibid., 8 (47), November 29, 1958, pp. 6–8, 30–31.

The first volume was also serialized in the *Toronto Telegram* under the title 'The Mackenzie King Story':

219 As early as October 1952 Dawson had decided to work on the 1944 crisis. NAC, WLMK Papers, MG 26, J 18 Series, vol. 1, Folder 2, F.A. McGregor to Norman A. Robertson, October 23, 1952.

220 For bibliographical details, see Section D, entries D1, D2, D3, and D4, in this volume.

221 The *Weekend Magazine* was included as a supplement to about forty daily newspapers in Canada.

DD5 [Part 1] 'Granddad's enemies in 1837 Rebellion.' *Toronto Telegram*, November 10, 1958, p. 27.

DD6 [Part 2] 'Willie was "big man" on U of T campus.' Ibid., November 11, 1958, p. 17.

DD7 [Part 3] 'I am a most peculiar compound.' Ibid., November 12, 1958, p. 23.

DD8 [Part 4] 'I intend to be a politician.' Ibid., November 13, 1958, p. 5.

DD9 [Part 5] 'Postmaster's offer changed his whole life.' Ibid., November 14, 1958, p. 14.

DD10 [Part 6] 'The great conciliator emerges.' Ibid., November 17, 1958, p. 10.

DD11 [Part 7] 'Labor Act became world model.' Ibid., November 18, 1958, p. 13.

DD12 [Part 8] 'At home in the House as Minister of Labour.' Ibid., November 19, 1958, p. 23.

DD13 [Part 9] 'Rejected by voters, he takes Rockefeller job.' Ibid., November 20, 1958, p. 5.

DD14 [Part 10] 'Victor in first vital test: He's PM.' Ibid., November 24, 1958, p. 10.

DD15 [Part 11] 'Governor General centre of row.' Ibid., November 25, 1958, p. 11.

DD16 [Part 12] 'Isolation here born of war.' Ibid., November 26, 1958, p. 52.

DD17 [Part 13] 'Independence in foreign affairs was won in 1923.' Ibid., November 28, 1958, p. 29.

DD18 [Part 14] 'When his brother died, he lost a critic.' Ibid., November 29, 1958, p. 16.

Volume Two:

DD19 [Part 1] 'Loneliness was his burden – and his shield.' *Weekend Magazine*, 13 (42), October 19, 1963, pp. 2–4, 26, 29–31.

DD20 [Part 2] 'Lord Byng is challenged, Meighen is routed.' Ibid., 13 (43), October 26, 1963, pp. 28–30, 32–34.

DD21 [Part 3] 'How he survived the Beauharnois Scandal.' Ibid., 13 (44), November 2, 1963, pp. 28–33.

DD22 [Part 4] 'How the spirit world gave him reassurance.' Ibid., 13 (45), November 9, 1963, pp. 34, 36–39.

SECTION EE

Appendix 5: Memoranda Prepared for Use by the Official Biographer

Several historians and scholars who were experts on various aspects of the Mackenzie King era prepared detailed memoranda for the use of the official biographer. The studies are arranged alphabetically by author. Locations of copies of the studies are provided.

EE1 EAYRS, JAMES GEORGE. 'Canada and attempts at international disarmament. 1: From the Washington Conference to the London Naval Conference, 1930.' [Memorandum prepared for use by the official biographer]. [1954]. 47 p.
Location: QUA, Frederick Wellington Gibson Papers, Herbert Blair Neatby Papers.

EE2 – 'Canada and reparations. 1: 1919–1926.' [1953]. [Memorandum prepared for use by the official biographer]. [1953]. 115 p.
Location: QUA, Frederick Wellington Gibson Papers.

EE3 – 'Canada and the European crisis. I. The Italo-Ethiopan War.' [Memorandum prepared for use by the official biographer]. [1954]. 101 p.
Location: QUA, Herbert Blair Neatby Papers.

EE4 – 'Canada and the European crisis. II. Reoccupation of the Rhineland, 1936.' [Memorandum prepared for use by the official biographer]. [1954]. 21 p.
Location: QUA, Herbert Blair Neatby Papers.

EE5 – 'Canada and the European crisis. IV. The Spanish Civil War,

1936–39. [Memorandum prepared for use by the official biographer]. [1954]. 13 p.
Location: QUA, Herbert Blair Neatby Papers.

EE6 – 'Canada and the European crisis. V. Mr King at Washington, March, 1937.' [Memorandum prepared for use by the official biographer]. [1954]. 15 p.
Location: QUA, Herbert Blair Neatby Papers.

EE7 – 'Canada and the European crisis. VI. Imperial Conference of 1937. [Memorandum prepared for use by the official biographer]. [1954]. 99 p.
Location: QUA, Herbert Blair Neatby Papers.

EE8 – 'Canada and the European crisis. VII. Mackenzie King's visit to Europe, June–July, 1937.' [Memorandum prepared for use by the official biographer]. [1954]. 31 p.
Location: QUA, Herbert Blair Neatby Papers.

EE9 – 'Canada and the European crisis. VIII. 1938 – The year of Munich.' [Memorandum prepared for use by the official biographer]. [1954]. 43 p.
Location: QUA, Herbert Blair Neatby Papers.

EE10 – 'Canada and the European crisis. IX. 1939 – The road to war.' [Memorandum prepared for use by the official biographer]. [1954]. 57 p.
Location: QUA, Herbert Blair Neatby Papers.

EE11 – 'Canadian external relations in Second World War.' [Memorandum prepared for use by the official biographer]. [Undated]. 315 p.
Location: QUA, Herbert Blair Neatby Papers.

EE12 – 'Canadian–American relations, 1921–1927. I. Aspects of peace with friction.' [Memorandum prepared for use by the official biographer]. [Undated]. 27 p.
Location: QUA, Herbert Blair Neatby Papers.

EE13 – 'Canadian–American relations, 1921–1927. II. Appointment of Canadian minister at Washington.' [Memorandum prepared for use by the official biographer]. [1953]. 56 p.
Location: QUA, Herbert Blair Neatby Papers.

EE14 – 'Chanak affair – Halibut fisheries.' [Memorandum prepared for use by the official biographer]. [Undated]. 77 p.
Location: QUA, Frederick Wellington Gibson Papers.

EE15 – 'Canada and the Far Eastern crisis, 1931–1939.' [Memorandum prepared for use by the official biographer]. [1954]. 64 p.
Location: QUA, Herbert Blair Neatby Papers.

EE16 – 'Canada and the Kellogg Pact.' [Memorandum prepared for use by the official biographer]. [1954]. 18 p.
Location: QUA, Herbert Blair Neatby Papers.

EE17 – 'Canada and the Locarno Pact.' [Memorandum prepared for use by the official biographer]. [1953]. 55 p.
Location: QUA, Frederick Wellington Gibson Papers.

EE18 – 'Canada and the Washington Conference, 1921–1922.' [Memorandum prepared for use by the official biographer]. [1954]. 34 p.
Location: QUA, Herbert Blair Neatby Papers.

EE19 – 'Canada's relations with the Soviet Union during the first King administration.' [Memorandum prepared for use by the official biographer]. [1953]. 40 p.
Location: QUA, Frederick Wellington Gibson Papers.

EE20 – 'Canadian–Soviet relations: (II) The expulsion of the Soviet Trade Mission, 1927.' [Memorandum prepared for use by the official biographer]. [1953]. 63 p.
Location: QUA, Frederick Wellington Gibson Papers.

EE21 – 'Mackenzie King and the development of the machinery of Canadian external policy, 1921–1930.' [Memorandum prepared for use by the official biographer]. [1954]. 43 p.
Location: QUA, Herbert Blair Neatby Papers.

EE22 – 'The St Lawrence Waterway: From the origin of the project to the Treaty of 1932.' [Memorandum prepared for use by the official biographer]. [1954]. 114 p.
Location: QUA, Frederick Wellington Gibson Papers.

EE23 – 'The Imperial Conference of 1930. 1. The conference and constitutional problems. 2. The conference and economic problems.

[Memorandum prepared for use by the official biographer]. [1954]. 48 p.
Location: QUA, Frederick Wellington Gibson Papers.

EE24 – 'The Imperial Conference at Ottawa, 1932.' [Memorandum prepared for use by the official biographer]. [1954]. 62 p.
Location: QUA, Frederick Wellington Gibson Papers.

EE25 – 'Canadian external relations in the Second World War.' [Memorandum prepared for use by the official biographer]. [Undated]. 315 p.
Location: QUA, Frederick Wellington Gibson Papers.

EE26 – 'Canada and the League of Nations. I. [?] [First page and title missing]. [Memorandum prepared for use by the official biographer]. [Undated]. 43 p.
Location: QUA, Herbert Blair Neatby Papers.

EE27 – 'Canada and the League of Nations. II. From draft treaties to Protocol of Geneva.' [Memorandum prepared for use by the official biographer]. [1953]. 50 p.
Location: QUA, Herbert Blair Neatby Papers.

EE28 – 'Canada & League of Nations. III. From the rejection of the Protocol to the acceptance of optional clause, 1925–1929.' [Memorandum prepared for use by the official biographer]. [1954]. 86 p.
Location: QUA, Herbert Blair Neatby Papers.

EE29 [EAYRS, JAMES GEORGE?] 'Defence policy, 1935–39 [including Bren Gun].' [Memorandum prepared for use by the official biographer]. [Undated]. 62 p.
Location: QUA, Frederick Wellington Gibson Papers.

EE30 – 'British Commonwealth Air Training Plan.' [Memorandum prepared for use by the official biographer]. [Undated]. 10 p.
Location: QUA, Frederick Wellington Gibson Papers.

EE31 FORSTER, DONALD FREDERICK. 'The Imperial Economic Conference of 1932 and opposition economic policy.' [Memorandum prepared for use by the official biographer]. [Undated]. 121 p.
Location: QUA, Frederick Wellington Gibson Papers.

EE32 – 'Opposition economic policy: Parliamentary session of 1932.' [Memorandum prepared for use by the official biographer]. [Undated]. 59 p.
Location: QUA, Frederick Wellington Gibson Papers.

EE33 – 'Opposition economic policy, 1933.' [Memorandum prepared for use by the official biographer]. [Undated]. 95 p.
Location: QUA, Frederick Wellington Gibson Papers.

EE34 – 'Stevens resignation and emergence of Bennett New Deal.' [Memorandum prepared for use by the official biographer]. [Undated]. 95 p.
Location: QUA, Frederick Wellington Gibson Papers.

EE35 – 'The "New Deal" broadcasts and Liberal reaction.' [Memorandum prepared for use by the official biographer]. [Undated]. 48 p.
Location: QUA, Frederick Wellington Gibson Papers.

EE36 – 'The National Liberal Federation.' [Memorandum prepared for use by the official biographer]. [Undated]. 9 p.
Location: QUA, Frederick Wellington Gibson Papers.

EE37 – 'Parliamentary session of 1935. I. January 17–March 1.' [Memorandum prepared for use by the official biographer]. [Undated]. 85 p.
Location: QUA, Frederick Wellington Gibson Papers.

EE38 – 'Parliamentary session of 1935. II. March 1 to April 17.' [Memorandum prepared for use by the official biographer]. [Undated]. 86 p.
Location: QUA, Frederick Wellington Gibson Papers.

EE39 – 'Parliamentary session of 1935. III. June 1 to July 5.' [Memorandum prepared for use by the official biographer]. [Undated]. 109 p.
Location: QUA, Frederick Wellington Gibson Papers.

EE40 – 'The trade agreement with the United States. II: The first phase, 1933.' [Memorandum prepared for use by the official biographer]. [Undated]. 37 p.
Location: QUA, Frederick Wellington Gibson Papers.

EE41 – 'The trade agreement with the United States, 1935. III: Develop-

ments in 1934.' [Memorandum prepared for use by the official biographer]. [Undated]. 39 p.
Location: QUA, Frederick Wellington Gibson Papers.

EE42 – 'The trade agreement with the U.S., 1935. IV: Negotiations as an election issue.' [Memorandum prepared for use by the official biographer]. [Undated]. 55 p.
Location: QUA, Frederick Wellington Gibson Papers.

EE43 – 'The trade agreement with the U.S., 1935. V: Negotiations under the Liberal Government, October 14–November 16, 1935. [Memorandum prepared for use by the official biographer]. [Undated]. 89 p.
Location: QUA, Frederick Wellington Gibson Papers.

EE44 – 'The trade agreement with the U.S.A., 1935. VII: Press and public reaction to the agreement.' [Memorandum prepared for use by the official biographer]. [Undated]. 36 p.
Location: QUA, Frederick Wellington Gibson Papers.

EE45 – 'The North Atlantic trade triangle. I: The background of the Anglo–American negotiations and Mr King's visit to Washington, March, 1937.' [Memorandum prepared for use by the official biographer]. [Undated]. 39 p.
Location: QUA, Frederick Wellington Gibson Papers.

EE46 – 'The North Atlantic trade triangle. II: Trade discussions, Imperial Conference of 1937.' [Memorandum prepared for use by the official biographer]. [Undated]. 76 p.
Location: QUA, Frederick Wellington Gibson Papers.

EE47 – 'The North Atlantic trade triangle. III: The announcement of a new Canada–U.S. trade agreement.' [Memorandum prepared for use by the official biographer]. [Undated]. 113 p.
Location: QUA, Frederick Wellington Gibson Papers.

EE48 – 'The North Atlantic trade triangle. IV: Reaction to announcement of a new Can.–U.S. agreement.' [Memorandum prepared for use by the official biographer]. [Undated]. 18 p.
Location: QUA, Frederick Wellington Gibson Papers.

EE49 – 'The North Atlantic trade triangle. V: Developments during the 1938 session.' [Memorandum prepared for use by the official biographer]. [Undated]. 61 p.
Location: QUA, Frederick Wellington Gibson Papers.

EE50 – 'Canada–U.K. Trade Agreement, 1937. I: The first phase of the negotiations and the removal of the Canadian embargo on Russian trade.' [Memorandum prepared for use by the official biographer]. [Undated]. 101 p.
Location: QUA, Frederick Wellington Gibson Papers.

EE51 – 'Canada–U.K. Trade Agreement, 1937. II: Completion and ratification of the Agreement.' [Memorandum prepared for use by the official biographer]. [Undated]. 70 p.
Location: QUA, Frederick Wellington Gibson Papers.

EE52 – 'Dominion–Provincial Conference of 1935.' [Memorandum prepared for use by the official biographer]. [Undated]. 60 p.
Location: QUA, Frederick Wellington Gibson Papers.

EE53 – 'Dominion–Provincial relations: 1935–39. The unemployment insurance amendment, 1937–39.' [Memorandum prepared for use by the official biographer]. [Undated]. 76 p.
Location: QUA, Frederick Wellington Gibson Papers.

EE54 – 'Dominion–Provincial financial relations: 1935–39. The financial condition of the western provinces and the announcement of the Royal Commission on Dominion–Provincial Relations, 1936–37.' [Memorandum prepared for use by the official biographer]. [Undated]. 100 p.
Location: QUA, Frederick Wellington Gibson Papers.

EE55 – [Mitchell Hepburn and Mackenzie King]. [Memorandum prepared for use by the official biographer]. [Undated]. 74 p.
Location: QUA, Frederick Wellington Gibson Papers.

EE56 – 'Unemployment & relief policy, 1935–1939. 1936 Parl[iamentary] session.' [Memorandum prepared for use by the official biographer]. [Undated]. 97 p.
Location: QUA, Frederick Wellington Gibson Papers.

EE57 – 'Unemployment & relief policy, 1935–39: First report of the National Employment Commission & the unemployment issue, 1938 session.' [Memorandum prepared for use by the official biographer]. [Undated]. 73 p.
Location: QUA, Frederick Wellington Gibson Papers.

EE58 – 'Unemployment and relief policy, 1935–1939. The unemployment issue in the 1938 session.' [Memorandum prepared for use by the official biographer]. [Undated]. 122 p.

Location: QUA, Frederick Wellington Gibson Papers.

EE59 – 'Unemployment and relief policy, 1935–1939. Unemployment Insurance Amendment, 1937–1939. [Memorandum prepared for use by the official biographer]. [Undated]. 64 p.
Location: QUA, Herbert Blair Neatby Papers.

EE60 – 'Bank of Canada Amendment Act of 1936.' [Memorandum prepared for use by the official biographer]. [Undated]. 53 p.
Location: QUA, Frederick Wellington Gibson Papers.

EE61 – 'Bank of Canada Amendment Act of 1938.' [Memorandum prepared for use by the official biographer]. [Undated]. 22 p.
Location: QUA, Frederick Wellington Gibson Papers.

EE62 – 'Dominion–Provincial Relations: Alberta. II: Alberta disallowance and the Quebec Padlock Law, 1938.' [Memorandum prepared for use by the official biographer]. [Undated]. 101 p.
Location: QUA, Frederick Wellington Gibson Papers.

EE63 – 'Dominion–Provincial Relations. The Oshawa strike.' [Memorandum prepared for use by the official biographer]. [Undated]. 96 p.
Location: QUA, Herbert Blair Neatby Papers.

EE64 – 'Dominion–Provincial Relations. Mackenzie King, the Ontario election of 1937 and the closing of Government House.' [Memorandum prepared for use by the official biographer]. [Undated]. 63 p.
Location: QUA, Herbert Blair Neatby Papers.

EE65 – 'Dominion–Provincial financial relations, 1935–1939.' [Memorandum prepared for use by the official biographer]. [Undated]. 82 p.
Location: QUA, Herbert Blair Neatby Papers.

EE66 GIBSON, FREDERICK WELLINGTON. 'Cabinet formation of 1921.' [Memorandum prepared for use by the official biographer]. [Undated]. 131 + 4 p.
Location: QUA, Frederick Wellington Gibson Papers.

EE67 – 'The Great War and Canadian society.' [Memorandum prepared for use by the official biographer]. [Undated]. 17 p.
Location: NAC, WLMK Papers, MG 26, J 21 Series, vol. 5, Folder 14.

EE68 – 'Mackenzie King and naval policy, 1909–1913.' [Memorandum prepared for use by the official biographer]. [Undated]. 381 p.
Location: QUA, Frederick Wellington Gibson Papers.

EE69 – 'Mackenzie King and the crisis of 1917.' [Memorandum prepared for use by the official biographer]. [Undated]. 270 p.
Location: NAC, WLMK Papers, MG 26, J 17 Series, vol. 5, Folder 13.

EE70 – 'The general election of 1921.' [Memorandum prepared for use by the official biographer]. [1952]. 159 p.
Location: QUA, Frederick Wellington Gibson Papers.

EE71 – 'The first administration, 1921–23.' [Memorandum prepared for use by the official biographer]. [Undated]. 94 p.
Location: QUA, Frederick Wellington Gibson Papers.

EE72 – 'The election and cabinet formation, 1921.' [Memorandum prepared for use by the official biographer]. [Undated]. 36 p.
Location: QUA, Frederick Wellington Gibson Papers.

EE73 – 'The first administration, 1923.' [Memorandum prepared for use by the official biographer]. [Undated]. 182 p.
Location: QUA, Frederick Wellington Gibson Papers.

EE74 – 'Liberals and Progressives.' [Memorandum prepared for use by the official biographer]. [Undated]. 954 p.
Location: QUA, Frederick Wellington Gibson Papers.

EE75 – 'General election of 1925 and the aftermath.' [Memorandum prepared for use by the official biographer]. [1956]. 109 p.
Location: QUA, Frederick Wellington Gibson Papers.

EE76 – 'The Liberals and Progressives in the 1926 session of Parliament.' [Memorandum prepared for use by the official biographer]. [Undated]. 154 p.
Location: QUA, Frederick Wellington Gibson Papers.

EE77 – 'Some problems of King Administrations, 1921–1926.' [Memorandum prepared for use by the official biographer]. [September 15, 1953]. 45 p.
Location: QUA, Frederick Wellington Gibson Papers.

EE78 LANE, A.W.A. 'Fiscal and tariff policy, 1926–1930.' [Memorandum prepared for use by the official biographer]. [Undated]. 131 p.
Location: QUA, Herbert Blair Neatby Papers.

EE79 – [Freight rates – Petersen contract]. [Memorandum prepared for use by the official biographer]. [Undated]. 244 p.
Location: QUA, Frederick Wellington Gibson Papers.

EE80 – 'Hudson Bay Railway.' [Memorandum prepared for use by the official biographer]. [Undated]. 71 p.
Location: QUA, Herbert Blair Neatby Papers.

EE81 – 'The railway freight rates question, 1921–26.' [Memorandum prepared for use by the official biographer]. [Undated]. 200 p.
Location: NAC, WLMK Papers, MG 26, J 17 Series, vol. 5.

EE82 – 'The railway problem: Its genesis and history to the early part of 1922.' [Memorandum prepared for use by the official biographer]. [Undated]. 78 p.
Location: QUA, Herbert Blair Neatby Papers.

EE83 – 'The strike of postal employees 1924.' [Memorandum prepared for use by the official biographer]. [Undated]. 46 p.
Location: NAC, WLMK Papers, MG 26, J 17 Series, vol. 6, Folder 1.

EE84 – [Trade and fiscal program, 1921–26]. [Memorandum prepared for use by the official biographer]. [Undated]. 203 p.

EE85 McGREGOR, FREDERICK ALEXANDER. 'WLMK and labour.' [Memorandum prepared for use by the official biographer]. [Undated]. 207 p.
Location: NAC, WLMK Papers, MG 26, J 17 Series, vol. 5, Folder 15.

EE86 WALKER, HARRY JAMES. 'Labour – Memoranda Nos. 1–11.' [Memoranda prepared for use by the official biographer]:
Location: NAC, WLMK Papers, MG 26, J 17 Series, vol. 5, Folder 17.

EE87 – 'Memorandum No. 1: Establishing the Department of Labour.' [1956]. 25 p.

EE88 – 'Memorandum No. 2: Labour legislation and organization in Canada at the close of the 19th Century.' [1956]. 20 p.

EE89 – 'Memorandum No. 3: The Valleyfield strike.' [Undated]. 37 p.

EE90 – 'Memorandum No. 4: Labour Department attacked on its first estimates.' [Undated]. 6 p.

EE91 – 'Memorandum No. 5: The Rossland strike.' [Undated]. 19 p.

EE92 – 'Memorandum No. 6: Re the Alien Labour Act.' [Undated]. 8 p.

EE93 – 'Memorandum No. 7: Royal Commission on Industrial Disputes in the Province of British Columbia, 1903.' [Undated]. 21 p.

EE94 – 'Memorandum No. 8: Compulsory investigation in railway disputes (Railway Labour Disputes Act, 1903). [Undated]. 14 p.

EE95 – 'Memorandum No. 9: The Industrial Disputes Investigation Act, 1903.' [1956]. 26 p.

EE96 – 'Supplement 'A' to Memorandum No. 9.' [1956]. 3 p.

EE97 – 'Supplement 'B' to Memorandum No. 9.' [1956]. 8 p.

EE98 – 'Supplement 'C' to Memorandum No. 9: Re-action in United States to the Industrial Disputes Investigation Act.' [1956]. 8 p.

EE99 – 'Memoranda No. 10: W.L. Mackenzie King's investigation into Oriental immigration and opium trade.' [Undated]. 50 p.

EE100 – 'Memorandum No. 11: The Grand Trunk Strike of 1910 and its aftermath – The Pensions Resolution of 1922.' [Undated]. 138 p.

SECTION FF

Appendix 6: Books in the Mackenzie King Library

While Mackenzie King's library has unfortunately not been kept intact at Laurier House, several lists of his books have been prepared. This section contains information about these lists.

FF1 *Catalogue of pamphlets, reports and journals in the library of the Right Honourable W.L. Mackenzie King, C.M.G., Prime Minister of Canada, Laurier House, arranged in numerical order, with a key to the sections* [by Gustave Lanctot]. Ottawa, 1923. 72 p.

FF2 'Library of William Lyon Mackenzie King.' [List prepared by V. Benoit, 1983–1986]. 208 p.

In 1952 three hundred and forty-nine books that were part of John King's library were transferred to Woodside.[222] In an unsigned memorandum to the trustees of his estate written in March 1950, King mentioned that 'the books from my father's library' 'which were at my home at Woodside' should go to their old home there.[223]

Late in the 1960s several thousand volumes were transferred to the National Library of Canada from Laurier House. A separate card index of these books is maintained at the National Library.

In addition to the books transferred to the National Library, about four thousand volumes were transferred to the National Archives Library.

---

222 NAC, WLMK Papers, MG 26, J 18 Series, vol. 1, Folder 2, F.A. McGregor to Literary Executors, October 1, 1952.

223 Ibid., Folder 1.

Index

This index includes entries for authors of books, periodical articles, and theses, as well as for important subjects. It does not include entries for the editors or authors of books that contain contributed chapters about King; that material is indexed only under the names of the authors of the specific chapters.

References are to item numbers. All references that have no letters preceding them relate to the page of textual material as opposed to individual titles of works.

www.ingramcontent.com/pod-product-compliance
Lightning Source LLC
LaVergne TN
LVHW040756070826
844660LV00025B/1160

* 9 7 8 1 4 4 2 6 5 7 2 0 5 *